SOLIDWORKS Sheet Metal and Surface Design 2026 for Beginners and Intermediate Users

CADArtifex

The premium provider of learning products and solutions

www.cadartifex.com

SOLIDWORKS Sheet Metal and Surface Design 2026 for Beginners and Intermediate Users

Author: Sandeep Dogra
Email: info@cadartifex.com

Published by
CADArtifex
www.cadartifex.com

ISBN: 978-9394074446

www.cadartifex.com

Dedication

First and foremost, I would like to thank my parents for being a great support throughout my career and while writing this book.

Heartfelt gratitude goes to my wife and my sisters for their patience and endurance in supporting me to take up and successfully accomplish this challenge.

I would also like to acknowledge the efforts of the employees at CADArtifex for their dedication in editing the contents of this textbook.

Video Courses by CADArtifex

CADArtifex offers a range of video courses designed to support students, educators, and professionals in developing practical CAD skills through structured, project-based learning. Available video courses include:

- SOLIDWORKS Mastery Pack – 11 Courses in 1 | Complete Beginner to Industry Training
- Fusion 360 Mastery Pack: Design, Sculpt & Build Real Projects (6-in-1 Course Combo)
- SOLIDWORKS for Beginners and Intermediate Users
- Learn SOLIDWORKS Sheet Metal: From Concept to Creation
- SOLIDWORKS Mechanical Design & Assemblies Masterclass
- Complete Fusion 360 All-in-One Course for Beginners (2025)
- Fusion 360 Surface Design & T-Spline Sculpting
- Complete FreeCAD for Beginners – No Experience Needed
- Complete Onshape for Beginners: Project-Based Approach
- Master Autodesk Inventor: From Basics to Advanced
- Mastering AutoCAD 2D & 3D for Beginners

For full course details and access, visit: ***cadartifex.com***

Contents at a Glance

Table of Contents

Preface

SOLIDWORKS, developed by Dassault Systèmes SOLIDWORKS Corp., world leader in engineering software, offers a complete set of 3D software tools that let you create, simulate, publish, and manage your data. By providing advanced solid modeling techniques, SOLIDWORKS helps engineers to optimize performance while designing with capabilities, that cut down on costly prototypes, and eliminate rework and delays, thereby saving time as well as development costs.

SOLIDWORKS is a feature-based, parametric solid-modeling mechanical design and automation software which allows you to convert 2D sketches into 3D models by using simple but highly effective modeling tools. The 3D components and assemblies created in SOLIDWORKS can be converted into 2D drawings within a few mouse clicks. In addition, you can validate your designs by simulating their real-world conditions and assessing the environmental impact of products.

SOLIDWORKS Sheet Metal and Surface Design 2026 for Beginners and Intermediate Users textbook has been designed for instructor-led courses and self-paced learning. It intends to help engineers and designers interested in learning SOLIDWORKS to create real-world sheet metal components and surface designs. This textbook is a great help for SOLIDWORKS users new to sheet metal and surface designs. It consists of a total of 224 pages covering the sheet metal and surface design environments of SOLIDWORKS. It teaches users to use SOLIDWORKS mechanical design software for creating parametric 3D sheet metal components and complex shapes of surface models.

This textbook not only focuses on using the tools and commands of SOLIDWORKS for creating sheet metal components and surface models but also on the concept of design. It contains theory followed by tutorials that provide users with step-by-step instructions for creating sheet metal components and surface models. Moreover, it ends with Hands-on Test Drives that allow users to experience the user-friendly interface and technical capabilities of SOLIDWORKS.

Prerequisites

You should be familiar with SOLIDWORKS user interface and the basics of creating 3D solid parts. You can refer to **SOLIDWORKS 2026: A Power Guide for Beginners and Intermediate Users** textbook by **CADArtifex** for learning different design techniques of creating 3D solid parts, assemblies, and 2D drawings.

What Is Covered in This Textbook

SOLIDWORKS Sheet Metal and Surface Design 2026 for Beginners and Intermediate Users textbook is designed to help you understand everything you need to know to start using SOLIDWORKS 2026 for creating real-world sheet metal components and surface models.

Who Should Read This Textbook

This textbook is written with a wide range of SOLIDWORKS users in mind, varying from beginners to advanced users as well as SOLIDWORKS instructors interested in learning sheet metal and surface design techniques. The easy-to-follow instructions of this textbook allow you to clearly understand different design techniques, SOLIDWORKS sheet metal design tools, SOLIDWORKS surface design tools, and design principles.

Icons/Terms used in This Textbook

The following icons and terms are used in this textbook:

Note

Note: Notes highlight information requiring special attention.

Tip

Tip: Tips provide additional advice, which increases the efficiency of the users.

Flyout

A Flyout is a list in which a set of tools are grouped together, see Figure 1.

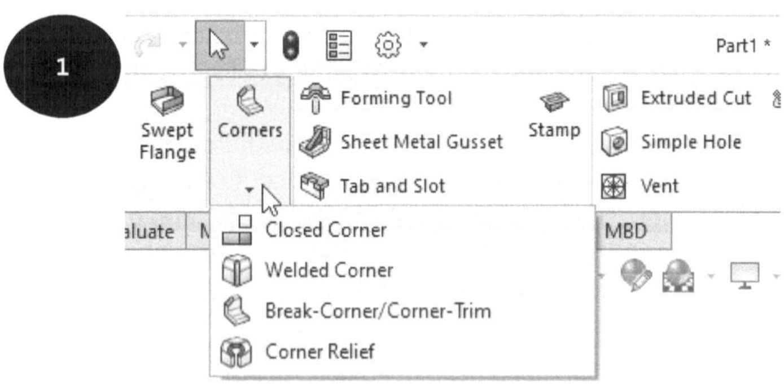

Drop-down List

A drop-down list is a list in which a set of options is grouped together, see Figure 2.

Rollout

A rollout is an area in which drop-down list, fields, buttons, check boxes are available to specify various parameters, see Figure 2. A rollout can either be in expanded or in collapsed form. You can expand/collapse a rollout by clicking on the arrow available on the right of its title bar.

Field

A Field allows you to enter new value, or modify an existing/default value, as per your requirement, see Figure 2. Also, a field allows you to select entities from the graphics area.

Check box

A Check box allows you to turn on or off the functions of a particular option, see Figure 2.

2

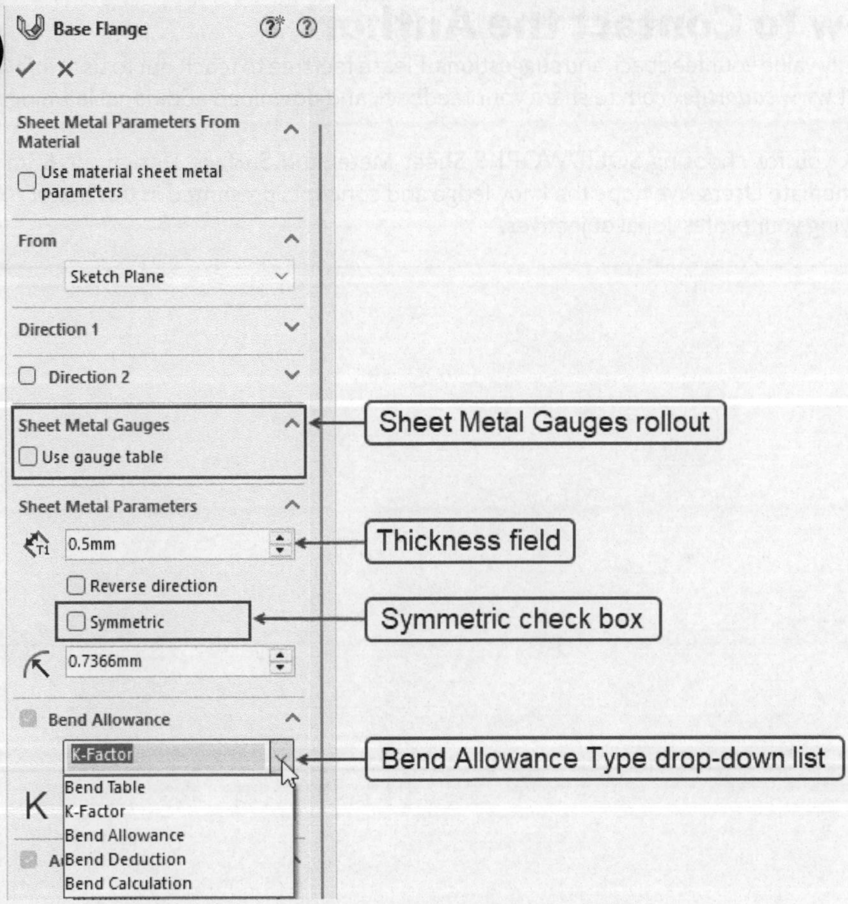

How to Download Online Resources

Students and faculty members can **download all parts/models** used in the illustrations, Tutorials and Hands-on Test Drives (exercises) of the textbook. In addition, faculty can also download PowerPoint Presentations (PPTs) of each chapter of the textbook.

To download the free online teaching and learning resources of the textbook, log in to our website (*cadartifex.com/login*) and navigate to the respective textbook page to access and download the resources. If you are a new user, you need to first sign up (*cadartifex.com/register*) for downloading the online resources of the textbook.

Interactive Support for Your Learning

In the book, you'll find **QR codes** next to key tutorial steps for certain tutorials. Scan these codes to access video demonstrations, designed to help you through any challenging parts of the process.

How to Contact the Author

We truly value your feedback and suggestions. Please feel free to reach out to us at *info@cadartifex*.com or visit *www.cadartifex.com* to share your feedback and download additional learning resources.

Thank you for choosing **SOLIDWORKS Sheet Metal and Surface Design 2026 for Beginners and Intermediate Users**. We hope the knowledge and concepts presented in this textbook support you in achieving your professional objectives.

CHAPTER

1

Introduction to SOLIDWORKS

In this book, the following topics will be discussed:

- Installing SOLIDWORKS
- Getting Started with SOLIDWORKS
- Invoking the Part Modeling Environment
- Understanding User Interface Components
- Customizing to Add CommandManager
- Saving Documents
- Opening an Existing Document

Welcome to the world of Computer Aided Design (CAD) with SOLIDWORKS. SOLIDWORKS, a product of Dassault Systèmes SOLIDWORKS Corp., and a world leader in engineering software, offers a complete set of 3D software tools that lets you create, simulate, publish, and manage your data. By providing advanced solid modeling techniques, SOLIDWORKS helps engineers to optimize performance while designing with capabilities, that cut down on costly prototypes and eliminate rework and delays, thereby saving time as well as development costs.

SOLIDWORKS is a feature-based, parametric solid-modeling mechanical design and automation software that allows you to convert 2D sketches into solid models by using simple but highly effective modeling tools. SOLIDWORKS provides a wide range of tools that allow you to create real-world components and assemblies. These real-world components and assemblies can then be converted into 2D engineering drawings for production. In addition, you can validate your designs by simulating their real-world conditions and assessing the environmental impact of products.

SOLIDWORKS utilizes a parametric feature-based approach for creating models. With SOLIDWORKS you can share your designs with your partners, subcontractors, and colleagues in smart new ways, which improves knowledge transfer and shortens the design cycle.

Installing SOLIDWORKS

If you do not have SOLIDWORKS installed on your system, you first need to get it installed. However, before you start installing SOLIDWORKS, you need to evaluate the system requirements and ensure that you have a system capable of running SOLIDWORKS adequately. Below are the system requirements for installing SOLIDWORKS 2026.

1. Operating Systems: Windows 10 - 64-bit, Windows 11 - 64-bit
2. RAM: 8 GB or more (16 GB or more recommended)
3. Disk Space: 10 GB or more
4. Processor: 3.3 GHz or higher
5. Graphics Card: SOLIDWORKS certified graphics cards and drivers

For more information about the system requirements for SOLIDWORKS, visit the SOLIDWORKS website at *https://www.solidworks.com/support/system-requirements*

Once the system is ready, install SOLIDWORKS by using the SOLIDWORKS DVD or by using the downloaded SOLIDWORKS setup files.

Getting Started with SOLIDWORKS

Once SOLIDWORKS 2026 is installed on your system, start SOLIDWORKS 2026 by double-clicking on the **SOLIDWORKS** 2026 icon on the desktop of your system. As soon as you double-click on the SOLIDWORKS 2026 icon, the system prepares to start SOLIDWORKS by loading all required files. Once all the required files have been loaded, the startup user interface of SOLIDWORKS 2026 appears along with the **Welcome** dialog box, see Figure 1.1.

1.1

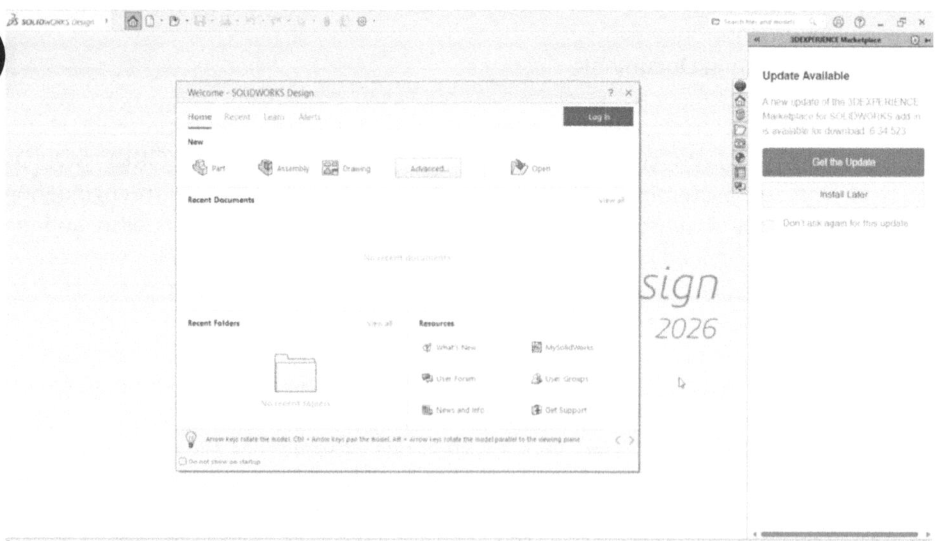

If you are starting SOLIDWORKS for the first time after installing the software, the **SOLIDWORKS License Agreement** window appears, see Figure 1.2. Click on the **Accept** button in the **SOLIDWORKS License Agreement** window to accept the license agreement and start SOLIDWORKS 2026.

1.2

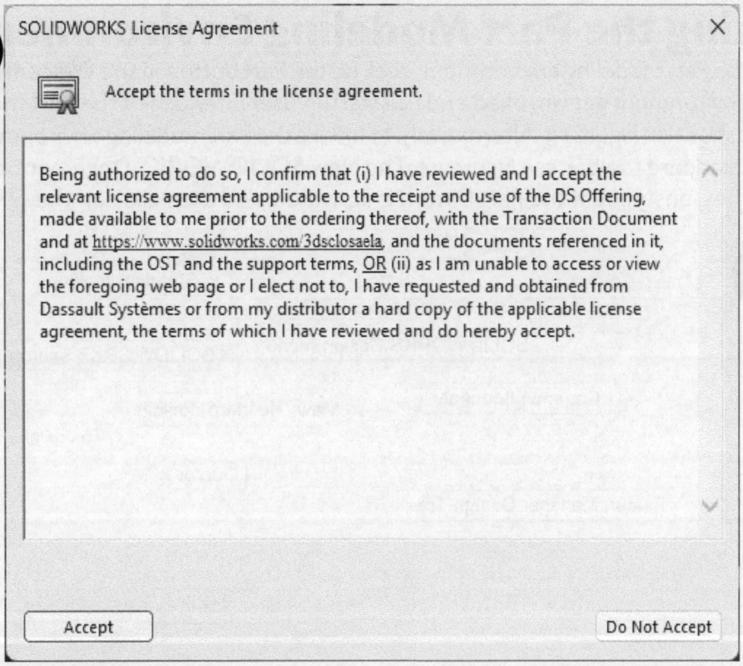

In SOLIDWORKS, the **Welcome** dialog box appears every time you start SOLIDWORKS and provides a convenient way to invoke new SOLIDWORKS documents, open existing documents, view recent documents and folders, access SOLIDWORKS resources, and stay updated on SOLIDWORKS news.

The **Welcome** dialog box has four tabs: **Home**, **Recent**, **Learn**, and **Alerts**. The options in the **Home** tab are used for invoking new SOLIDWORKS documents (**Part**, **Assembly**, and **Drawing**), opening existing documents, viewing recent documents and folders, and accessing SOLIDWORKS resources. The **Recent** tab displays a list of recent documents and folders. The **Learn** tab is used for accessing instructional resources such as tutorials, sample models, access to 3D Content Center, certification program, and so on to help you learn more about SOLIDWORKS. The **Alerts** tab is used for updating you with SOLIDWORKS news and provides different types of alerts in different sections including **Troubleshooting** and **Technical Alerts.**

Tip: If the **Welcome** dialog box does not appear on the screen, then you can invoke it by clicking on the **Welcome to SOLIDWORKS** tool in the **Standard** toolbar. Alternatively, you can click on **Help > Welcome to SOLIDWORKS** in the SOLIDWORKS Design Menus or the **Welcome to SOLIDWORKS** option in the **SOLIDWORKS Resources Task Pane** to invoke the **Welcome** dialog box. You will learn more about **Standard** toolbar, SOLIDWORKS Design Menus, and **SOLIDWORKS Resources Task Pane** later.

In SOLIDWORKS, you can create surface models and sheet metal components within the Part modeling environment, therefore it is important to first get familiar with different components of the Part modeling environment. The method for invoking the Part modeling environment is discussed next.

Invoking the Part Modeling Environment

To invoke the Part modeling environment, click on the **Part** button in the **Welcome** dialog box. The Part modeling environment gets invoked and the startup user interface of the Part modeling environment appears, as shown in Figure 1.3. Alternatively, to invoke the Part modeling environment, click on the **New** tool in the **Standard** toolbar, see Figure 1.4. The **New SOLIDWORKS Document** dialog box appears. In this dialog box, ensure that the **Part** button is activated, and then click on the **OK** button.

1.3

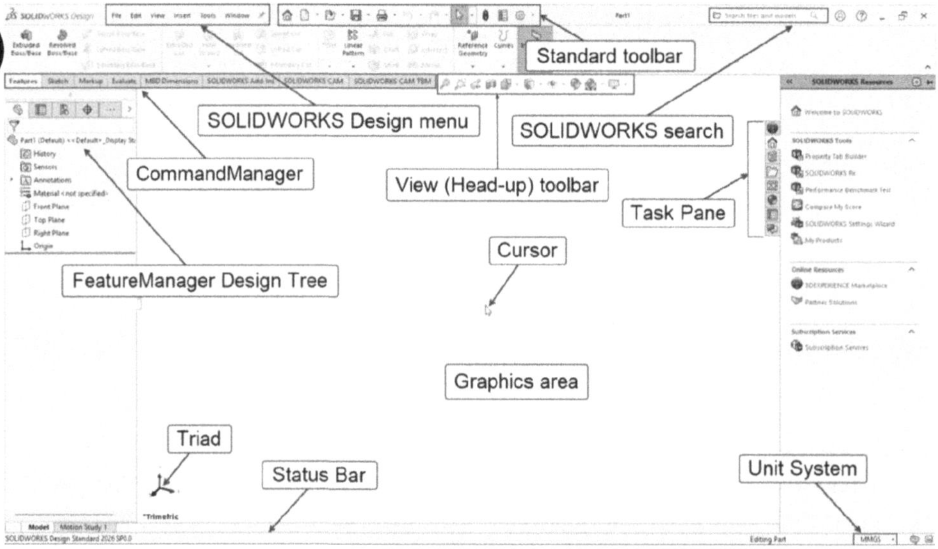

1.4

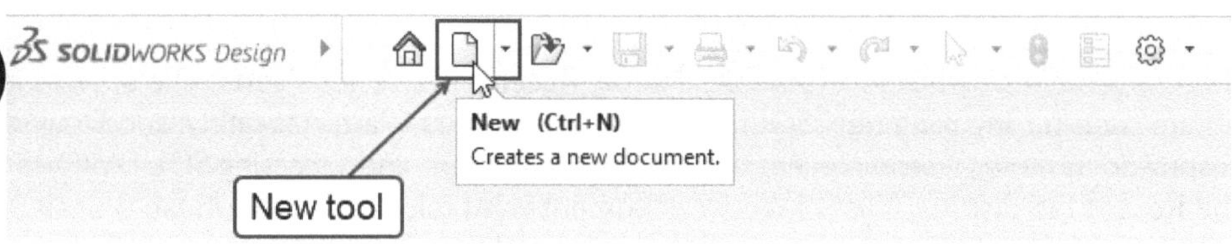

Note: If you are invoking the Part modeling environment for the first time after installing the software, the **Units and Dimension Standard** dialog box appears, see Figure 1.5. In this dialog box, you can specify the default unit system for SOLIDWORKS documents.

1.5

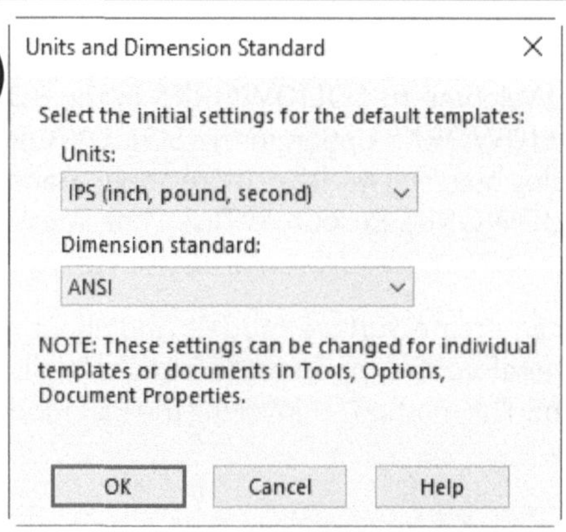

Tip: Similar to invoking the Part modeling environment for creating parts/components, you can invoke the Assembly environment for creating assemblies and the Drawing environment for creating 2D drawings by using the Assembly and Drawing buttons of the **Welcome** dialog box, respectively.

Understanding User Interface Components

Some of the components of the startup user interface of the Part modeling environment are discussed next.

Standard Toolbar

The **Standard** toolbar contains a set of the most frequently used tools such as **New**, **Open**, and **Save**, see Figure 1.6.

1.6

SOLIDWORKS Design Menus

The SOLIDWORKS Design Menus contains different menus such as **File**, **View**, and **Tools** for accessing different tools of SOLIDWORKS, see Figure 1.7.

1.7

Note that the SOLIDWORKS Design Menus appears when you move the cursor on the SOLIDWORKS logo, which is available at the top left corner of the screen. You can keep the SOLIDWORKS Design Menus visible all the time by clicking on the push-pin button available at the end of the SOLIDWORKS Design Menus. Note that the tools in the different menus are dependent upon the type of environment invoked.

SOLIDWORKS Search

The SOLIDWORKS Search is a search tool for searching commands/tools, knowledge base (help topics), community forums, files, models, and so on, see Figure 1.8.

1.8

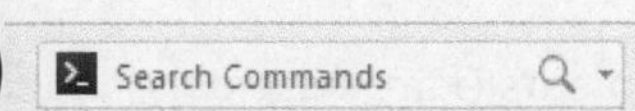

CommandManager

CommandManager is available at the top of the graphics area. It provides access to different sets of SOLIDWORKS tools. There are various CommandManagers such as **Features CommandManager**, **Sketch CommandManager**, **Sheet Metal CommandManager**, and **Evaluate CommandManager** available in the Part modeling environment. You can access these CommandManagers by clicking on the respective tabs. On clicking the **Features** tab, the **Features CommandManager** appears, which provides access to various tools for creating a 3D solid component, see Figures 1.9 and 1.10. Figure 1.9 shows the partial view of the **Features CommandManager** and Figure 1.10 shows a 3D solid component created by creating all its features one by one by using the solid modeling tools.

1.9

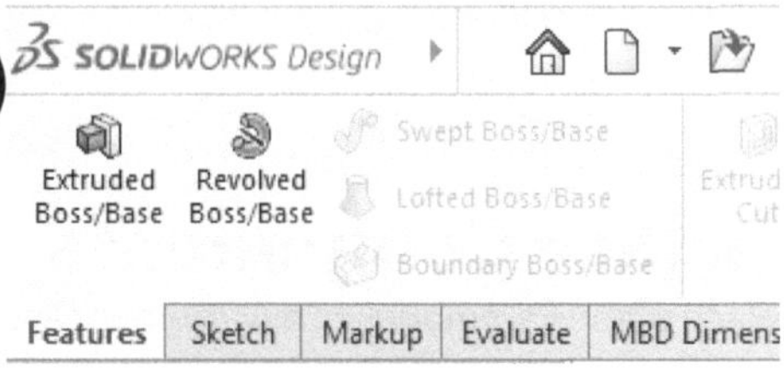

1.10

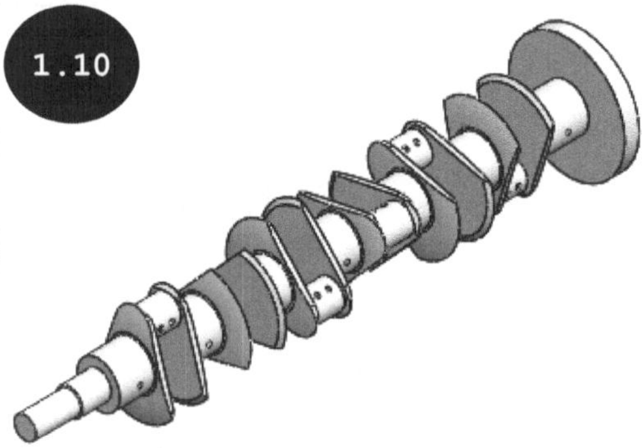

Note: To learn creating 3D solid components, assemblies, and 2D drawings, refer to **SOLIDWORKS 2026: A Power Guide for Beginners and Intermediate Users** textbook by CADArtifex.

Similarly, on clicking the **Sheet Metal** tab, the **Sheet Metal CommandManager** appears, which provides access to various tools for creating a sheet metal component, see Figures 1.11 and 1.12. Figure 1.11 shows the partial view of the **Sheet Metal CommandManager** and Figure 1.12 shows a sheet metal component. If the **Sheet Metal** tab is not available in the CommandManager, then you need to customize it to add it. You will learn more about adding the **Sheet Metal CommandManager** and its tools later in this chapter.

1.11

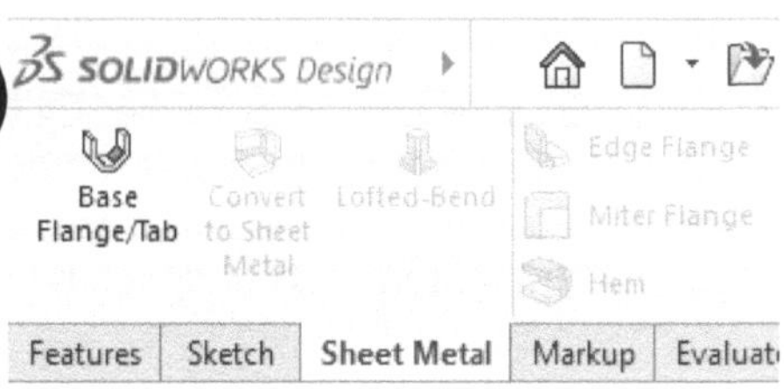

1.12

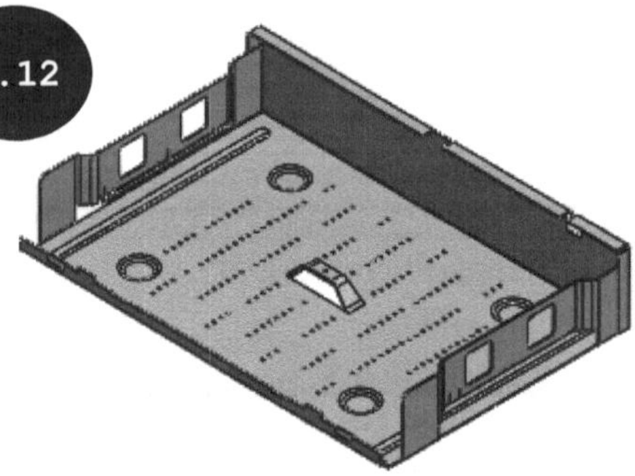

Tip: The different environments (Part, Assembly, and Drawing) of SOLIDWORKS are provided with different sets of CommandManagers.

FeatureManager Design Tree

FeatureManager Design Tree appears on the left of the graphics area and keeps a record of all operations or features used for creating a model, see Figure 1.13. Note that the first created feature appears at the top and the next created features appear one after the other in the FeatureManager Design Tree. Also, in the FeatureManager Design Tree, three default planes and an origin appear, by default.

1.13

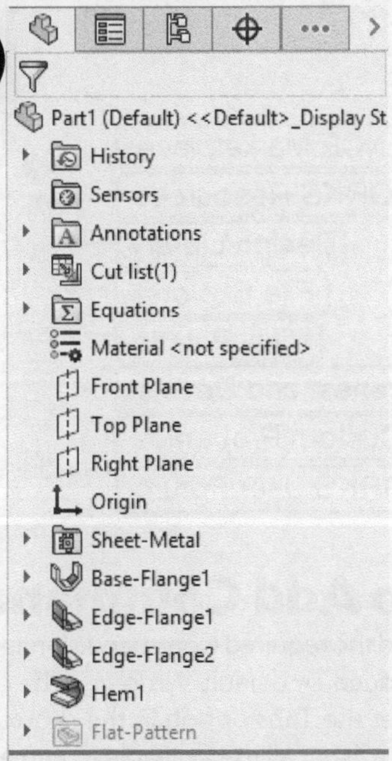

View (Heads-Up) Toolbar

The View (Heads-Up) toolbar is available at the top center of the graphics area, see Figure 1.14. It is provided with different sets of tools that are used for manipulating the view and display of a model available in the graphics area.

1.14

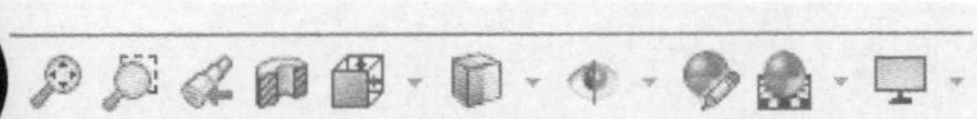

Status Bar

The Status Bar is available at the bottom of the graphics area and provides information about the action to be taken based on the currently active tool. It also displays the current state of the sketch being created, the coordinate system, and so on.

Task Pane

Task Pane appears on the right side of the screen with various tabs such as **SOLIDWORKS Resources**, **Design Library**, **File Explorer**, **Appearances, Scenes, and Decals**, and **Custom Properties** for accessing various online resources of SOLIDWORKS, several applications, subscription services, library, and so on, see Figure 1.15.

1.15

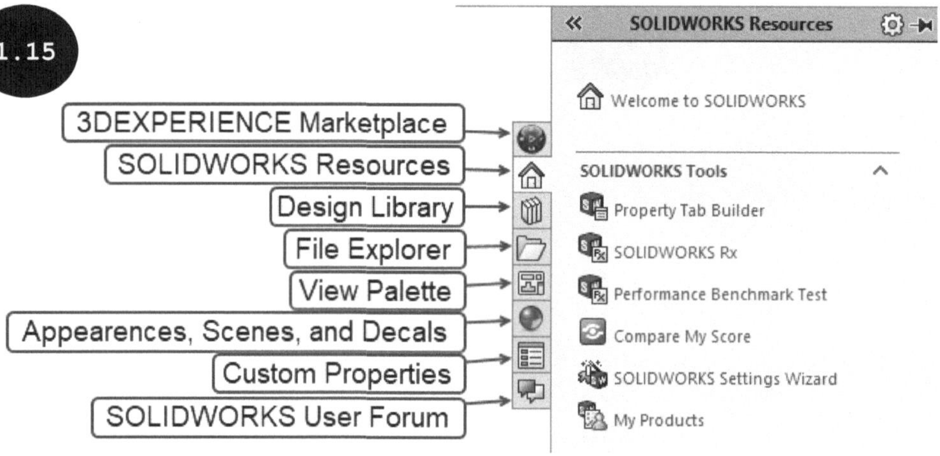

Customizing to Add CommandManager

In SOLIDWORKS, you can add the required CommandManager tab such as **Surface** and **Sheet Metal** in the CommandManger, if not added, by default. To do so, right-click anywhere on the CommandManager and then move the cursor over the **Tabs** option in the shortcut menu that appears, see Figure 1.16. A cascading menu appears with a list of all the available CommandManagers, see Figure 1.16. Note that a tick-mark in front of the CommandManager name in this cascading menu indicates that the respective CommandManager is already added. Click on the required CommandManager in the cascading menu to be added or removed, respectively.

1.16

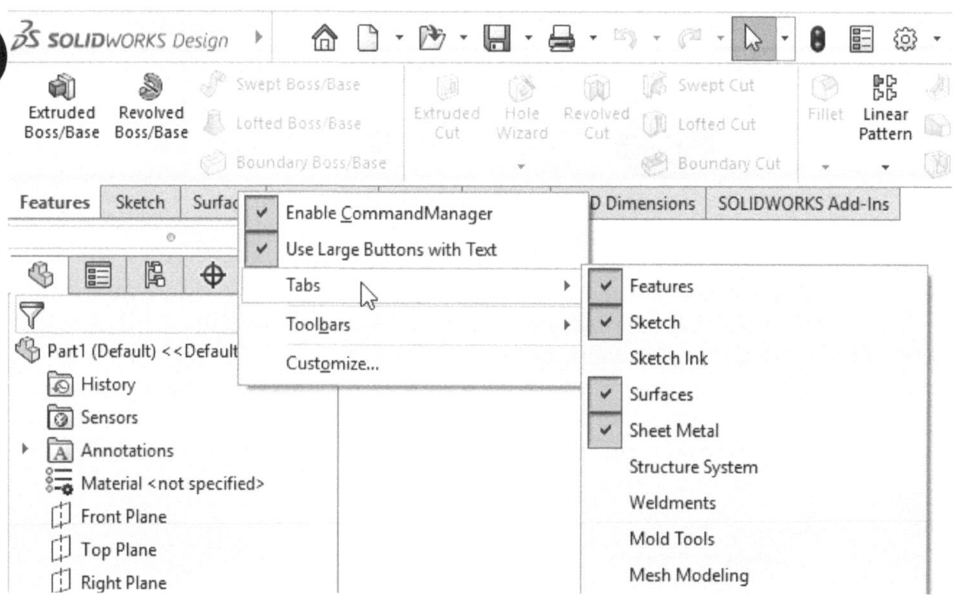

Saving Documents

To save a document created in any of the environments of SOLIDWORKS, click on the **Save** tool in the **Standard** toolbar or click on **File > Save** in the SOLIDWORKS Design Menus. The **Save As** dialog box appears. Enter the name of the document in the **File name** field of the dialog box and then browse to the location where you want to save the document. Next, click on the **Save** button.

Opening an Existing Document

To open an existing SOLIDWORKS Document, click on the **Open** button in the **Welcome** dialog box. Alternatively, click on the **Open** tool in the **Standard** toolbar or click on **File > Open** in the SOLIDWORKS Design Menus. The **Open** dialog box appears. In this dialog box, select the **SOLIDWORKS Files (*.sldprt; *.sldasm; *.slddrw)** file extension in the **File Type** drop-down list. Note that you can select the file extension depending on the type of document to be opened. After selecting the required file extension, browse to the location where the SOLIDWORKS document is saved and then click on the document to be opened. Next, click on the **Open** button in the dialog box. The selected document gets opened.

Similar to opening existing SOLIDWORKS documents, you can also open/import documents created in other CAD applications. SOLIDWORKS allows you to open documents created in CATIA V5, PTC Creo, Unigraphics/NX, Inventor, Solid Edge, CADKEY, Rhino, DWG, and so on by selecting the respective file extension in the **File Type** drop-down list of the **Open** dialog box. In addition to this, you can also open documents saved in universal CAD formats such as IGES, STEP, STL, and Parasolid.

Summary

In this chapter, you have learned about system requirements for installing SOLIDWORKS. You have also learned how to invoke the Part Modeling environment, and various components of the Part Modeling environment, customize to add the required CommandManager tab, save documents, and open an existing document in SOLIDWORKS.

Questions

Complete and verify the following sentences:

- The _________ contains different menus such as File, View, and Tools for accessing different tools of SOLIDWORKS.
- The surface modeling environment and the Sheet Metal environment of SOLIDWORKS can be invoked within the _________ environment.
- The Features CommandManager is provided with different sets of tools that are used for creating _________.

- The _________ toolbar is used for manipulating the view and display of the model in the graphics area.
- In SOLIDWORKS, you can open IGES and STEP files. (True/False)
- The FeatureManager Design Tree is used for keeping a record of all operations/features in an order. (True/False)
- In SOLIDWORKS, you cannot customize the tools in a CommandManager. (True/False)

CHAPTER

2

Creating Sheet Metal Components

In this chapter, the following topics will be discussed:

- Creating a Sheet Metal Component
- Creating a Base Flange
- Understanding Nodes of FeatureManager Design Tree
- Creating an Edge Flange
- Creating a Tab Feature
- Creating a Miter Flange
- Creating a Sketched Bend
- Creating a Jog Bend
- Creating a Hem Feature
- Closing Corners
- Welding Corners
- Breaking Corners
- Adding Corner Reliefs
- Creating a Lofted Bend
- Creating an Extruded Cut Feature
- Creating a Forming Tool
- Inserting a Forming Tool
- Creating a Vent
- Converting a 3D Solid Part into a Sheet Metal
- Converting a 3D Shelled Part into a Sheet Metal
- Mirroring and Patterning a Sheet Metal Feature
- Creating a Flat Pattern of a Sheet Metal Part
- Flattening Selected Bends of a Sheet Metal Part
- Folding Selected Bends of a Sheet Metal Part
- Creating Cuts Across the Bends
- Defining Sheet Parameters to a Custom Material
- Generating a Drawing View of the Flat Pattern

A sheet metal component is a thin and flat piece of metal that has a uniform thickness ranging from 0.154 mm (0.006 in) to 6.35 mm (0.25 in). In SOLIDWORKS, you can create a sheet metal component by using various tools of the **Sheet Metal CommandManager** and then generate its flat pattern layout with a single click, see Figures 2.1 and 2.2. The flat pattern layout provides a flattened view of the sheet metal component which helps in computing the overall sheet size required for creating the sheet component. Figure 2.1 shows a sheet metal component and Figure 2.2 shows its flat pattern layout.

2.1

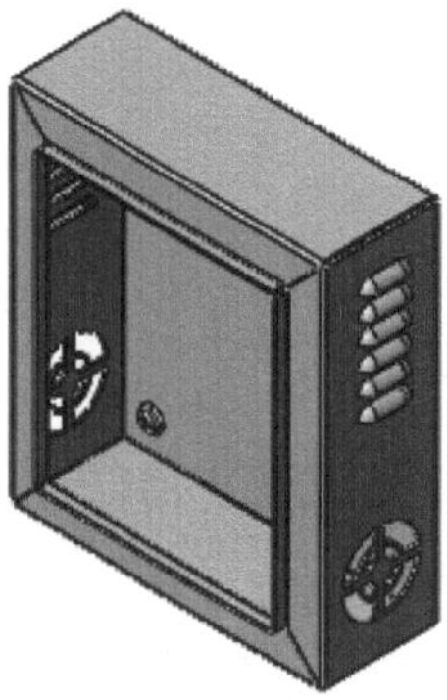

2.2

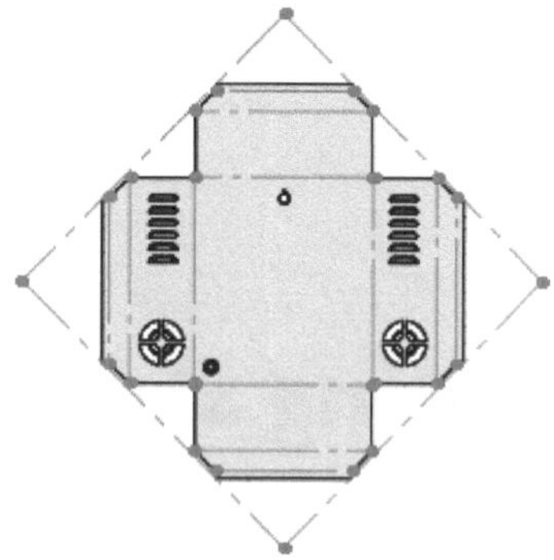

Creating a Sheet Metal Component

In SOLIDWORKS, you can create sheet metal components within the Part modeling environment by using various tools available in the **Sheet Metal CommandManager**. To display the tools of the **Sheet Metal CommandManager**, click on the **Sheet Metal** tab in the CommandManager, see Figure 2.3.

2.3

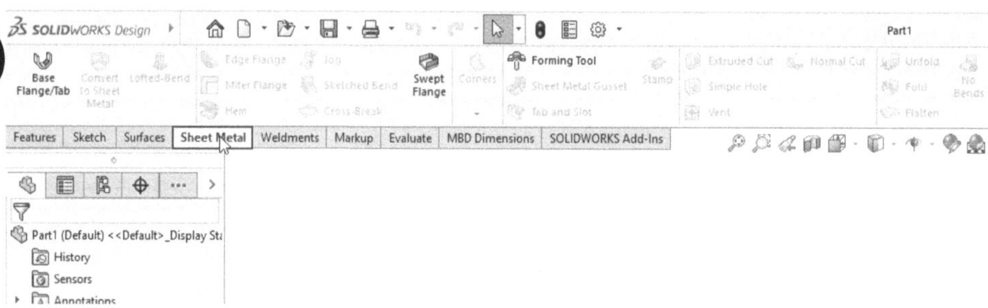

If the **Sheet Metal** tab is not available in the CommandManager then right-click anywhere on the CommandManager. Next, click on the **Tabs > Sheet Metal** option in the shortcut menu that appears, see Figure 2.4. The **Sheet Metal** tab becomes available in the CommandManager.

Note that initially, most of the tools of the **Sheet Metal CommandManager** are not activated. These tools get activated as soon as you create a base flange of a sheet metal component.

2.4

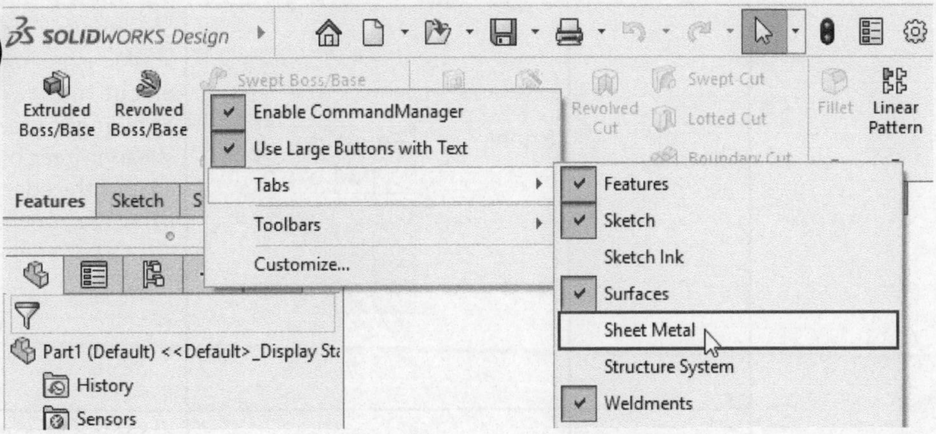

Tip: In the shortcut menu shown in Figure 2.4, a tick-mark in front of the CommandManager name indicates that the respective CommandManager is already added. You can add any CommandManager that is not available by default, by clicking on its name.

Note that in the tool room or a machine shop, you need to perform various operations such as bending, cutting, and drawing on a flat sheet of uniform thickness to create a sheet metal component of a desired shape, see the below table.

Techniques	Types	Illustration	Description
Bending	V-bending	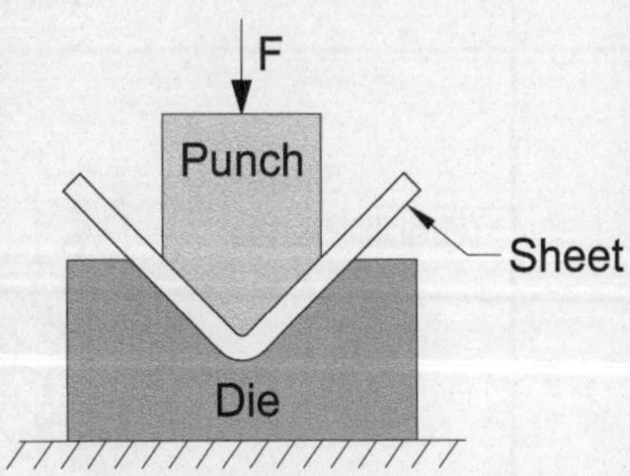	V-bending is a bending process in which the punch pushes the sheet into a V-shaped groove of the die causing it to bend.
	Edge bending	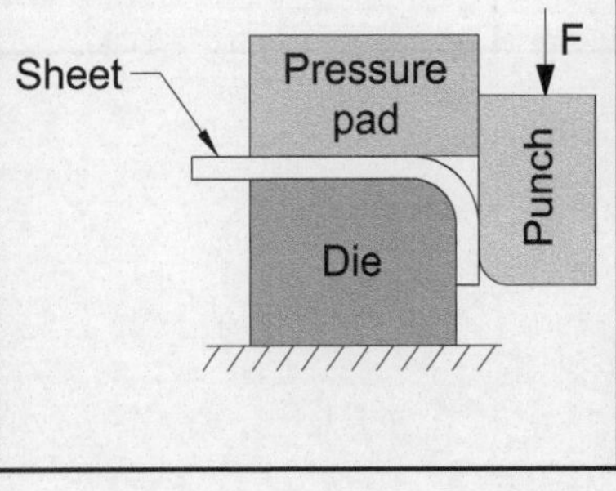	Edge bending is a process in which the punch pushes the sheet that extends beyond the die and pad, against the edge of the die causing it to bend.

Cutting	Shearing	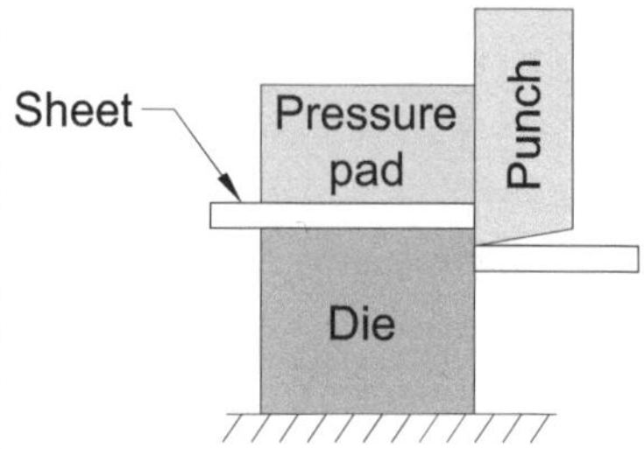	Shearing is a cutting process in which the sheet is divided or cut into two parts by applying a great enough shearing force on the sheet, against the edge of the die, using the punch.
	Blanking	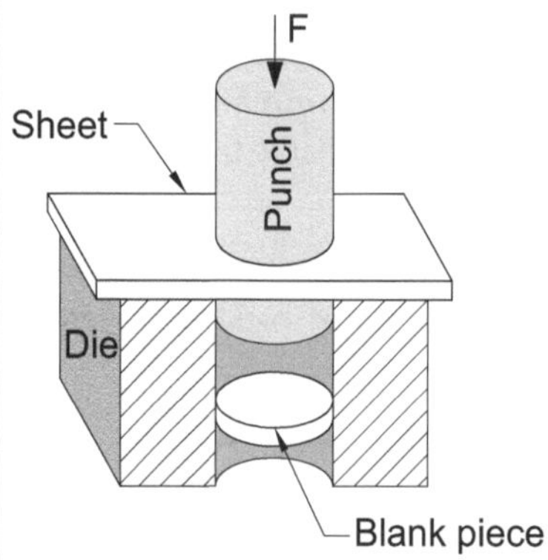	Blanking is a process in which a piece of sheet is removed from a large stock. This removed piece is also called blank and is not scrap, but rather a desired part that will be used for further processing.
	Punching	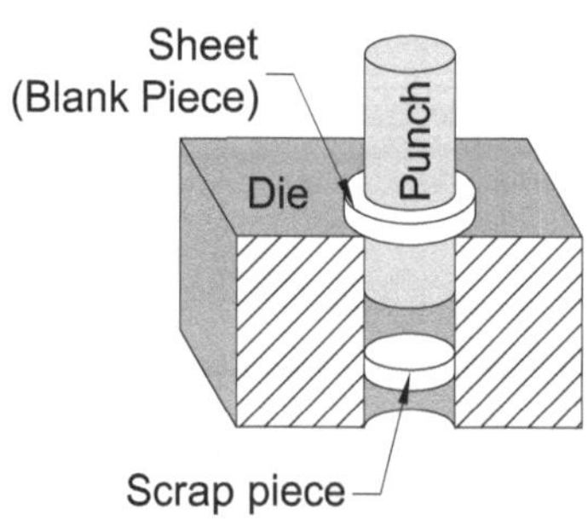	Punching is a cutting process in which a piece of sheet is removed from a large stock and creates a hole in the sheet. The removed piece is scrap.

Drawing	Drawing (Before and After operations)	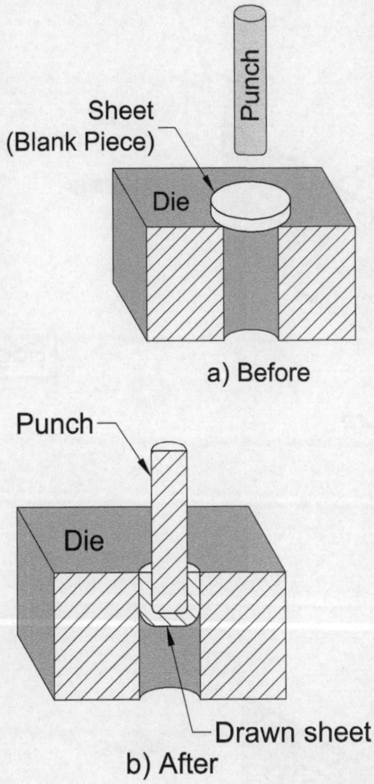	Drawing is a process in which a sheet is stretched into a desired shape by pushing it into the cavity of the die in the shape of the desired part. The drawing process requires a blank, which is a pre-cut piece of a stock (sheet).

Tip: An extremely thin metal whose thickness is less than 0.154 mm (0.006 in) is known as a foil and a thicker metal whose thickness is greater than 6.35 mm (0.25 in) is known as a plate.

It is evident from the above table that a sheet metal component is created by performing various operations such as bending, cutting, and drawing on a flat sheet of uniform thickness.

In SOLIDWORKS, to create sheet metal, you need to create all its features one by one, see Figure 2.5. The first created feature of a sheet metal component is known as the base flange. Figure 2.5 depicts the process for creating a sheet metal component and Figure 2.6 shows its flat pattern.

2.5

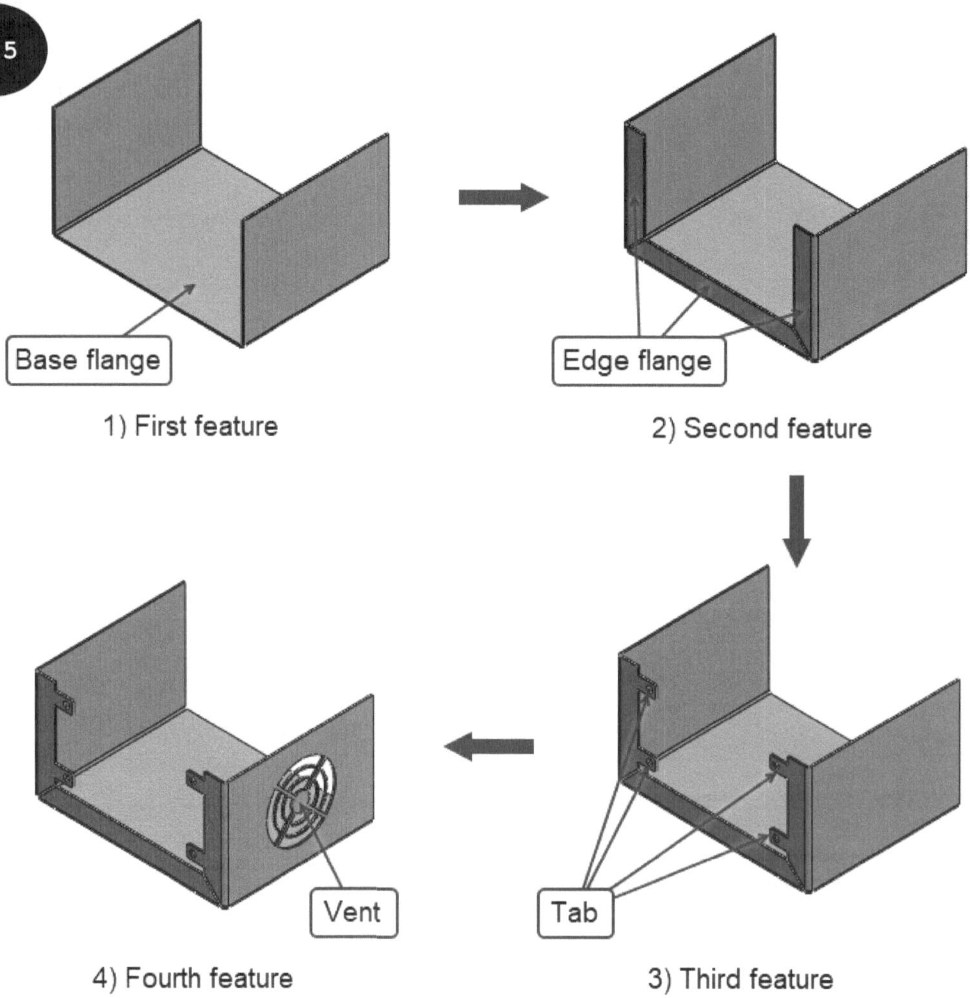

2.6

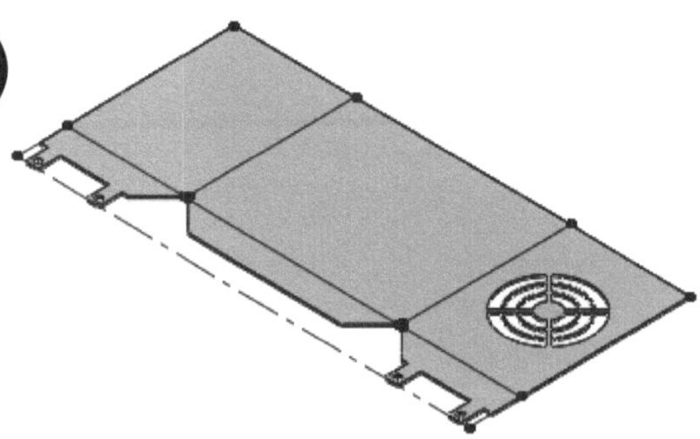

In SOLIDWORKS, the sheet metal parameters such as material thickness, bend radius, and bend allowance are defined while creating the base flange, and the same are used for all the remaining flanges or features of the sheet metal component as the default parameters. These sheet metal parameters are used for calculating the total flattened length of the sheet metal component.

Creating a Base Flange

The first created feature of a sheet metal component is known as the base flange. You can create a base flange by using an open or a closed sketch, see Figures 2.7 and 2.8.

2.7

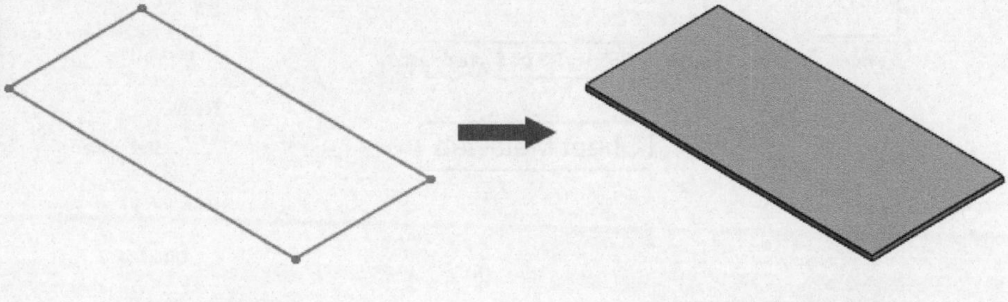

Closed Sketch Base flange

2.8

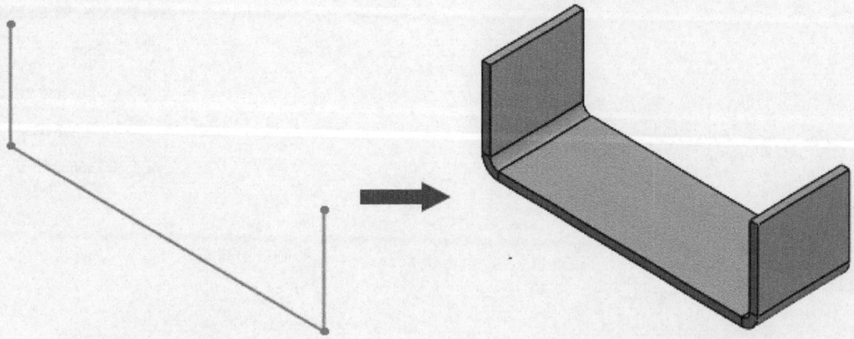

Open sketch Base flange

To create a base flange, invoke the Sketching environment and then create an open sketch or a closed sketch by using the sketching tools.

Tip: To invoke the Sketching environment, click on the **Sketch** tool in the **Sketch CommandManager** and then select a plane as the sketching plane for creating the sketch of the base flange. Refer to "**SOLIDWORKS 2026: A Power Guide for Beginners and Intermediate Users**" textbook by **CADArtifex** to learn about creating sketches, 3D solid parts, assemblies, and 2D drawings.

After creating a sketch, click on the **Sheet Metal** tab in the CommandManager and then click on the **Base Flange/Tab** tool, see Figure 2.9. The **Base Flange PropertyManager** appears, see Figure 2.10. Also, the preview of the base flange as per the default sheet metal parameters appears in the graphics area, see Figure 2.11. Note that the **Direction 1** and **Direction 2** rollouts of the PropertyManager are available only if the sketch of the base flange is an open sketch. The options in the **Base Flange PropertyManager** are used for defining the sheet metal parameters such as material thickness, bend radius, and bend allowance, which are also used as default parameters for the entire sheet metal component. However, you can edit these default parameters at any point in time of the designing process. You will learn about editing the default parameters of the sheet metal component later in this chapter. The options in the **Base Flange PropertyManager** are discussed next.

2.9

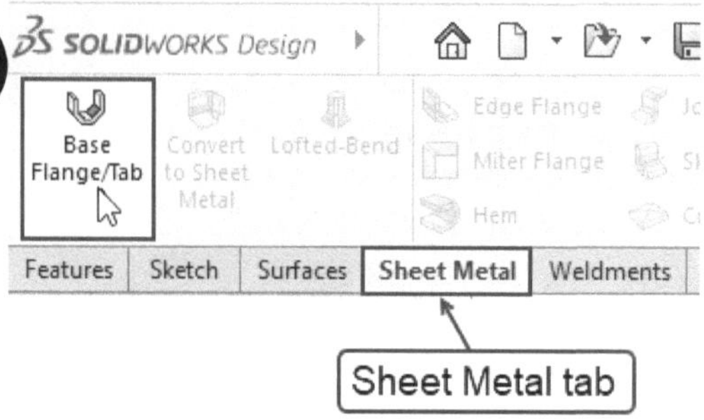

2.10

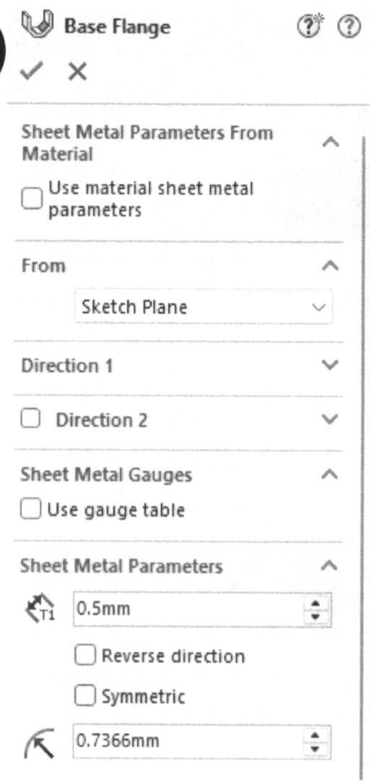

2.11

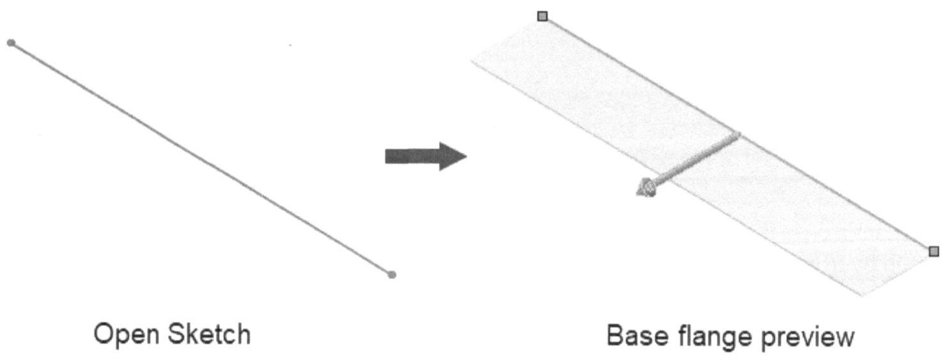

Note: If you exit the Sketching environment after creating the sketch and the sketch is not selected in the graphics area, then on invoking the **Base Flange/Tab** tool, the **Message PropertyManager** appears, and you are prompted to select either a sketch or a sketching plane. Select the sketch in the graphics area. The **Base Flange PropertyManager** and the preview of the base flange appear. However, if the sketch is not created then you can select a sketching plane for creating the sketch in the Sketching environment.

Use material sheet metal parameters

On selecting the **Use material sheet metal parameters** check box, the sheet metal parameters that are defined with the assigned custom material of the current part document will be used for the sheet metal component being created. If a material is not defined to the current part document, then on selecting this check box, a message appears that "**There is no material applied to the part**". Also, if a material is defined without the sheet metal parameters, then on selecting this check box, a message appears that "**There are no valid sheet metal parameters defined with the material**". You will learn about defining sheet metal parameters to a custom material of a part document later.

From Rollout

The options in the **Start Condition** drop-down list of the **From** rollout are used for specifying the start condition for the base flange, see Figure 2.12. By default, the **Sketch Plane** option is selected in this drop-down list. As a result, the base flange starts exactly from the sketching plane of the sketch.

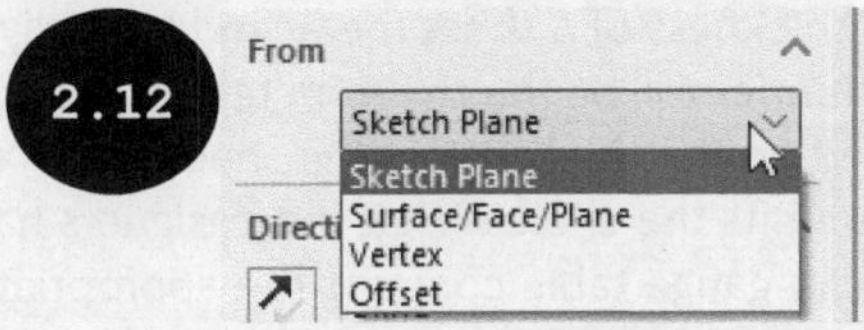

The **Surface/Face/Plane**, **Vertex**, and **Offset** options of the drop-down list are used for defining the start condition of the base flange up to a selected surface, face, or plane; up to a selected vertex; or at a specified offset distance, respectively. Note that these options are applicable when creating the second and subsequent flanges of a sheet metal component.

Direction 1

The options in the **Direction 1** rollout of the PropertyManager are used for defining the end condition or termination of the base flange in one direction. Note that this rollout is available only if the sketch of the base flange is an open sketch.

Tip: If the **Direction 1** rollout is in collapsed form, you need to expand it by clicking on the arrow available in its title bar for displaying its options.

By default, the **Blind** option is selected in the **End Condition** drop-down list of the **Direction 1** rollout. As a result, you can specify the end condition of the base flange in one direction by specifying its depth value in the **Depth** field of the rollout, see Figure 2.13. The **Reverse Direction** button is used to flip the direction of extrusion to either side of the sketching plane.

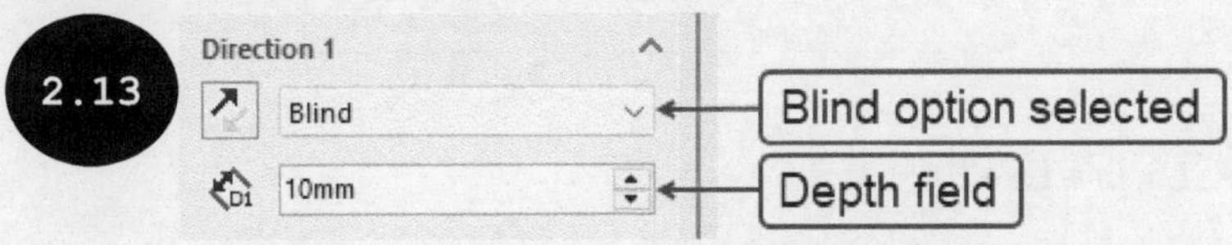

The **Mid Plane** option in the **End Condition** drop-down list is used for extruding the base flange symmetrically about the sketching plane. The **Up To Vertex**, **Up To Surface**, and **Offset From Surface** options of the drop-down list are used for extruding the base flange up to a selected vertex, surface, and at an offset distance from a selected surface, respectively. Note that these options are used while creating the second and further flanges of a sheet metal component.

Direction 2

The options in the **Direction 2** rollout are the same as those in the **Direction 1** rollout of the PropertyManager with the only difference that the options of the **Direction 2** rollout are used for specifying the end condition of the base flange in the second direction of the sketching plane.

Note: As discussed earlier, the **Direction 1** and **Direction 2** rollouts of the PropertyManager are available only if the sketch of the base flange is an open sketch.

Sheet Metal Gauges

In SOLIDWORKS, you can select a gauge table with pre-defined sheet metal parameters for creating a sheet metal component. A gauge table is simply a Microsoft Excel spreadsheet, which enables you to choose an appropriate sheet metal thickness, based on the material and the gauge numbers. A gauge number refers to the standard thickness of a sheet metal and typically is in the range of 3 to 38. The higher the gauge number, the thinner will be the sheet metal thickness. A gauge table also contains a list of available bend radii, based on the thickness of the sheet metal and the available tooling to be used in the bending process. It limits the choices that the designers have for selecting a bend radius based on availability. Moreover, a gauge table contains the appropriate K-factor for calculating the bend allowance, which represents the stretch of the sheet metal in the bent regions, see Figure 2.14. Alternatively, it can contain the calculated bend allowance or bend deduction values to represent the stretch of sheet metal in the bend regions for calculating the total flat length of the sheet, refer to Figures 2.14 and 2.15. Figure 2.14 illustrates the concept of bend allowance for calculating the flat length of sheet metal.

2.14

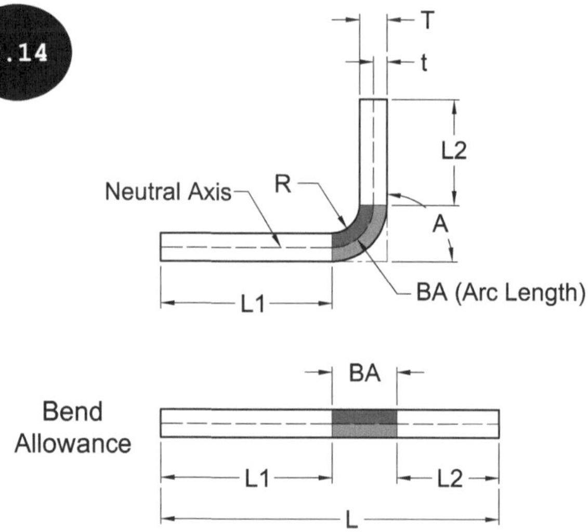

L = L1 + L2 + BA

Where,

L = Total flat length
L1 = Leg length 1
L2 = Leg length 2
BA = Bend allowance

Bend allowance (BA) = A (π / 180) (R + (K x T))

Where,

A = Bend angle

R = Inside bend radius
K = K-factor
T = Material Thickness

K-factor (K) = t / T

Where,

T = Material Thickness
t = Distance from the neutral axis to the inside face

Note: The K-factor is defined as the ratio between the distance from the neutral axis to the inner bend face and the material thickness. Note that when a sheet is bent, its inner portion gets compressed, and its outer portion gets expanded/stretched. The line where the transition from the compression to the expansion occurs is known as the neutral axis, refer to Figures 2.14 and 2.15. The original position of the neutral axis is at 50 percent (center) of the material thickness of a flat sheet. However, when bending the sheet, the position of the neutral axis gets shifted towards the inner face of the bend and it varies depending on the bend angle, bend radius, material properties, and the method of bending.

Figure 2.15 illustrates the concept of bend deduction for calculating the flat length of sheet metal.

2.15

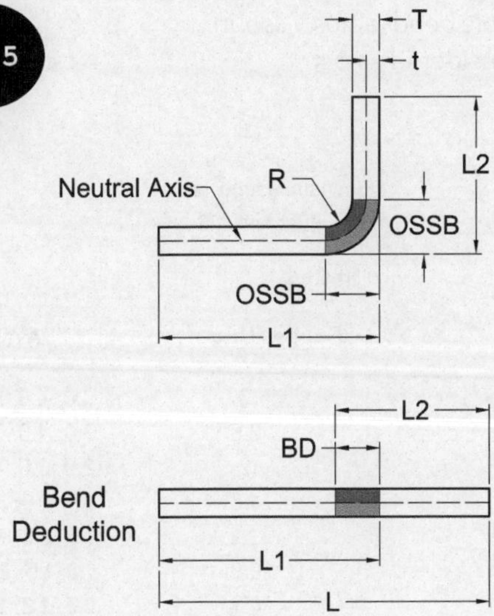

L = L1 + L2 - BD

Where,

L = Total flat length
L1 = Leg length 1
L2 = Leg length 2
BD = Bend deduction

Bend deduction (BD) = (2 X OSSB) - BA

Where,

OSSB = Outside setback
BA = Bend allowance

Outside setback (OSSB) = (R + T) Tan A/2

Where,

R = Inside bend radius
T = Material Thickness
A = Bend angle

To select a gauge table with pre-defined sheet metal parameters, select the **Use gauge table** check box in the **Sheet Metal Gauges** rollout of the PropertyManager. The **Select Table** drop-down list is enabled below this check box. This drop-down list displays a list of all the available gauge tables, see Figure 2.16. Select the required gauge table in this drop-down list. Figure 2.17 shows the default "**SAMPLE TABLE - ALUMINUM - METRIC UNITS**" gauge table. In this table, the gauge numbers are available in the range from 10 to 26. Also, each gauge number represents a standard thickness and the available bend radius. Also, in this gauge table, the K-factor is considered as 0.5.

2.16

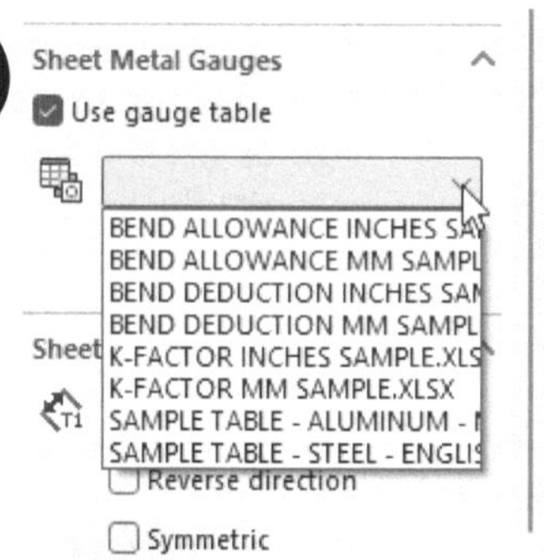

2.17

	A	B	C
1			
2	**Type:**	Aluminum Gauge Table	
3	**Process**	Aluminum - Coining	
4	**K-Factor**	0.5	
5	**Unit:**	millimeters	
6			
7	**Gauge No.**	**Gauge (Thickness)**	**Available Bend Radius**
8	Gauge 10	3	3.0; 4.0; 5.0; 8.0; 10.0
9	Gauge 12	2.5	3.0; 4.0; 5.0; 8.0; 10.0
10	Gauge 14	2	2.0; 3.0; 4.0; 5.0; 8.0; 10.0
11	Gauge 16	1.5	1.5; 2.0; 3.0; 4.0; 5.0; 8.0; 10.0
12	Gauge 18	1.2	1.5; 2.0; 3.0; 4.0; 5.0; 8.0; 10.0
13	Gauge 20	0.9	1.0; 1.5; 2.0; 3.0; 4.0; 5.0
14	Gauge 22	0.7	0.8; 1.0; 1.5; 2.0; 3.0; 4.0; 5.0
15	Gauge 24	0.6	0.8; 1.0; 1.5; 2.0; 3.0; 4.0; 5.0
16	Gauge 26	0.5	0.5; 0.8; 1.0; 1.5; 2.0; 3.0; 4.0; 5.0
17			

Figure 2.18 shows an upper portion of the default "**BEND ALLOWANCE MM SAMPLE**" gauge table. In this table, the available gauge numbers are 3, 4, and 5. Also, the calculated bend allowance is defined as corresponding to the bend angle and the bend radius. For example, the bend allowance corresponding to the bend angle of 90 degrees and the bend radius of 3 mm is defined as 0.27 mm in the case of gauge 5.

2.18

	A	B	C	D	E	F
1	**Type:**	Steel Gauge Table				
2	**Process**	Steel Air Bending				
3	**Bend Type:**	Bend Allowance				
4	**Unit:**	millimeters				
5	**Material:**	Steel				
6						
7						
8	**Gauge No.**	**Gauge 5**				
9	**Thickness:**	**1**				
10	**Angle**	**Radius**				
11		1.00	2.00	3.00	4.00	
12	15	0.25	0.26	0.27	0.28	
13	30	0.25	0.26	0.27	0.28	
14	45	0.25	0.26	0.27	0.28	
15	60	0.25	0.26	0.27	0.28	
16	75	0.25	0.26	0.27	0.28	
17	90	0.25	0.26	0.27	0.28	
18						
19						
20	**Gauge No.**	**Gauge 4**				
21	**Thickness:**	**1.5**				
22	**Angle**	**Radius**				
23		1.00	2.00	3.00	4.00	
24	15	0.30	0.31	0.32	0.33	
25	30	0.30	0.31	0.32	0.33	
26	45	0.30	0.31	0.32	0.33	
27	60	0.30	0.31	0.32	0.33	
28	75	0.30	0.31	0.32	0.33	
29	90	0.30	0.31	0.32	0.33	

In SOLIDWORKS, you can edit the parameters of a default gauge table or create a new gauge table in the Microsoft Excel spreadsheet. To do so, browse to *C:\Program Files\SOLIDWORKS Corp\SOLIDWORKS\lang\english\Sheet Metal Gauge Tables* location in the installation directory of your system, see Figure 2.19. Next, double-click on an existing gauge table to open it as a Microsoft Excel spreadsheet and then edit its properties, as required. Next, save the modified gauge table with a new name in the **Sheet Metal Gauge Tables** folder at the same location. Note that the Microsoft Excel spreadsheet files that are saved in the **Sheet Metal Gauge Tables** folder are displayed in the **Select Table** drop-down list of the **Sheet Metal Gauges** rollout in the PropertyManager as gauge tables.

2.19

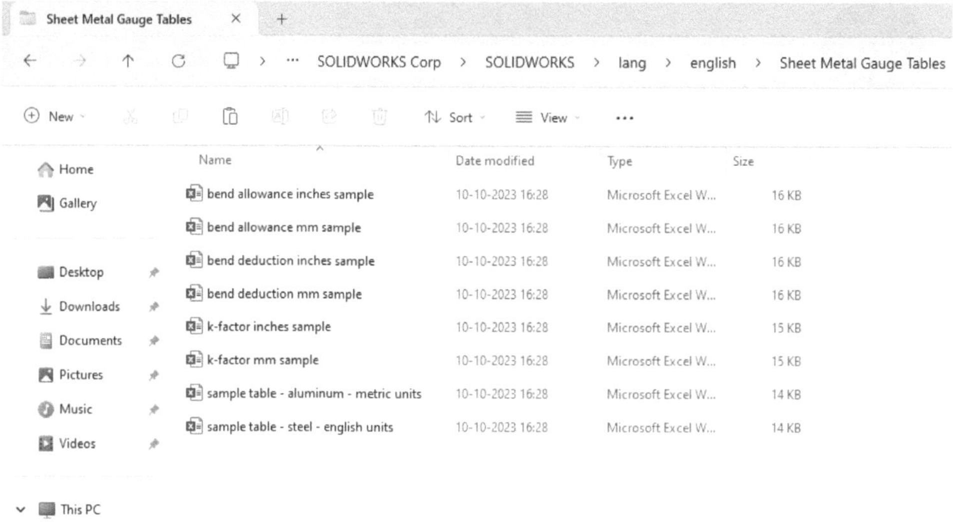

After selecting a gauge table in the **Select Table** drop-down list of the **Sheet Metal Gauges** rollout in the PropertyManager, the options for defining the material thickness, bend radius, and bend allowance become available in the respective drop-down lists of the PropertyManager, see Figure 2.20.

2.20

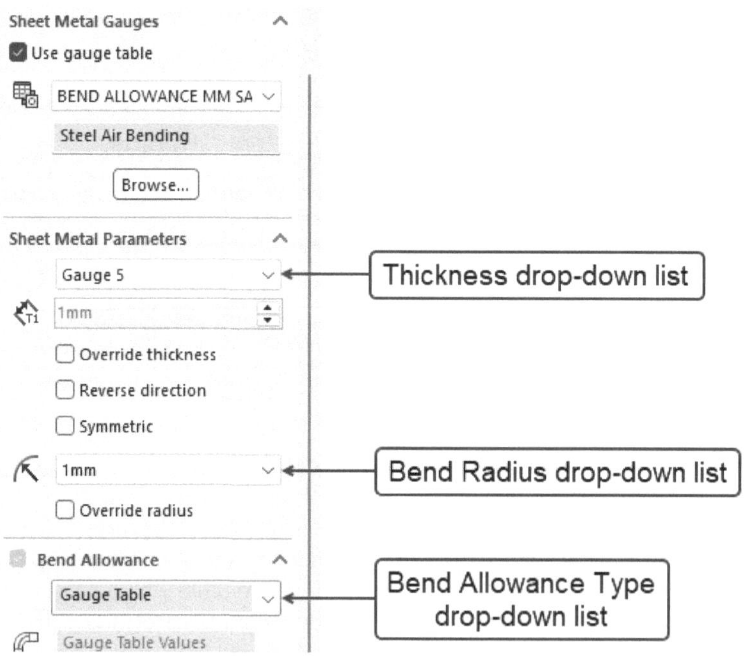

The availability of these options depends upon the data specified in the selected gauge table. Select the required option to define the material thickness in terms of a gauge number and the bend radius of the sheet in the respective drop-down list. Also, the **Gauge Table** option is selected in the **Bend Allowance Type** drop-down list, by default. As a result, the value for calculating the flat length of the sheet metal in terms of bend allowance, bend deduction, or K-factor is imported from the selected gauge table. You can select any other option in the **Bend Allowance Type** drop-down list to manually define the respective value for calculating the flat length of the sheet.

Note: The selection of a gauge table limits the choice that the designers have for defining the sheet metal thickness and the bend radius based on availability. However, you can override the thickness and bend radius values by selecting the **Override thickness** and **Override radius** check boxes in the **Sheet Metal Parameters** rollout, respectively.

Tip: Without using a gauge table, you can define the sheet metal parameters, manually in the **Sheet Metal Parameters** and **Bend Allowance** rollouts of the PropertyManager.

Sheet Metal Parameters

The options in the **Sheet Metal Parameters** rollout are used for defining the material thickness and the bend radius, see Figure 2.21. The options are discussed next.

2.21

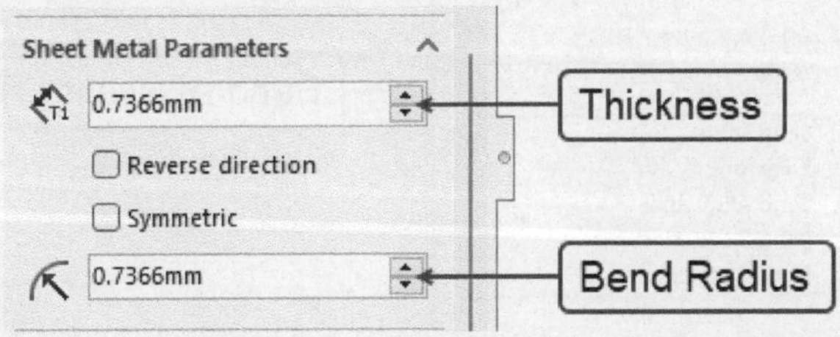

Note: The availability of options in the **Sheet Metal Parameters** rollout for defining the sheet metal thickness and bend radius depends on whether a gauge table is selected or not. Figure 2.21 shows the **Sheet Metal Parameters** rollout when a gauge table is not selected.

Thickness

The **Thickness** field of the **Sheet Metal Parameters** rollout is used for specifying a uniform thickness for the sheet metal component to be created.

Bend Radius

The **Bend Radius** field is used for specifying a default bend radius for the sheet metal. You can enter a bend radius in this field, based on the thickness of the sheet metal and the available tooling to be used in the bending process, refer to Figure 2.22. In this figure, a typical punch and die set is used for bending a sheet of uniform thickness. Note that the punch and die have a radius at their peak, and these radii cause a specific bend radius in the sheet metal when forming a bend in the bending process.

2.22

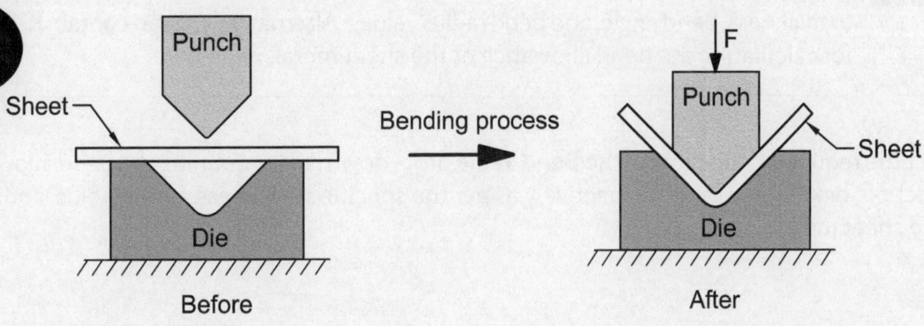

Reverse direction

The **Reverse direction** check box is used for flipping the direction of material thickness to the other side of the sketch in the graphics area.

Symmetric

The **Symmetric** check box is used for adding material thickness equally on both sides of the sketch in the graphics area.

Bend Allowance

The **Bend Allowance Type** drop-down list in the **Bend Allowance** rollout is used for selecting an option to define the bend allowance, which represents the stretch of the sheet metal in the bent regions. Figure 2.23 shows the expanded **Bend Allowance Type** drop-down list. The options in this drop-down list are discussed next.

2.23

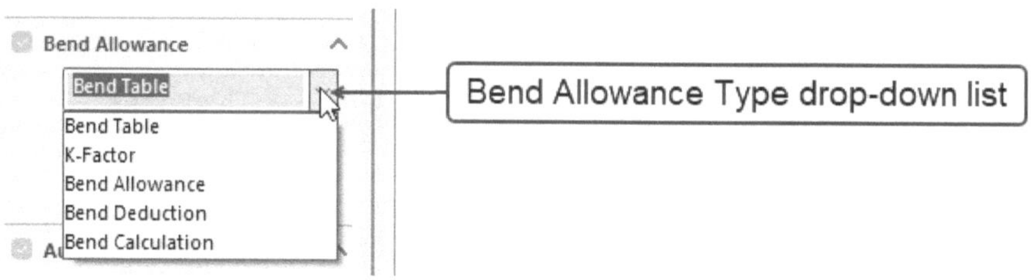

Bend Table

The **Bend Table** option is used for selecting a bend table, which is simply a Microsoft Excel spreadsheet for defining the bend allowance of the sheet metal. On selecting this option, the **Bend Table** drop-down list becomes available in the rollout with a list of all the available bend tables, see Figure 2.24. In this figure, a list of default bend tables is displayed in the drop-down list.

2.24

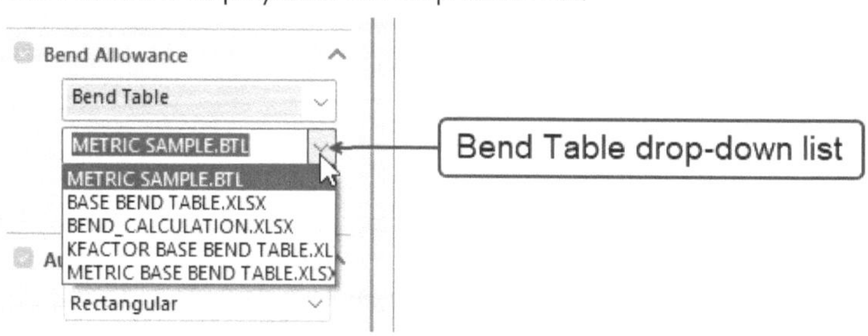

Note: A bend table contains calculated bend allowance or bend deduction values corresponding to thickness, bend angle, and bend radius values. Alternatively, it can contain K-Factor values for calculating the bend allowance of the sheet metal.

Select the required bend table in the **Bend Table** drop-down list for defining the bend allowance, bend deduction, or K-factor value, respectively as per the specified thickness, bend radius, and bend angle of the sheet metal.

Note: You can edit a default bend table or create a new bend table in the Microsoft Excel spreadsheet. For doing so, browse to *C:\Program Files\SOLIDWORKS Corp\SOLIDWORKS\lang\english\Sheetmetal Bend Tables* location in the installation directory of your system. Next, double-click on an existing bend table to open it as a Microsoft Excel spreadsheet and then edit its properties or enter new properties, as required. Next, save the modified bend table with a new name in the **Sheetmetal Bend Tables** folder at the same location. Note that the Microsoft Excel spreadsheet files that are saved in the **Sheetmetal Bend Tables** folder are displayed in the **Bend Table** drop-down list as bend tables. In addition to the Microsoft Excel file, a bend table can also be created as a text file with ***.btl*** file extension.

K-Factor

On selecting the **K-Factor** option in the **Bend Allowance Type** drop-down list, you need to manually enter the required K-factor value in the field that appears below the drop-down list, see Figure 2.25. The concept of K-Factor is discussed earlier under the heading **Sheet Metal Gauges**.

Note: The concepts of bend allowance, bend deduction, and K-Factor are discussed earlier with illustrations discussing the topic **Sheet Metal Gauges**, refer to page 32.

Bend Allowance

On selecting the **Bend Allowance** option, you need to manually enter the bend allowance value in the field that appears below the drop-down list, see Figure 2.26.

2.25

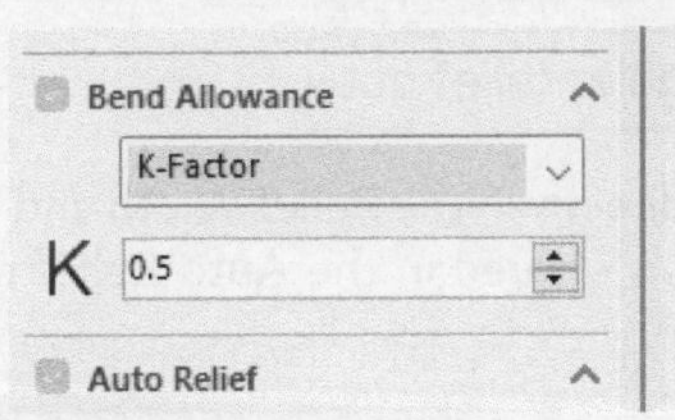

2.26

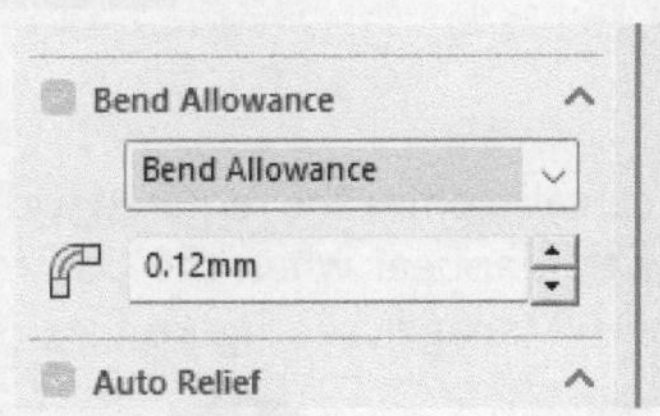

Bend Deduction

On selecting the **Bend Deduction** option in the **Bend Allowance Type** drop-down list, you need to manually enter the bend deduction value in the field that appears below the drop-down list.

Bend Calculation

On selecting the **Bend Calculation** option, the bend allowance, bend deduction, or K-factor value gets imported from the table selected in the drop-down list that appears below the **Bend Allowance Type** drop-down list.

Auto Relief

The **Auto Relief Type** drop-down list in the **Auto Relief** rollout is used for selecting a relief type (rectangular, tear, or obround) to be added automatically in bend regions for preventing or avoiding unwanted deformation or tear in the sheet metal. Figure 2.27 shows the options in the **Auto Relief Type** drop-down list and the same are discussed next.

2.27

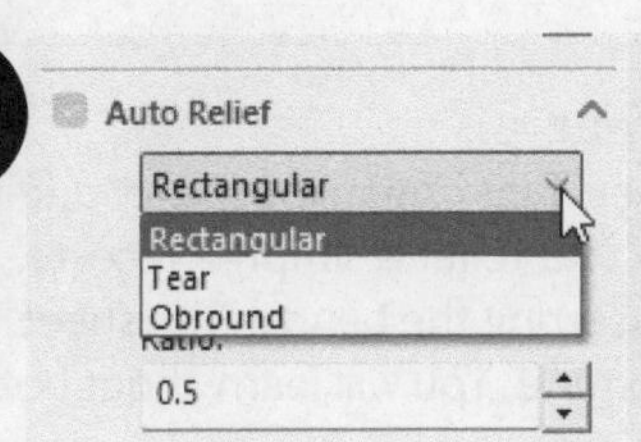

Rectangular

The **Rectangular** option is used for adding rectangular relief cuts in the bend regions of a sheet, refer to Figure 2.28. When you select this option, you need to define the width and depth values of the rectangular relief cut. By default, the **Use relief ratio** check box is selected in the **Auto Relief** rollout. As a result, the relief ratio is used for calculating the width and depth values of the relief cut. You can enter the relief ratio in the range from 0.05 to 2.0 in the **Relief Ratio** field of the rollout. The higher the value of the relief ratio, the larger the size (depth and width) of the relief cut added in the bend region. The equations for calculating the width and depth values by using the relief ratio are given below:

Width value = Relief ratio x Material Thickness

Depth value = Relief ratio x Material Thickness

2.28

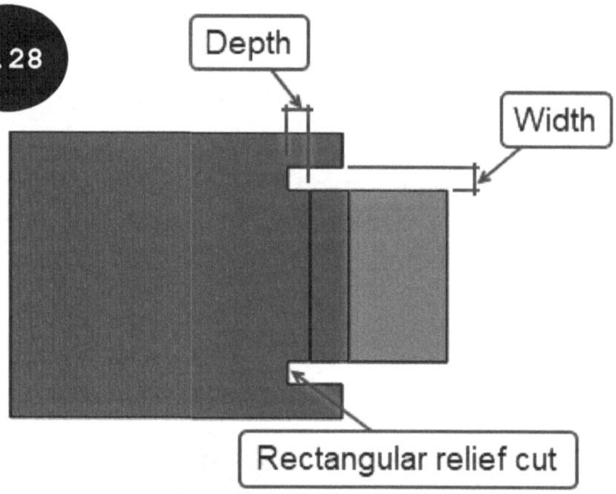

You can also enter the required width and depth values directly in the **Relief Width** and **Relief Depth** fields that appear when the **Use relief ratio** check box is cleared in the **Auto Relief** rollout of the PropertyManager, see Figure 2.29.

2.29

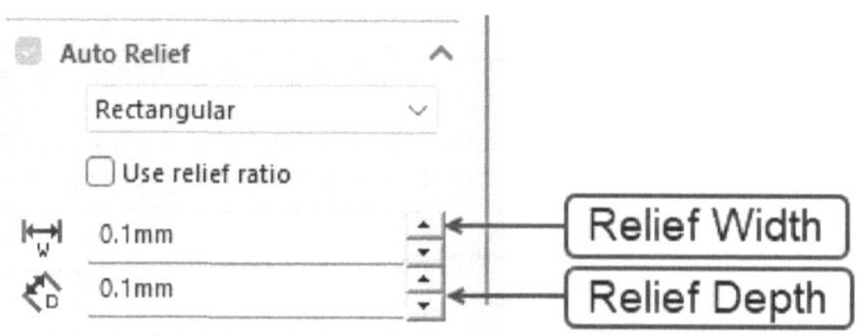

Note: In Figure 2.28, an edge flange is created at an angle on an existing edge of the sheet with rectangular relief cut. You will learn more about creating edge flange and the application of adding reliefs in the bends later.

Tear

The **Tear** option is used for adding tear relief cuts in the bend regions of the sheet, refer to Figure 2.30. A tear relief is simply a face-to-face shear of the material with no gap. It requires a minimum size for inserting the bend in the sheet. In SOLIDWORKS, you can add two types of tear relief cuts: **Rip** and **Extend**. You will learn about both these types of tear reliefs later.

2.30

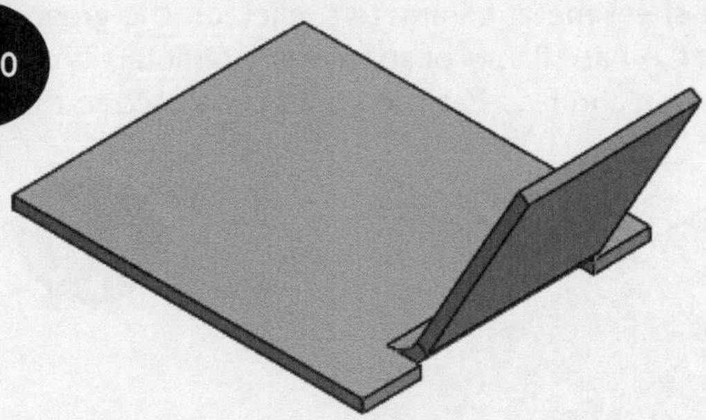

Obround

The **Obround** option is used for adding obround relief cuts in the bend regions of a sheet, refer to Figure 2.31. When you select this option, you need to define the width and depth values of the obround relief cut. By default, the **Use relief ratio** check box is selected in the **Auto Relief** rollout. As a result, the relief ratio is used for calculating the width and depth values of the relief cut. You can enter the relief ratio in the range from 0.05 to 2.0 in the **Relief Ratio** field of the rollout. The higher the value of the relief ratio, the larger the size (depth and width) of the relief cut added in the bend region. The equations for calculating the width and depth values by using the relief ratio are the same as discussed earlier while creating the rectangular relief cut.

2.31

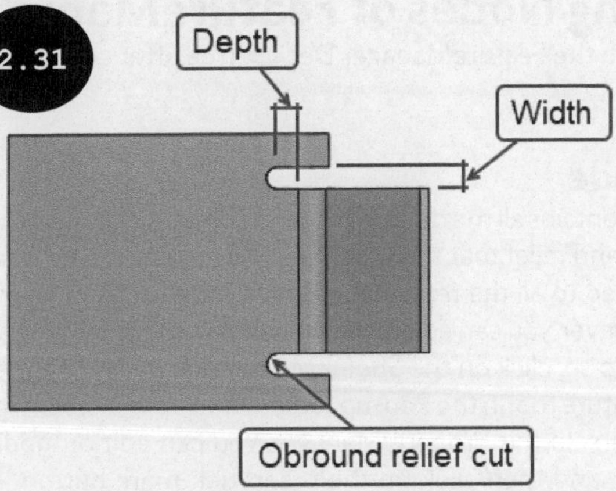

You can also enter the required width and depth values directly in the **Relief Width** and **Relief Depth** fields that appear when the **Use relief ratio** check box is cleared in the **Auto Relief** rollout of the PropertyManager.

Note: All the sheet metal parameters such as material thickness, bend radius, bend allowance, and relief that are specified while creating a base flange in the **Base Flange PropertyManager** will be used as default parameters for creating all the remaining flanges or features of the sheet metal component.

After specifying all the sheet metal parameters, click on the green tick-mark button in the **Base Flange PropertyManager**. A base flange of specified parameters is created, see Figure 2.32. Also, the **Sheet-Metal**, **Base-Flange1**, and **Flat-Pattern** nodes get added to the FeatureManager Design Tree, see Figure 2.33.

2.32

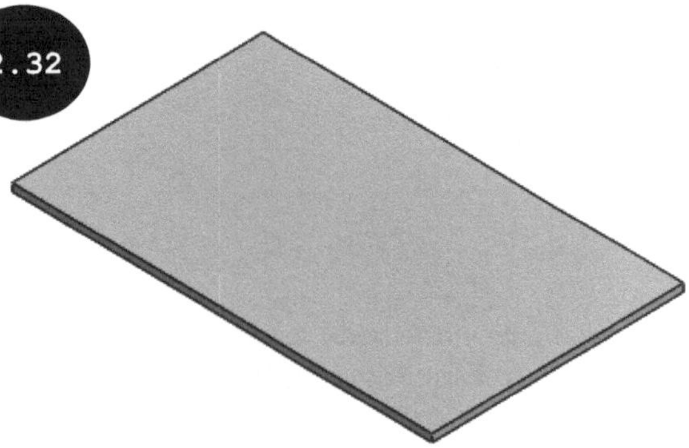

2.33

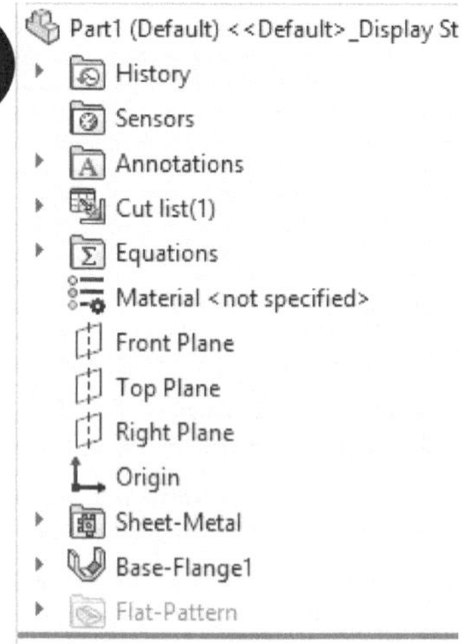

Understanding Nodes of FeatureManager Design Tree

Different nodes added to the FeatureManager Design Tree after creating a base flange are discussed next.

Sheet-Metal Node

The **Sheet-Metal** node contains all the default sheet-metal parameters such as material thickness, bend radius, bend allowance, and relief that are specified while creating the base flange. These parameters are automatically assigned to all the remaining flanges or features of the sheet metal component as default parameters. However, you can edit these default parameters of a sheet metal component at any stage of the design. To do so, click on the **Sheet-Metal** node in the FeatureManager Design Tree and then click on the **Edit Feature** tool in the Pop-up toolbar that appears, see Figure 2.34. The **Sheet-Metal PropertyManager** appears. In this PropertyManager, you can edit or modify the default sheet metal parameters, as required, and then click on the green tick-mark button in the PropertyManager to confirm the changes made and exit the PropertyManager.

2.34

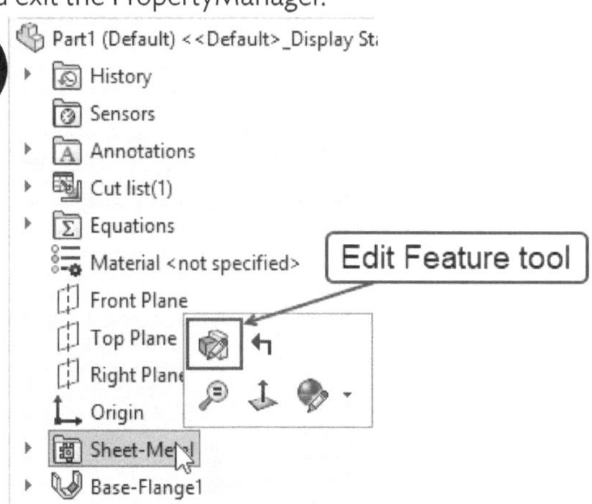

Base-Flange1 Node

The **Base-Flange1** node represents the base feature of the sheet metal component and gets added to the FeatureManager Design Tree after creating the base flange. It is used for editing or overriding the default parameters of the base flange as well as editing its sketch. To override the default parameters of the base flange, click on the **Base-Flange1** node in the FeatureManager Design Tree and then click on the **Edit Feature** tool in the Pop-up toolbar that appears, see Figure 2.35. The **Base-Flange1 PropertyManager** appears. In this PropertyManager, select the **Override default parameters** check box and then override the default parameters of the base flange by entering new values in the respective fields that are enabled in the PropertyManager. After overriding the default parameters, click on the green tick-mark button in the PropertyManager to confirm the changes made and exit the PropertyManager.

Similarly, to edit the sketch of the base flange, click on the **Base-Flange1** node and then click on the **Edit Sketch** tool in the Pop-up toolbar that appears, see Figure 2.36. The Sketching environment gets invoked. Now, you can edit the sketch of the base flange by using the sketching tools, as required in the Sketching environment.

2.35

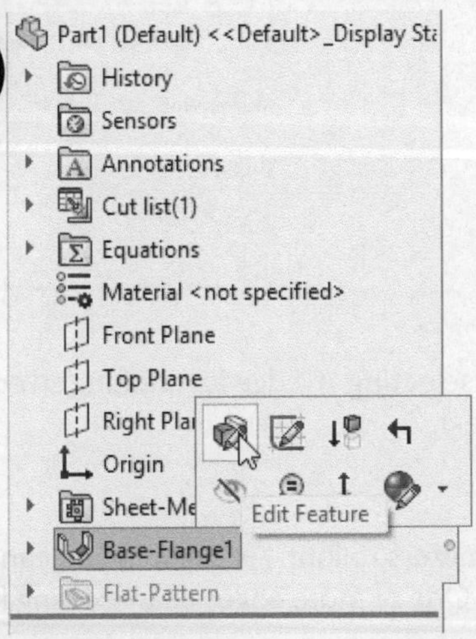

2.36

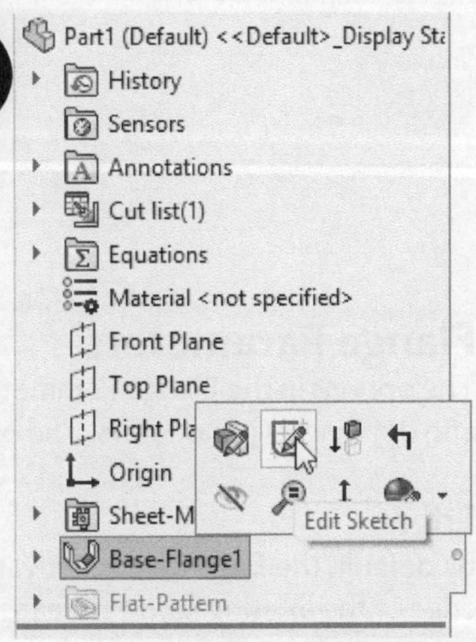

Flat-Pattern Node

The **Flat-Pattern** node is used for creating the flat pattern of the sheet metal component. By default, this node is in suppressed mode and appears in a light grey in the FeatureManager Design Tree. You will learn more about creating a flat pattern of a sheet metal component later.

Creating an Edge Flange

A flange that is created on the edge of an existing flange of a sheet metal component is known as the edge flange. To create an edge flange, click on the **Edge Flange** tool in the **Sheet Metal CommandManager**, see Figure 2.37. The **Edge-Flange1 PropertyManager** appears, see Figure 2.38. Also, you are prompted to select an edge of a planar face for creating an edge flange, since the **Edge** field is activated in the PropertyManager, by default. The options in the PropertyManager are discussed next.

2.37

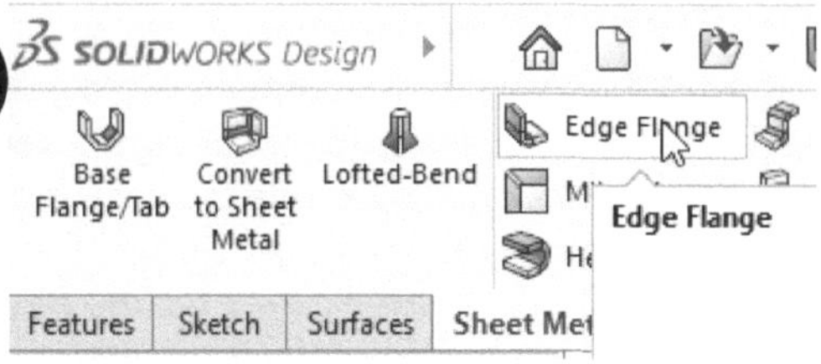

2.38

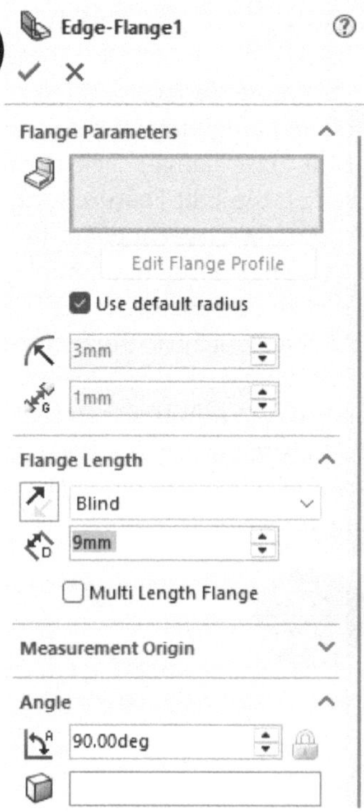

Flange Parameters

The options in the **Flange Parameters** rollout are used for selecting an edge for creating an edge flange and defining its parameters. The options are discussed next.

Edge

By default, the **Edge** field is activated in the **Flange Parameters** rollout. As a result, you can select an edge of the existing flange or feature in the graphics area. One or more edges of an existing flange can be selected.

After selecting an edge, the preview of an edge flange appears along its entire length in the graphics area with two arrows, see Figure 2.39. Also, the name of the selected edge appears in the **Edge** field of the **Flange Parameters** rollout. Next, move the cursor to either side of the selected edge to define the direction of flange creation and then click to define the length of the edge flange arbitrarily in the graphics area. Note that as you move the cursor, the length of the flange gets increased or decreased, dynamically in the graphics area. You can select one or more edges to create a flange.

2.39

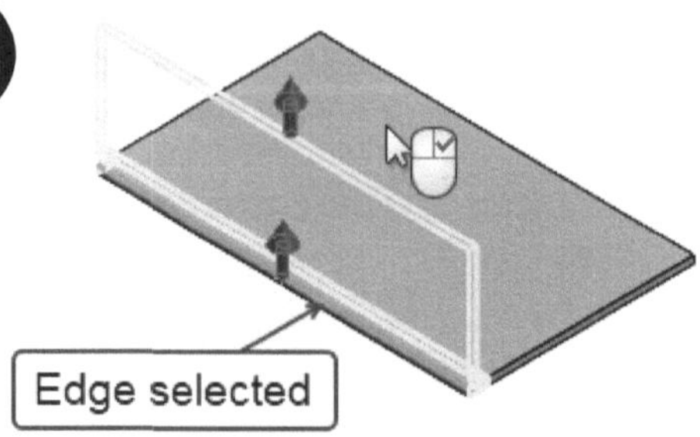

Note: After defining the length of the edge flange by clicking the left mouse button, you can select other edges of existing flanges as well for creating multiple edge flanges along the selected edges.

Edit Flange Profile

The **Edit Flange Profile** button in the **Flange Parameters** rollout is used for editing the profile of the edge flange. By default, the edge flange is created along the entire length of the selected edge, refer to Figure 2.39. To edit the profile of the edge flange, click on the **Edit Flange Profile** button. The Sketching environment gets invoked. Also, the **Profile Sketch** dialog box appears, informing the sketch is valid, see Figure 2.40.

2.40

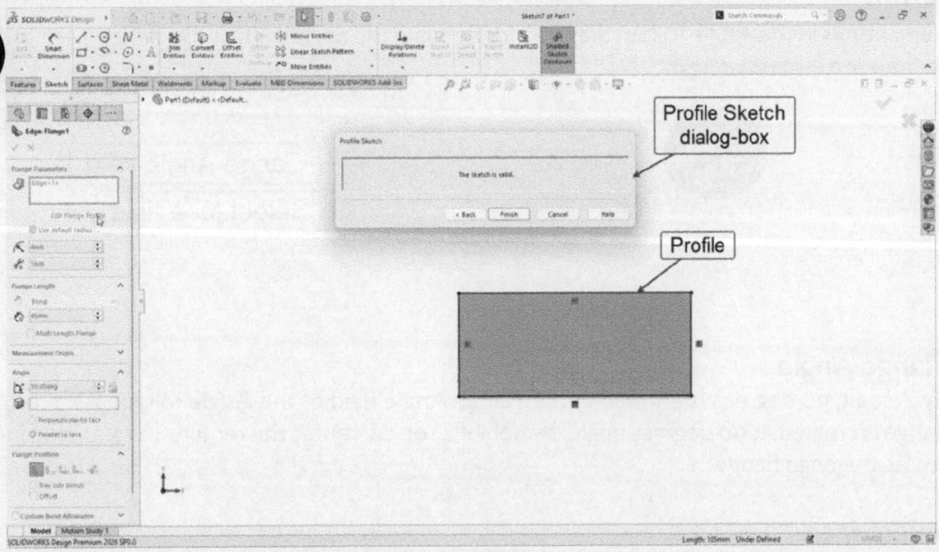

Now, you can edit the sketch of the profile by using the sketching tools in the Sketching environment, as required. You can also drag the entities of the sketch to edit the width of the flange along the selected edge or the length of the flange. After editing the sketch, ensure that the sketch of the profile is valid. A message for the same appears in the **Profile Sketch** dialog box. Next, click on the **Back** button in the **Profile Sketch** dialog box to switch back to the **Edge Flange PropertyManager** for defining the remaining parameters of the edge flange. Note that if you click on the **Finish** button in this dialog box, then an edge flange of modified profile and specified parameters gets created on the selected edge. Figure 2.41 shows the preview of an edge flange after modifying its width along the selected edge.

2.41

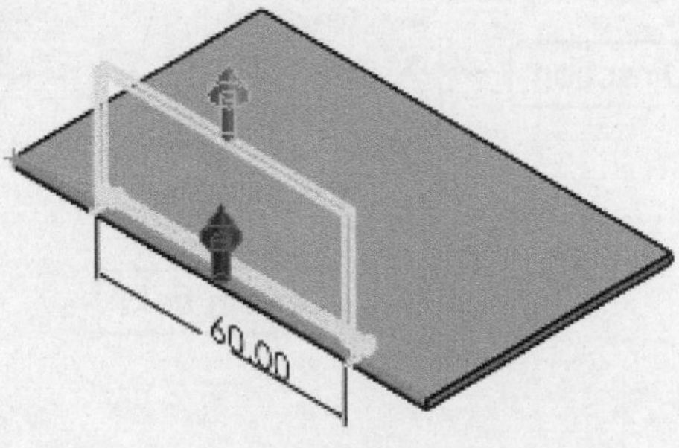

Use default radius

By default, the **Use default radius** check box is selected in the **Flange Parameters** rollout. As a result, the default bend radius is used for creating the edge flange. However, you can edit or override the default bend radius. To do so, clear the **Use default radius** check box and then enter a new bend radius value in the **Bend Radius** field that is enabled in the **Flange Parameters** rollout.

Use gauge table

The **Use gauge table** check box is used for selecting a new bend radius from the list of available bend radii in the selected gauge table. Note that this check box is enabled only if a gauge table is selected for defining the sheet metal parameters while creating the base flange of the component.

Angle

The options in the **Angle** rollout are used for defining the angle of the edge flange, see Figure 2.42. The options are discussed next.

2.42

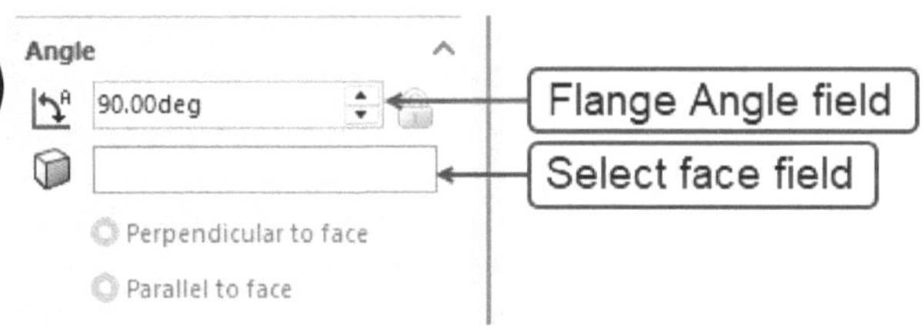

Flange Angle

By default, **90** degrees is entered in the **Flange Angle** field of the **Angle** rollout. As a result, the edge flange is created at 90 degrees angle, by default. You can enter the required angle value in this field to create the edge flange.

Select face

The **Select face** field is used for creating an edge flange, perpendicular or parallel to a selected face. To do so, click on the **Select face** field and then select a face in the graphics area. The **Perpendicular to face** and **Parallel to face** radio buttons are enabled in the rollout. Select the required radio button for creating the edge flange perpendicular or parallel to the selected face of the component, respectively.

Flange Length

The options in the **Flange Length** rollout are used for defining the length of the edge flange, see Figure 2.43. The options are discussed next.

2.43

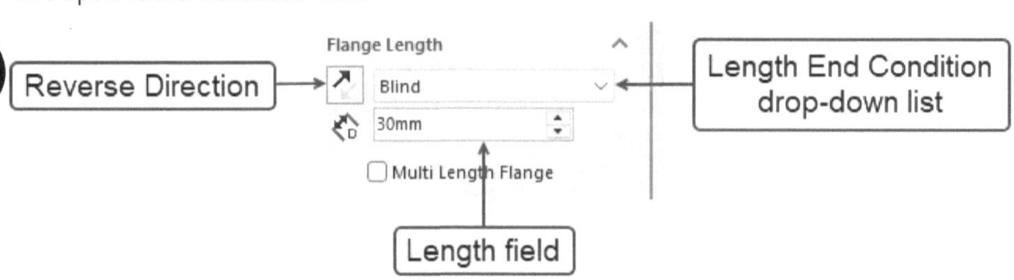

Length End Condition Drop-down List

By default, the **Blind** option is selected in the **Length End Condition** drop-down list of the **Flange Length** rollout, refer to Figure 2.43. As a result, you can enter the length of the edge flange in the **Length** field. You can also click on the Direction arrow that appears in the graphics area and then move the cursor upward or downward to define the length of the flange, dynamically, see Figure 2.44. The **Up To Vertex** option of the **Length End Condition** drop-down list is used for defining the length of the edge flange up to a selected vertex. The **Up To Edge And Merge** option defines the length of the edge flange up to an edge of another body and merges the bodies. This option is used when working with multi-body parts.

2.44

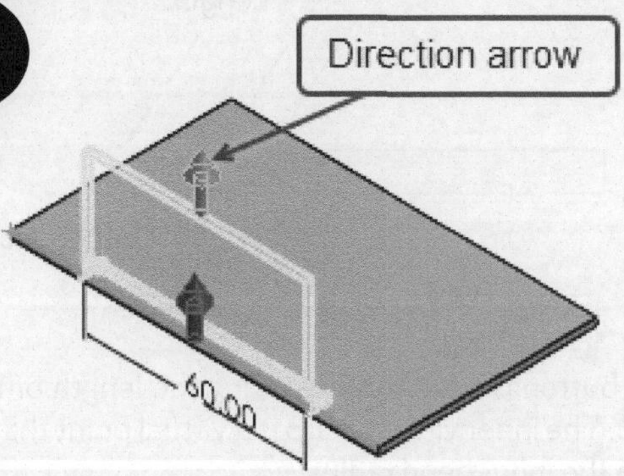

Reverse Direction

The **Reverse Direction** button in the **Flange Length** rollout is used for flipping the direction of an edge flange to the other side of the selected edge. You can also click on the Reverse Direction arrow that appears in the graphics area to flip the direction of the edge flange in the graphics area, see Figure 2.45.

2.45

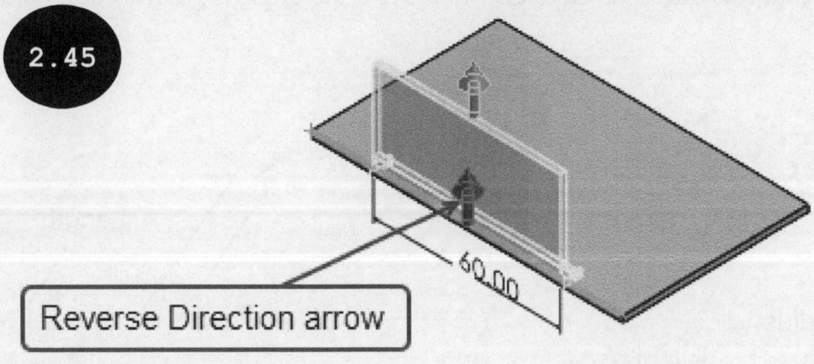

Multi Length Flange

By default, the **Multi Length Flange** check box is cleared in the **Flange Length** rollout. Therefore, if multiple edges are selected, flanges of equal length are created on all the selected edges.

When this check box is selected, you can assign different flange lengths to each selected edge. This option enables you to create flanges with varying lengths on different edges within the same feature.

Measurement Origin

The options in the **Measurement Origin** rollout are used for measuring the length of the flange, see Figure 2.46. The options are discussed next.

2.46

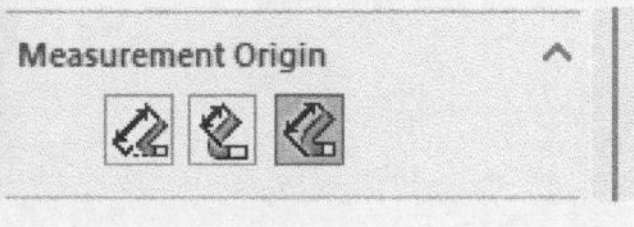

Outer Virtual Sharp

The **Outer Virtual Sharp** button in the **Flange Length** rollout is used for measuring the length of the flange from the outer virtual sharp, refer to Figure 2.47. The outer virtual sharp is a virtual point that is created at the intersection of edges that are tangent to the outer bend radius.

2.47

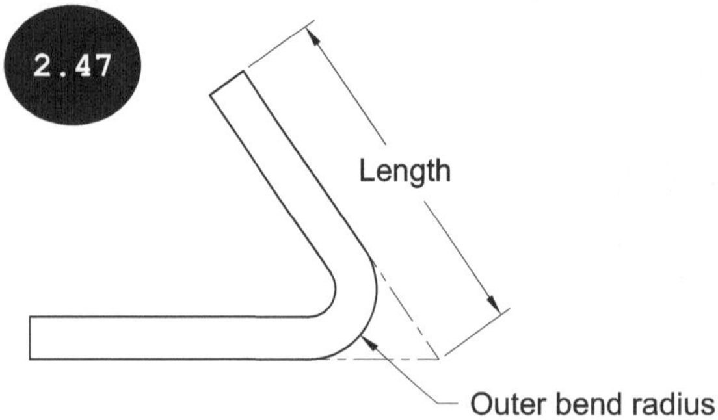

Inner Virtual Sharp

The **Inner Virtual Sharp** button is used for measuring the length of the flange from the inner virtual sharp, refer to Figure 2.48. The inner virtual sharp is a virtual point that is created at the intersection of edges that are tangent to the inner bend radius.

Tangent Bend

The **Tangent Bend** button is used for measuring the length of the flange from an imaginary line that is tangent to the outer bend radius and parallel to the end edge of the flange being created, refer to Figure 2.49. Note that this button is enabled when the bend angle is greater than 90 degrees and less than 180 degrees.

2.48

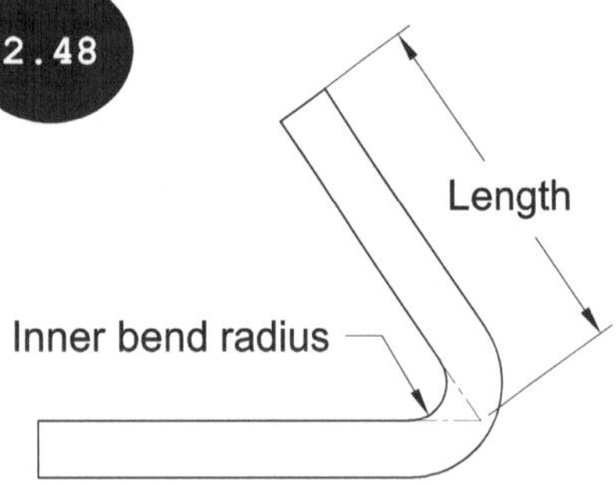

2.49

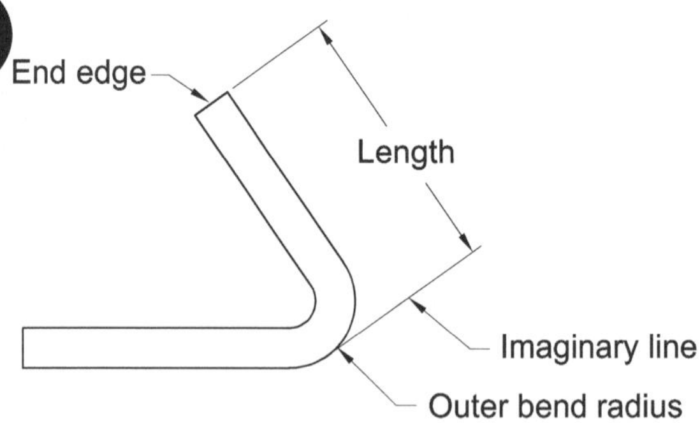

Flange Position

The options in the **Flange Position** rollout are used for defining the position of the edge flange, see Figure 2.50. The options are discussed next.

2.50

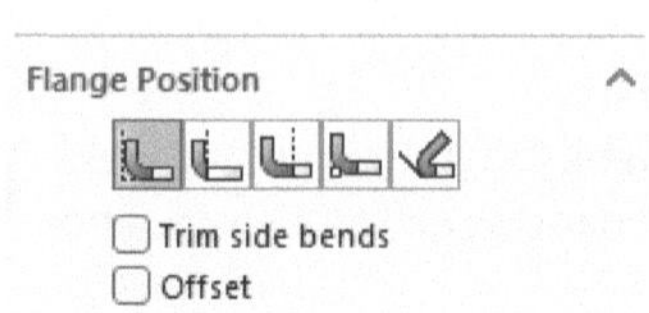

Material Inside

The **Material Inside** button is used for adding flange thickness inside the maximum limit of the sheet, see Figure 2.51.

2.51

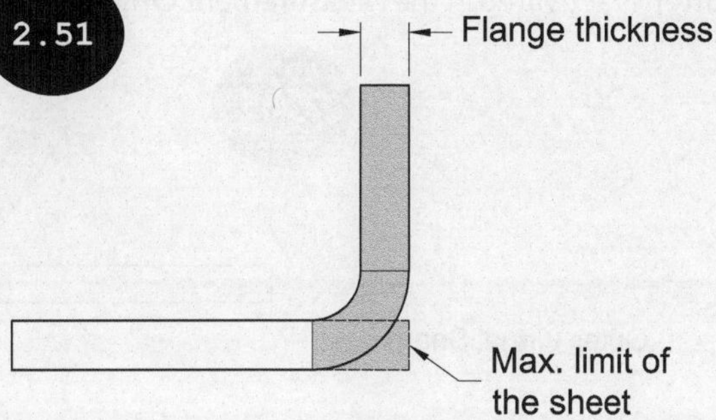

Material Outside

The **Material Outside** button is used for adding the flange thickness outside the maximum limit of the sheet, see Figure 2.52.

2.52

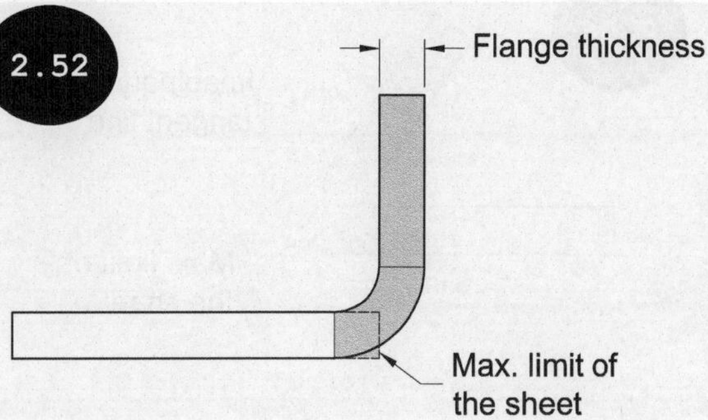

Bend Outside

The **Bend Outside** button is used for creating an edge flange such that its bend starts from the end of the maximum limit of the sheet, see Figure 2.53.

2.53

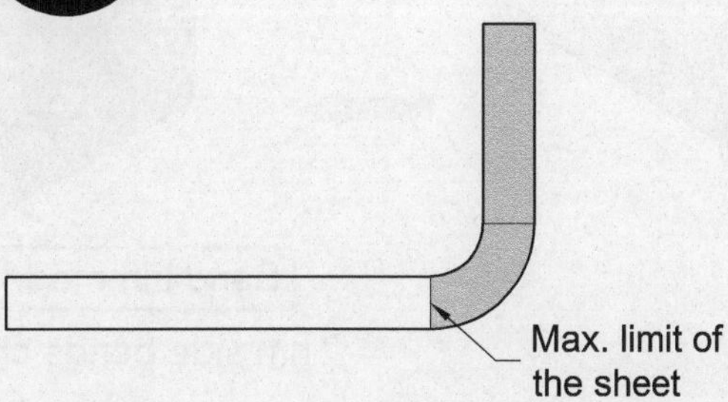

Bend from Virtual Sharp

The **Bend from Virtual Sharp** button is used for creating an edge flange such that the bending (bend angle) starts from the virtual sharp, see Figures 2.54 and 2.55. Note that the virtual sharp can either be the outer virtual sharp or the inner virtual sharp depending upon whether the **Outer Virtual Sharp** or the **Inner Virtual Sharp** button is activated in the **Measurement Origin** rollout of the PropertyManager.

2.54

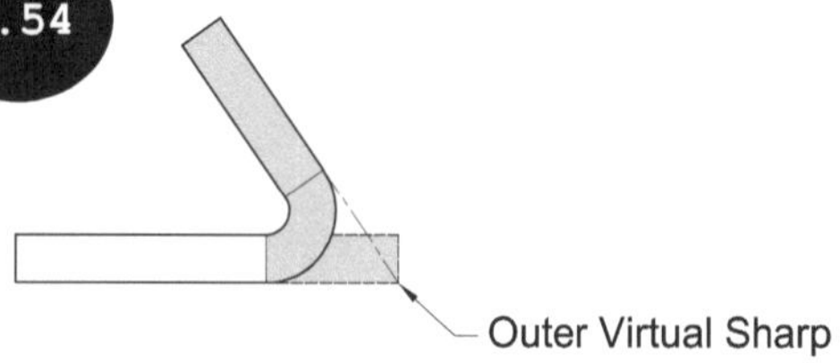

2.55

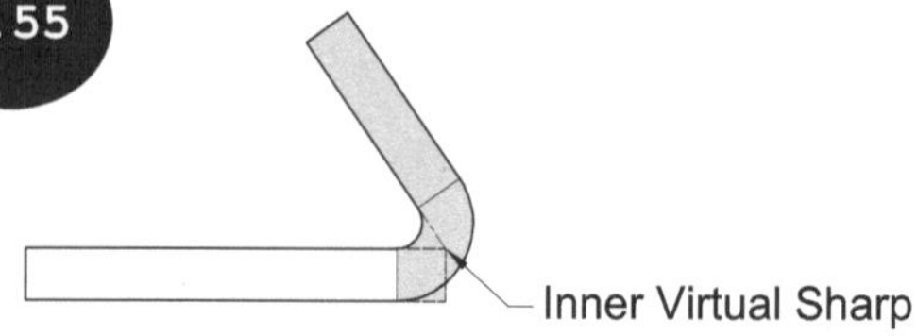

Tangent to Bend

The **Tangent to Bend** button is used for creating an edge flange such that the bend of the flange lies tangent to the maximum limit of the sheet, see Figure 2.56. Note that this button is enabled when the bend angle is greater than 90 degrees and less than 180 degrees.

2.56

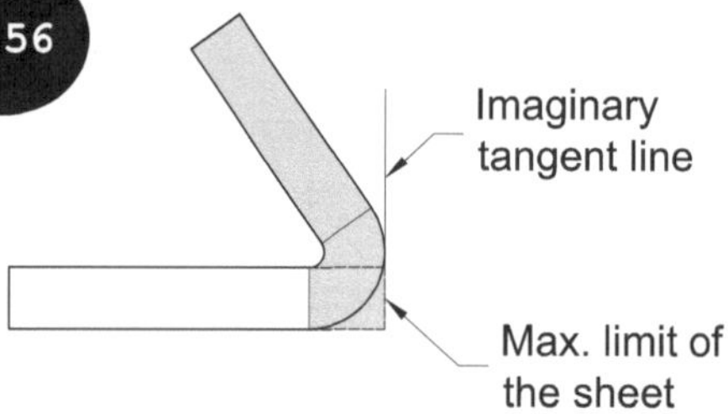

Trim side bends

The **Trim side bends** check box in the **Flange Position** rollout is used for trimming or removing the extra material from the bends of the existing side flanges, see Figures 2.57 and 2.58. In Figure 2.57, an edge flange is created by selecting the **Trim side bends** check box, whereas in Figure 2.58, an edge flange is created by clearing the **Trim side bends** check box.

2.57

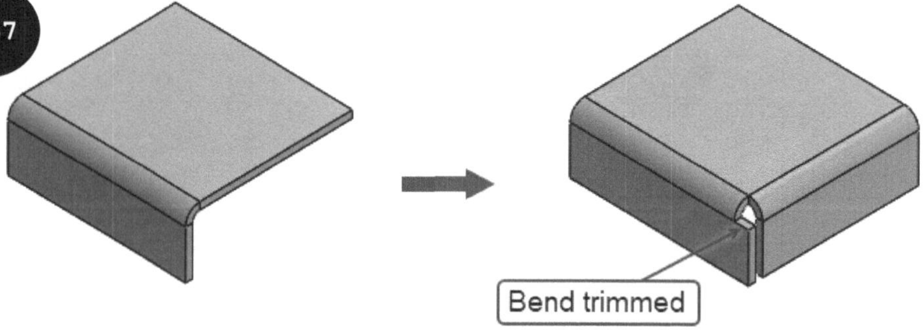

Trim side bends check box is selected

2.58

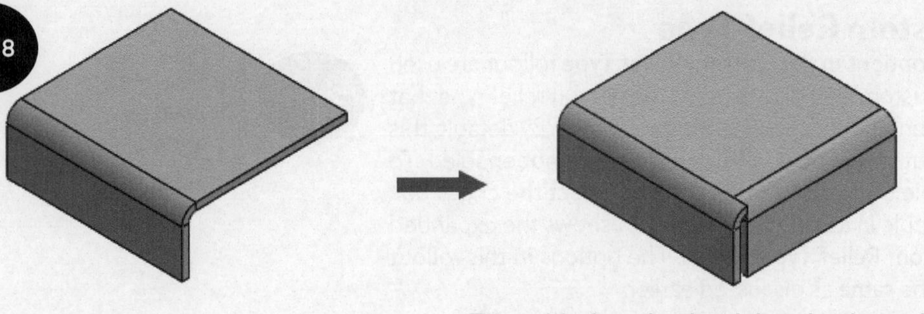

Tip: In Figures 2.57 and 2.58, the edge flange is created by defining its position (flange thickness) inside the maximum limit of the sheet.

Offset

The **Offset** check box is used for creating an edge flange at an offset distance from the selected edge, see Figure 2.59. When this check box is selected, the **Offset End Condition** drop-down list and the **Offset Distance** field become available in the **Flange Position** rollout. By default, the **Blind** option is selected in the **Offset End Condition** drop-down list. As a result, you can specify an offset distance in the **Offset Distance** field of the rollout for creating an edge flange. You can also select the **Up To Vertex**, **Up To Surface**, or **Offset From Surface** option in this drop-down list for defining the end condition of an edge flange, respectively.

2.59

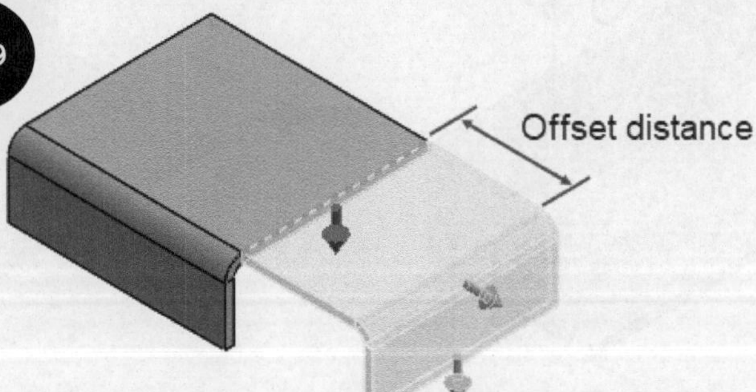

Note: The **Offset** check box is not available when the **Bend from Virtual Sharp** button is selected for defining the position of the edge flange in the **Flange Position** rollout.

Custom Bend Allowance

The options in the **Custom Bend Allowance** rollout are used for customizing or overriding the default bend allowance that is defined while creating the base flange. By default, this rollout is collapsed and its options are not enabled. To enable the options of this rollout, select the check box available in its title bar. Figure 2.60 shows the expanded **Custom Bend Allowance** rollout. The options in this rollout are the same as discussed earlier.

2.60

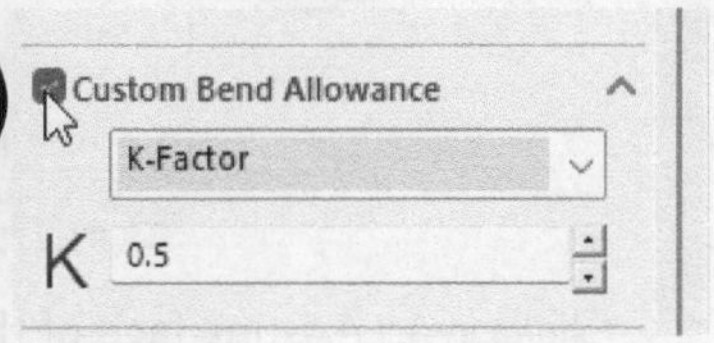

Custom Relief Type

The options in the **Custom Relief Type** rollout are used for customizing or overriding the default relief type that is defined while creating the base flange. By default, this rollout is collapsed, and its options are not enabled. To enable the options of this rollout, select the check box available in its title bar. Figure 2.61 shows the expanded **Custom Relief Type** rollout. The options in this rollout are the same as discussed earlier.

2.61

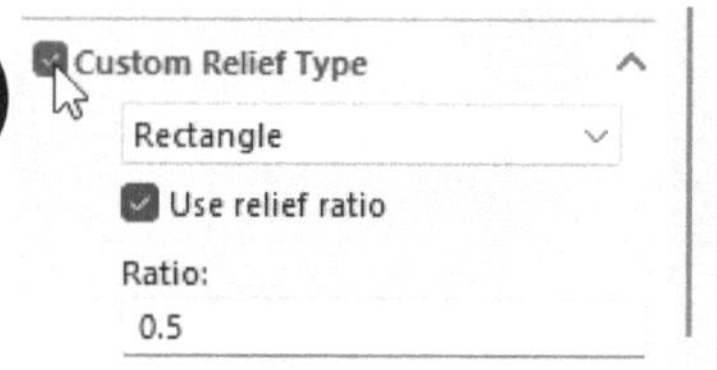

After defining all the required options for creating an edge flange, click on the green tick-mark button in the **Edge Flange PropertyManager**. An edge flange with specified parameters is created in the graphics area.

Creating a Tab Feature

A tab feature is created by adding material equivalent to the thickness of the sheet metal component. The thickness of a tab feature is defined automatically as equivalent to the thickness of the sheet and its profile or outline is defined by a sketch geometry, see Figure 2.62. The method for creating a tab feature is discussed below:

2.62

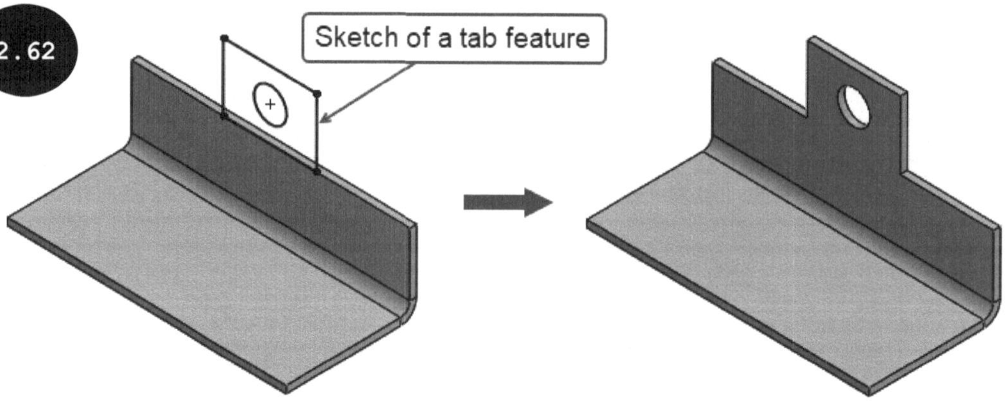

1. Click on the **Base Flange/Tab** tool in the **Sheet Metal CommandManager**, see Figure 2.63. The **Message PropertyManager** appears, and you are prompted to either select a plane or a planar face for creating a sketch of the tab feature or an existing sketch.

2.63

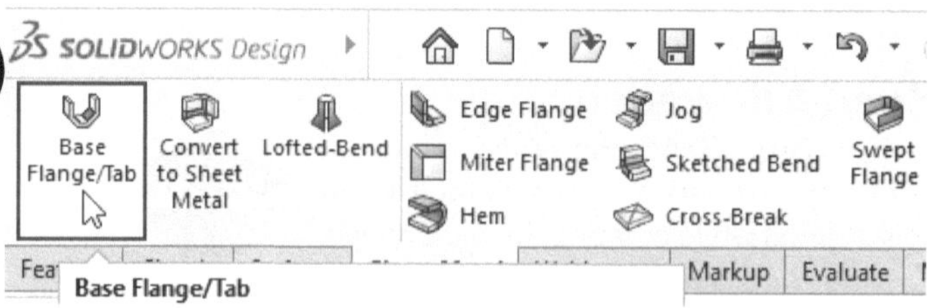

2. Click on an existing face of the sheet metal component to create the sketch of the tab feature. The Sketching environment gets invoked and the selected face gets oriented normal to the viewing direction.

Tip: If the sketch is already created in the graphics area, then you can select it as the sketch of the tab feature before or after invoking the **Base Flange/Tab** tool.

As the name of the **Base Flange/Tab** tool suggests, it is used for creating a base feature as well as a tab feature of a sheet metal component.

3. Create a sketch of the tab feature in the graphics area by using the sketching tools, refer to Figure 2.64.

2.64

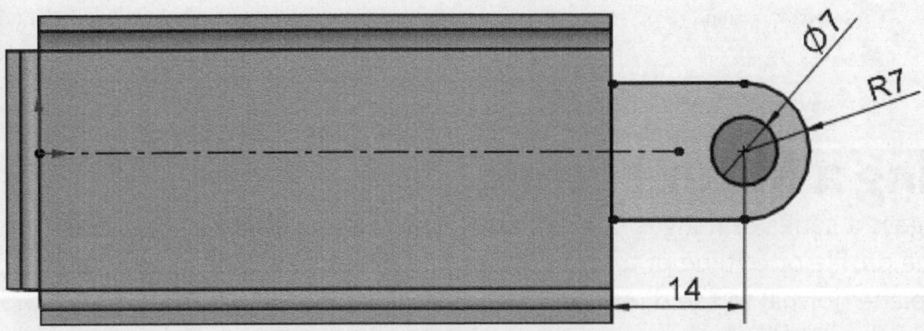

Note: The sketch of a tab feature should be a closed sketch. If you create an open sketch, the base flange will be created as a new sheet body.

4. After creating the sketch, exit the Sketching environment by clicking on the **Exit Sketch** tool in the **Sketch CommandManager**. The **Base Flange PropertyManager** appears, see Figure 2.65. Also, a preview of the tab feature appears in the graphics area having the same thickness as the thickness of the sheet.

Note: By default, the direction of the tab feature is defined automatically to make it coincident with the thickness of the sheet for preventing any disjoint in the component. However, if needed, you can reverse its direction to the other side of the sketching plane by selecting the **Reverse direction** check box in the PropertyManager.

Also, the **Merge result** check box is selected in the PropertyManager, by default. As a result, the resultant tab feature gets merged with the sheet. If you clear this check box, the tab feature does not merge with the sheet and creates a separate body.

5. Accept the default options and then click on the green tick-mark in the PropertyManager. The tab feature gets created, refer to Figure 2.66.

2.65

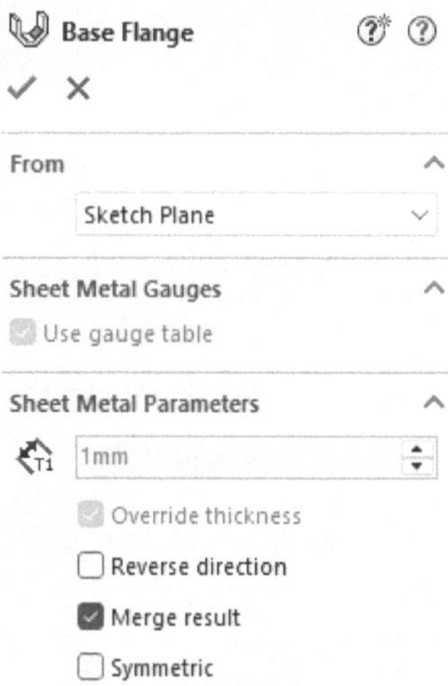

2.66

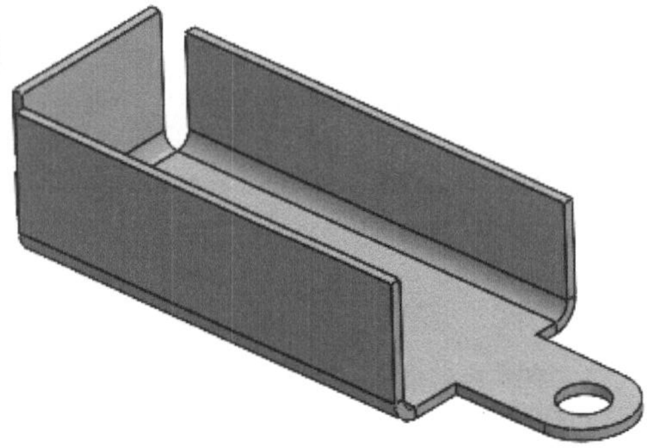

Creating a Miter Flange

A miter flange is a series of flanges created along the existing edges of the sheet metal component. Note that the profile or outline of a miter flange is defined by a sketch geometry that is created on a sketching plane normal to the direction of its extrusion, see Figure 2.67. The method for creating a miter flange is discussed below:

2.67

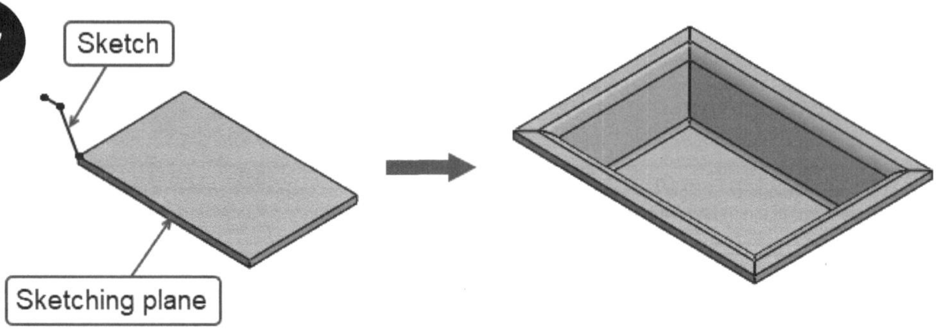

1. Click on the **Miter Flange** tool in the **Sheet Metal CommandManager**, see Figure 2.68. The **Message PropertyManager** appears, and you are prompted to either select a plane or a planar face for creating a sketch of a miter flange or an existing sketch.

2.68

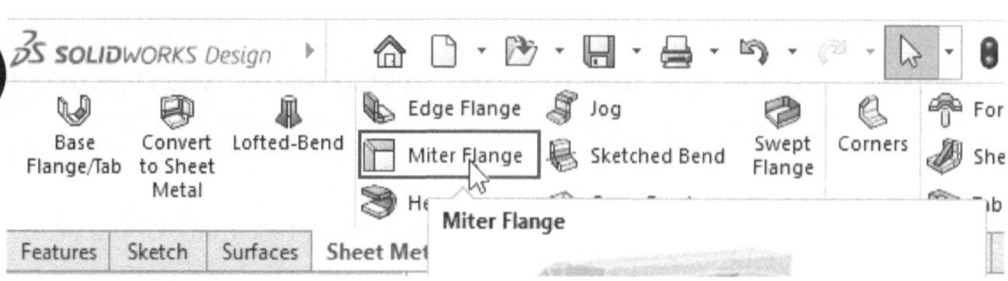

2. Click on a planar face of the sheet metal component that is normal to the direction of extrusion of the miter flange. The Sketching environment gets invoked and the selected planar face gets oriented normal to the viewing direction.

Tip: If the sketch is already created in the graphics area, then you can select it as the sketch of the miter flange before or after invoking the **Miter Flange** tool.

3. Create a sketch of the miter flange by using the sketching tools, refer to Figure 2.69.

2.69

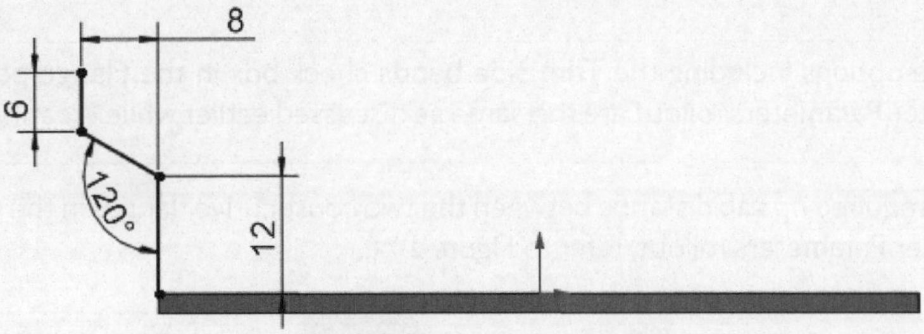

Note: The sketch of a tab feature should be a valid open sketch.

4. After creating the sketch, exit the Sketching environment by clicking on the **Exit Sketch** tool in the **Sketch CommandManager**. The **Miter Flange PropertyManager** appears, see Figure 2.70. Also, a preview of the miter flange appears in the graphics area along an edge normal to the sketching plane of the sheet, see Figure 2.71. In this figure, the orientation of the model is changed to isometric.

2.70

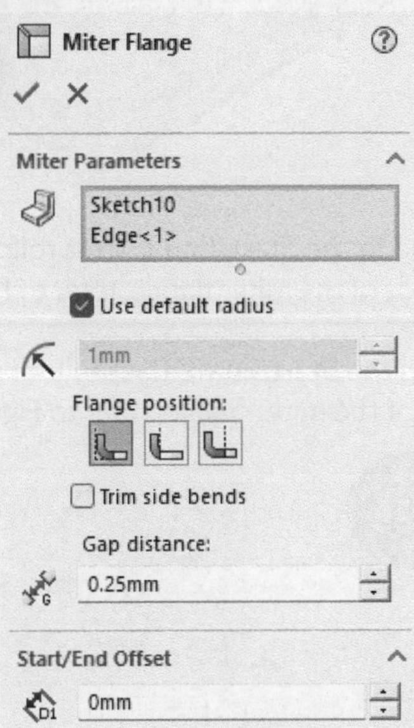

2.71

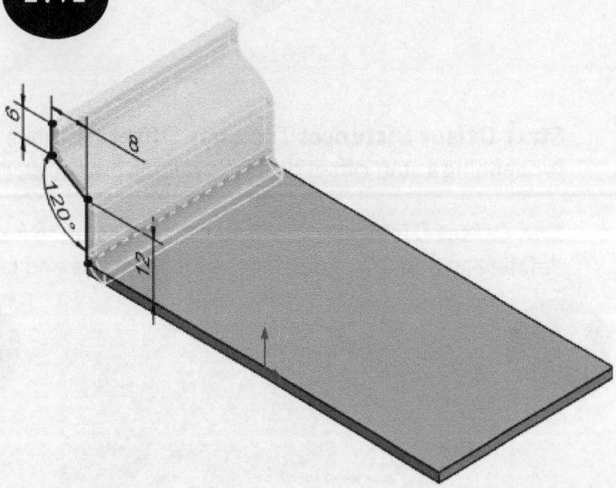

Note: By default, the **Use default radius** check box is selected in the **Miter Flange PropertyManager**. As a result, the default bend radius is used for the miter flange. However, you can override the default bend radius value by clearing the **Use default radius** check box and then entering a new bend radius in the **Bend Radius** field that is enabled below this check box in the PropertyManager.

5. Click to select other connected edges of the sheet one by one to create a series of flanges. The preview appears along all the selected edges of the sheet, see Figure 2.72. Also, the names of all the selected edges appear in the **Along Edges** field of the **Miter Parameters** rollout.

6. Define the position of the flanges by activating the required button (**Material Inside**, **Material Outside**, or **Bend Outside**) in the **Flange position** area of the **Miter Parameters** rollout.

Note: The options including the **Trim side bends** check box in the **Flange position** area of the **Miter Parameters** rollout are the same as discussed earlier while creating an edge flange.

7. Enter the required rip gap distance between the two consecutive flanges in the **Gap distance** field of the **Miter Parameters** rollout, refer to Figure 2.73.

2.72

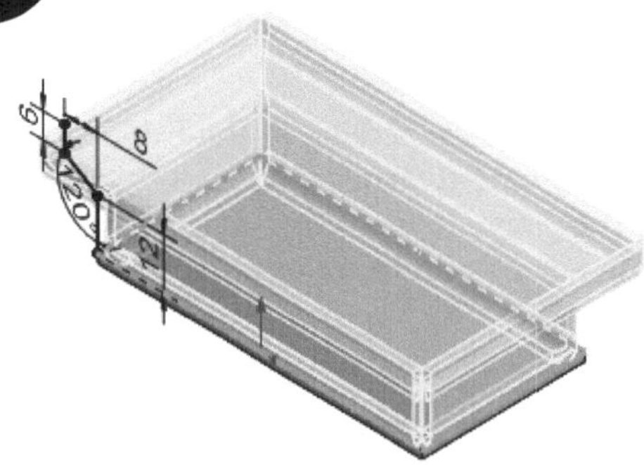

2.73

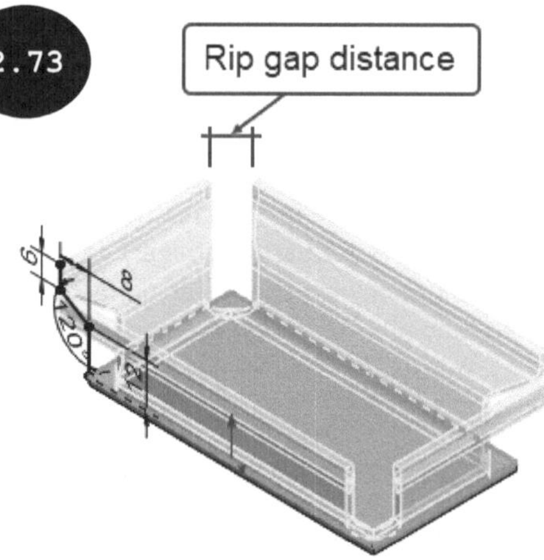

Start Offset Distance: The Start Offset Distance field in the **Start/End Offset** rollout is used for defining a start offset distance value from the start face of the miter flange, refer to Figure 2.74.

End Offset Distance: The End Offset Distance field in the **Start/End Offset** rollout is used for defining an end offset distance value from the end face of the miter flange, refer to Figure 2.75.

2.74

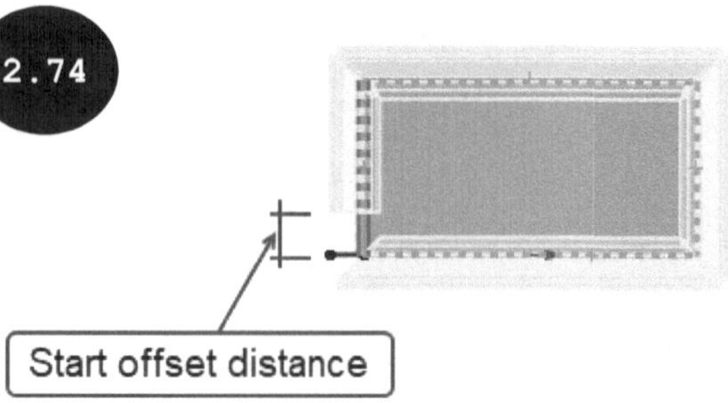

2.75

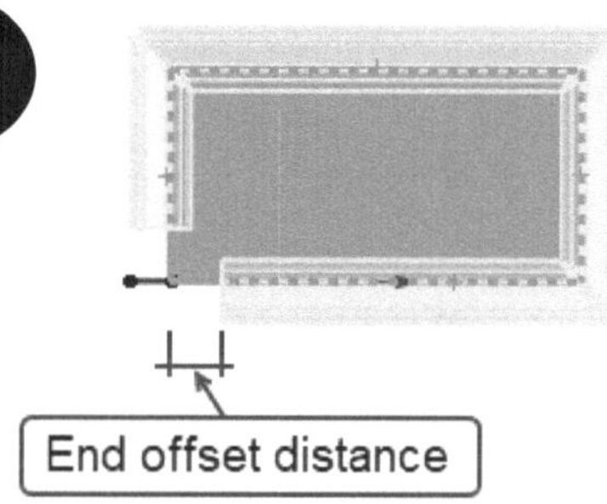

Note: The start offset distance is applied to the first selected edge, whereas the end offset distance is applied to the last selected edge of a series of continuous flanges.

By default, 0 (zero) is entered in the **Start Offset Distance** and **End Offset Distance** fields. As a result, the flanges on the first and last selected edges are created along their full length without any offset distance.

8. If needed, enter the required start and end offset distance values in the **Start Offset Distance** and the **End Offset Distance** fields of the **Start/End Offset** rollout, respectively.

Note: The options in the **Custom Bend Allowance** and **Custom Relief Type** rollouts of the PropertyManager are used for customizing or overriding the default bend allowance and relief type that are defined while creating the base flange. The options are same as discussed earlier.

9. Click on the green tick-mark button in the PropertyManager. The miter flange is created on the selected edges of the sheet, see Figure 2.76.

2.76

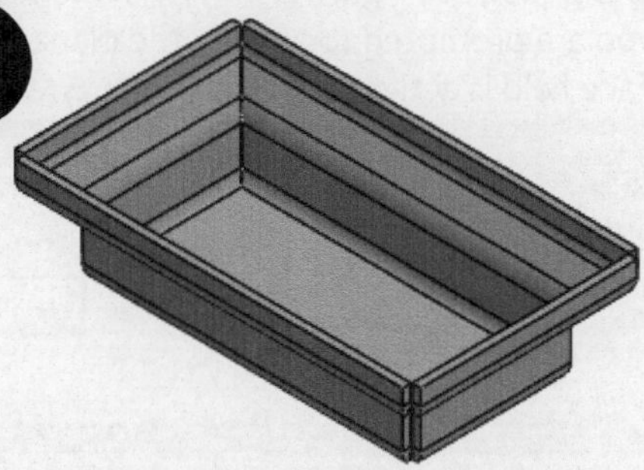

Creating a Sketched Bend

A sketched bend is a bend created by using a sketch line as the bending line, see Figure 2.77. The method for creating a sketched bend is discussed below:

2.77

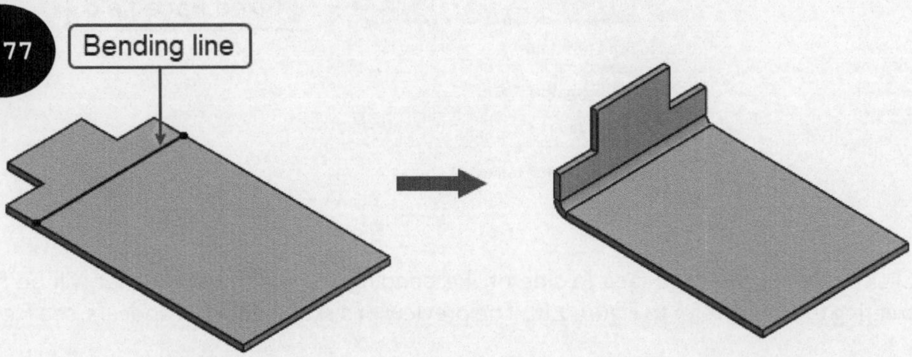

1. Invoke the Sketching environment by selecting a planar face of the sheet on which a bending line is to be created.

2. Create a line as the bending line by using the **Line** tool, refer to Figure 2.78.

2.78

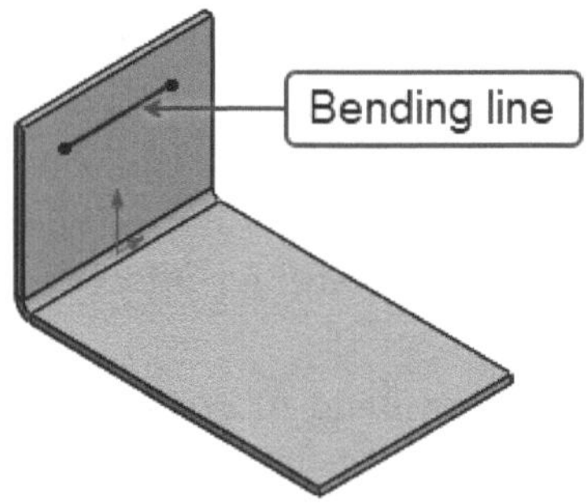

Tip: The bending line does not necessarily need to be created through the entire length of the sheet. Also, you can create it before or after invoking the **Sketched Bend** tool.

3. After creating a bending line, click on the **Sheet Metal** tab in the CommandManager and then click on the **Sketched Bend** tool, see Figure 2.79. The **Sketched Bend PropertyManager** appears, see Figure 2.80. Also, you are prompted to specify the planar face to be fixed when creating the bend, since the **Fixed Face** field is activated in the PropertyManager, by default.

2.79

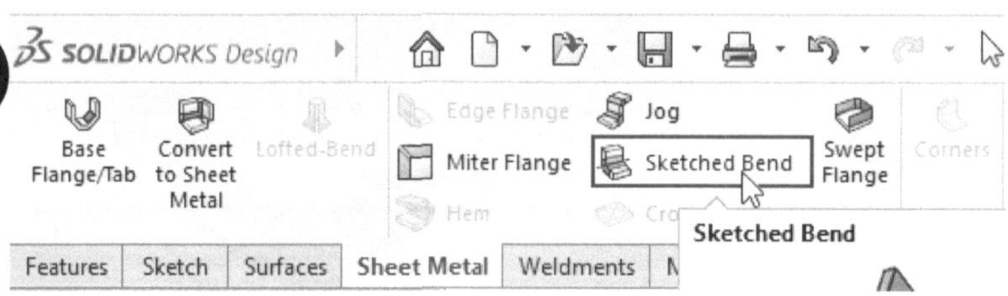

2.80

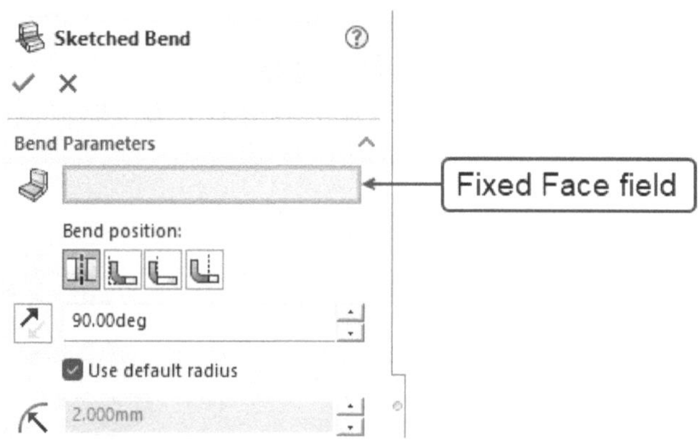

4. Click to define the fixed face (a side of the bending line) of the sheet that will be fixed after creating the bend, refer to Figure 2.81. The preview of a sketched bend appears, see Figure 2.82.

2.81

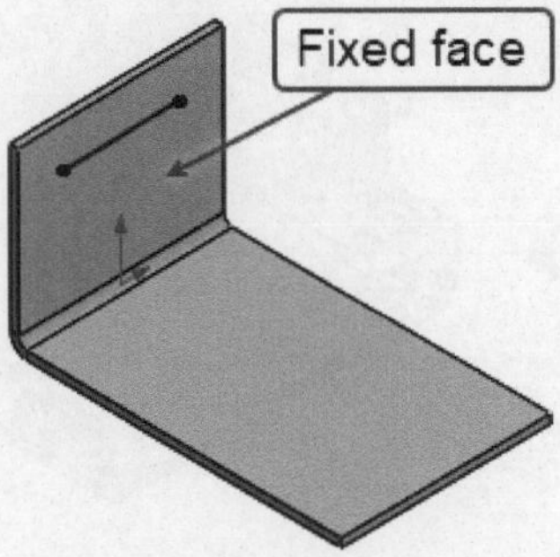

2.82

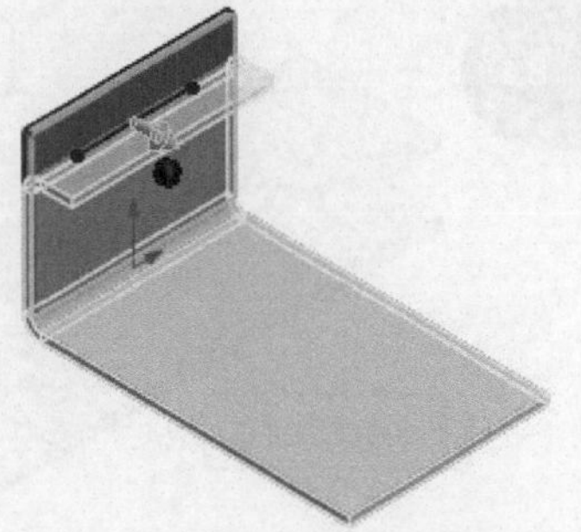

5. Define the position of the bend by activating the required button (**Bend Centerline, Material Inside, Material Outside**, or **Bend Outside**) in the **Bend position** area of the **Bend Parameters** rollout.

Note: By default, the **Bend Centerline** button is activated in the **Bend position** area of the **Bend Parameters** rollout. As a result, the sheet thickness is added equally on both the sides of the bending line. The remaining options in this area are the same as discussed earlier.

6. Enter the bend angle in the **Bend Angle** field of the **Bend Parameters** rollout, as required.

7. Click on the **Reverse Direction** button in the **Bend Parameters** rollout of the PropertyManager to flip the bend direction to the other side of the sheet, if needed.

Note: By default, the **Use default radius** check box is selected in the **Sketched Bend PropertyManager**. As a result, the default bend radius is used for the sketched bend. However, you can override the default bend radius value by clearing the **Use default radius** check box and then entering a new bend radius in the **Bend Radius** field that is enabled below this check box in the PropertyManager.

8. Click on the green tick-mark button in the PropertyManager. A sketched bend is created, see Figure 2.83.

2.83

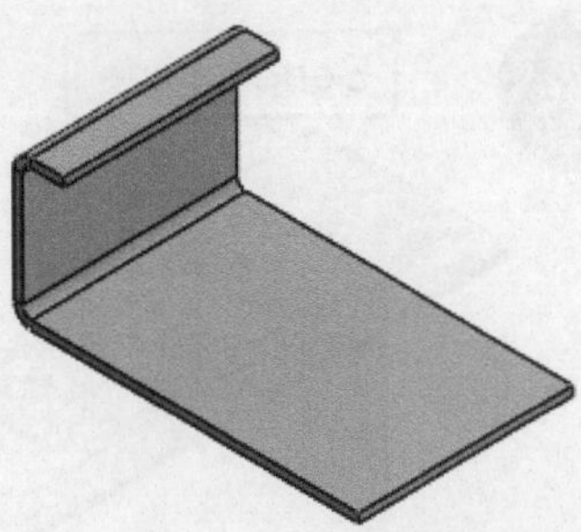

Note: You can also create multiple sketched bends by using a single sketch. For doing so, create more than one sketch line as the bending lines on the selected planar face, refer to Figure 2.84. This figure shows two bending lines created as a single sketch, a fixed face, and the resultant sketched bends.

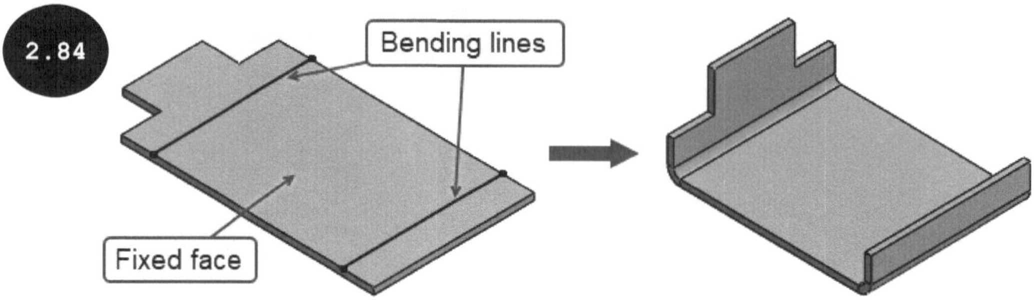

Creating a Jog Bend

A jog bend consists of two bends created by using a single bending line, see Figure 2.85. The method for creating a sketched bend is discussed below:

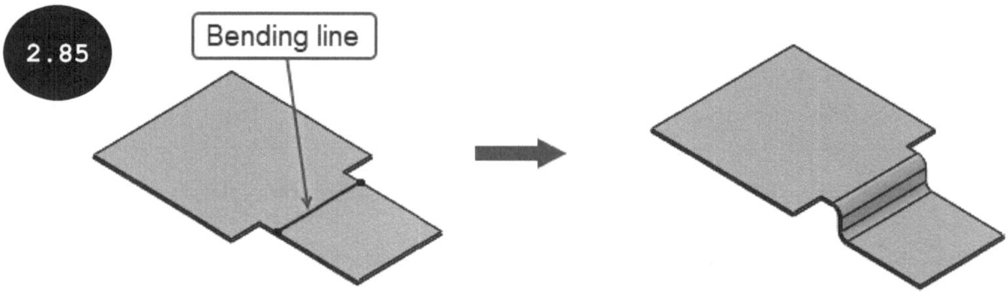

1. Invoke the Sketching environment by selecting a planar face of the sheet on which a bending line is to be created.

2. Create a line as the bending line by using the **Line** tool, refer to Figure 2.86.

Note: The sketch of the jog bend must contain a single line. It is not necessary to be created through the entire length of the face, refer to Figure 2.86. Also, it is not necessary to be horizontal or vertical.

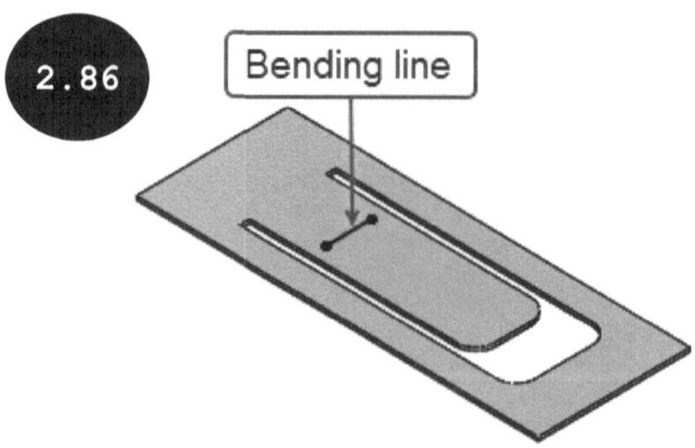

3. After creating a bending line, click on the **Sheet Metal** tab in the CommandManager and then click on the **Jog** tool, see Figure 2.87. The **Jog PropertyManager** appears, see Figure 2.88. Also, you are prompted to specify the planar face to be fixed when creating the jog bend, since the **Fixed Face** field is activated in the PropertyManager, by default.

2.87

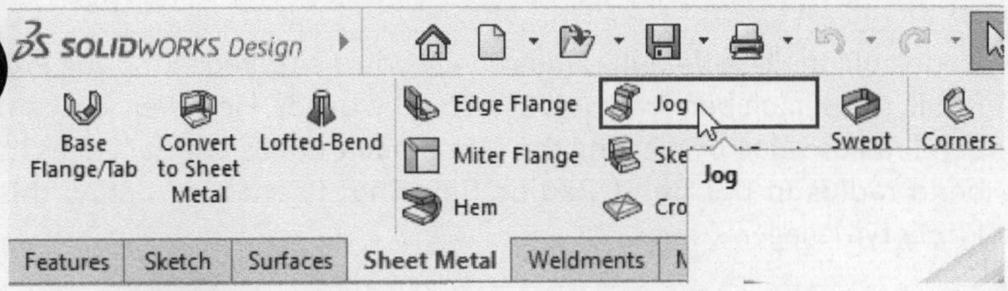

2.88

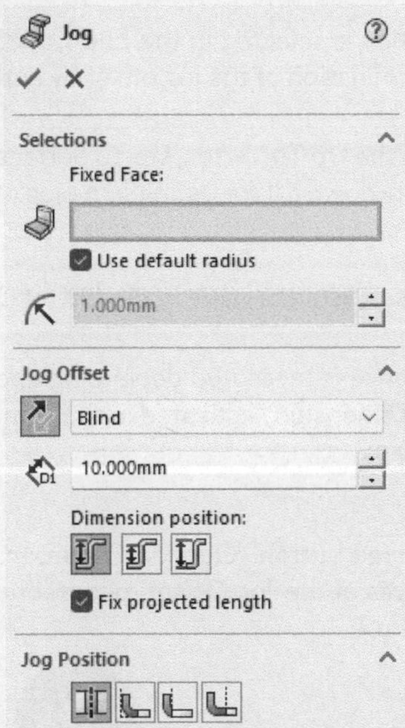

Tip: You can create the bending line before and after invoking the **Jog** tool.

4. Click to define the fixed face of the sheet that will be fixed after creating the jog bend. The preview of a jog bend which consists of two bends appears in the graphics area, see Figure 2.89.

2.89

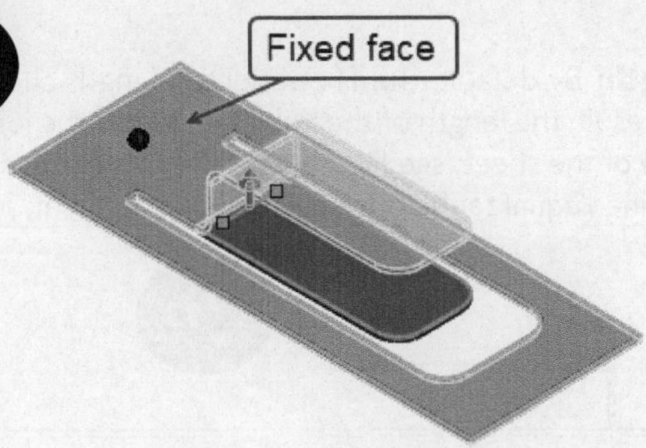

Note: By default, the **Use default radius** check box is selected in the **Jog PropertyManager**. As a result, the default bend radius is used for the bends. However, you can override the default bend radius value by clearing the **Use default radius** check box and then entering a new bend radius in the **Bend Radius** field that is enabled below this check box in the PropertyManager.

5. Ensure that the **Blind** option is selected in the **End Condition** drop-down list of the **Jog Offset** rollout for defining the termination of the jog offset by entering an offset distance value.

Note: You can also select the **Up To Vertex**, **Up To Surface**, or **Offset From Surface** option in the **End Condition** drop-down list for defining the jog offset, respectively.

6. Enter the required jog offset distance value in the **Offset Distance** field, refer to Figure 2.90.

Note: The jog offset distance is measured depending upon the button (**Outside Offset**, **Inside Offset**, or **Overall Dimension**) activated in the **Dimension position** area of the **Jog Offset** rollout, see Figure 2.91.

7. Click to activate the required button (**Outside Offset**, **Inside Offset**, or **Overall Dimension**) in the **Dimension position** area of the **Jog Offset** rollout for measuring the jog offset dimension, as required, refer to Figure 2.91.

2.90

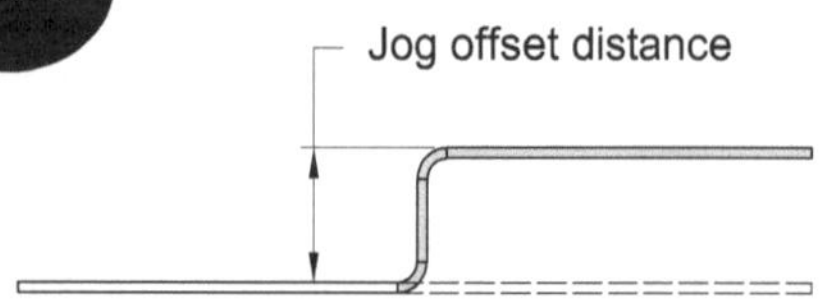

2.91

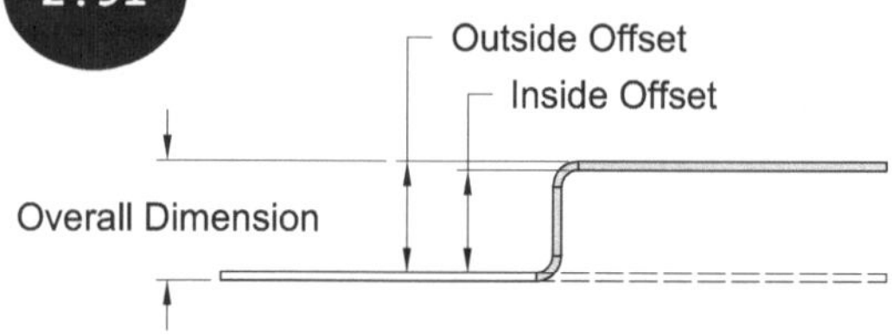

Fix projected length: By default, the **Fix projected length** check box is selected in the **Jog Offset** rollout. As a result, the length of the bent sheet after the jog bend is maintained equal to the projected length of the sheet, see Figure 2.92. If you clear this check box, the length of the bent sheet is maintained equal to the original length of the sheet, see Figure 2.93.

2.92

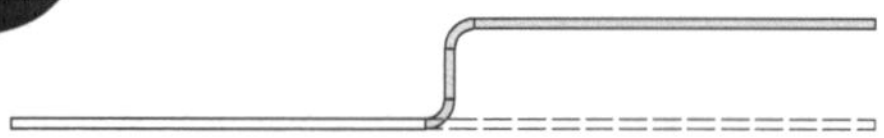

Fix projected length check box selected

2.93

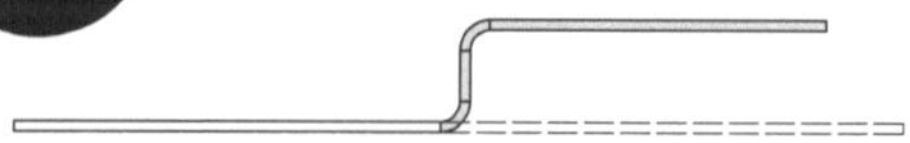

Fix projected length check box cleared

8. Select or clear the **Fix projected length** check box in the **Offset** rollout, as required.

9. Define the position of the bends by activating the required button (**Bend Centerline, Material Inside, Material Outside**, or **Bend Outside**) in the **Jog Position** rollout. All these buttons are the same as discussed earlier.

10. Enter the required angle of the jog bend in the **Jog Angle** field of the **Jog Angle** rollout, see Figures 2.94 and 2.95. In Figure 2.94, the jog angle is defined as 90 degrees, whereas in Figure 2.95, the jog angle is defined as 135 degrees.

2.94

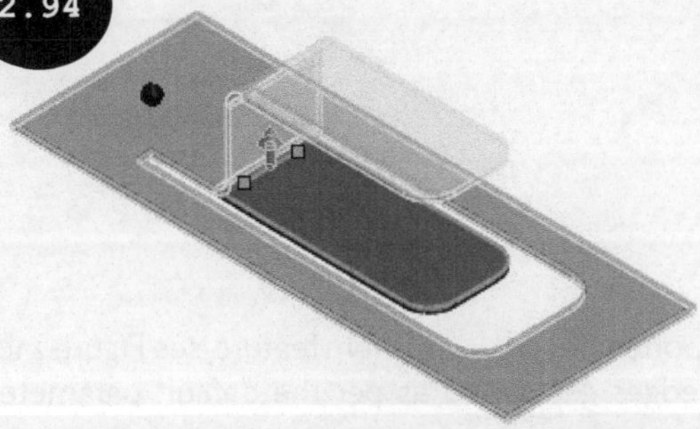

2.95

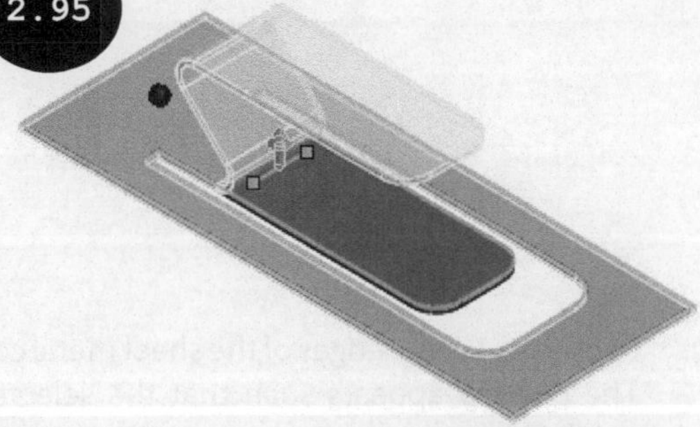

11. Click on the green tick-mark button in the PropertyManager. A jog bend of specified parameters is created, see Figure 2.96.

2.96

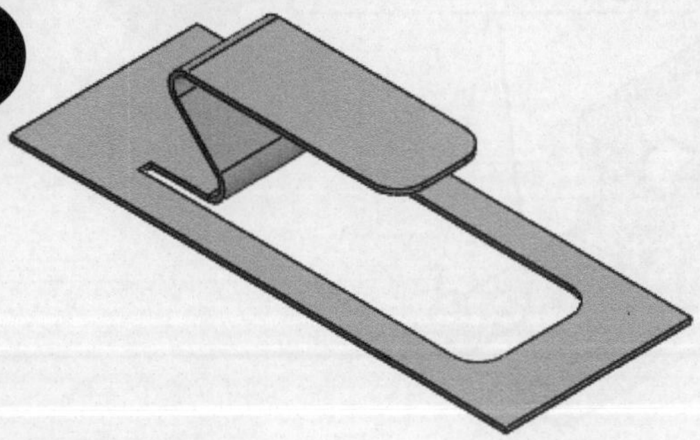

Creating a Hem Feature

A hem feature is created by curling a sheet to remove its sharp edges that may cause injury while handling the component, see Figure 2.97. The method for creating a hem feature is discussed below:

2.97

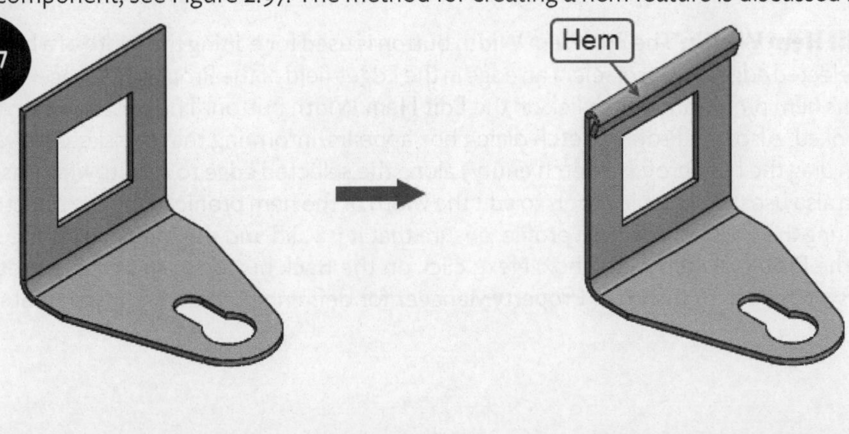

1. Click on the **Hem** tool in the **Sheet Metal CommandManager**, see Figure 2.98. The **Hem PropertyManager** appears, see Figure 2.99.

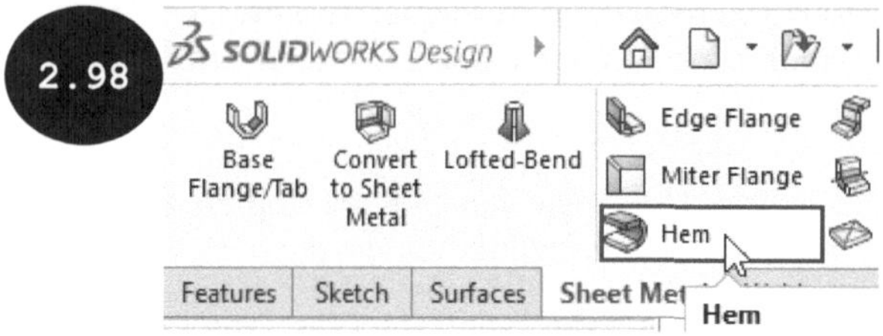

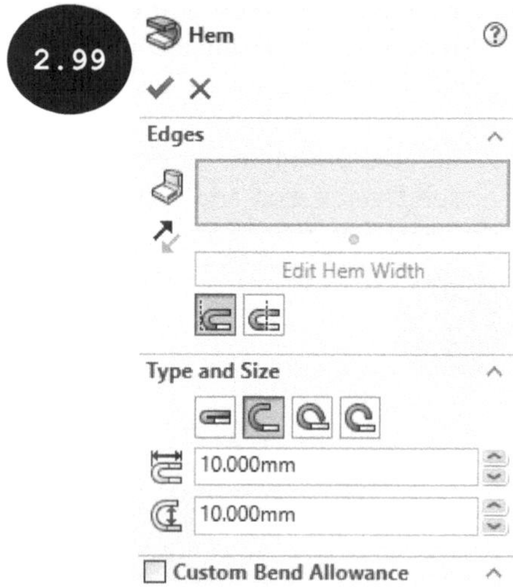

2. Click to select the edges of the sheet metal component for creating a hem feature, see Figure 2.100. The preview appears such that the selected edges get curled as per the default parameters, see Figure 2.101.

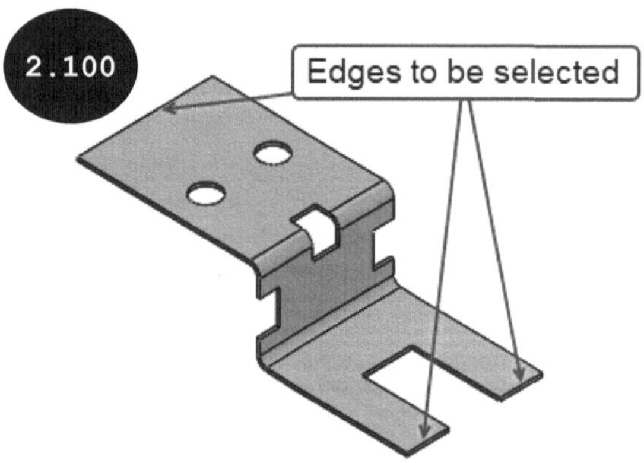

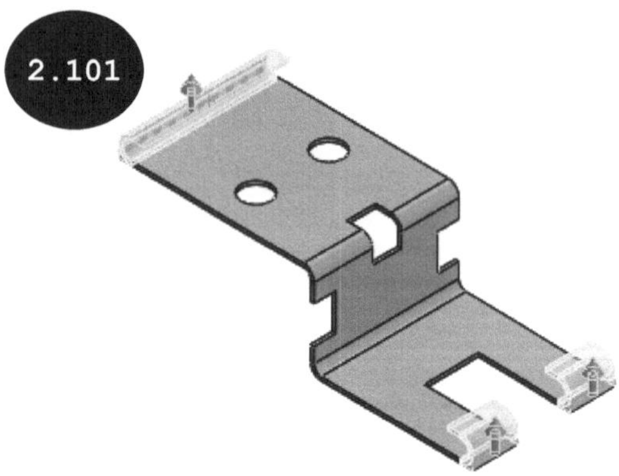

Note: The selected edge for creating a hem must be a linear edge.

Edit Hem Width: The **Edit Hem Width** button is used for editing the width of a hem profile along a selected edge. To do so, select an edge in the **Edges** field of the PropertyManager to edit the width of its hem profile and then click on the **Edit Hem Width** button. The Sketching environment gets invoked. Also, the **Profile Sketch** dialog box appears, informing that the sketch is valid. Now, you can drag the hem profile (sketch entity) along the selected edge to edit its width, as required. You can also use the sketching tools to edit the width of the hem profile along the selected edge. After editing the width of the hem profile, ensure that it is valid and the message for the same appears in the **Profile Sketch** dialog box. Next, click on the **Back** button in the **Profile Sketch** dialog box to switch back to the **Hem PropertyManager** for defining the remaining parameters of the hem feature. Note that if you click on the **Finish** button in the **Profile Sketch** dialog box, then the hem feature with specified parameters gets created on the selected edge or edges. Figure 2.102 shows the preview of a hem feature after editing the width of a hem profile along an edge.

2.102

3. Edit the width of the hem profile for one or more selected edges one by one by using the **Edit Hem Width** button, if needed.

4. Click on the required button (**Material Inside** or **Material Outside**) in the **Edges** rollout of the PropertyManager to define the material thickness inside or outside the maximum limit of the sheet, as required.

5. Click on the **Reverse Direction** button in the **Edges** rollout of the PropertyManager to reverse the direction of hem, if needed.

6. Select the required type of hem to be created by clicking on the required button (**Closed, Open, Tear Drop**, or **Rolled**) in the **Type and Size** rollout of the PropertyManager, see Figure 2.103.

2.103

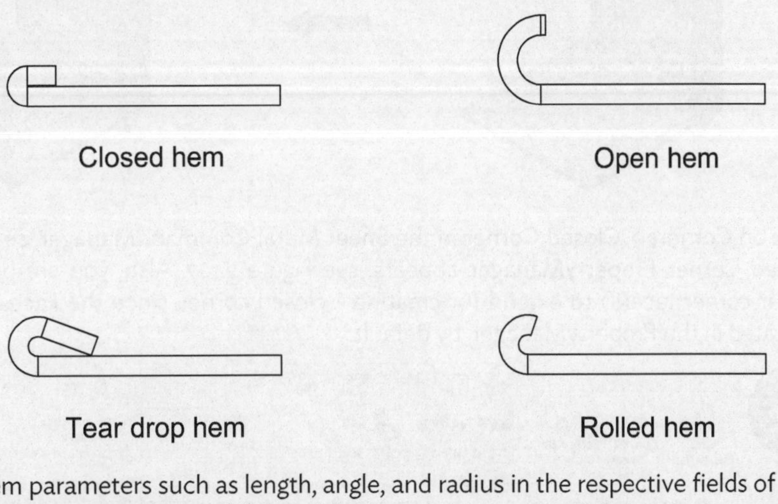

7. Define the hem parameters such as length, angle, and radius in the respective fields of the **Type and Size** rollout. Note that the availability of fields in this rollout for defining the hem parameters depends upon the type of hem selected.

Note: You can also customize or override the bend allowance and relief type by using the **Custom Bend Allowance** and **Custom Relief Type** rollout of the PropertyManager, as discussed earlier.

8. Click on the green tick-mark button in the PropertyManager. A hem feature with specified parameters is created, see Figure 2.104.

2.104

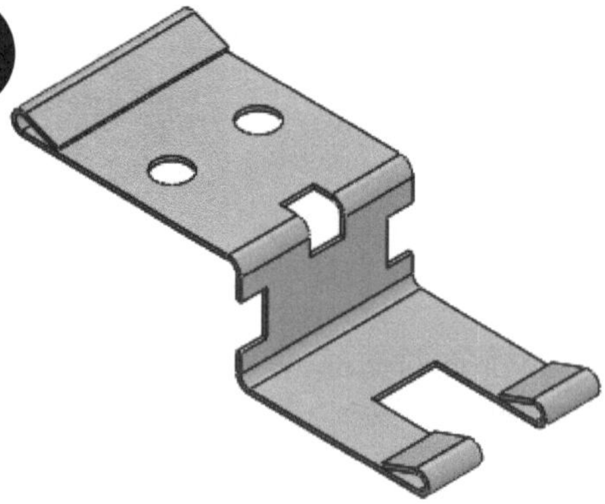

Closing Corners

A closed corner is created by filling the gap between adjacent flanges of a sheet metal component, see Figure 2.105. The method for creating a closed corner is discussed below:

2.105

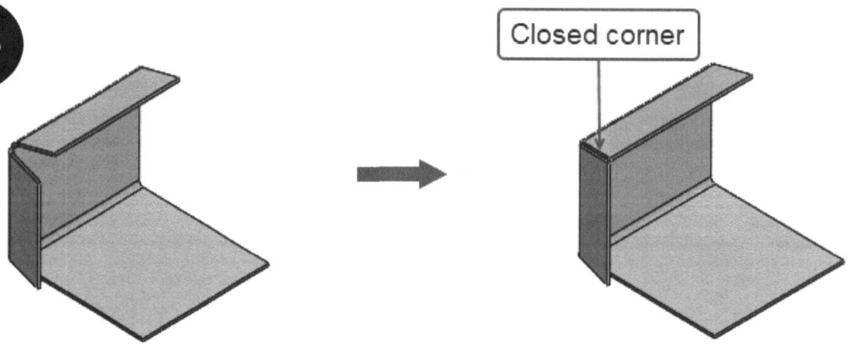

1. Click on **Corners > Closed Corner** in the **Sheet Metal CommandManager**, see Figure 2.106. The **Closed Corner PropertyManager** appears, see Figure 2.107. Also, you are prompted to select planar corner face(s) to extend for creating a closed corner, since the **Faces to Extend** field is activated in the PropertyManager, by default.

2.106

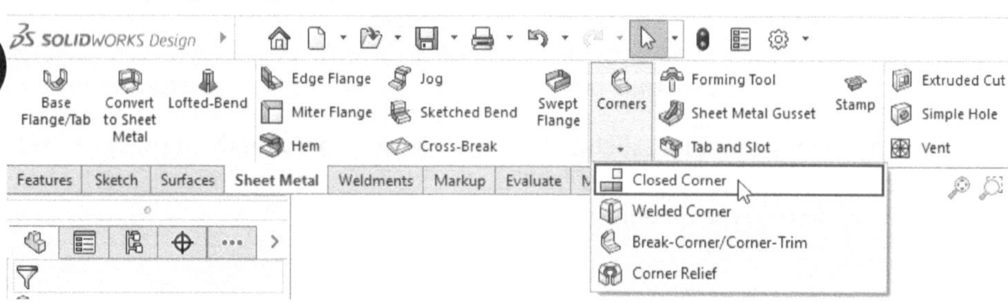

2.107

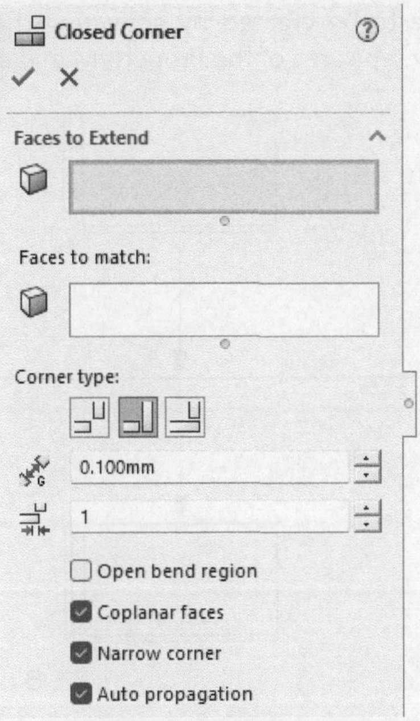

2. Select a planar face of a corner as the face to be extended, see Figure 2.108. The preview of a closed corner appears in the graphics area, since SOLIDWORKS automatically attempts to find the face to match with it for creating a closed corner, see Figure 2.109. It is because, the **Auto propagation** check box is selected in the PropertyManager, by default. Note that the names of the matched faces are displayed in the **Faces to Match** field of the PropertyManager.

2.108

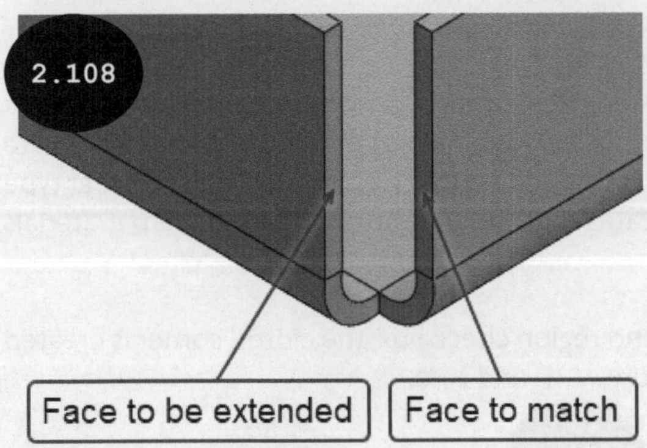

2.109

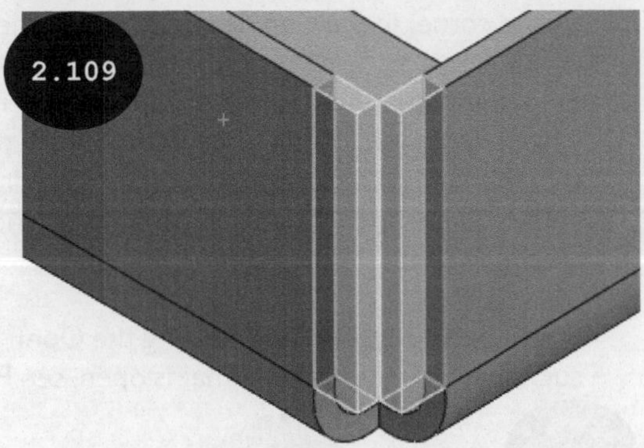

Note: If SOLIDWORKS is unable to find matching faces automatically, then you need to manually select them by using the **Faces to Match** field of the PropertyManager.

You can select one or more planar faces to be extended one after another for creating multiple closed corners in the **Faces to Extend** field of the PropertyManager.

3. Define the corner type to be created by activating the required button (**Butt, Overlap**, or **Underlap**) in the **Corner type** area of the PropertyManager, see Figure 2.110.

2.110

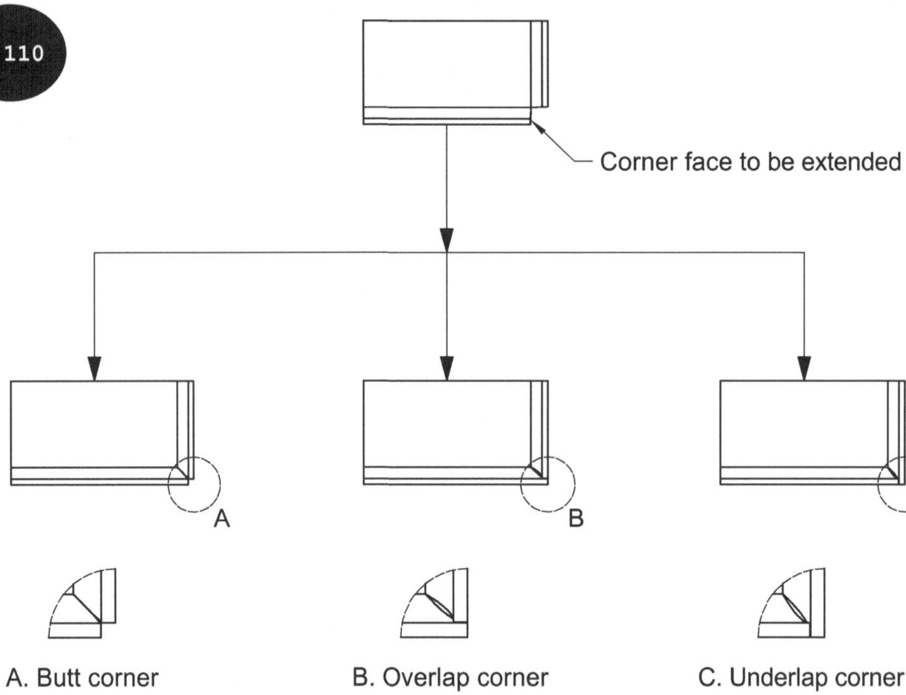

4. Enter the required gap distance between the two faces (extended face and matched face) of the closed corner in the **Gap distance** field of the PropertyManager.

5. Enter the overlap/underlap ratio between the material that overlaps and the material that underlaps while creating a closed corner in the **Overlap/underlap ratio** field of the PropertyManager. Note that this field is enabled only when the **Overlap** or **Underlap** button is activated in the **Corner type** area of the PropertyManager. Also, ratio 1 indicates that the overlap and the underlap materials are equivalent.

   Open bend region: On selecting the **Open bend region** check box, the closed corner is created such that its bend region remains open, see Figures 2.111 and 2.112.

2.111

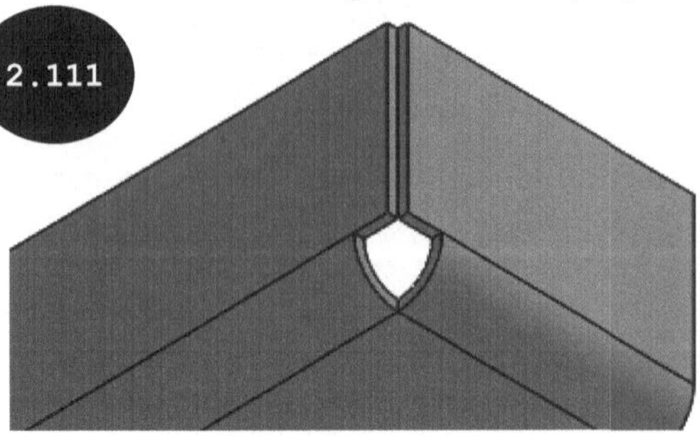

Open bend region check box is selected

2.112

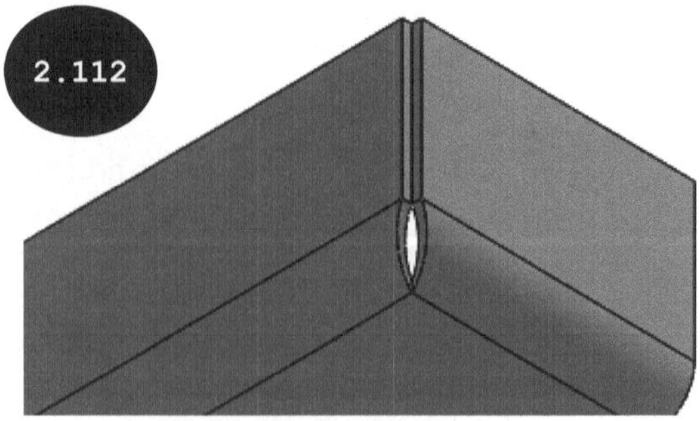

Open bend region check box is cleared

Coplanar faces: On selecting the **Coplanar faces** check box, the closed corner is created such that all the faces that are coplanar to the selected extended face get selected for creating the closed corner, see Figures 2.113 and 2.114.

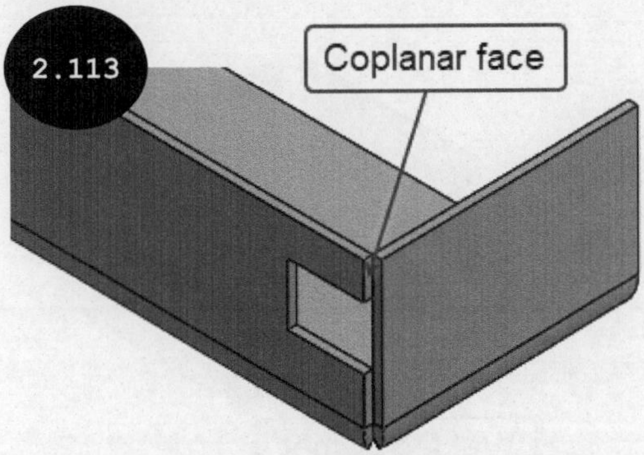

Coplanar faces check box is selected

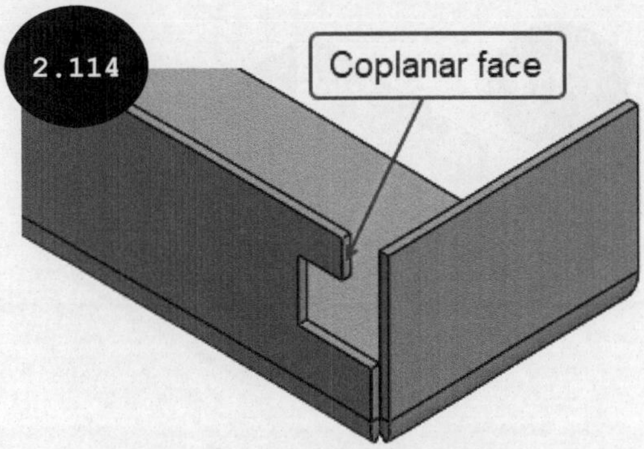

Coplanar faces check box is cleared

Narrow corner: On selecting the **Narrow corner** check box, the closed corner is created such that its bend area gets narrow by using an algorithm in the large bend radii, see Figures 2.115 and 2.116.

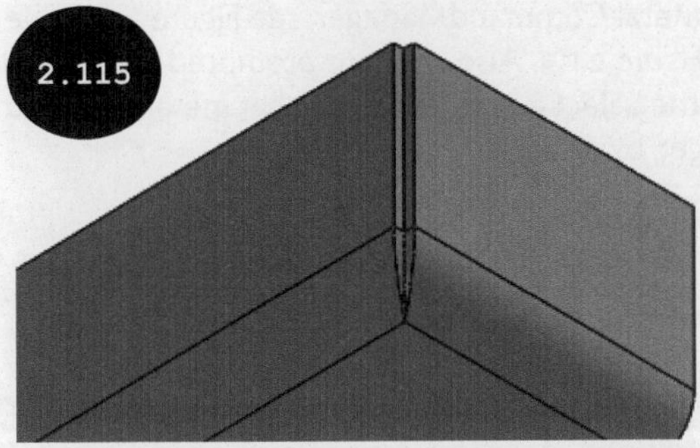

Narrow corner check box is selected

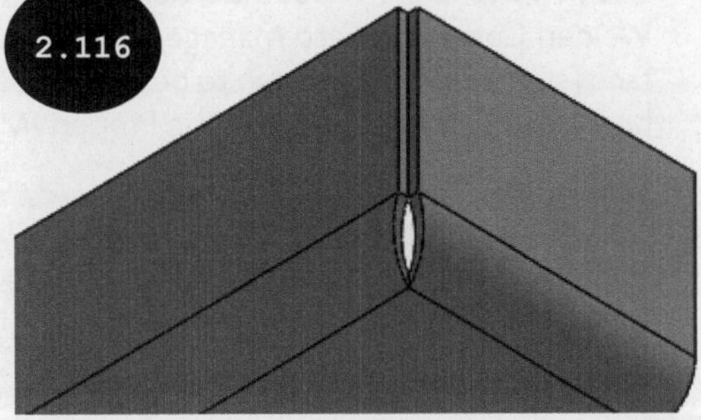

Narrow corner check box is cleared

Auto propagation: By default, the **Auto propagation** check box is selected. As a result, the faces to be matched get selected automatically on selecting the faces to be extended for creating closed corners.

6. Select or clear the **Open bend region**, **Coplanar faces**, **Narrow corner**, and **Auto propagation** check boxes in the PropertyManager, as required.

7. Click on the green tick-mark button in the PropertyManager. A closed corner is created between the selected faces of the sheet metal component.

Welding Corners

A welded corner is created by adding a weld bead at the corner of a sheet metal component, see Figure 2.117. The method for creating a welded corner is discussed below:

2.117

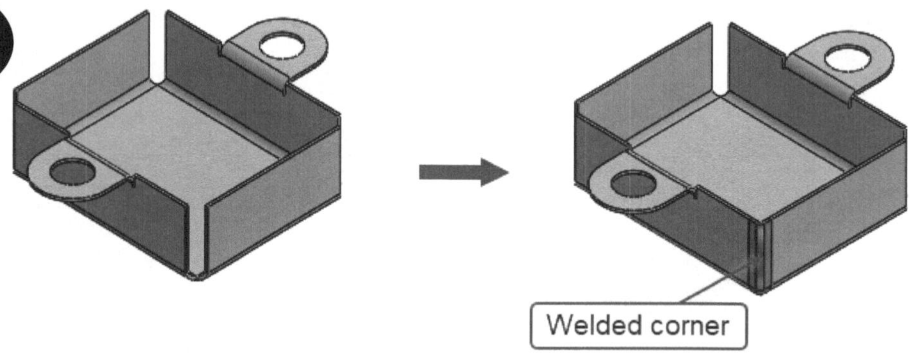

Note: A welded corner can be created between two flanges which includes miter flanges, edge flanges, and closed corner flanges.

1. Click on **Corners > Welded Corner** in the **Sheet Metal CommandManager**, see Figure 2.118. The **Welded Corner PropertyManager** appears, see Figure 2.119. Also, you are prompted to select a face (side face) of the corner to be welded, since the **Select a side face of a sheet metal corner to be welded** field is activated in the PropertyManager, by default.

2.118

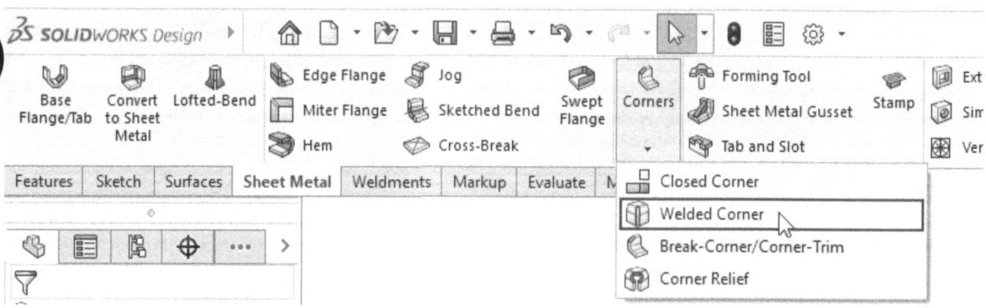

2.119

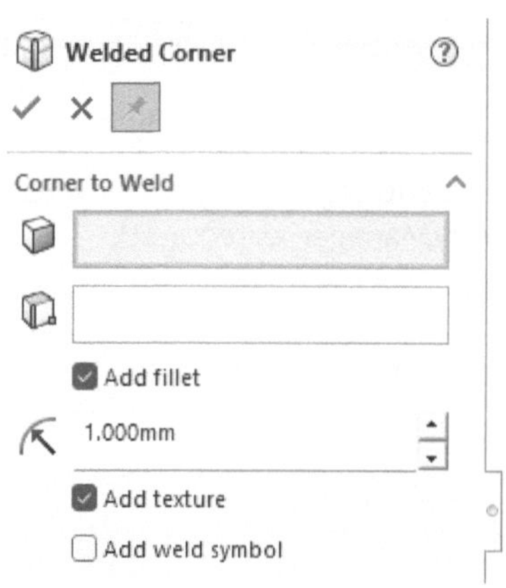

2. Select a face (side face) of the corner to be welded in the graphics area, see Figure 2.120. The preview of a welded corner appears in the graphics area, see Figure 2.121. Also, the name of the selected face is displayed in the **Select a side face of a sheet metal corner to be welded** field of the PropertyManager.

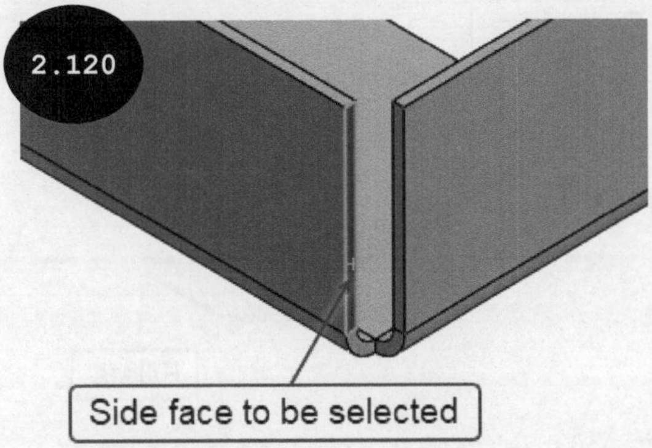

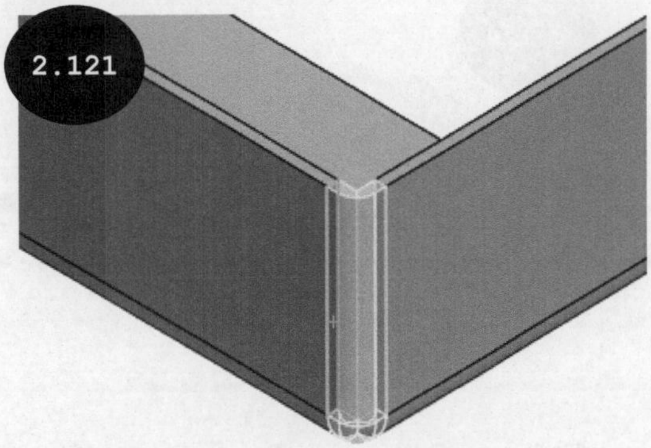

Stopping point: The Stopping point field in the PropertyManager is used for selecting a vertex, an edge, or a face to define a stopping point where the weld bead ends.

3. Click on the **Stopping point** field in the PropertyManager and then select a vertex, an edge, or a face as the stopping point for ending the weld bead, if needed.

Add fillet: On selecting the Add fillet check box, a fillet of specified radius value gets added in the resultant welded corner, see Figures 2.122 and 2.123.

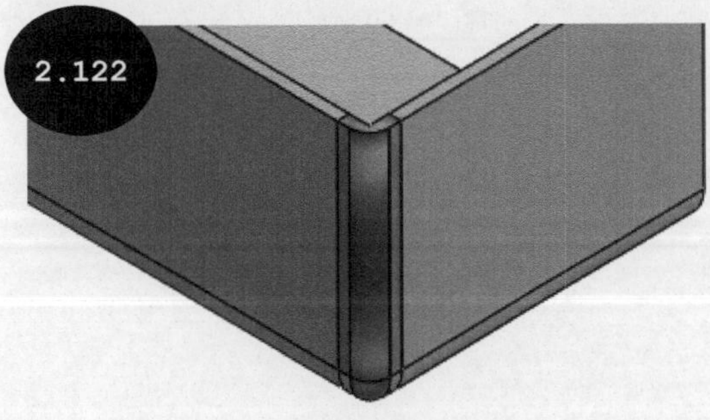

Add fillet check box is selected

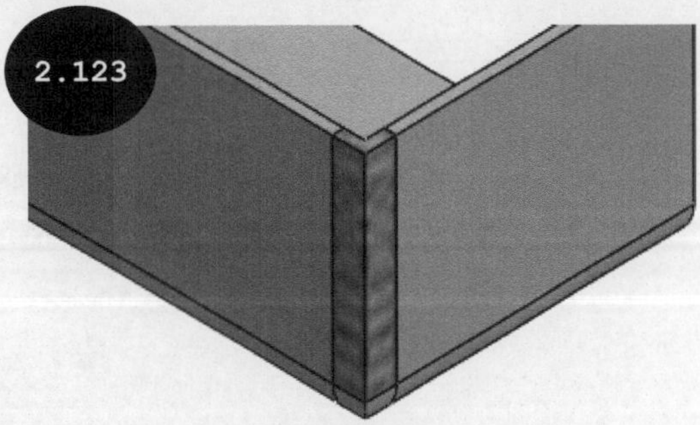

Add fillet check box is cleared

4. Select or clear the **Add fillet** check box in the PropertyManager, as required.

5. Enter the required fillet radius in the **Fillet radius** field of the PropertyManager. Note that this field is enabled only when the **Add fillet** check box is selected.

6. Select the **Add texture** check box in the PropertyManager to add a texture to the weld bead.

7. Select the **Add weld symbol** check box in the PropertyManager for adding a weld symbol.

8. Click on the green tick-mark button in the PropertyManager. A welded corner is created.

Breaking Corners

In SOLIDWORKS, you can break the corner edges of a sheet metal component by creating chamfers or fillets, see Figure 2.124. The method for breaking corners is discussed below:

2.124

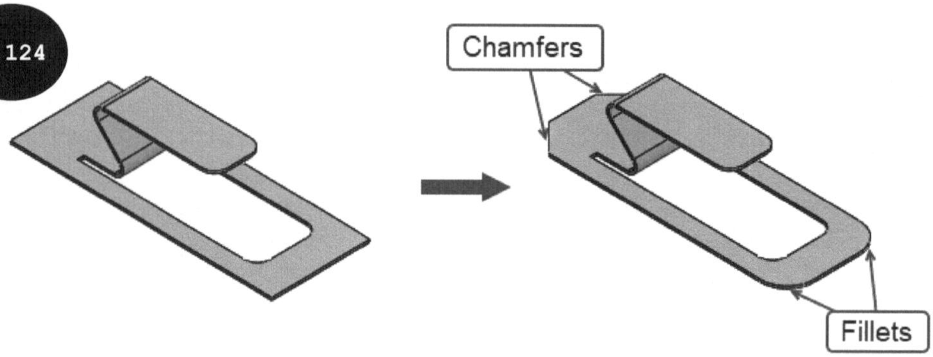

1. Click on **Corners > Break-Corner/Corner-Trim** in the **Sheet Metal CommandManager**, see Figure 2.125. The **Break Corner PropertyManager appears**, see Figure 2.126. Also, you are prompted to select corner edge(s) or flange face(s), since the **Corner Edges and/or Flange Faces** field is activated in the PropertyManager, by default.

2.125

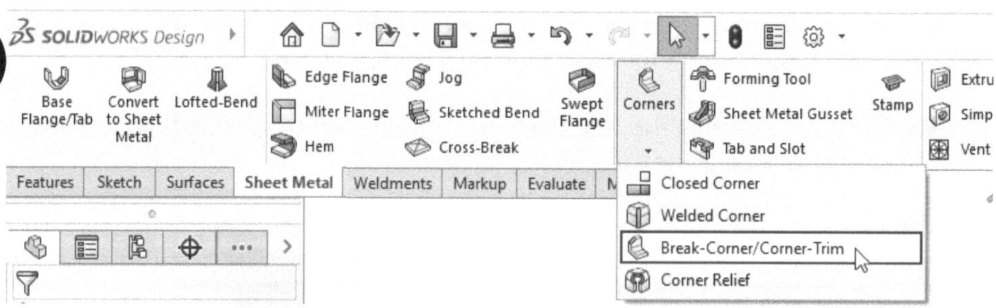

2.126

2. Select one or more corner edges or faces of a sheet metal component. The preview of chamfers or fillets appears on the selected edges depending upon whether the **Chamfer** or **Fillet** button is activated in the **Break type** area of the PropertyManager, see Figure 2.127.

   Note that clicking the **Collect all corners** button in the **Break Corner Options** rollout automatically selects all the available corners, and their names appear in the Corner edge selecting field.

Note: On selecting a face, all the outer corners of the selected face are chamfered or filleted by default, see Figure 2.128. If you select the **Internal corners only** check box, the chamfer or fillet is applied to the internal corners.

2.127

2.128

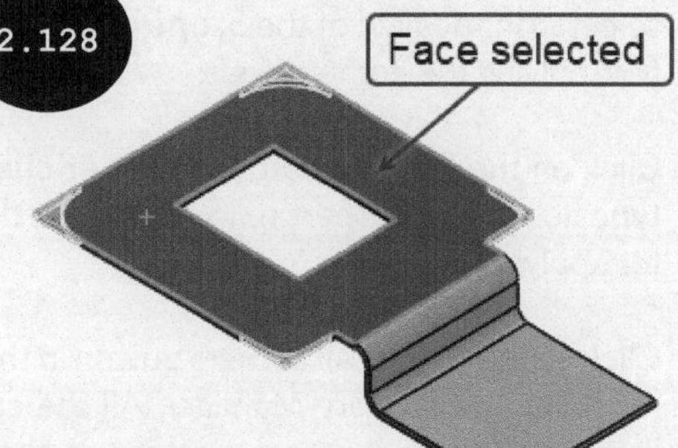

3. Click on the **Chamfer** or **Fillet** button in the **Break type** area of the PropertyManager to create chamfers or fillets on the selected edges, respectively.

4. Enter the chamfer distance or fillet radius in the **Distance** or **Radius** field of the PropertyManager, respectively. Note that the availability of the field depends upon whether the **Chamfer** or **Fillet** button is activated in the **Break type** area of the PropertyManager.

5. Click on the green tick-mark button in the PropertyManager. The selected corner edges get broken such that the fillets or chamfers are created.

Adding Corner Reliefs

You can add corner relief treatments between 2 or 3 bend corners of a sheet metal component by using the **Corner Relief** tool. It helps to prevent unwanted deformation in the sheet metal component while creating its flat pattern. The method for adding corner reliefs is discussed below:

1. Click on **Corners > Corner Relief** in the **Sheet Metal CommandManager**, see Figure 2.129. The **Corner Relief PropertyManager** appears, see Figure 2.130.

2.129

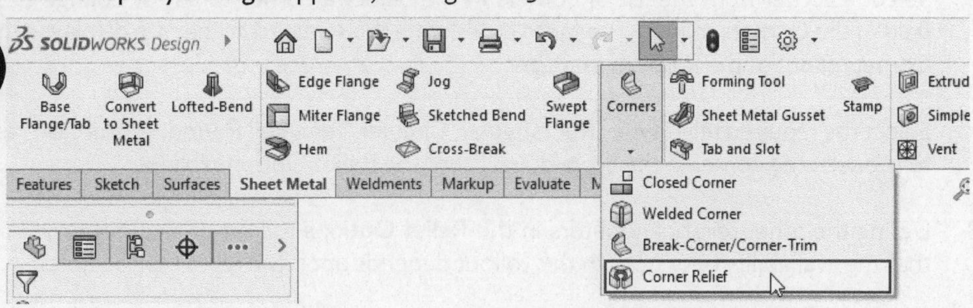

2. Select the **2 Bend Corner** or **3 Bend Corner** radio button in the **Corner Type** rollout for adding corner reliefs between 2 bend corners or 3 bend corners of the sheet, respectively.

3. Ensure that the sheet metal component (body) is selected in the field of the **Scope** rollout as the body for applying the corner reliefs.

4. Click on the **Select a corner to set or change relief type** field in the **Corners** rollout to select the corners for applying the reliefs.

5. Click on the **Collect all corners** button in the **Corners** rollout of the PropertyManager. All the corners get listed in the **Select a corner to set or change relief type** field of the **Corners** rollout depending upon whether the **2 Bend Corner** or **3 Bend Corner** radio button is selected. Also, the same gets highlighted in the graphics area, see Figure 2.131. In this figure, two corners (3 bend corners) are highlighted in the graphics area.

2.130

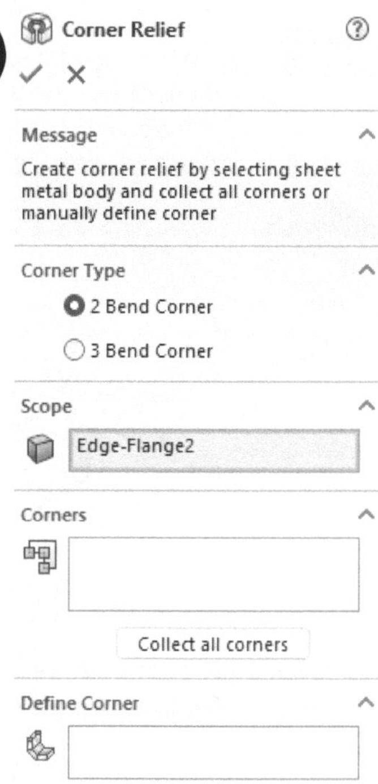

2.131

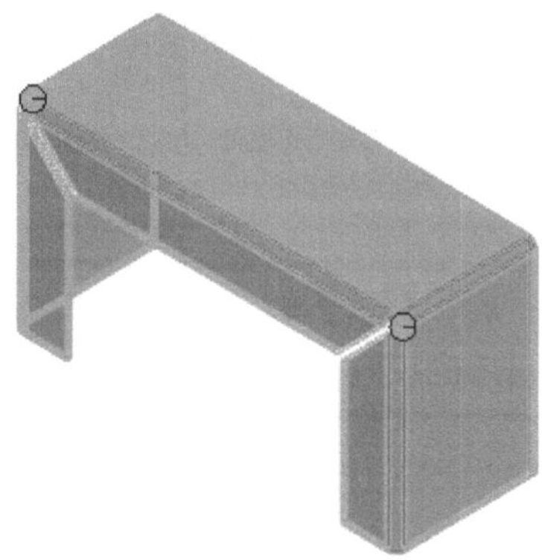

6. Select a corner from the list of corners in the **Select a corner to set or change the relief type** field of the **Corners** rollout. The faces that define the selected corner are displayed in the **Define Corner** rollout of the PropertyManager.

7. Select the required relief type (**Rectangular**, **Circular**, **Tear**, **Full Round**, or **Suitcase**) to be applied to the selected corner in the drop-down list of the **Relief Options** rollout.

8. Define the other relief parameters in the **Relief Options** rollout of the PropertyManager. Note that the availability of options in this rollout depends upon the relief type selected.

9. Similarly, define the relief type and its parameters for other corners of the sheet.

10. Click on the green tick-mark button in the PropertyManager. The corner reliefs with specified parameters get applied to the selected corners in the sheet metal component, see Figure 2.132. This figure shows 3 bend corners before and after applying the circular corner relief with specific parameters.

2.132

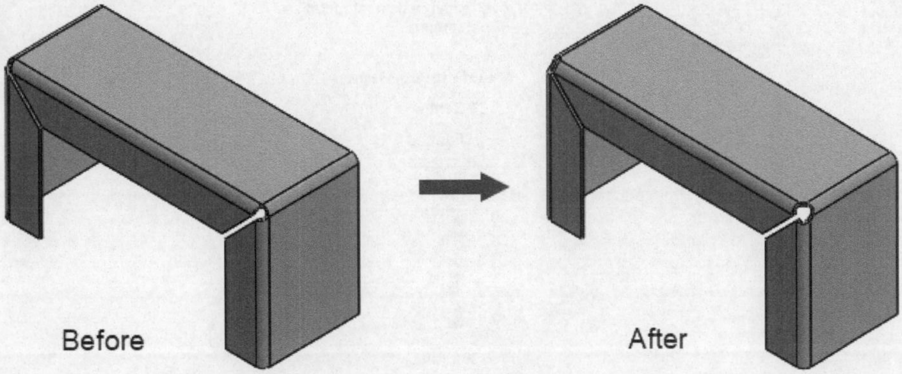

Creating a Lofted Bend

A lofted bend is created by lofting two open sections (sketches) such that the sheet transits from one section to another, see Figure 2.133. This figure shows two open sections and the resultant lofted bend. The method for creating a lofted bend is discussed below:

2.133

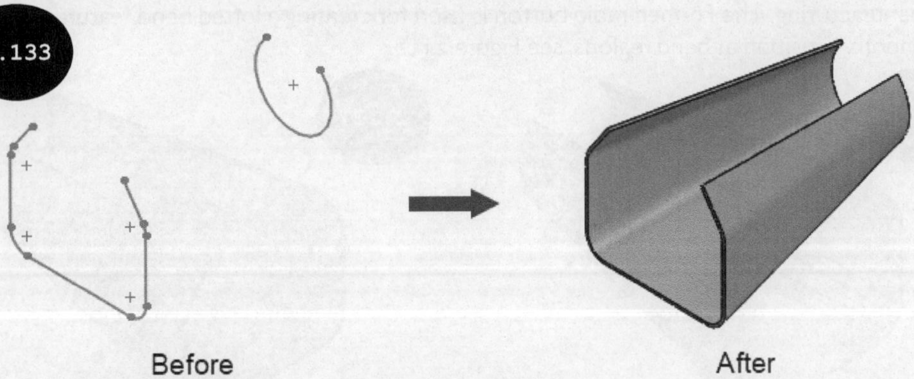

1. Click on the **Lofted-Bend** tool in the **Sheet Metal CommandManager**, see Figure 2.134. The **Lofted Bends PropertyManager** appears, see Figure 2.135.

2.134

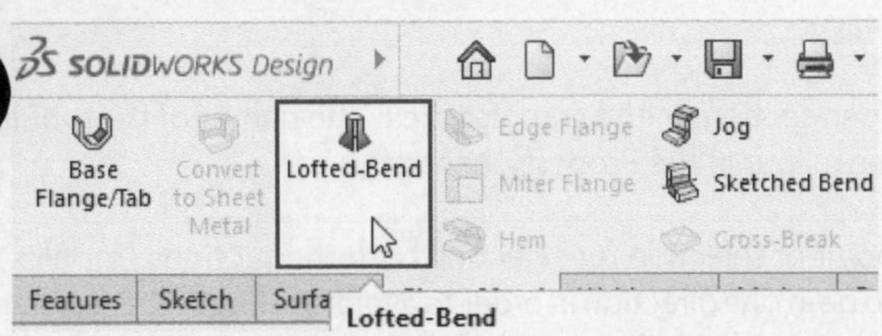

2.135

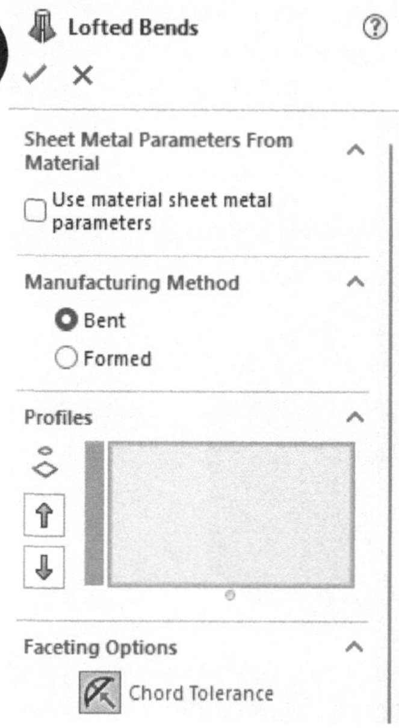

Manufacturing Method: The **Bent** radio button in the **Manufacturing Method** rollout is used for creating a lofted bend feature with real physical bends at the bend regions, see Figure 2.136. It forms a realistic transition between the two sections to facilitate instruction for press brake manufacturing. The **Formed** radio button is used for creating a lofted bend feature with rolled or smooth transition at bend regions, see Figure 2.137.

2.136

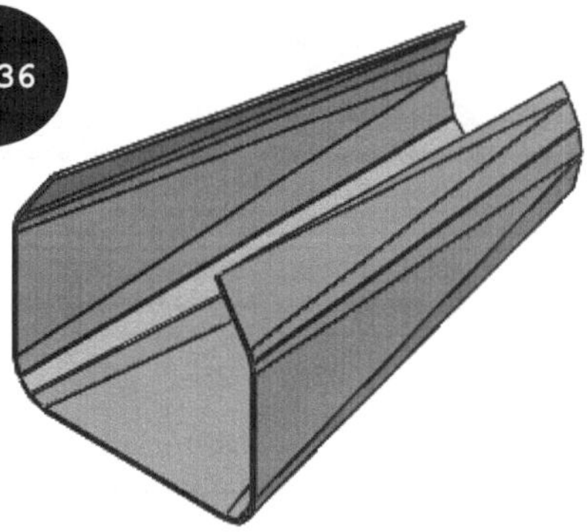

2.137

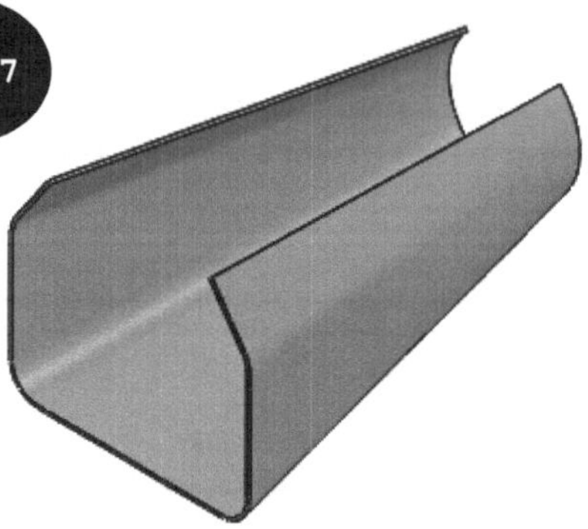

2. Select the required radio button (**Bent** or **Formed**) in the **Manufacturing Method** rollout in the PropertyManager.

3. Select two open sections in the graphics area. The names of the profiles appear in the **Profile** field of the **Profiles** rollout in the PropertyManager.

Note: The point of selection for selecting both the sections (profiles) of the lofted bend feature should be in one direction in order to avoid twisting in the resultant feature. Also, the sections (profiles) should not have vertices for creating a formed lofted bend feature. If the sections have vertices, you can replace them with fillets.

Faceting Options: The **Faceting Options** rollout appears only when the **Bent** radio button is selected in the **Manufacturing Method** rollout of the PropertyManager and is used for defining the faceting option for the bends. The **Chord Tolerance** button is used for defining the maximum distance or deviation between the original sketch geometry and the facet face in a bend region, refer to Figure 2.138. The **Number of Bends** button is used for defining the number of bends in a bend region. The **Segment Length** button is used for defining the maximum length of the facet face (linear segment) in a bend region. The **Segment Angle** button is used for defining the maximum angle between two adjacent facet faces in a bend region.

2.138

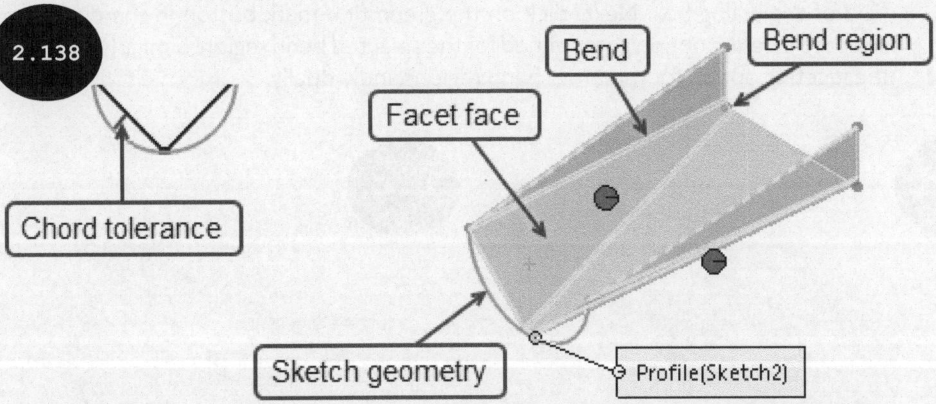

4. Click on the required button (**Chord Tolerance**, **Number of Bends**, **Segment Length**, or **Segment Angle**) in the **Faceting Options** rollout of the PropertyManager, as discussed above.

5. Depending upon the faceting option selected in the **Faceting Options** rollout, enter the facet value in the field of the **Facet Value** rollout. For example, if the **Number of Bends** button is selected in the **Faceting Options** rollout, then you can enter the number of bends to be created in a bend region as the facet value in the field of the **Facet Value** rollout.

Refer to endpoint: By default, the **Refer to endpoint** check box is selected in the **Facet Value** rollout. As a result, the lofted bend segments get translated such that a sharp corner is formed at the bend regions, see Figure 2.139. If this check box is cleared, the sharp corner gets replaced with adjacent bends such that an approximated arc is created at the corner, see Figure 2.140.

2.139

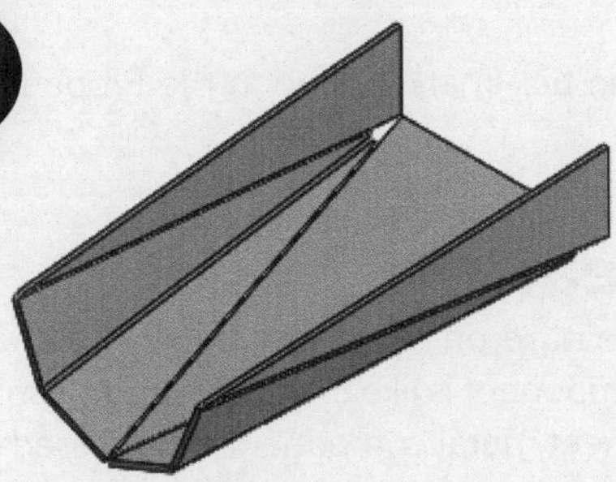

Refer to endpoint check box is selected

2.140

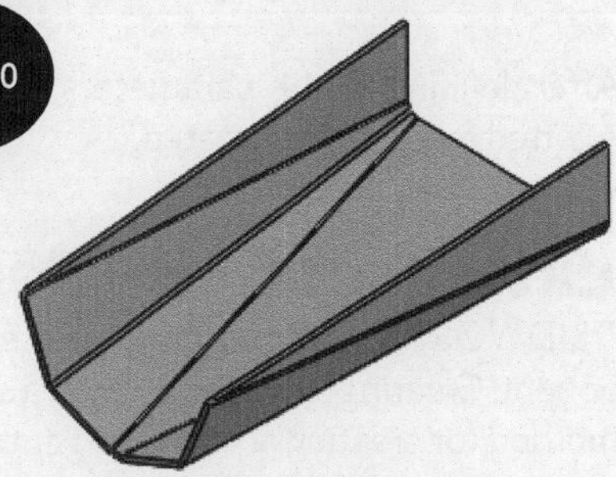

Refer to endpoint check box is cleared

6. Select or clear the **Refer to endpoint** check box in the **Facet Value** rollout, as discussed above.

Note: By default, the defined faceting option applies to all bend regions of the lofted bend feature. However, you can also define the faceting option individually to a bend region. To do so, click on the pink dot of a bend region in the graphics area whose faceting option is to be defined, see Figure 2.141. The **Faceting options** dialog box appears, see Figure 2.142. In this dialog box, select the required button (**Chord Tolerance, Number of Bends, Segment Length,** or **Segment Angle**) as the faceting option and then enter its facet value in the **Facet value** field of the dialog box. Next, click on the green tick-mark button in the dialog box. The selected faceting option gets defined for the selected bend region. Similarly, you can define the faceting option for the other bend regions, individually.

2.141

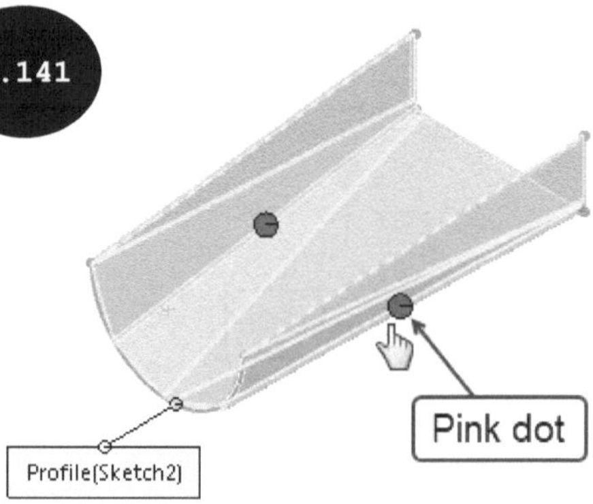

2.142

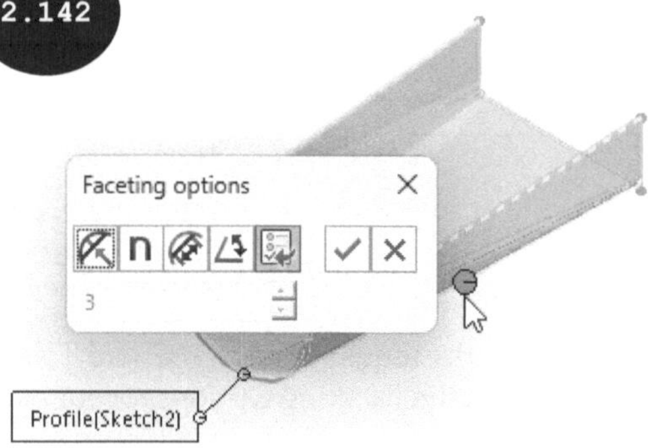

Tip: You can also customize the sheet metal parameters, bend allowance, and relief by using the options available in the **Sheet Metal Parameters, Bend Allowance,** and **Auto Relief** rollouts of the PropertyManager. The options in these rollouts are same as discussed earlier.

Note: In SOLIDWORKS 2026, you can add material thickness equally on both sides of the sketch in the graphics area by selecting the **Symmetric** check box in the **Sheet Metal Parameters** rollout of the PropertyManager.

7. After defining all the parameters, click on the green tick-mark button in the PropertyManager. A lofted feature gets created.

Creating an Extruded Cut Feature

In SOLIDWORKS, you can create an extruded cut feature on the planar face of a sheet metal component. Creating extruded cuts on a sheet metal component is like creating cuts on a solid model. The method for creating an extruded cut feature on a sheet metal component is discussed below:

1. Click on the **Extruded Cut** tool in the **Sheet Metal CommandManager**, see Figure 2.143. The **Extrude PropertyManager** appears. Also, you are prompted to either select a plane or a planar face for creating a sketch of the extruded cut feature or select an existing sketch.

2.143

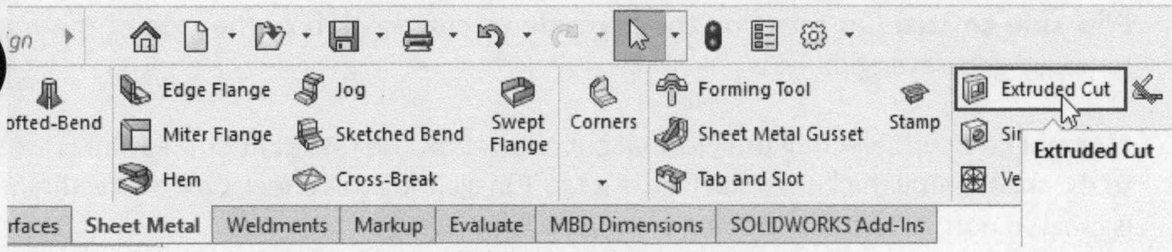

Tip: If the sketch is already created in the graphics area, then you can select it as the sketch of the extruded cut feature before or after invoking the **Extruded Cut** tool.

2. Select a planar face of the sheet metal component or a plane as the sketching plane. The Sketching environment gets invoked and the selected planar face gets orientated normal to the viewing direction.

3. Create a sketch of the extruded cut feature by using the sketching tools, see Figure 2.144.

4. After creating the sketch, exit the Sketching environment. The **Cut-Extrude PropertyManager** appears, see Figure 2.145. Also, a preview of the cut feature appears in the graphics area.

2.144

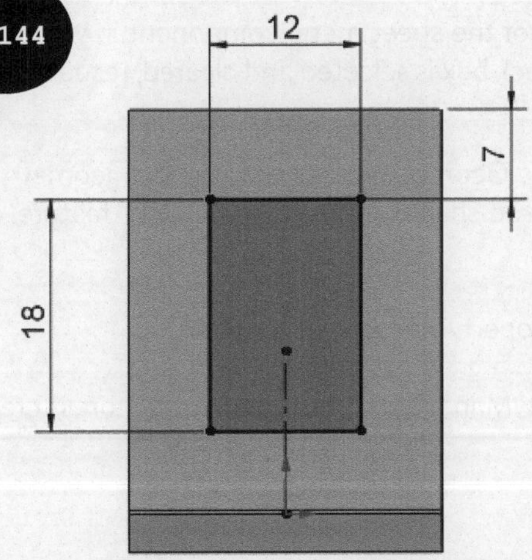

2.145

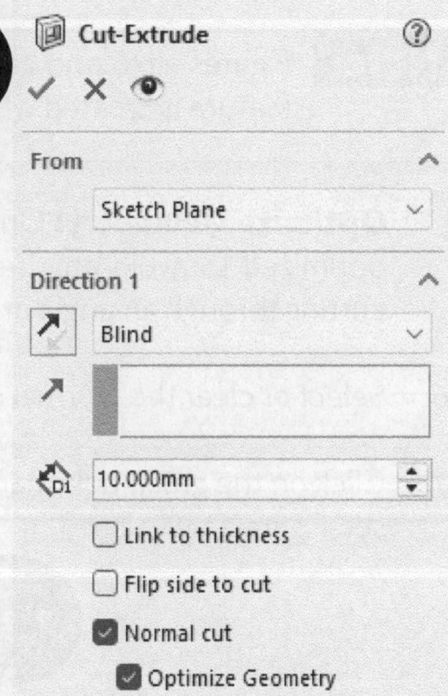

5. Define the depth of the extruded cut feature by selecting the required option: **Blind, Through All, Up To Next**, or **Up To Surface** in the **End Condition** drop-down list of the PropertyManager. The options for defining the depth of the extrude cut feature on a sheet metal component are same as those defining the depth of the extrude cut feature on a solid model.

Note: You can also define the depth of the cut feature equal to the thickness of the sheet metal component by selecting the **Link to thickness** check box in the PropertyManager. This check box is available only when the **Blind** option is selected in the **End Condition** drop-down list of the PropertyManager. When the **Link to thickness** check box is selected, the depth of the extruded cut feature gets automatically adjusted or defined equal to the thickness of the sheet.

Flip side to cut: On selecting the **Flip side to cut** check box, the side of the material to be removed gets reversed.

Normal cut: On selecting the **Normal cut** check box, the resultant cut feature is created normal to the sheet metal thickness, see Figure 2.146. On clearing this check box, the resultant cut feature is created normal to the sketching plane, see Figure 2.147.

2.146

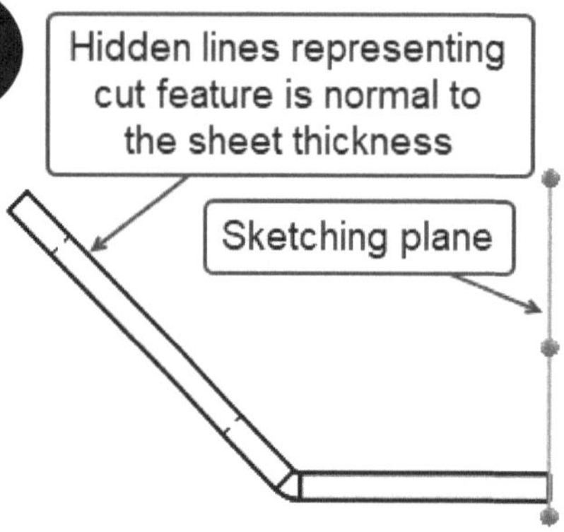

2.147

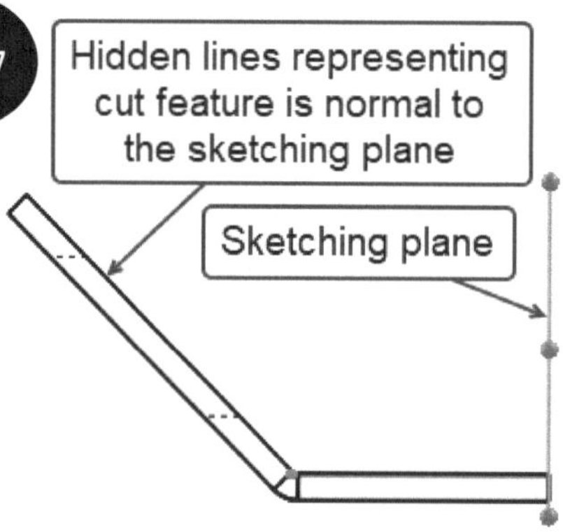

Note: Figures 2.146 and 2.147 show the side view of the sheet metal component in which a cut feature is created when the **Normal cut** check box is selected and cleared, respectively.

Optimize Geometry: On selecting the **Optimize Geometry** check box, the cut geometry gets optimized to avoid any irregularities or problematic shapes in the resultant cut feature when cutting through an angle or curved face.

6. Select or clear the **Normal cut** check box in the PropertyManager, as required.
7. Click on the green tick-mark button in the PropertyManager. An extruded cut feature is created, see Figure 2.148.

2.148

Creating a Forming Tool

A forming tool is a solid part that acts as a die for creating formed features like embosses, louvers, and lances. These formed features are not straight-line bends, rather they represent the features that are created by stamping, punching, or drawn operations, refer to Figure 2.149. SOLIDWORKS is provided with some sample forming tool parts to get started with creating formed features on a sheet metal component. You can access these forming tool parts in the **forming tools** sub-folder of the **design library** folder in the **Design Library Task Panel**, refer to Figure 2.150

2.149

2.150

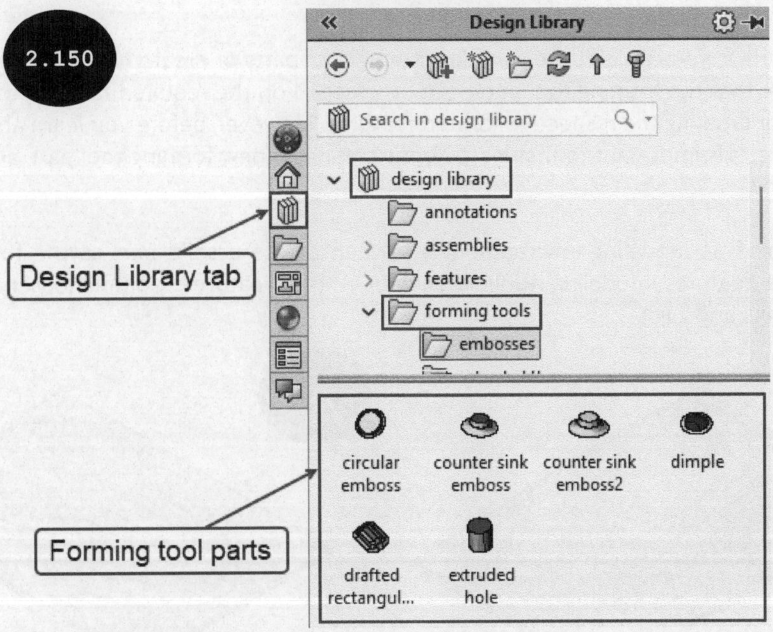

Note: If the **Design library** folder is not available in the **Design Library Task Panel**, then you need to customize to add it. For doing so, click on the **Options** tool in the **Standard** toolbar. The **System Options** dialog box appears. In this dialog box, click on the **File Locations** option in its left panel and then select the **Design Library** option in the **Show folders for** drop-down list that appears in the right panel of the dialog box, see Figure 2.151. Next, click on the **Add** button in the dialog box. The **Choose Folder** dialog box appears. In this dialog box, browse to the location *C:\ProgramData\SOLIDWORKS\SOLIDWORKS* 2026 and then select the **design library** folder. Next, click on the **OK** button in the dialog box. The location for **Design Library** gets defined to *C:\ProgramData\SOLIDWORKS\SOLIDWORKS* 2026*\design library*. Next, click on the **OK** button in the dialog box. The **SOLIDWORKS** message window appears. Click on the **Yes** button to accept the changes and display the **design library** folder in the **Design Library Task Panel**.

2.151

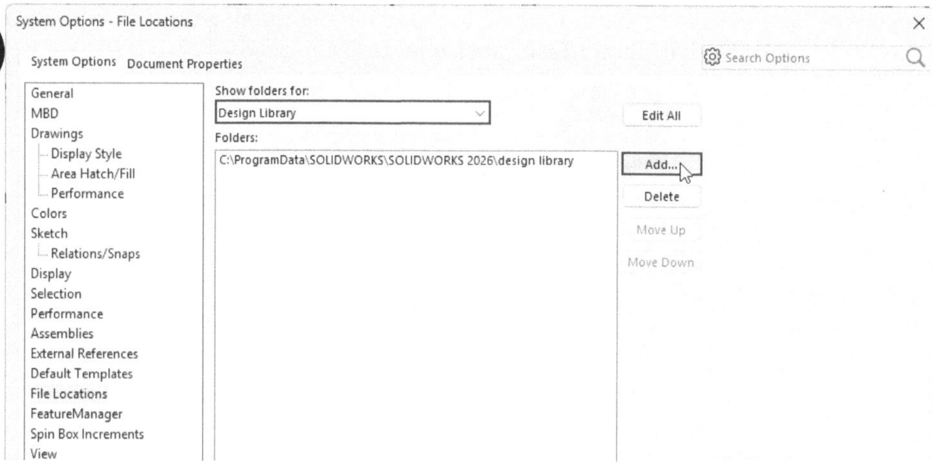

In SOLIDWORKS, you can edit the sample forming tool parts or create new forming tool parts, as required. Note that the forming tool parts can be dragged on the required faces of the sheet metal component for creating the respective formed features. However, before you learn about creating a formed feature, it is important to first learn about creating a new forming tool part, and the same is discussed below:

1. Invoke the Part modeling environment and then create a solid part as the forming tool by using the features modeling tools available in the **Features CommandManager**, refer to Figures 2.152 and 2.153.

2.152

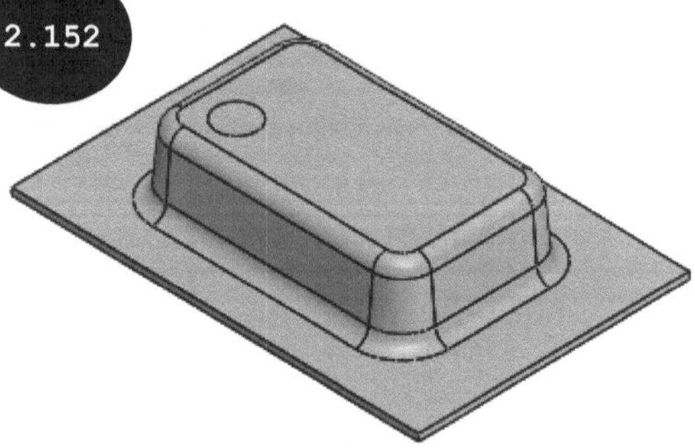

2.153

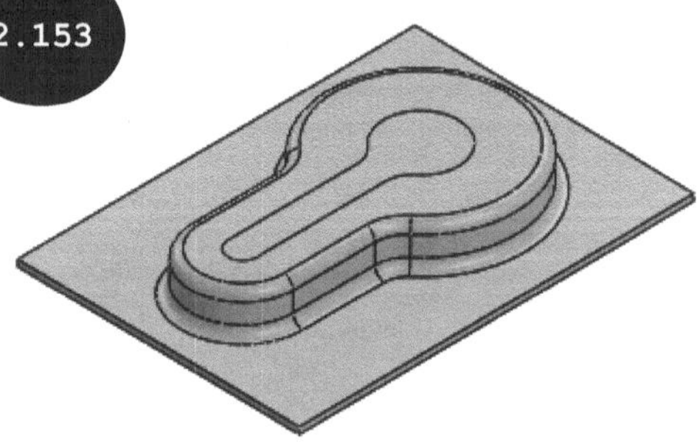

Note: To learn creating 3D solid parts, assemblies, and drawings, refer to "**SOLIDWORKS 2026: A Power Guide for Beginners and Intermediate Users**" textbook by **CADArtifex**.

After creating a 3D solid part, you can convert it into a forming tool.

2. Click on the **Forming Tool** tool in the **Sheet Metal CommandManager** to create a forming tool, see Figure 2.154. The **Form Tool PropertyManager** appears, see Figure 2.155. Also, you are prompted to select a stopping face, since the **Stopping Face** field is activated in the PropertyManager, by default.

2.154

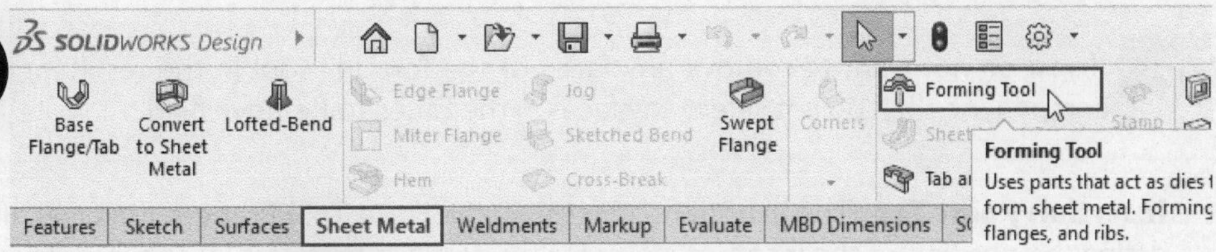

2.155

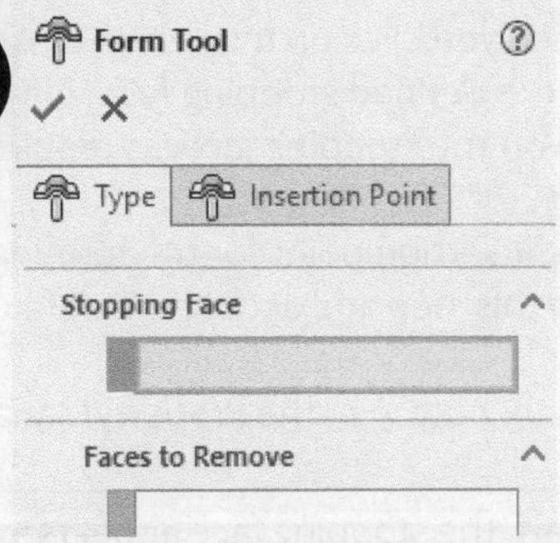

Stopping Face: The **Stopping Face** field is used for defining the stopping face of the forming tool where it stops when inserted on a sheet metal component, see Figures 2.156 and 2.157.

Faces to Remove: The **Faces to Remove** field is used for defining a face or faces of the forming tool to be removed when inserted on a sheet metal component, see Figures 2.156 and 2.157. Note that you can also create a forming tool without selecting any face to be removed. In doing so, none of the faces of the forming tool gets removed in the resultant sheet metal component.

Note: You will learn about inserting a formatting tool on a sheet metal component for creating a formed feature later in this chapter.

3. Click to define a stopping face of the forming tool, see Figures 2.156 and 2.157.
4. After defining the stopping face, click on the **Faces to Remove** field in the PropertyManager and then select one or more faces of the forming tool to be removed when it is inserted into a sheet metal component, see Figures 2.156 and 2.157.

2.156

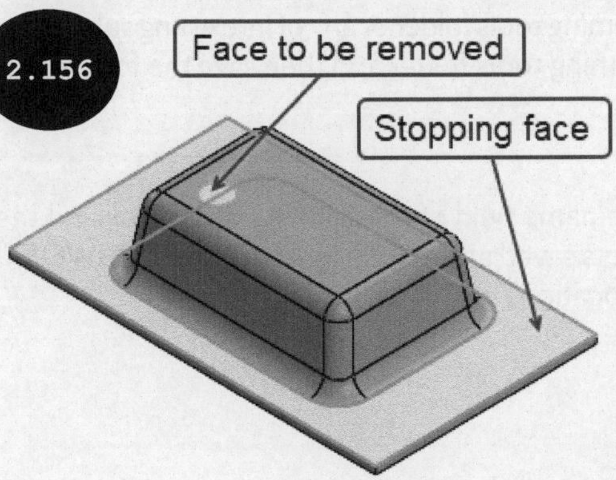

2.157

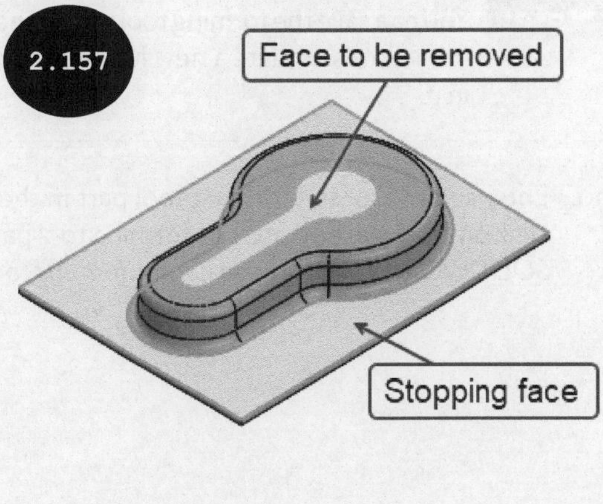

Tip: If you do not want to remove any faces of the forming tool in the resultant sheet metal component, then do not select any faces in the **Faces to Remove** field.

Insertion Point Tab: The **Insertion Point** tab in the **Form Tool PropertyManager** allows you to define the position of the insertion point for the forming tool part by applying dimensions and relations, as required. When you click on this tab, the insertion point for the forming tool appears at its default position on the defined stopping face. Now, you can apply dimensions or relations to define its new position on the stopping face, as required.

5. Define the position of the insertion point for the forming tool by using the **Insertion Point** tab, if needed. You can also skip this step and accept the default position of the insertion point.

6. Click on the green tick-mark button in the PropertyManager. A forming tool part gets created.

Note: In a forming tool part, the stopping face appears in cyan color and the faces to be removed appear in red color.

After creating a forming tool part, you need to save it as a forming tool.

7. Press the CTRL + S keys or click on the **Save** tool in the **Standard** toolbar. The **Save As** dialog box appears.

Tip: If the part file is already saved, then you need to click on **File > Save As** in the SOLIDWORKS Design Menus to invoke the **Save As** dialog box.

8. Select the **Form Tool (*.sldftp)** as the file type in the **Save as type** drop-down list of the **Save As** dialog box. The location to save the forming tool gets browsed automatically to the **design library** folder at *C:\ProgramData\SOLIDWORKS\SOLIDWORKS 2026\design library* in the dialog box.

9. Double-click on the **forming tools** folder in the **design library** folder of the **Save As** dialog box.

Note: You can save the forming tool part in the **forming tools** folder or any of its existing sub-folders. You can also create a new folder in the **forming tools** folder and then save the forming tool in it.

10. Enter a name for the forming tool part in the **File name** field of the **Save As** dialog box and then click on the **Save** button. The forming tool part gets saved at the *C:\ProgramData\SOLIDWORKS\SOLIDWORKS 2026\design library\forming tools* location.

Inserting a Forming Tool

After creating a forming tool part and saving it at the desired location, you can insert it on the face of a sheet metal component to create the respective formed feature, refer to Figures 2.158 and 2.159. The method for inserting a forming tool part is discussed below:

2.158

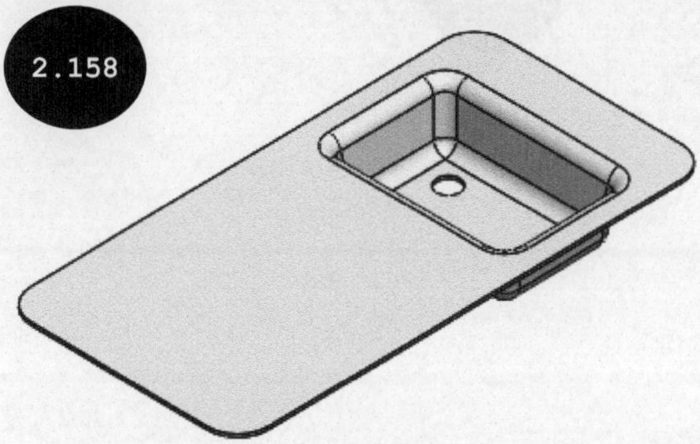

2.159

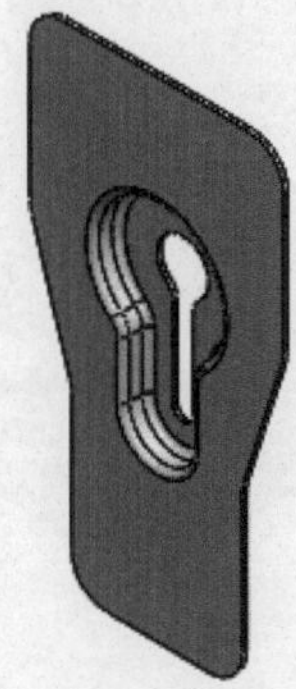

1. Invoke the **Design Library Task Panel** by clicking on the **Design Library** tab in the Task Panel, see Figure 2.160.

2. Expand the **design library** folder and then the **forming tools** sub-folder in the **Design Library Task Panel**. A list of all available different categories of forming tool parts appears in the expanded **forming tools** sub-folder, refer to Figure 2.160.

2.160

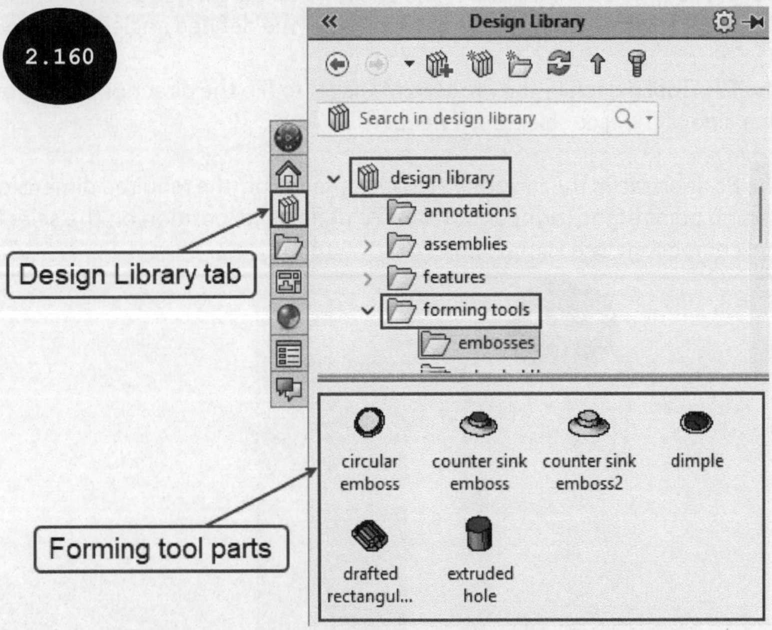

3. Select the required category in it. The forming tool parts that are available in the selected category appear on the lower part of the **Design Library Task Panel**, refer to Figure 2.160. In this figure, the **embosses** category is selected. As a result, all the forming tool parts that are available in the **embosses** category appear on the lower part of the **Design Library Task Panel**.

4. Drag and drop the required formed tool part from the lower part of the **Design Library Task Panel** to the face of the sheet metal component in the graphics area, see Figure 2.161. Also, the **Form Tool Feature PropertyManager** appears, see Figure 2.162.

2.161

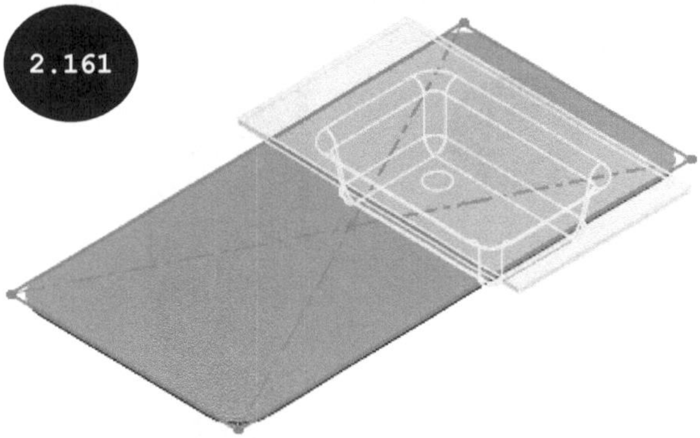

2.162

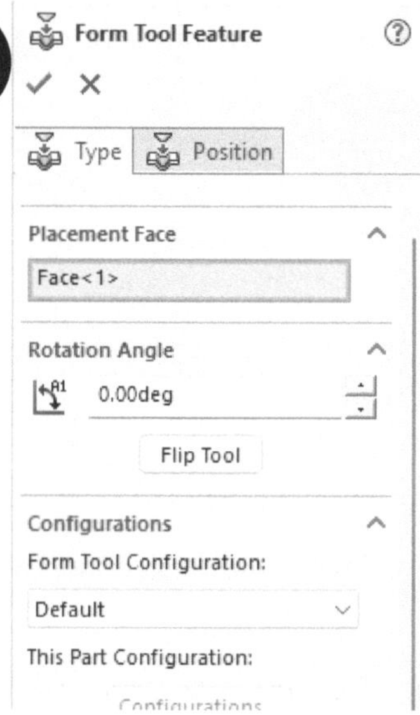

5. Enter the required angle in the **Rotation Angle** field of the PropertyManager for rotating the formed tool part on the selected face of the sheet metal part, if needed. Next, click anywhere in the graphics area. The formed tool gets rotated as per the defined angle of rotation.

6. Click on the **Flip Tool** button in the PropertyManager to flip the direction of the formed tool part on the other side of the face selected, if needed.

7. Click on the **Position** tab in the PropertyManager, then apply the required dimensions or relations to the insertion point of the formed tool part for defining its position on the selected face of the sheet metal component, see Figure 2.163.

2.163

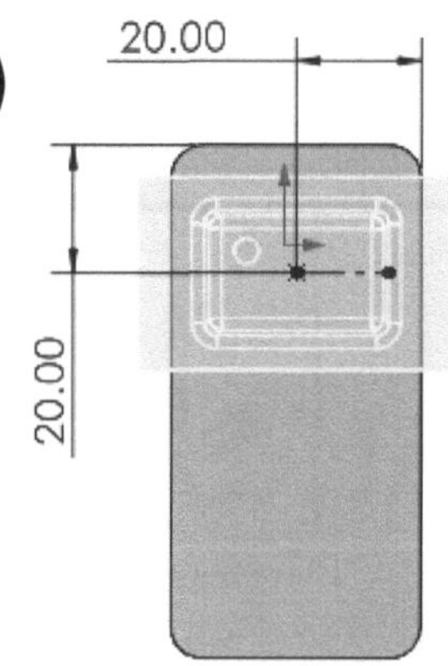

Note: You can also insert multiple sub-instances of the formed tool part by clicking on the selected face of the sheet metal component.

8. After defining the position of the formed tool part on the selected face of the sheet metal component, click on the green tick-mark button. The formed feature gets created, see Figure 2.164.

2.164

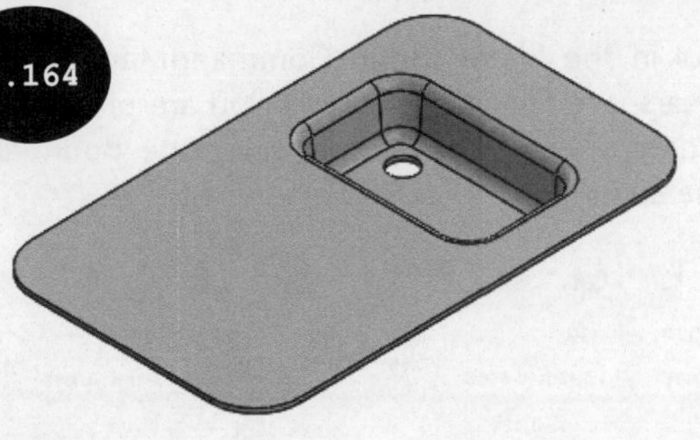

Creating a Vent

In SOLIDWORKS, you can create a vent feature on the face of a sheet metal component by using the **Vent** tool in the **Sheet Metal CommandManager**, see Figure 2.165. A vent feature uses a closed sketch segment as its boundary and the open or closed sketch segments inside the selected boundary as its ribs and spars, see Figure 2.165. The method for creating a vent feature is discussed below:

2.165

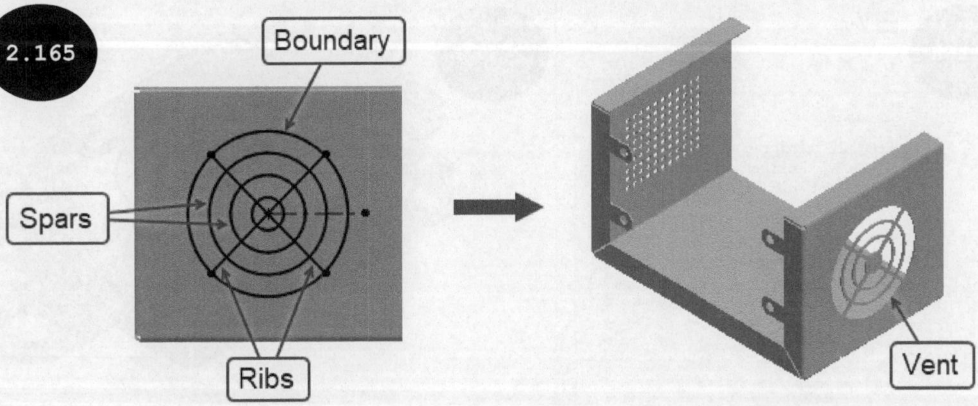

1. Invoke the Sketching environment by selecting a face of the sheet metal component where you want to create a vent feature.

2. Create a sketch of the vent feature which includes a closed sketch segment as a boundary and closed or open sketch segments inside the boundary as ribs and spars segments, refer to Figures 2.165 and 2.166. Note that you can create a vent of any shape by creating its sketch, accordingly.

2.166

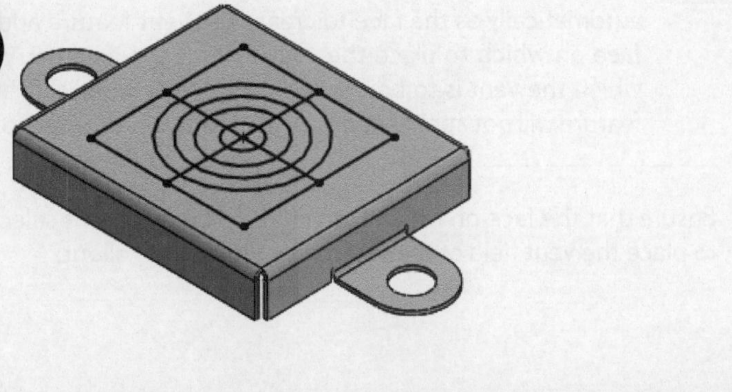

3. After creating the sketch of the vent feature, exit the Sketching environment. Next, click anywhere in the graphics area to exit the current selection set.

4. Click on the **Vent** tool in the **Sheet Metal CommandManager**, see Figure 2.167. The **Vent PropertyManager** appears, see Figure 2.168. Also, you are prompted to select a closed sketch segment as the boundary of the vent feature, since the **Boundary** field is activated in the PropertyManager, by default.

2.167

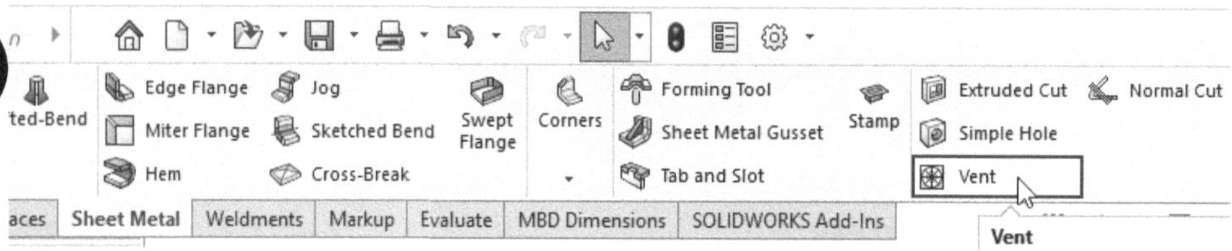

5. Select the sketch segment that forms a closed loop as the boundary of the vent feature, refer to Figure 2.169. The preview of a vent feature appears such that the material that lies inside the defined boundary gets removed from the face of the sheet metal component. In Figure 2.169, the outer four sketch segments are selected to define the boundary of the vent feature.

2.168

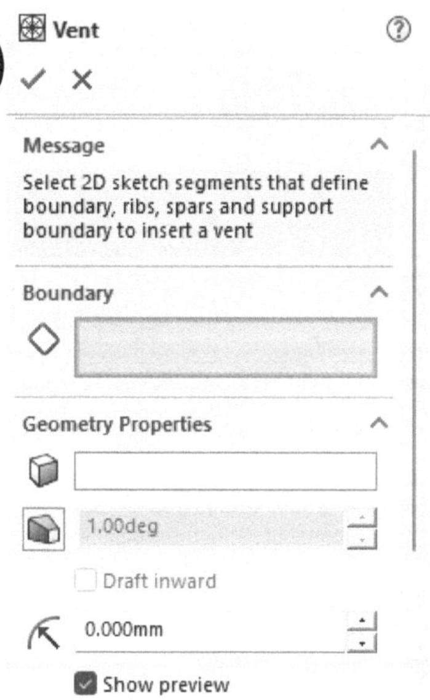

2.169

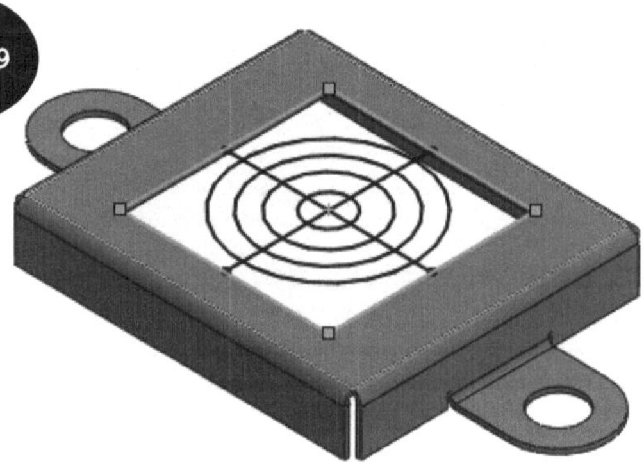

Note: The face of the sheet metal component on which the sketch is created gets selected automatically as the face to create the vent feature and its name appears in the **Select a face on which to place the vent** field of the **Geometry Properties** rollout. If the face on which the vent is to be created is not selected in this field, then the preview of the vent feature will not appear and you need to select the face to create the vent feature, manually.

6. Ensure that the face on which the vent is to be created is selected in the **Select a face on which to place the vent** field of the **Geometry Properties** rollout.

Draft On/Off: The **Draft On/Off** button is used for adding draft angle (tapering) to the vent feature. By default, this button is not enabled. As a result, the resultant vent feature is created without having any tapering in it. To add tapering to a vent feature, click on the **Draft On/Off** button. The **Draft Angle** field and the **Draft inward** check box get enabled in the rollout of the PropertyManager. The **Draft Angle** field is used for entering the draft angle for the vent feature and the **Draft inward** check box is used for reversing the direction of the draft.

Radius for the fillets: The **Radius for the fillets** field is used for defining the fillet radius at the intersections between the boundary, ribs, and spars of the vent feature, refer to Figures 2.170 and 2.171. Figure 2.170 shows a resultant vent feature without any fillet radius (0 fillet radius), whereas Figure 2.171 shows a resultant vent feature with a fillet radius at the intersections among the boundary, ribs, and spars of the vent feature.

2.170

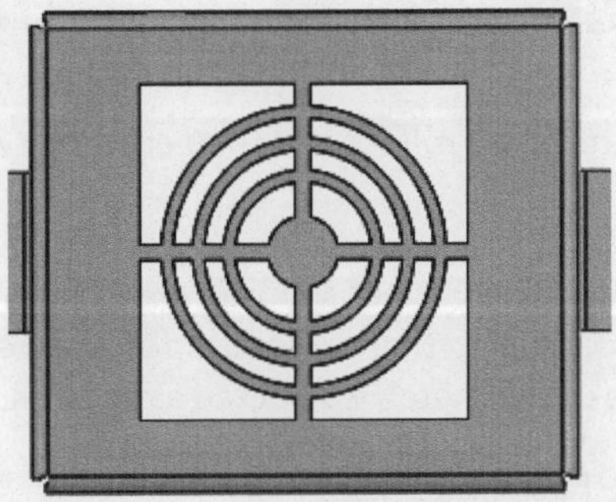

2.171

Show preview: By default, the **Show preview** check box is selected. As a result, while creating a vent feature, its preview appears in the graphics area.

Flow Area: The **Flow Area** rollout of the PropertyManager shows the total area available inside the boundary of the vent feature in square units, see Figure 2.172. It also shows the open area inside the boundary of the vent feature for the air flow in terms of the percentage of the total area. The value of the open area gets updated as you add vent entities such as fillets, ribs, and spars.

2.172

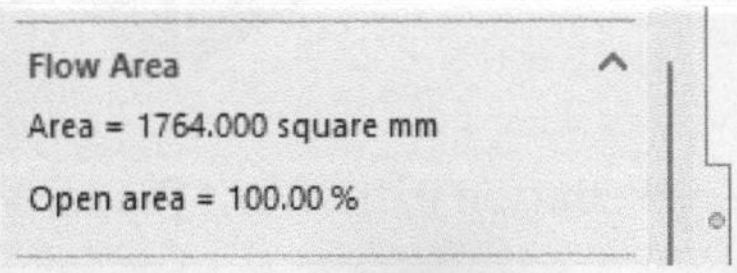

7. Click on the **Select 2D sketch segments that represent ribs of the vent** field in the **Ribs** rollout and then select the open or closed sketch segments inside the defined boundary as the ribs of the vent feature, see Figure 2.173. In this figure, two open sketch segments are selected as ribs.

2.173

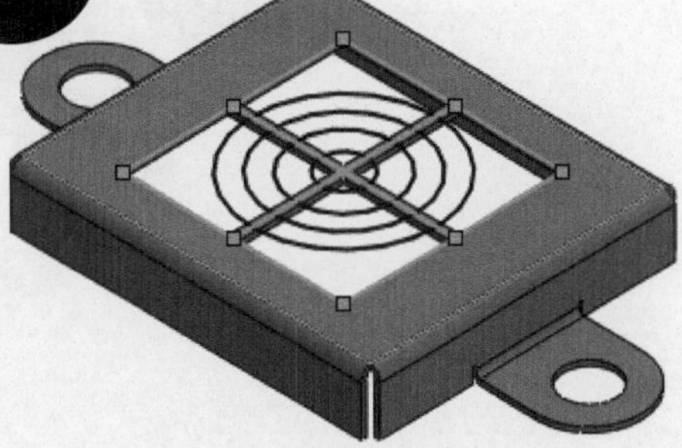

8. Click on the **Enter the width of the ribs** field in the **Ribs** rollout and then enter the width of the ribs in it.

9. Click on the **Select 2D sketch segments that represent spars of the vent** field in the **Spars** rollout and then select the open or closed sketch segments inside the boundary as the spars of the vent feature, see Figure 2.174. In this figure, three outer circular sketch segments are selected as spars.

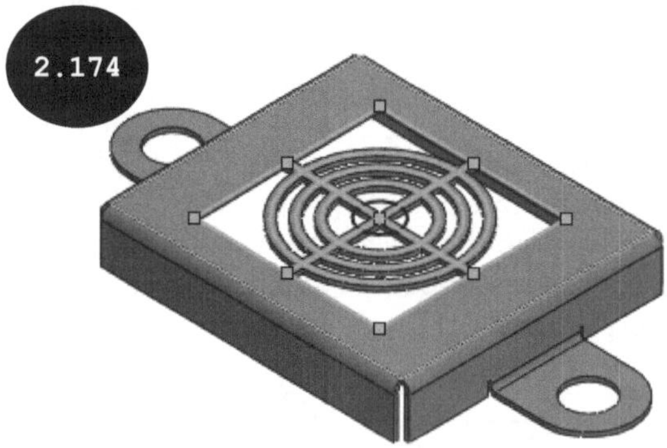

10. Click on the **Enter the width of the spars** field in the **Spars** rollout and then enter the width of the spars in it.

11. Click on the field in the **Fill-In Boundary** rollout and then select a closed sketch segment inside the boundary as the fill-in boundary acting as a supporting boundary for the vent feature, see Figure 2.175. In this figure, the innermost circle of the sketch is selected as the fill-in boundary.

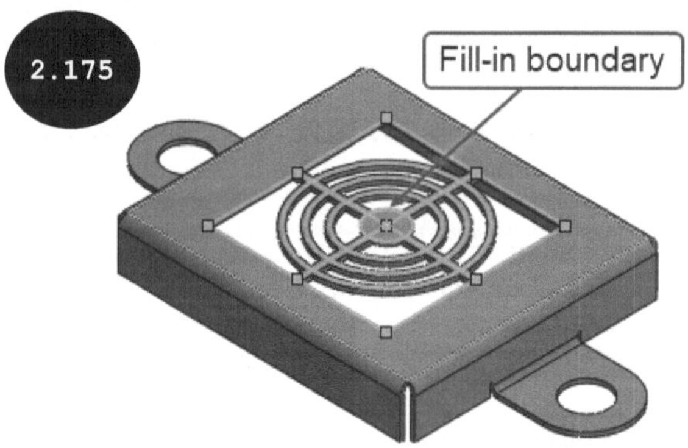

12. Click on the green tick-mark button in the **Vent PropertyManager**. A vent feature gets created, see Figure 2.176.

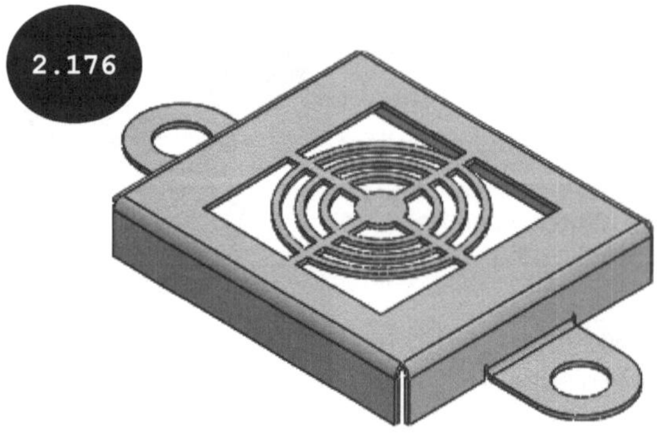

Converting a 3D Solid Part into a Sheet Metal

In SOLIDWORKS, you can also convert a 3D solid part into a sheet metal component by using the **Convert to Sheet Metal** tool, see Figure 2.177. The method for converting a 3D solid part into a sheet metal component is discussed below:

2.177

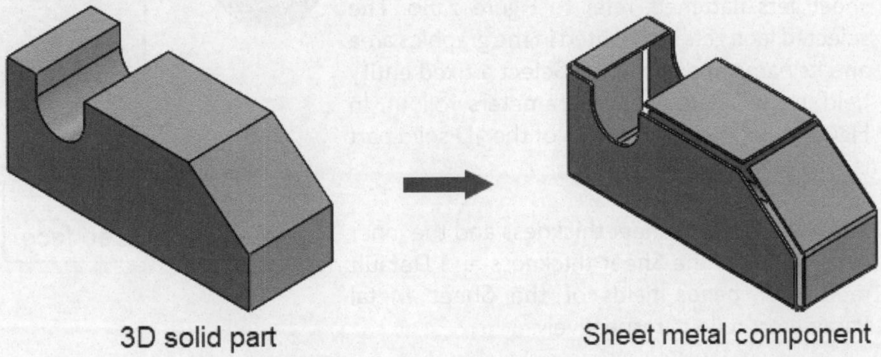

1. Create a 3D solid part in the Part modeling environment or open an existing 3D solid part to be converted into a sheet metal component.

Note: To learn creating 3D solid parts, assemblies, and drawings, refer to "**SOLIDWORKS 2026: A Power Guide for Beginners and Intermediate Users**" textbook by **CADArtifex**.

2. Click on the **Convert to Sheet Metal** tool in the **Sheet Metal CommandManager**, see Figure 2.178. The **Convert to Sheet Metal PropertyManager** appears, see Figure 2.179. Also, the available 3D solid part becomes transparent in the graphics area.

2.178

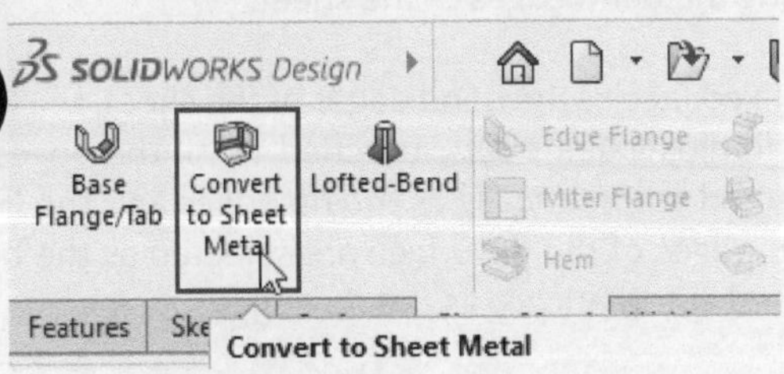

2.179

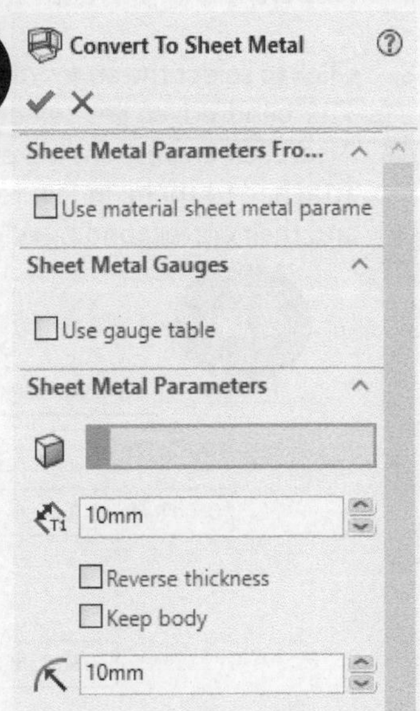

3. Ensure that the **Select a fixed entity** field is activated in the **Sheet Metal Parameters** rollout to select a face of the part as the fixed face of the resultant sheet while creating its flat pattern.

4. Select a face of the 3D solid part as the fixed face of the model that remains fixed when the resultant sheet gets flattened, refer to Figure 2.180. The selected face gets highlighted in the graphics area and its name appears in the **Select a fixed entity** field in the **Sheet Metal Parameters** rollout. In Figure 2.180, the bottom face of the 3D solid part is selected as the fixed face.

2.180

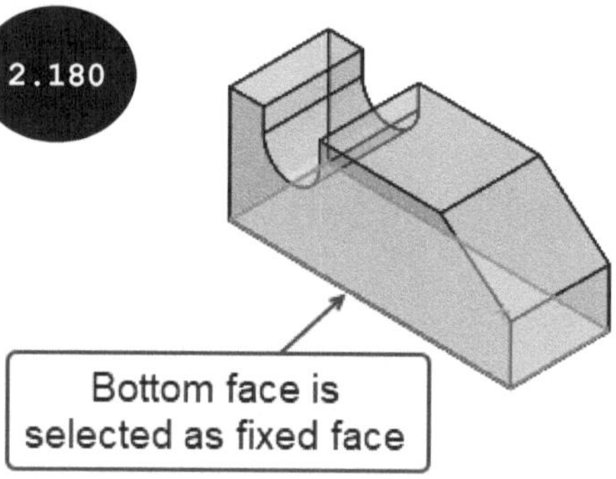

5. Enter the required sheet thickness and the inner bend radius in the **Sheet thickness** and **Default radius for bends** fields of the **Sheet Metal Parameters** rollout, respectively.

   Reverse thickness: The **Reverse thickness** check box is used for reversing the sheet metal thickness direction from inside to outside the part or vice-versa.

   Keep body: The **Keep body** check box is used for keeping the original solid part in the graphics area. By default, this check box is cleared. As a result, the original solid part gets consumed by the resultant sheet metal component.

6. Ensure that the **Keep body** check box is cleared in the **Sheet Metal Parameters** rollout.

7. Ensure that the **Select edges/faces that represent bends** field in the **Bend Edges** rollout of the PropertyManager is activated for selecting the bend edges of the sheet.

8. Click to select the edges of the selected fixed face as the bend edges of the sheet, see Figure 2.181. The bend edges get selected, and the **Radius** callout gets attached to all the edges selected. Also, their corresponding edges get selected automatically as the rip edges and the **Gap** callout attached to them. In Figure 2.181, all four edges of the fixed face are selected as the bend edges and their corresponding edges are selected automatically as the rip edges.

2.181

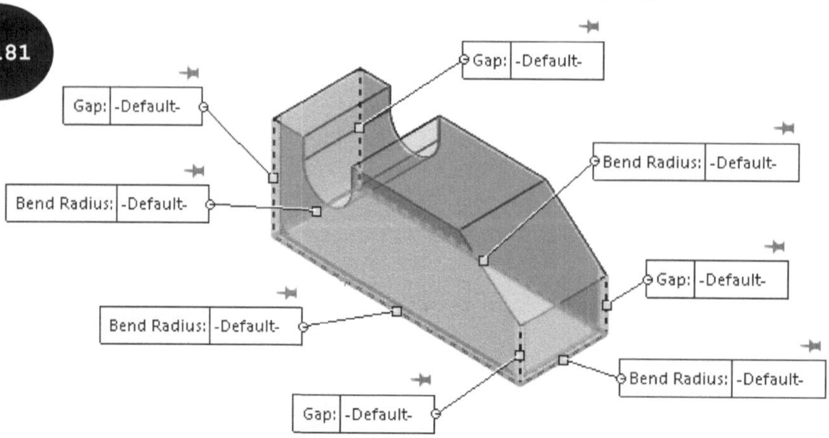

Tip: It is recommended to first select the edges of the fixed face and then continue with the selection of other edges of the part as the bend edges of the sheet.

After selecting the edges of the fixed face as the bend edges, you can also select other edges of the part as the bend edges.

9. Select the other required edges of the part as the bend edges, see Figure 2.182.

2.182

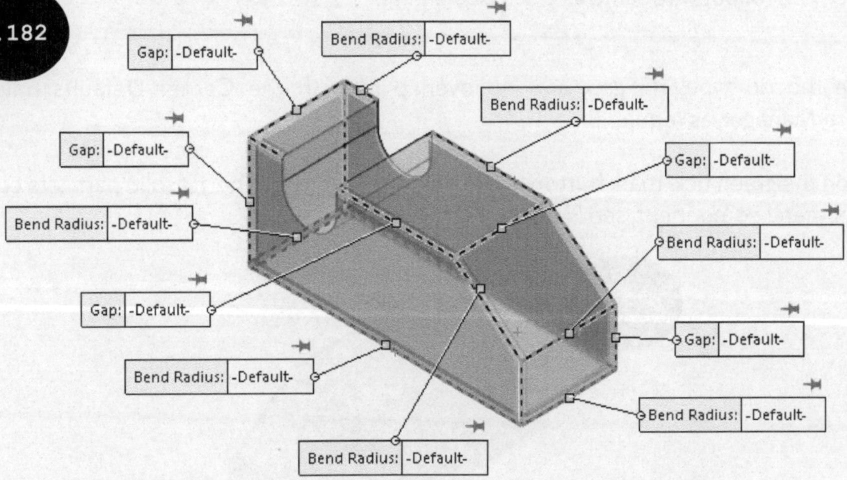

Note: The selected bend edges appear in blue color with Radius callout, whereas the rip (gap) edges appear in pink color with Gap callouts. Also, the names of the selected bend edges appear in the field of the **Bend Edges** rollout and the names of the rip edges appear in the field of the **Rip Edges found (Read-only)** rollout of the PropertyManager.

Show callouts: By default, the **Show callouts** check box is selected in the **Bend Edges** and **Rip Edges found (Read-only)** rollouts of the PropertyManager. As a result, the callouts for the bend edges and the rip edges are displayed in the graphics area. Note that the **Default** option is selected in each callout, which indicates that the default specified bend radius and the gap/rip value are used for bend edges and rip edges, respectively. You can edit or change the default bend radius and the rip value of an edge individually by clicking on the **Default** option of their respective callout in the graphics area.

Collect All Bends: The Collect All Bends button in the **Bend Edges** rollout is used for finding all the appropriate bends in the part, automatically. It works better in the case of an imported part with pre-existing bends in it.

Rip Sketches: The **Select a sketch to add a rip** field in the **Rip Sketches** rollout is used for selecting a sketch line or entity to define the required rip on the face of the part.

Corner Defaults: The options in the **Corner Default** rollout are used for defining the default rip type, rip gap, and rip overlap ratio for the corners of the resultant sheet metal component. You can define the rip type by clicking on the required button (**Open Butt**, **Overlap**, or **Underlap**) in this rollout. The **Default gap for all rips** field is used for specifying the default rip gap for the corners and the **Default overlap ratio for all rips** field is used for specifying the default rip overlap ratio for the corners.

Tip: You can also customize the bend allowance and relief by using the options available in the **Bend Allowance** and **Auto Relief** rollouts of the PropertyManager, respectively. The options in these rollouts are same as discussed earlier.

10. Define the rip type, rip gap, and rip overlap ratio in the **Corner Defaults** rollout of the PropertyManager, as required.

11. Click on the green tick-mark button in the PropertyManager. The 3D solid part gets converted to a sheet metal component, see Figure 2.183.

2.183

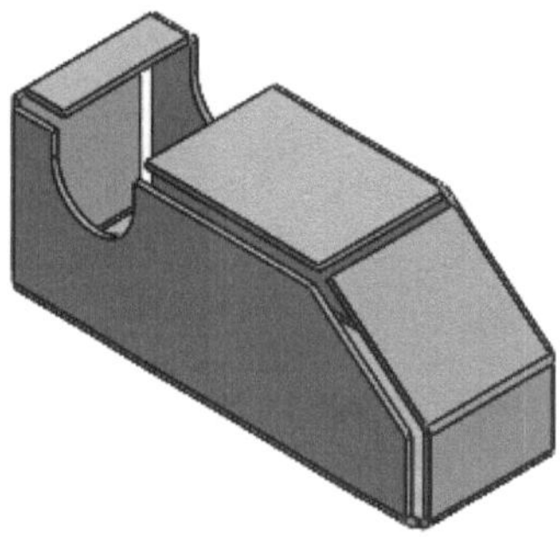

Converting a 3D Shelled Part into a Sheet Metal

In SOLIDWORKS, you can convert a 3D shelled part into a sheet metal component by adding rips and bends, see Figure 2.184. The method for converting a 3D shelled part into a sheet metal component is discussed below:

2.184

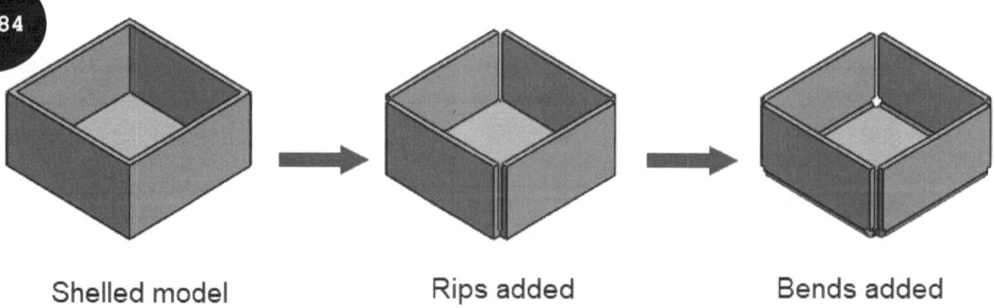

1. Create a 3D shelled model of uniform thickness by removing at least one of the faces of the model in the Part modeling environment, refer to Figure 2.185.

2.185

Now, you need to convert the shelled model into a sheet metal component by adding rips and bends.

2. Click on the **Rip** tool in the **Sheet Metal CommandManager**, see Figure 2.186. The **Rip PropertyManager** appears, see Figure 2.187. Also, you are prompted to select the edges of the shelled model to be ripped, since the **Edges to Rip** field is activated in the PropertyManager, by default.

2.186

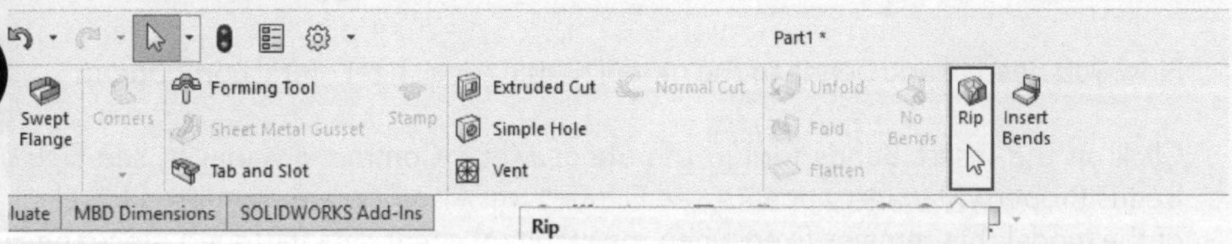

3. Click to select the internal or external edges of the model to be ripped, see Figure 2.188. Two arrows appear on each selected edge of the model indicating that rips are added in both directions. In this figure, outer five edges are selected.

2.187

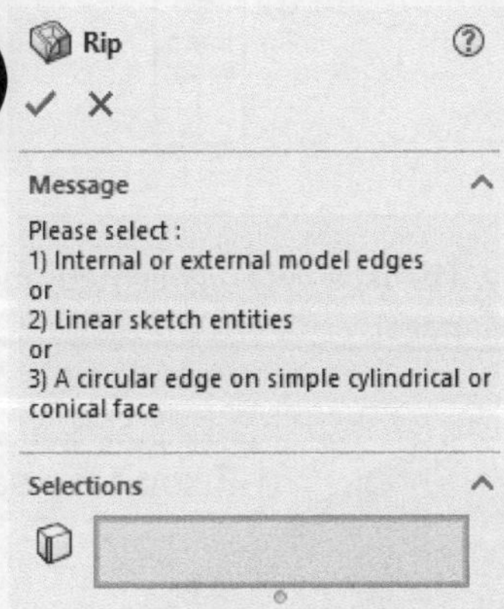

2.188

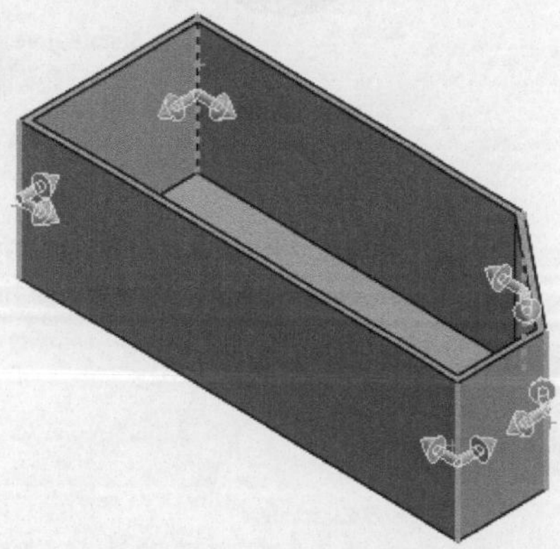

Change Direction: The **Change Direction** button is used for changing the rip direction of the selected edge sequences from one direction to the other direction, and then to both directions. To do so, you need to first select the name of the edge in the **Edges to Rip** field whose rip direction is to be changed and then click on the **Change Direction** button in the PropertyManager.

4. Change the rip directions for the selected edges by clicking on the **Change Direction** button, if needed, as discussed above.

5. Enter the required gap distance value in the **Rip Gap** field of the PropertyManager.

6. Click on the green tick-mark button in the PropertyManager. The rips of the defined gap value are added to the selected edges of the model, see Figure 2.189.

2.189

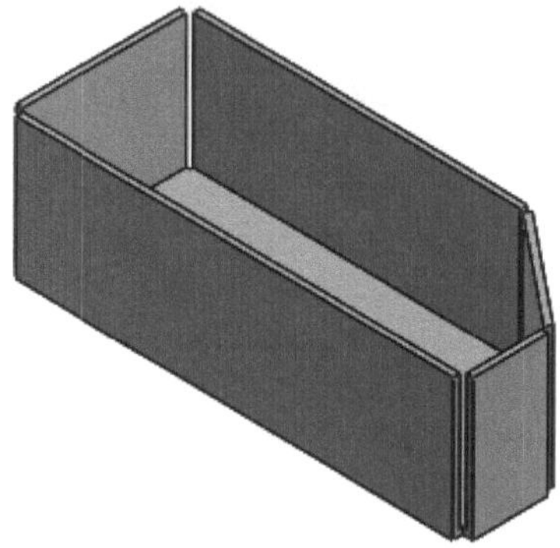

Now, you need to add bends to the model to make it a sheet metal component.

7. Click on the **Insert Bends** tool in the **Sheet Metal CommandManager**, see Figure 2.190. The **Bends PropertyManager** appears, see Figure 2.191. Also, you are prompted to select a fixed face of the model that remains fixed when the resultant sheet gets flattened, since the **Fixed Face or Edge** field is activated in the PropertyManager, by default.

2.190

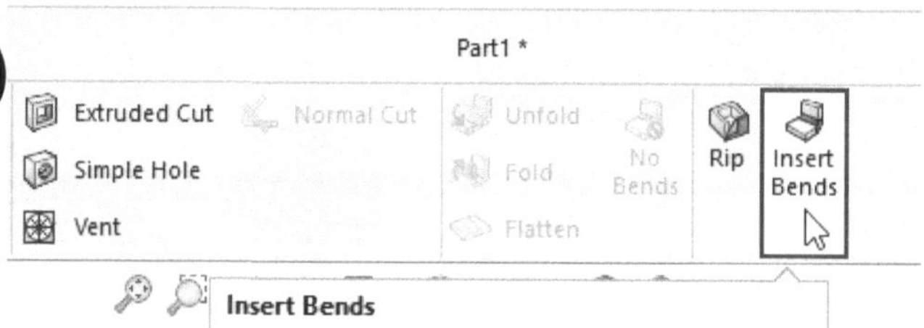

8. Click on select a fixed face of the model, see Figure 2.192. The face gets highlighted, and its name appears in the **Fixed Face or Edge** field of the PropertyManager.

2.191

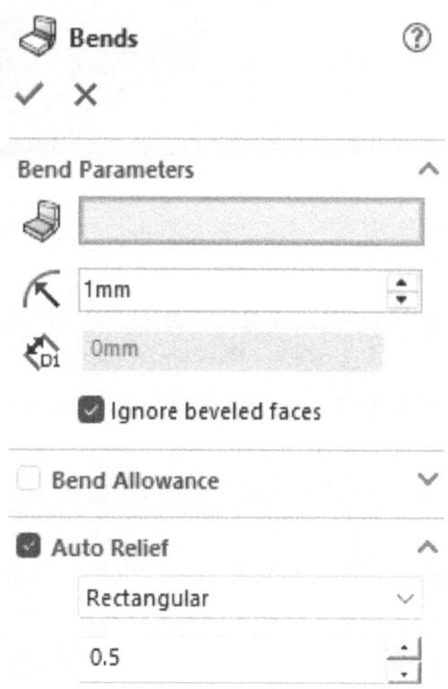

2.192

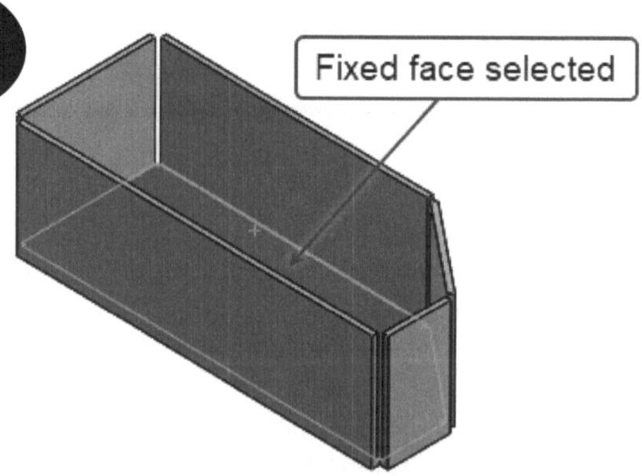

9. Enter the required bend radius in the **Bend Radius** field of the **Bend Parameters** rollout.

Tip: You can also add rips to the edges of a solid model by using the **Rip Parameters** rollout of the **Bends PropertyManager**. The method for adding rips is same as discussed earlier.

10. Accept the remaining default options and then click on the green tick-mark button in the PropertyManager. The **SOLIDWORKS** message window appears, which informs that the auto-relief cuts were made for one or more bends. Next, click on the **OK** button in this window. The bends of specified radius are added on all the edges of the selected fixed face, see Figure 2.193. Also, the **Sheet-Metal** node is added to the **FeatureManager Design Tree**, which indicates that the solid shelled model gets converted to a sheet-metal component.

2.193

Mirroring and Patterning a Sheet Metal Feature

In SOLIDWORKS, you can mirror and pattern a sheet metal feature by using the **Mirror**, **Linear Pattern**, and **Circular Pattern** tools of the **Features CommandManager**, respectively in the same manner as of mirroring and patterning a solid part feature while creating a 3D solid part.

Creating a Flat Pattern of a Sheet Metal Part

In a tool room or machine shop, the most important thing that you need before creating a sheet metal part/component is the flat pattern layout of the sheet. It defines the shape and size of the raw sheet before it is formed. It also helps in defining the manufacturing process for creating the finished sheet metal component.

In SOLIDWORKS, after creating a sheet metal component, you can generate its flat pattern. To do so, click on the **Flatten** tool in the **Sheet Metal CommandManager**, see Figure 2.194. The flat pattern layout of the sheet metal component gets generated in the graphics area, see Figure 2.195. Note that it is a toggle tool. You can click on this tool again to switch back to the sheet metal component.

2.194

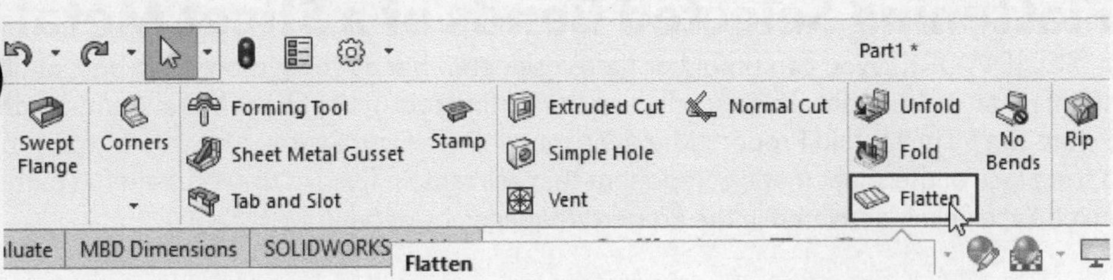

2.195

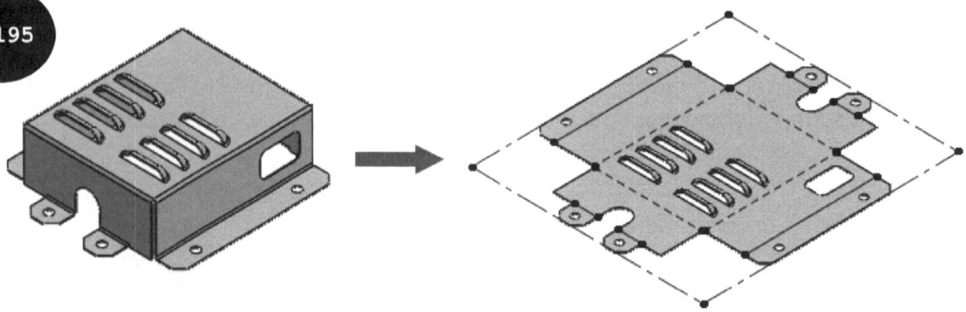

Alternatively, expand the **Flat-Pattern** node available at the end of all features in the **FeatureManager Design Tree**, see Figure 2.196. Next, click on the **Flat-Pattern1** feature in it and then click on the **Unsuppress** tool in the Pop-up toolbar that appears, see Figure 2.196. The **Flat-Pattern1** feature gets unsuppressed, and the flat pattern layout of the sheet metal component gets generated in the graphics area. Similarly, you can suppress the **Flat-Pattern1** feature for switching back to the sheet metal component.

2.196

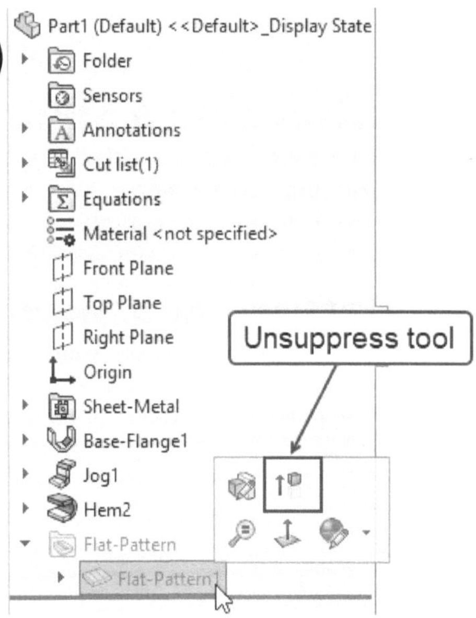

Flattening Selected Bends of a Sheet Metal Part

In SOLIDWORKS, you can unfold or flatten selected bends (one, more than one, or all bends) of a sheet metal component. To do so, click on the **Unfold** tool in the **Sheet Metal CommandManager**, see Figure 2.197. The **Unfold PropertyManager** appears, see Figure 2.198. Also, you are prompted to select a fixed face of the sheet metal component that will remain fixed in the resultant flat pattern, since the **Fixed Face** field is activated in the PropertyManager, by default.

2.197

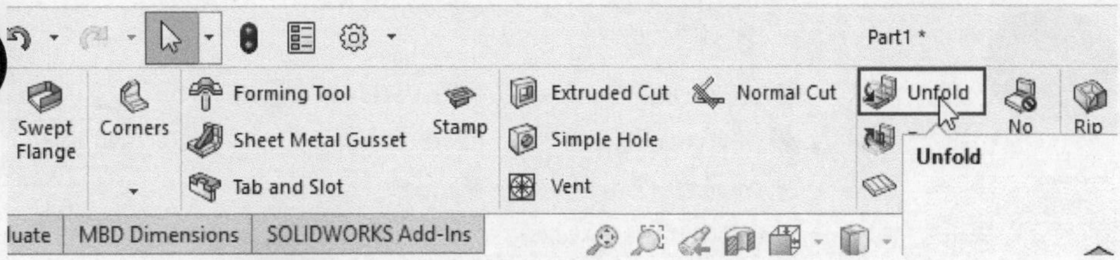

2.198

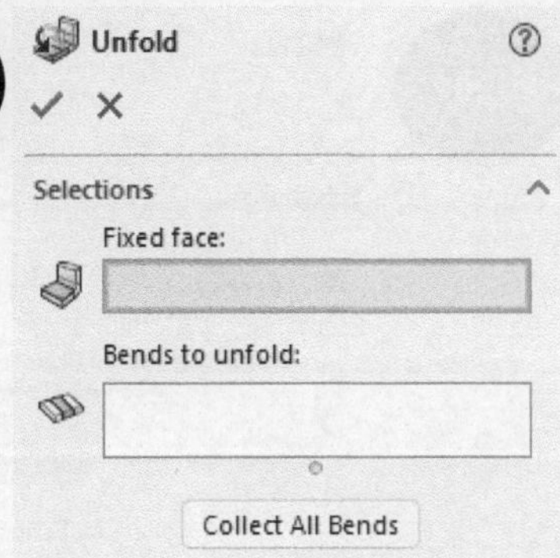

Click to select a face of the sheet metal component as the fixed face in the graphics area, see Figure 2.199. After selecting the fixed face, the **Bends to unfold** field gets activated in the PropertyManager for selecting the bends to be flattened. Select the bends of the sheet metal component to be flattened, see Figure 2.199. You can select one, more than one, or all the bends of the component to be flattened. In Figure 2.199, two bends are selected to be flattened. Note that to select all the bends of the sheet metal component, you need to click on the **Collect All Bends** button in the PropertyManager. After selecting the fixed face and bends to be flattened, click on the green tick-mark button in the PropertyManager. The selected bends get flattened, see Figure 2.200.

2.199

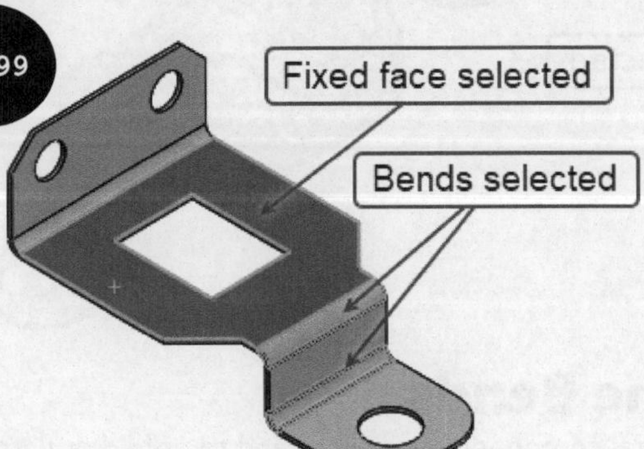

2.200

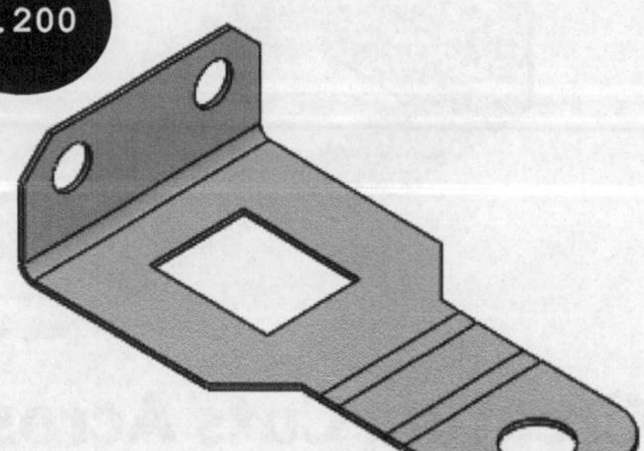

Folding Selected Bends of a Sheet Metal Part

In SOLIDWORKS, you can fold the selected unfolded or flattened bends of a sheet metal component. To do so, click on the **Fold** tool in the **Sheet Metal CommandManager**, see Figure 2.201. The **Fold PropertyManager** appears, and the fixed face of the sheet metal component gets selected automatically in its **Fixed face** field, see Figure 2.202. Also, you are prompted to select bends to be folded, since the **Bends to fold** field is activated in the PropertyManager, by default.

2.201

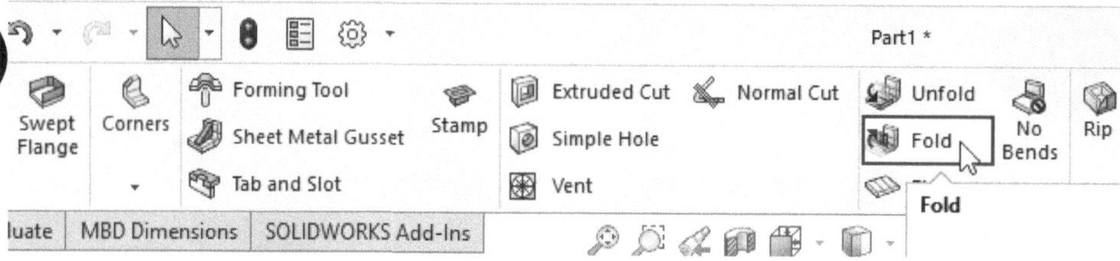

2.202

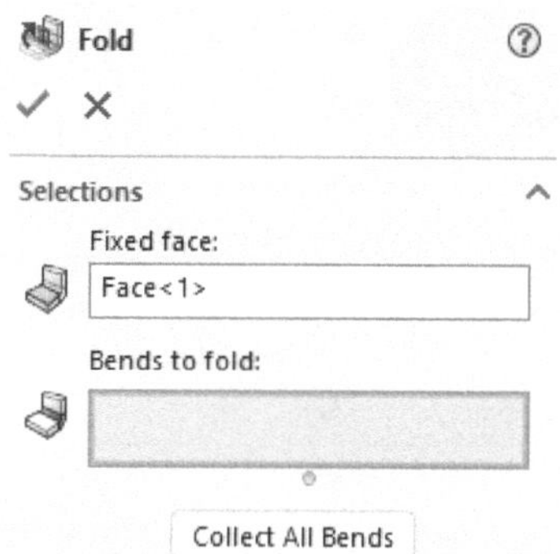

Select the unfolded or flattened bends of the sheet metal component to be folded in the graphics area, see Figure 2.203. You can select one, more than one, or all the unfolded bends of the component to be folded. In Figure 2.203, two unfolded bends are selected to be folded. Note that to select all the unfolded bends of the sheet metal component, you need to click on the **Collect All Bends** button in the PropertyManager. Next, click on the green tick-mark button in the PropertyManager. The selected bends get folded in the graphics area, see Figure 2.204.

2.203

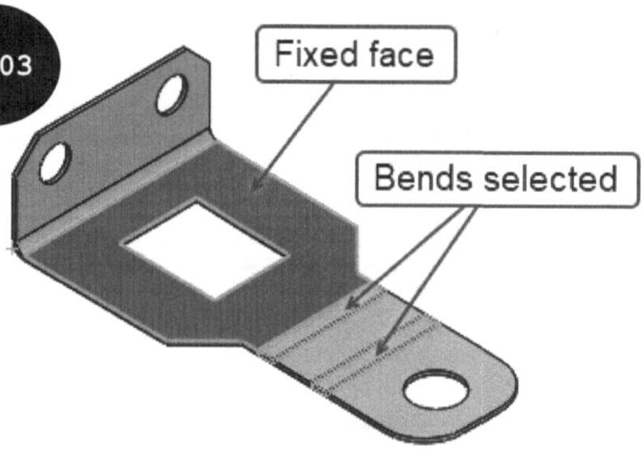

2.204

Creating Cuts Across the Bends

To create cuts across the bends of a sheet metal component, you first need to unfold or flatten the bends of the sheet metal component using the **Unfold** tool. After unfolding the bends, you can create cut features across the bends, as required by using the **Extruded Cut** tool, see Figure 2.205. In this figure, all three bends of a sheet metal component get unfolded by using the **Unfold** tool, and the cut feature is created on two of the unfolded bends.

2.205

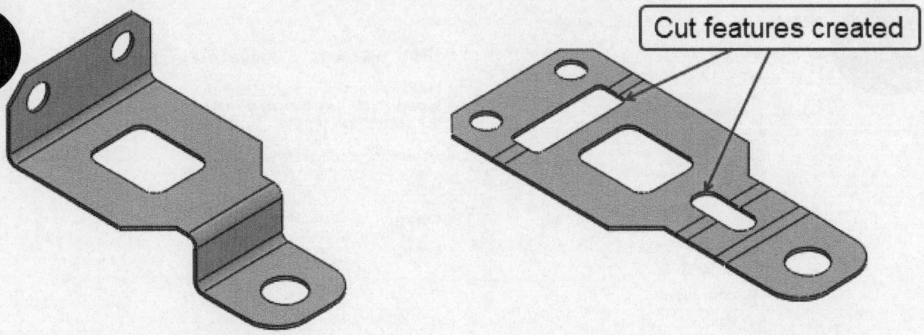

Sheet metal component

Cuts created on unfolded bends

After creating the cut feature on the unfolded bends of the sheet metal component, fold the bends by using the **Fold** tool, see Figure 2.206. The cut features are created across the bends of the sheet metal component.

2.206

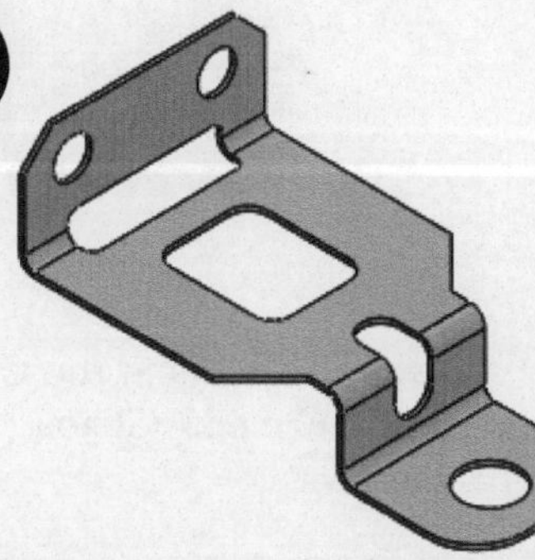

Defining Sheet Parameters to a Custom Material

In SOLIDWORKS, you can define the sheet metal parameters to a custom material of a part document and link these parameters with a sheet metal component. To do so, invoke a new part document of SOLIDWORKS and then right-click on the **Material <not specified>** option in the **FeatureManager Design Tree**, see Figure 2.207. A shortcut menu appears. In this shortcut menu, click on the **Edit Material** option. The **Material** dialog box appears, see Figure 2.208.

2.207

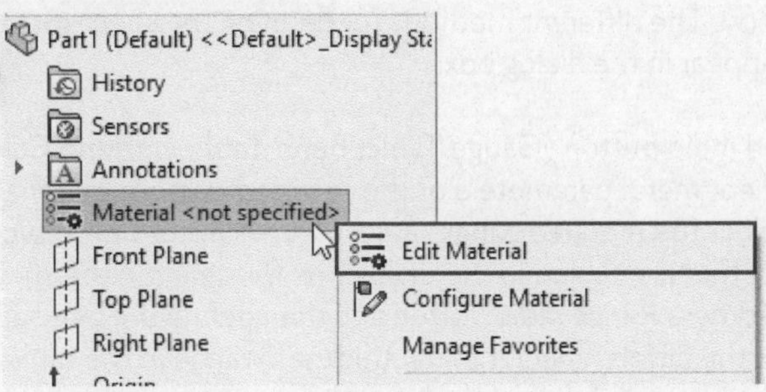

2.208

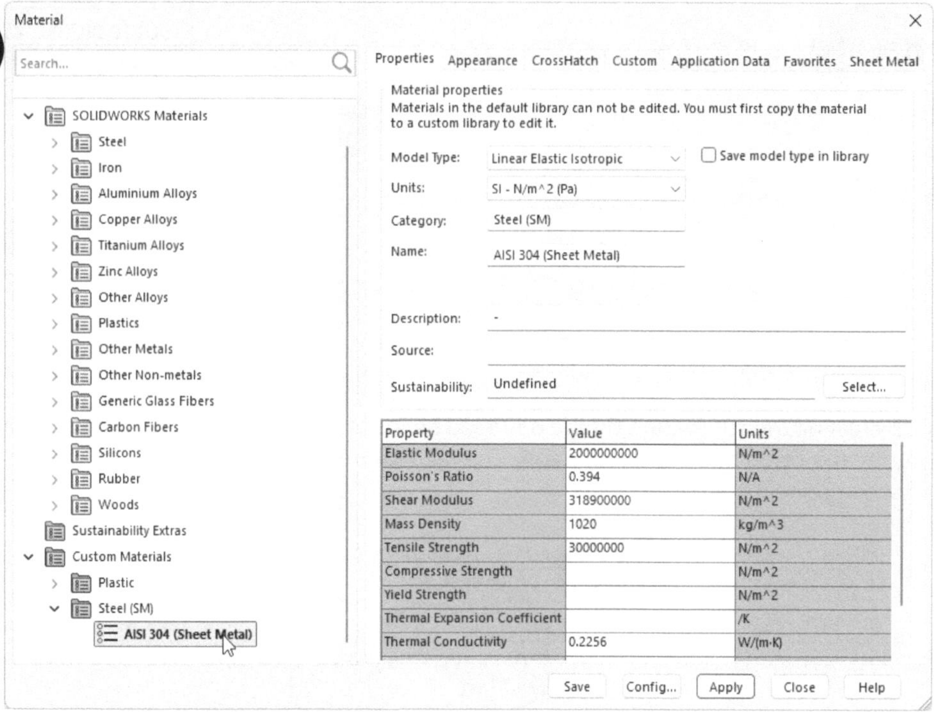

In the **Material** dialog box, create a custom material in the **Custom Materials** category, refer to Figure 2.208. In this figure, a custom material named **AISI 304 (Sheet Metal)** is created in the **Steel (SM)** category of the **Custom Materials** library.

Note: To create a custom material, you can also copy a standard material from the **SOLIDWORKS Materials** library and paste it inside the **Custom Materials** library of the **Material** dialog box. Next, edit its material properties, as required. To learn more about creating a new material category, custom material, and so on, refer to "**SOLIDWORKS 2026: A Power Guide for Beginners and Intermediate Users**" textbook by **CADArtifex**.

After creating a custom material, select it and then click on the **Sheet Metal** tab in the **Material** dialog box, see Figure 2.209. The different methods for defining the sheet metal parameters to the selected custom material appear in the dialog box.

Select the required radio button (**Gauge Table**, **Bend Table**, or **Bend Calculation Table**) as a method for defining the sheet metal parameters of the selected custom material. Depending upon the radio button chosen, select the required gauge table, bend table, or bend calculation table, respectively in the drop-down list that is enabled in the dialog box for defining the sheet metal properties. You can also select the **Thickness Range** radio button and then define the bend allowance, bend deduction, or k-factor values for the different sheet metal thickness range in the table that is enabled in the dialog box, refer to Figure 2.209. In this figure, the bend allowance values are defined for sheet metal thickness ranging from 0 to 6 in different rows of the table. Note that the thickness range specified in the different rows of the table must be continuous.

2.209

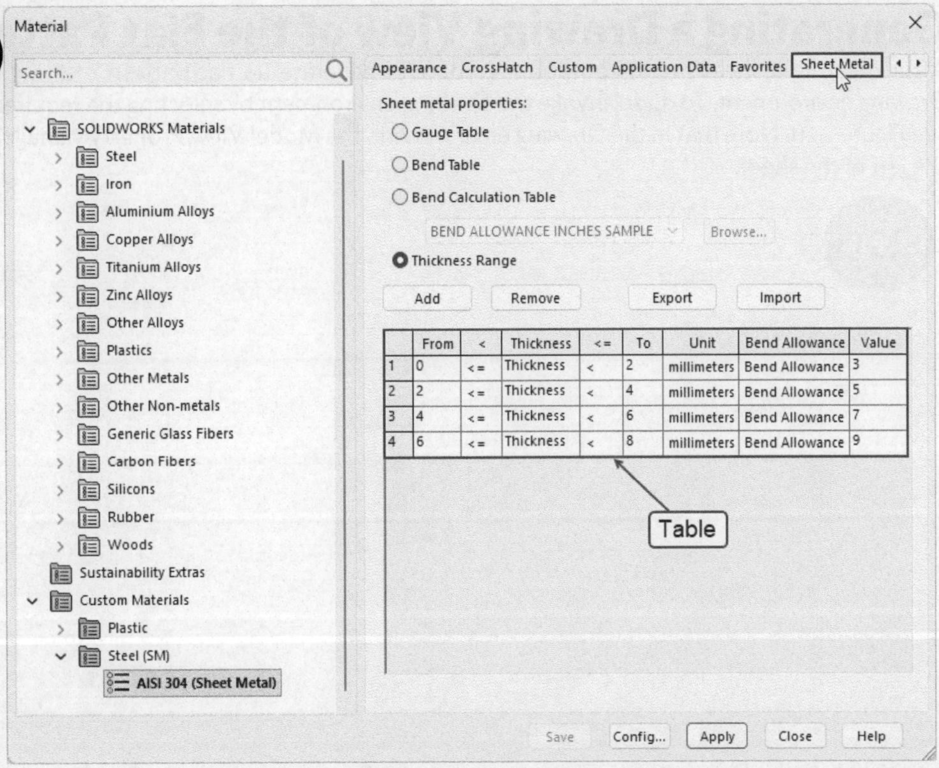

Note: You can use the **Add** button in the dialog box for adding a new row and the **Remove** button for removing a selected row in the table. You can also export the defined table with thickness range values in an excel spreadsheet by using the **Export** button. The **Import** button is used for importing an existing excel spreadsheet containing thickness range values in the table.

After defining the sheet metal parameters to a selected custom material, click on the **Apply** button and then the **Close** button in the dialog box. The sheet metal parameters are defined for the custom material. Now, you can use these parameters while creating a sheet metal component. For example, to use the sheet metal parameters defined for a custom material while creating a base flange, select the **Use material sheet metal parameters** check box in the **Base Flange PropertyManager**, see Figure 2.210.

2.210

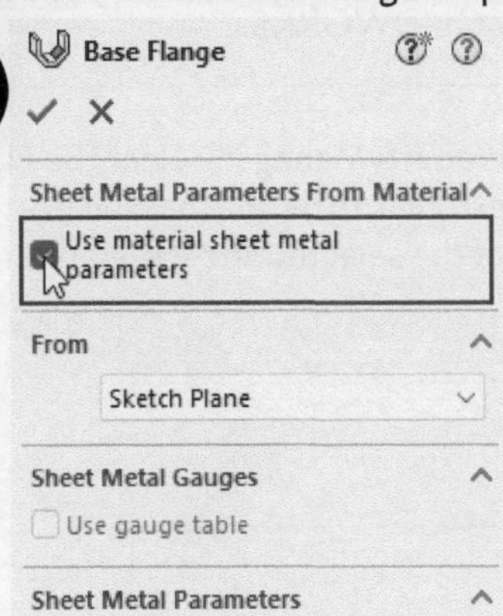

Generating a Drawing View of the Flat Pattern

After creating a sheet metal component, you can generate its flat pattern drawing view in the Drawing environment. To do so, invoke the Drawing environment by selecting the required sheet size, see Figure 2.211. Note that in the Drawing environment, the **Model View PropertyManager** appears to the left of the sheet.

2.211

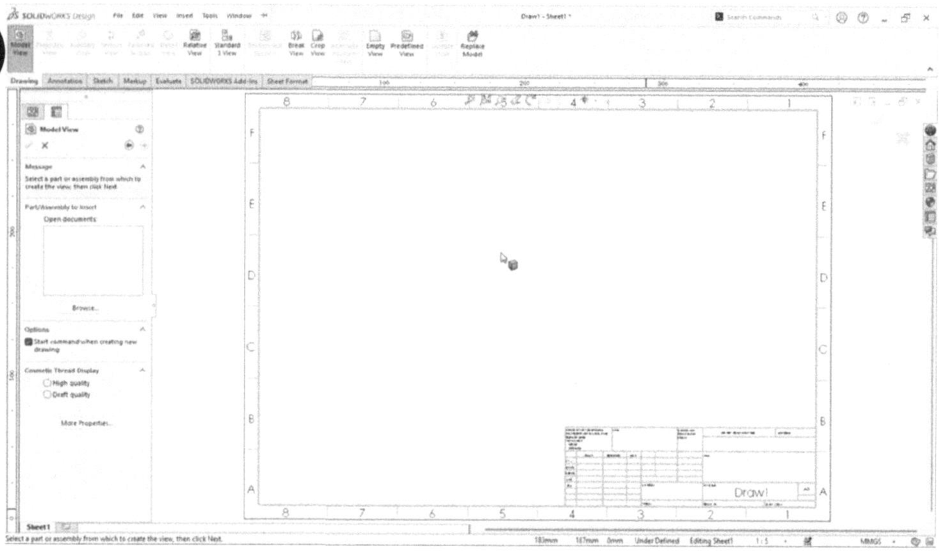

After invoking the Drawing environment, click on the **Browse** button in the **Part/Assembly to Insert** rollout of the **Model View PropertyManager**. The **Open** dialog box appears.

In the **Open** dialog box, browse to the location where the sheet metal component, whose flat pattern view is to be generated, has been saved, and then select it. Next, click on the **Open** button in the dialog box. A rectangular box representing the drawing view of the selected component is attached to the cursor. Also, the options of the PropertyManager get modified, see Figure 2.212.

Note: If the sheet metal component is listed or available in the **Open documents** field of the **Model View PropertyManager,** then you can double-click on it for generating its flat pattern view. Note that the **Open document** field displays only those components that are opened in the current session of SOLIDWORKS.

In the modified **Model View PropertyManager**, select the **Flat pattern** check box in the **Orientation** rollout, refer to Figure 2.212. Next, click to define the placement point of the drawing view on the sheet. The flat pattern drawing view of the selected sheet metal component gets generated, see Figure 2.213.

2.212

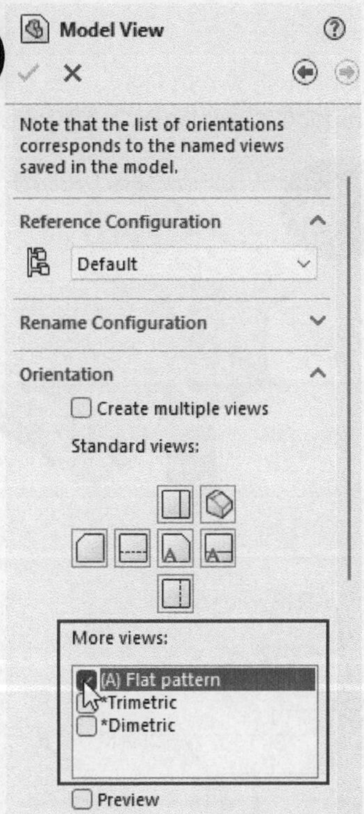
Model View
Note that the list of orientations corresponds to the named views saved in the model.
Reference Configuration
Default
Rename Configuration
Orientation
Create multiple views
Standard views:
More views:
(A) Flat pattern
*Trimetric
*Dimetric
Preview

2.213

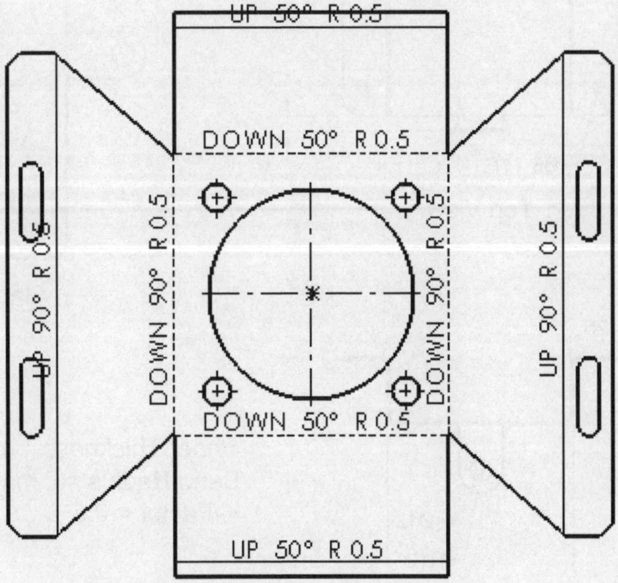
UP 50° R 0.5
DOWN 50° R 0.5
DOWN 90° R 0.5
DOWN 90° R 0.5
UP 90° R 0.5
UP 90° R 0.5
DOWN 50° R 0.5
UP 50° R 0.5

Tutorial 1

Create the sheet metal component shown in Figure 2.214. The different views, dimensions, and flat pattern of the sheet metal component are shown in Figure 2.215. All dimensions are in mm.

2.214

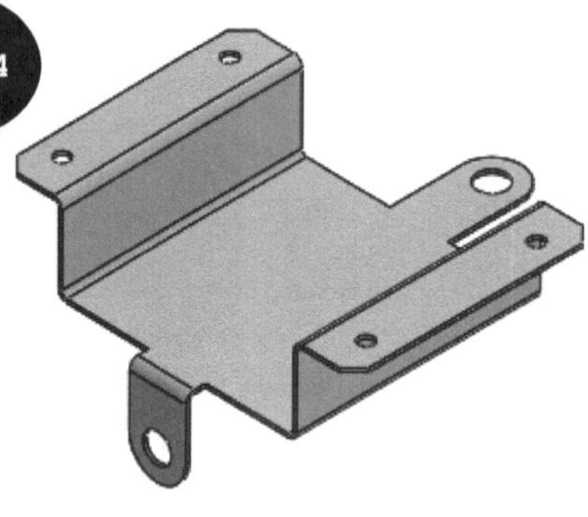

2.215

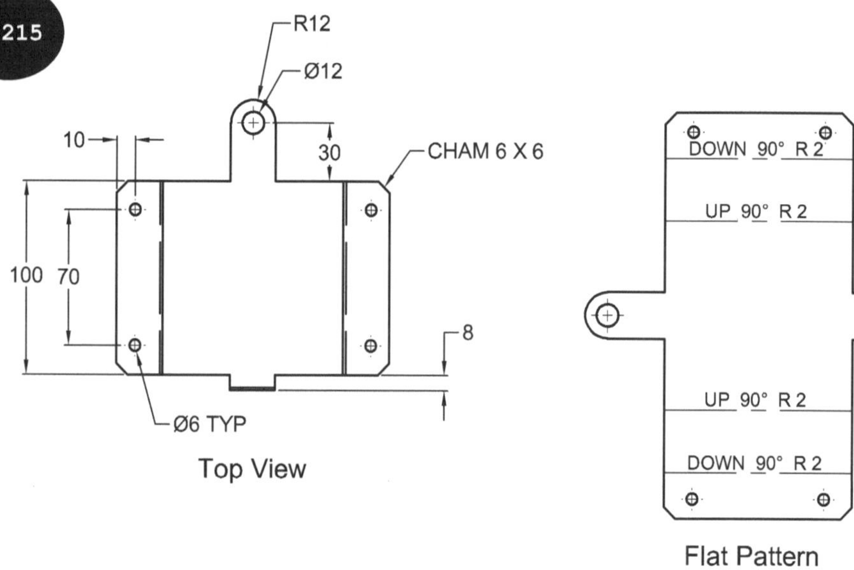

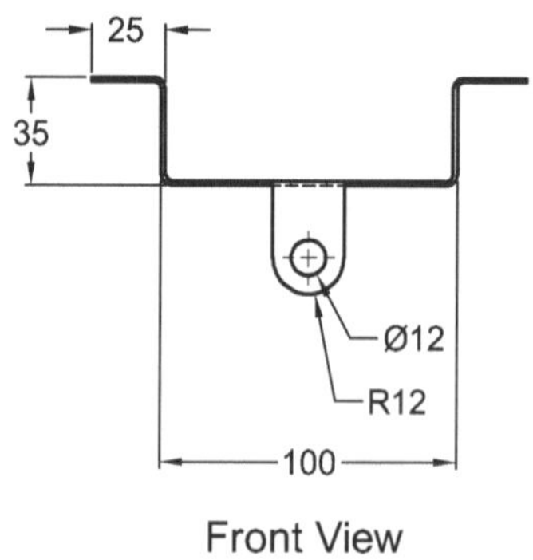

Sheet Thickness = 1.5 mm
Bend Radius = 2 mm
K-Factor = 0.5

Section 1: Invoking the Part Modeling Environment

1. Start SOLIDWORKS by double-clicking on the SOLIDWORKS icon on your desktop. The startup user interface of SOLIDWORKS appears along with the **Welcome** dialog box, see Figure 2.216.

2.216

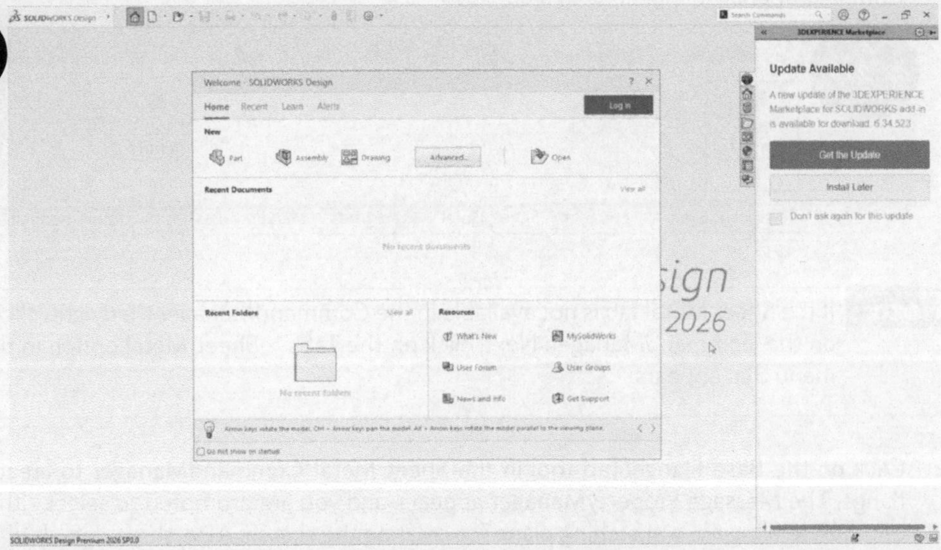

2. Click on the **Part** button in the **Welcome** dialog box. The Part modeling environment is invoked.

Note: If SOLIDWORKS is already open and the **Welcome** dialog box does not appear on the screen, then you can invoke the **Welcome** dialog box by clicking on the **Welcome to SOLIDWORKS** tool in the **Standard** toolbar. Alternatively, click on the **New** tool in the **Standard** toolbar and then double-click on the **Part** button in the **New SOLIDWORKS Document** dialog box that appears for invoking the Part modeling environment.

Section 2: Specifying Unit Settings

1. Move the cursor toward the lower right corner of the screen over the Status Bar and then click on the **Unit System** area, see Figure 2.217. The **Unit System** flyout appears.

2.217

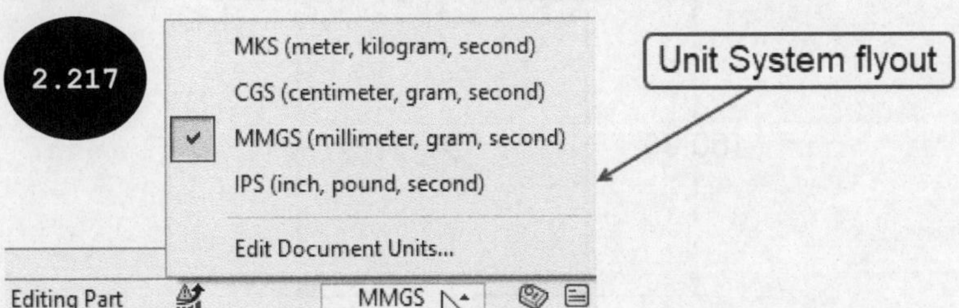

2. Ensure that the **MMGS (millimeter, gram, second)** option is tick-marked in the flyout as the unit system for the current part document.

Section 3: Creating the Base Flange of the Sheet Metal Component

Now, you need to create the base flange of the sheet metal component.

1. Click on the **Sheet Metal** tab in the CommandManager. The tools of the **Sheet Metal CommandManager** appear, see Figure 2.218.

2.218

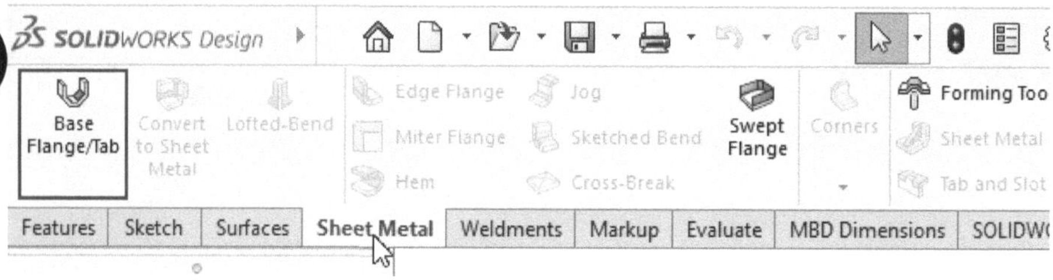

Note: If the **Sheet Metal** tab is not available in the CommandManager then right-click anywhere on the CommandManager. Next, click on the **Tabs > Sheet Metal** option in the shortcut menu that appears.

2. Click on the **Base Flange/Tab** tool in the **Sheet Metal CommandManager** to create the base flange. The **Message PropertyManager** appears, and you are prompted to select either a sketch of the base flange or a sketching plane for creating the sketch. Also, three default planes, which are mutually perpendicular to each other appear in the graphics area.

3. Click to select the Top plane as the sketching plane in the graphics area for creating the sketch of the base flange. The Sketching environment gets invoked and the Top plane becomes normal to the viewing direction.

4. Create the sketch of the base flange in the drawing area by using the sketching tools, see Figure 2.219.

2.219

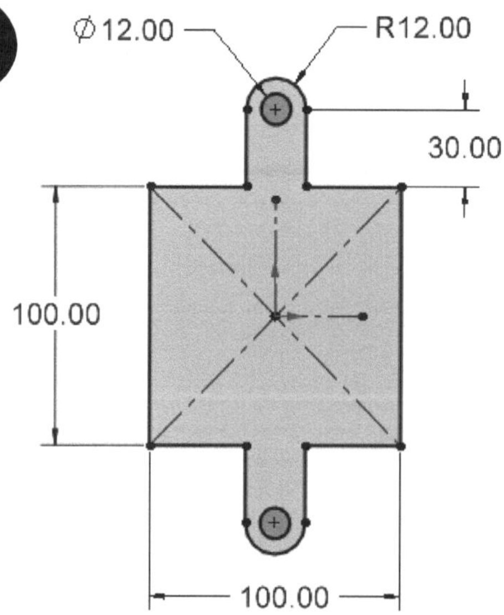

5. After creating the sketch of the base flange, exit the Sketching environment. The **Base Flange PropertyManager** appears, see Figure 2.220. Also, the preview of the base flange with default thickness appears in the graphics area.

   Now, you need to define the sheet metal parameters in the **Base Flange PropertyManager** and the same will be used as the default parameters for the entire sheet metal component.

2.220

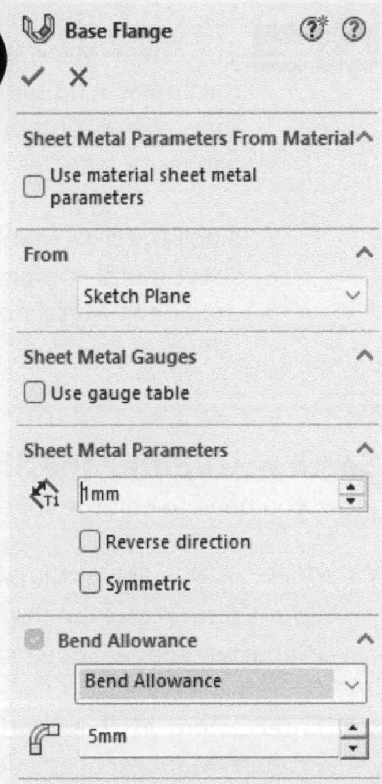

6. Enter **1.5** mm in the **Thickness** field of the **Sheet Metal Parameters** rollout as the thickness of the sheet metal component.

7. Select the **K-Factor** option in the **Bend Allowance Type** drop-down list of the **Bend Allowance** rollout for defining the bend allowance of the sheet metal component in the bent regions.

8. Enter **0.5** as the K-factor value in the **K-Factor** field of the **Bend Allowance** rollout.

9. Select the **Rectangular** option in the **Auto Relief Type** drop-down list of the **Auto Relief** rollout of the PropertyManager.

10. Ensure that the **Use relief ratio** check box is selected and **0.5** value is entered in the **Ratio** field of the **Auto Relief** rollout of the PropertyManager.

11. Click on the green tick-mark button in the PropertyManager. The base flange of the sheet metal component gets created, see Figure 2.221. Also, the **Sheet-Metal, Base-Flange1**, and **Flat-Pattern** nodes get added to the **FeatureManager Design Tree**, see Figure 2.222. Change the orientation of the model to isometric.

2.221

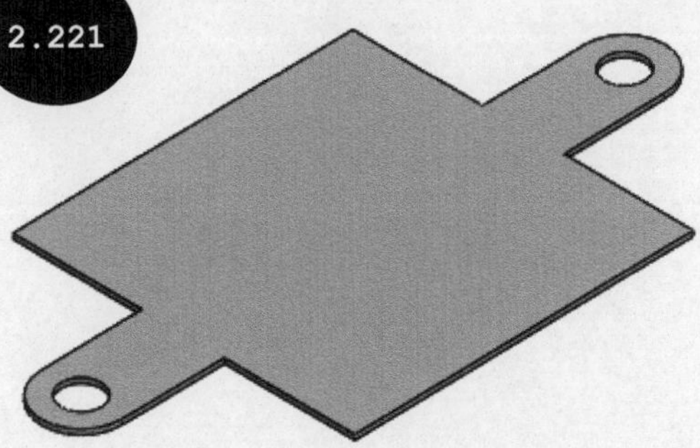

2.222

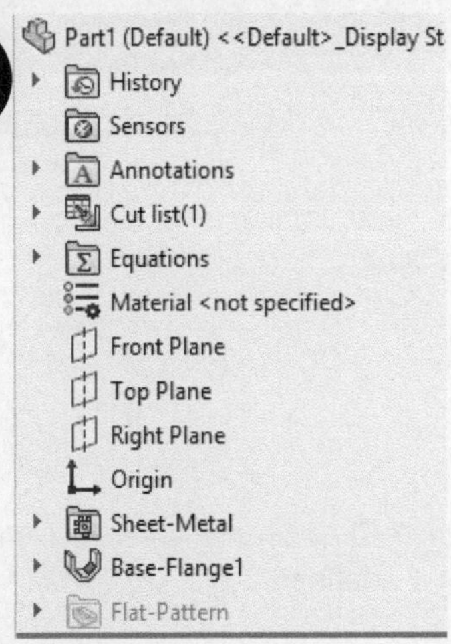

Note: The **Sheet-Metal** node contains all the default sheet metal parameters such as material thickness, bend allowance, and relief that are specified while creating the base flange of the sheet metal component. These parameters gets automatically assigned to all the remaining flanges or features of the sheet metal component as default parameters.

Since the base feature created above does not contain any bends, the bend radius for the sheet metal component is not defined while creating it. In such a case, you need to edit the **Sheet-Metal** node of the **FeatureManager Design Tree** for defining the default bend radius, as required.

Section 4: Editing the Sheet Metal Parameters

Now, you need to edit the sheet metal parameters to define the default bend radius to 2 mm.

1. Click on the **Sheet-Metal** node in the **FeatureManager Design Tree** and then click on the **Edit Feature** tool in the Pop-up toolbar that appears, see Figure 2.223. The **Sheet-Metal PropertyManager** appears.

2. Enter **2** mm in the **Bend Radius** field of the **Bend Parameters** rollout in the **Sheet-Metal PropertyManager** as the default bend radius of the sheet metal component, see Figure 2.224.

2.223

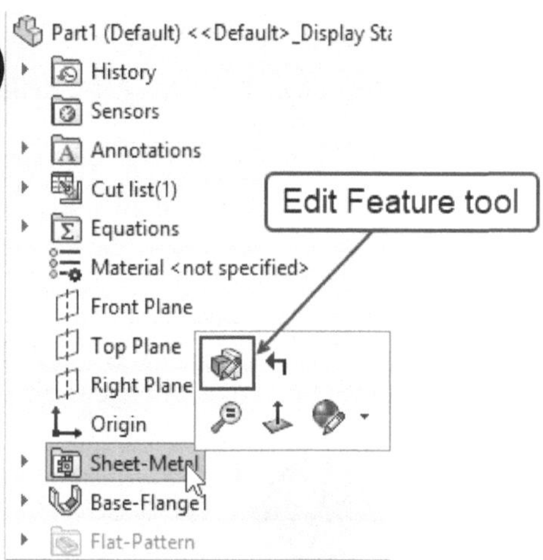

2.224

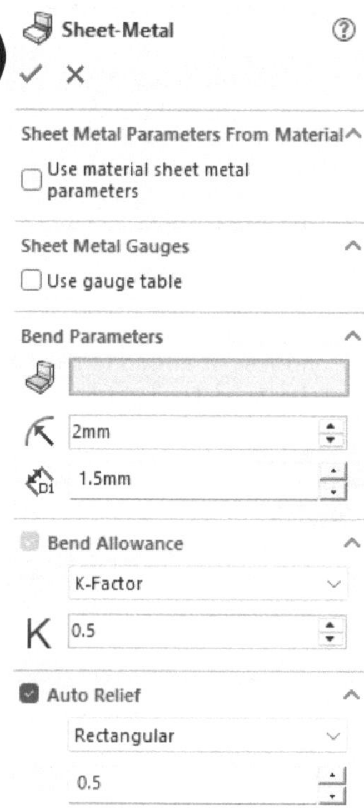

3. Click on the green tick-mark button in the PropertyManager. The default bend radius gets defined.

Section 5: Creating the Edge Flange

Now, you need to create edge flanges of the sheet metal component.

1. Click on the **Edge Flange** tool in the **Sheet Metal CommandManager**, see Figure 2.225. The **Edge-Flange PropertyManager** appears, see Figure 2.226. Also, you are prompted to select an edge of a planar face to create the edge flange, since the **Edge** field is activated in the PropertyManager, by default.

2.225

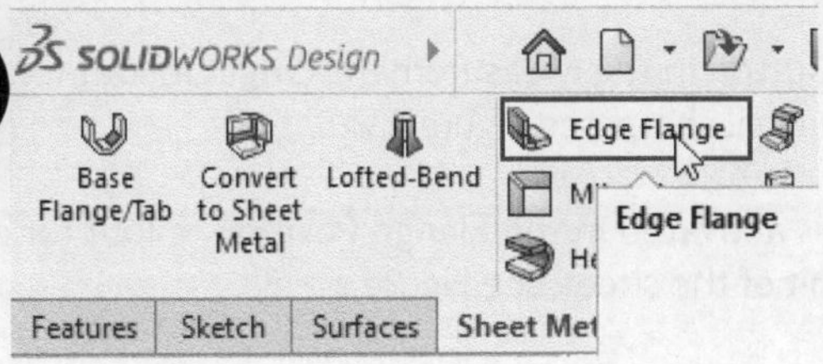

2.226

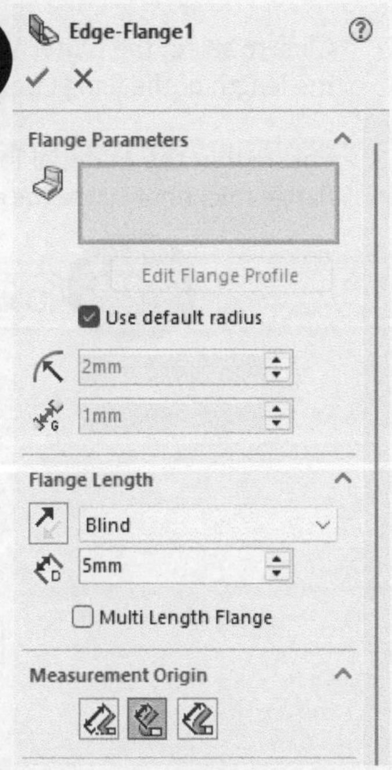

2. Click to select the upper right edge of the base flange in the graphics area, see Figure 2.227. The preview of an edge flange appears along the entire length of the selected edge, see Figure 2.227. Also, the name of the selected edge appears in the **Edge** field of the **Flange Parameters** rollout.

2.227

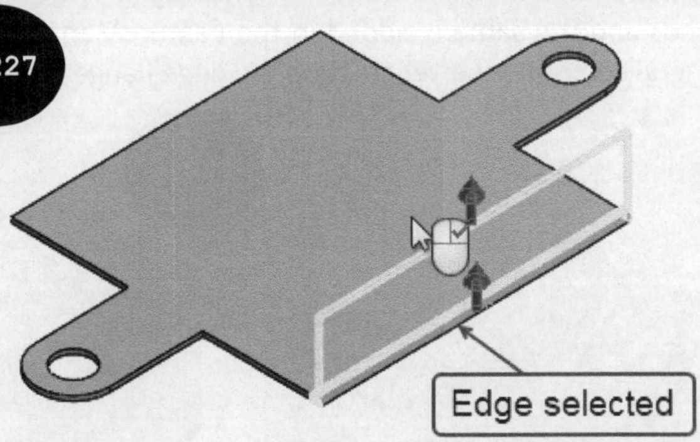

3. Move the cursor upward and then click to define the length of the edge flange arbitrarily in the graphics area.

4. Ensure that **90** degrees is specified as the angle of the edge flange in the **Flange Angle** field of the **Angle** rollout.

5. Ensure the **Blind** option is selected in the **End Condition** drop-down list of the **Flange Length** rollout.

6. Enter **35** mm in the **Length** field of the **Flange Length** rollout as the length of the edge flange.

7. Click to select the **Outer Virtual Sharp** button in the **Measurement Origin** rollout for measuring the length of the flange from the outer virtual sharp, see Figure 2.228.

8. Ensure that the **Material Inside** button is activated in the **Flange Position** rollout for adding the flange thickness inside the maximum limit of the sheet, see Figure 2.228.

2.228

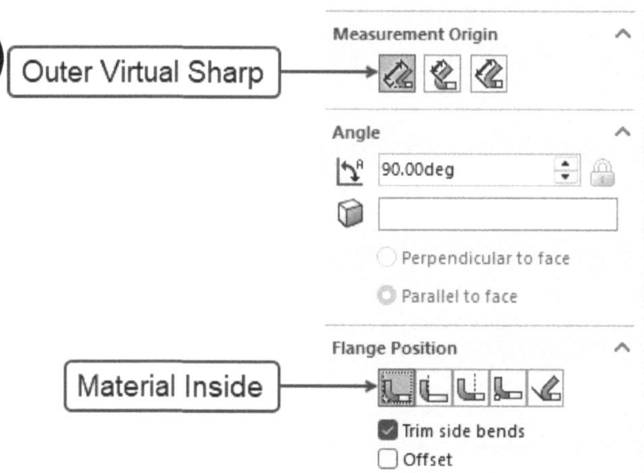

9. Click to select the upper left edge of the base flange for creating another edge flange of the same parameters, see Figure 2.229. The preview of another edge flange appears in the graphics area.

10. Click on the green tick-mark button in the PropertyManager. The edge flange feature is created with two edge bends and the same is added in the FeatureManager Design Tree. Figure 2.230 shows the sheet metal component after creating the edge flange feature.

2.229

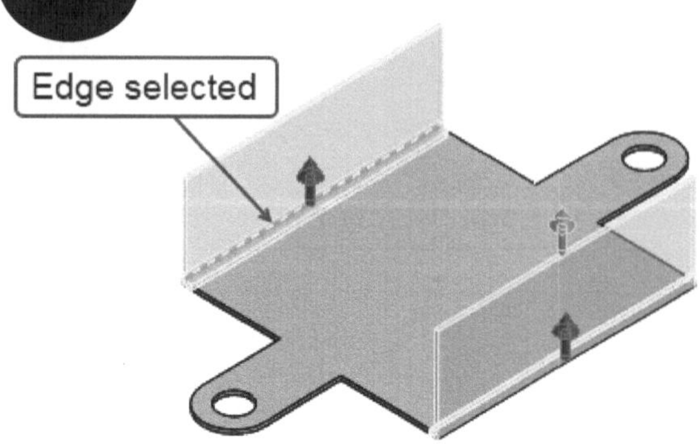

2.230

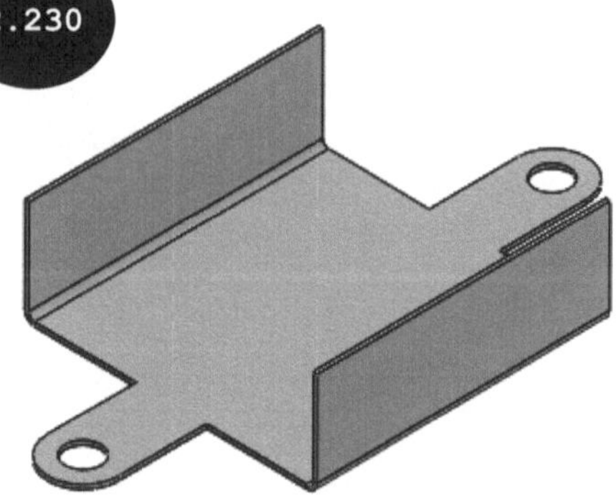

Section 6: Creating the Second Edge Flange Feature

Now, you need to create another edge flange feature on the edges of the previously created flanges.

1. Click on the **Edge Flange** tool in the **Sheet Metal CommandManager**. The **Edge-Flange PropertyManager** appears. Also, you are prompted to select an edge of a planar face to create the edge flange.

2. Select an edge of the previously created right edge flange in the graphics area, see Figure 2.231. The preview of an edge flange appears along the entire length of the selected edge.

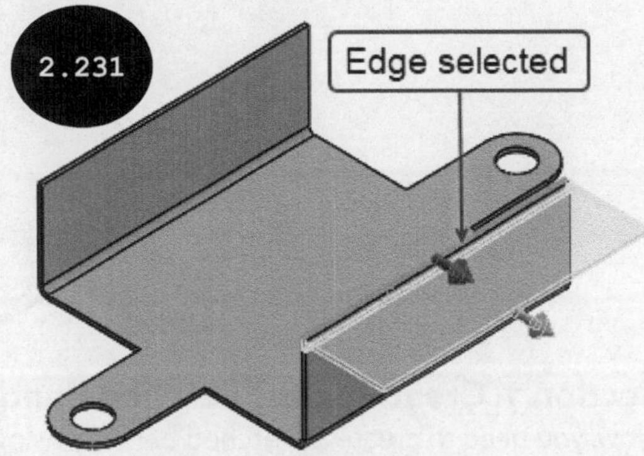

3. Move the cursor towards the right and then click to define the length of the edge flange arbitrarily in the graphics area.

4. Ensure that the **Blind** option is selected in the **End Condition** drop-down list of the **Flange Length** rollout.

5. Enter **25** mm in the **Length** field of the **Flange Length** rollout as the length of the edge flange.

6. Ensure that **90** degrees is specified as the angle of the edge flange in the **Flange Angle** field of the **Angle** rollout.

7. Click on the **Outer Virtual Sharp** button in the Flange Length rollout to measure the length of the flange from the outer virtual sharp.

8. Ensure that the **Material Inside** button is activated in the **Flange Position** rollout for adding the flange thickness inside the maximum limit of the sheet.

9. Select an edge of the previously created left edge flange in the graphics area, see Figure 2.232. The preview of another edge flange with the same parameters appears in the graphics area.

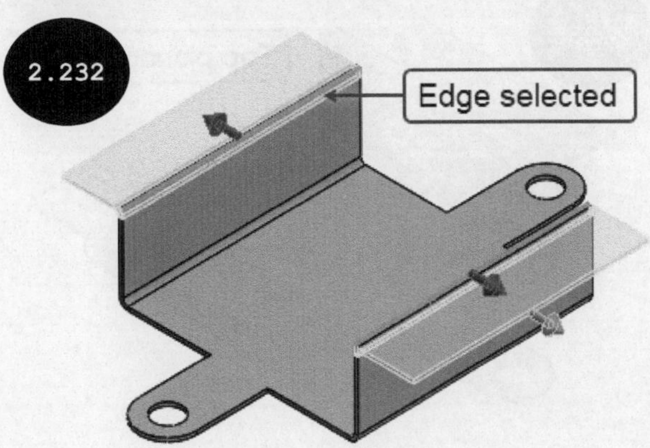

10. Click on the green tick-mark button in the PropertyManager. The second edge flange feature is created with two edge bends and the same is added in the FeatureManager Design Tree. Figure 2.233 shows the sheet metal component after creating the second edge flange feature.

2.233

Section 7: Creating the Sketched Bend

Now, you need to create a sketched bend by using a sketch line as the bending line.

1. Click on the **Sketched Bend** tool in the **Sheet Metal CommandManager** to create a sketched bend, see Figure 2.234. The **Message PropertyManager** appears, and you are prompted to either select a sketching plane for creating the sketch of the bending line or an existing sketch.

2.234

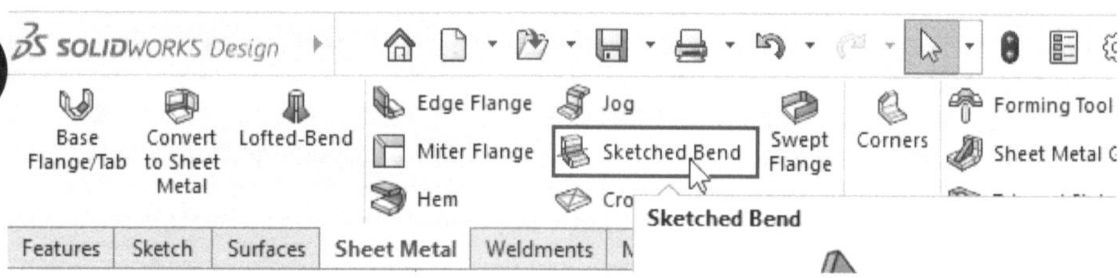

2. Select the top planar face of the base flange in the graphics area for creating the sketch of the bending line, see Figure 2.235. The Sketching environment gets invoked and the top planar face becomes normal to the viewing direction.

2.235

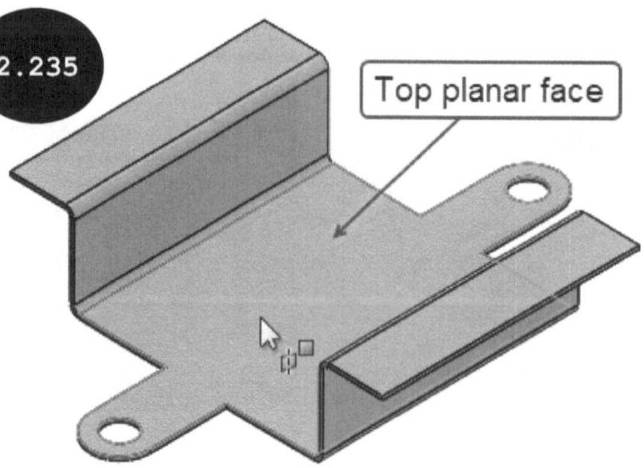

3. Create a line as the bending line for creating the sketched bend in the graphics area, see Figure 2.236.

4. After creating the bending line, exit the Sketching environment by clicking on the **Exit Sketch** tool in the **Sketch CommandManager**. The **Sketched Bend PropertyManager** appears, see Figure 2.237. Also, you are prompted to specify a planar face to be fixed when creating the bend.

2.236

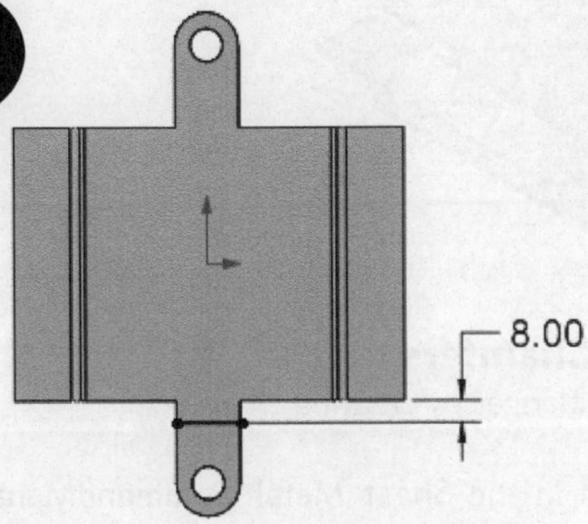

2.237

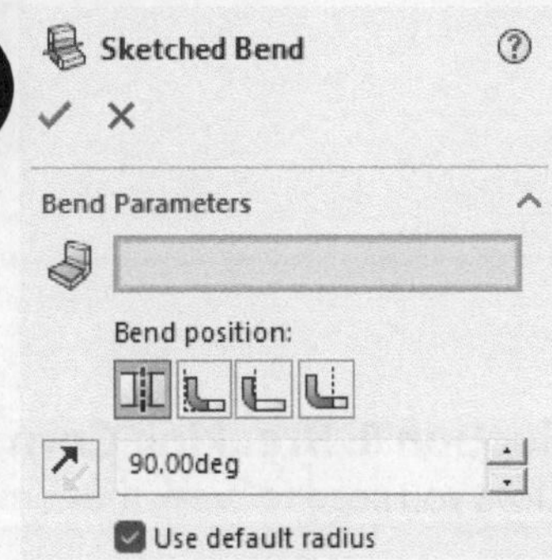

Tip: You can create the bending line before or after invoking the **Sketched Bend** tool.

5. Change the orientation of the model to isometric and then select the fixed face of the sheet, see Figure 2.238. The preview of the sketched bend appears in the graphics area, see Figure 2.239.

2.238

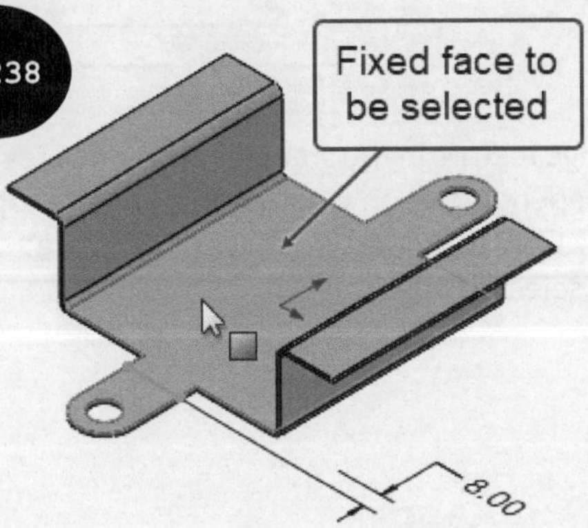

2.239

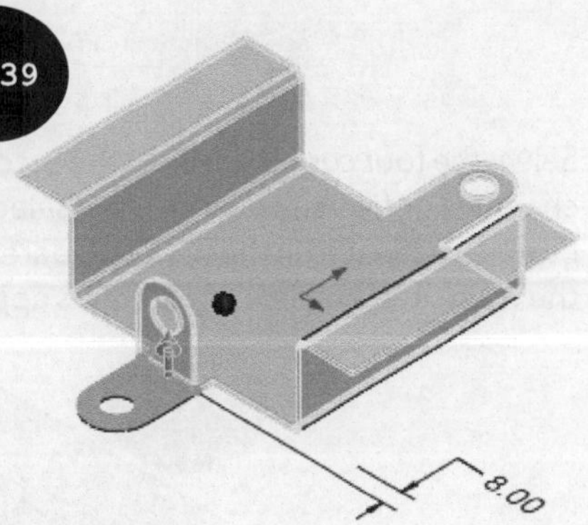

6. Click on the **Material Inside** button in the **Bend position** area of the **Bend Parameters** rollout to add the material thickness inside the maximum limit of the sheet.

7. Ensure that **90** degrees is specified in the **Bend Angle** field of the PropertyManager.

8. Click on the **Reverse Direction** button in the PropertyManager to reverse the direction of the bend to the downward direction.

9. Click on the green tick-mark button in the PropertyManager. A sketched bend is created, see Figure 2.2340.

2.240

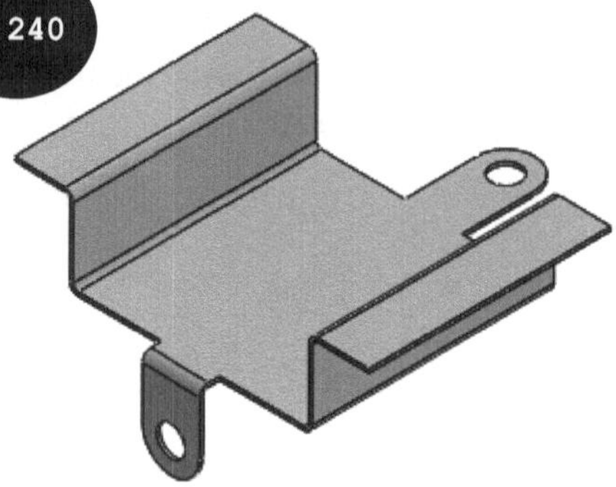

Section 8: Breaking Corners by Creating Chamfers

Now, you need to break the corner edges of the edge flanges by creating chamfers.

1. Click on **Corners > Break-Corner/Corner-Trim** in the **Sheet Metal CommandManager**, see Figure 2.241. The **Break Corner PropertyManager** appears.

2.241

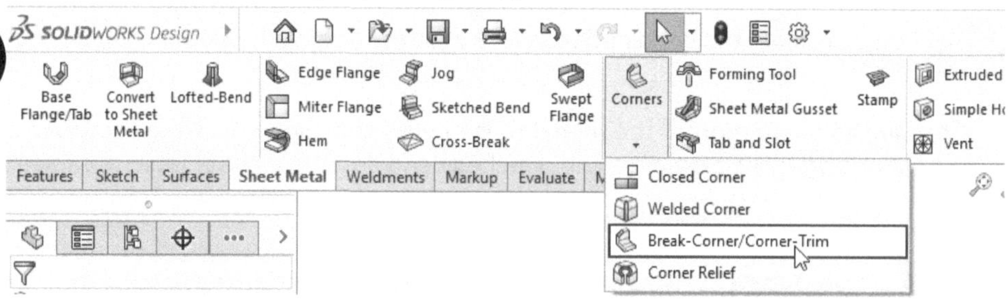

2. Select the four corner edges of the second edge flange feature in the graphics area. The preview of chamfers or fillets appears on the selected edges depending upon whether the **Chamfer** or **Fillet** button is activated in the **Break type** area of the **Break Corner PropertyManager**, see Figure 2.242. In the figure, the preview of chamfers appears on the selected edges.

2.242

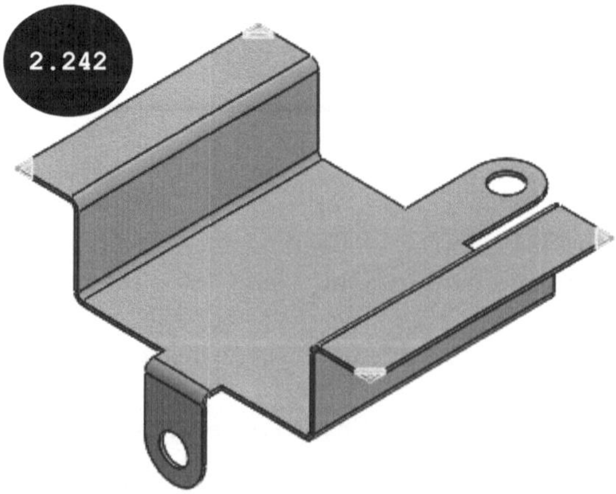

3. Click on the **Chamfer** button in the **Break type** area of the PropertyManager to create chamfers on the selected edges.

4. Enter 6 mm in the **Distance** field of the PropertyManager.

5. Click on the green tick-mark button in the PropertyManager. The chamfers are created on the selected corners, see Figure 2.243.

2.243

Section 9: Creating the Extruded Cut Feature

Now, you need to create the extruded cut feature on the top planar face of the edge flange.

1. Click on the **Extruded Cut** tool in the **Sheet Metal CommandManager**, see Figure 2.244. The **Extrude PropertyManager** appears.

2.244

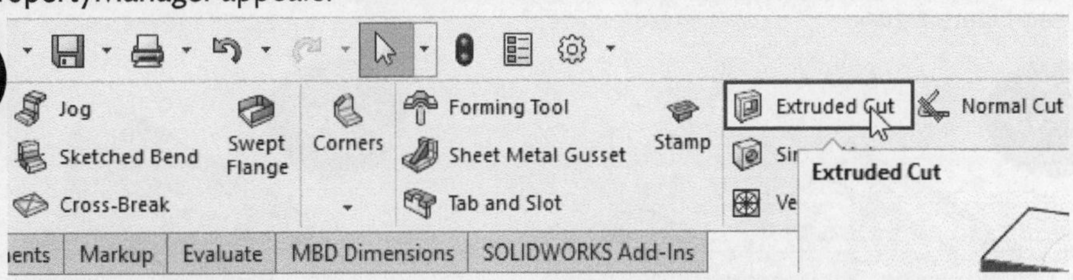

2. Select the top planar face of the edge flange as the sketching plane, see Figure 2.245. The Sketching environment gets invoked and the selected face becomes normal to the viewing direction.

3. Create four circles of equal diameter as the sketch of the cut feature, see Figure 2.246.

2.245

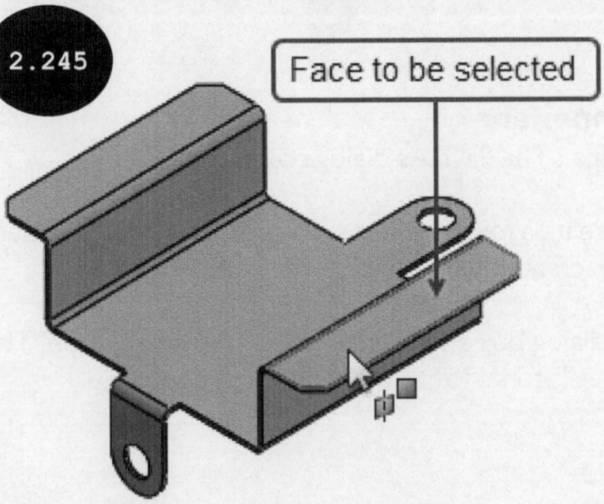

2.246

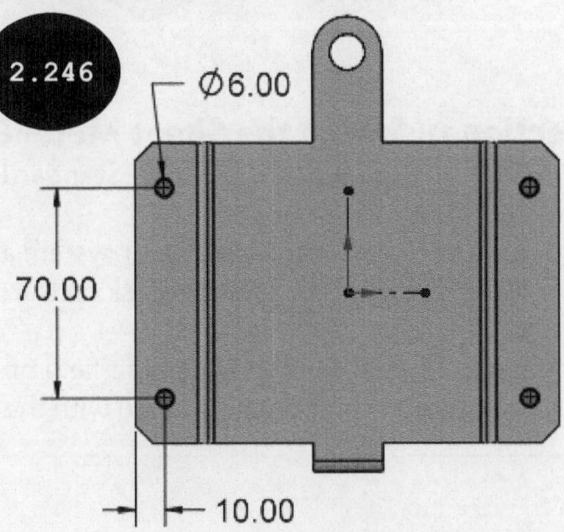

4. After creating the sketch, exit the Sketching environment. The **Cut-Extrude PropertyManager** appears. Also, the preview of the cut feature appears in the graphics area.

5. Change the orientation of the part to isometric.

6. Ensure that the **Link to thickness** check box is selected in the PropertyManager for linking the depth of the cut feature with the sheet thickness.

7. Click on the green tick-mark button in the PropertyManager. The extrude cut feature gets created, see Figure 2.247.

2.247

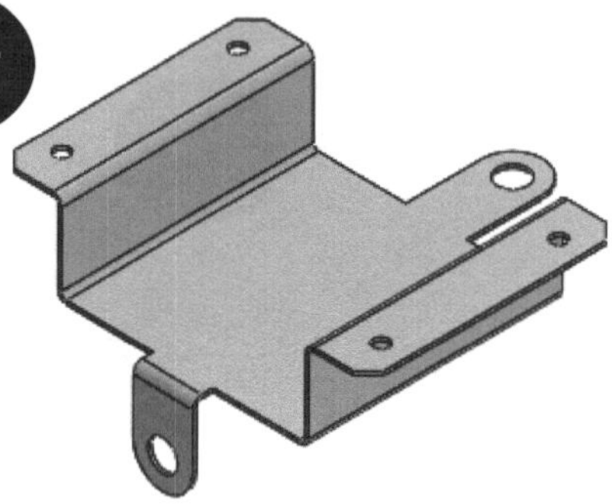

Section 10: Generating the Flat Pattern

Now, you need to create the flat pattern of the sheet metal component.

1. Click on the **Flatten** tool in the **Sheet Metal CommandManager**. The flat pattern of the sheet metal component gets generated in the graphics area, see Figure 2.248.

2. After reviewing the flat pattern of the sheet metal component, click on the **Flatten** tool again in the **Sheet Metal CommandManager** to switch back to the finished sheet metal component, see Figure 2.249.

2.248

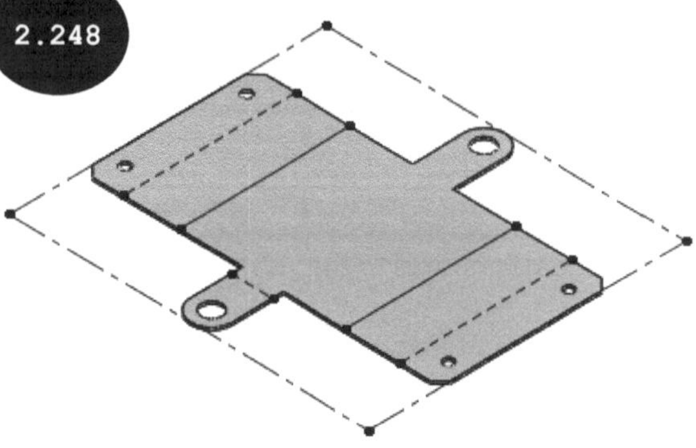

2.249

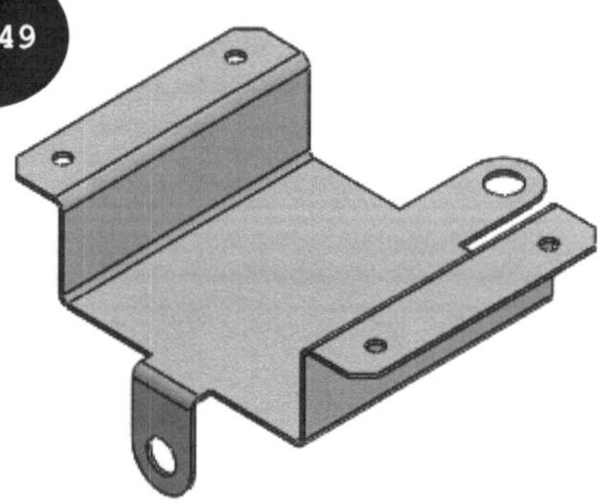

Section 11: Saving the Sheet Metal Component

1. Click on the **Save** tool in the **Standard** toolbar. The **Save As** dialog box appears.

2. Browse to the local drive of your system and create a folder with the name **SOLIDWORKS Sheet Metal Design**. Next, double-click on the newly created folder to save the component in it.

3. Enter **Tutorial 1** in the **File name** field of the dialog box and then click on the **Save** button. The sheet metal component is saved with the name Tutorial 1 at the specified location.

Tutorial 2

Create the sheet metal component shown in Figure 2.250. The different views, dimensions, and flat pattern of the sheet metal component are shown in Figure 2.251. After creating the component, you need to generate its flat pattern drawing view on the A3 sheet size. All dimensions are in mm.

2.250

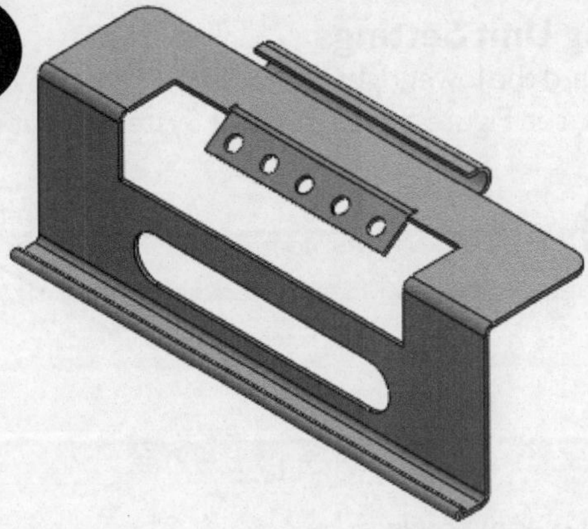

2.251

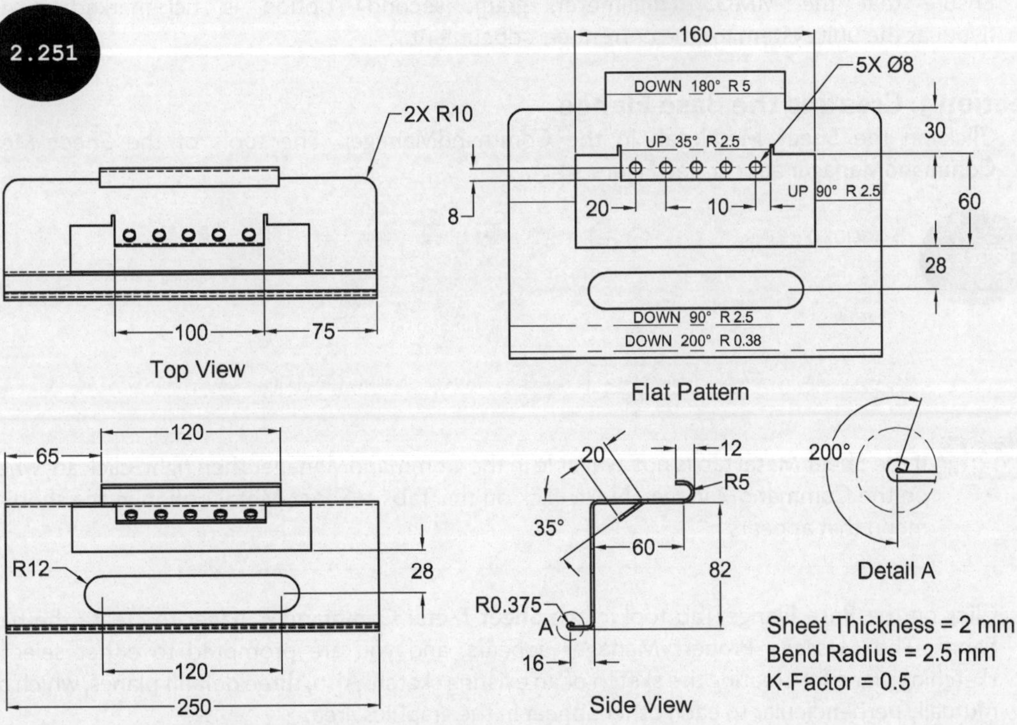

Section 1: Invoking the Part Modeling Environment

1. Start SOLIDWORKS by double-clicking on the SOLIDWORKS icon on your desktop. The startup user interface of SOLIDWORKS appears along with the **Welcome** dialog box.

2. Click on the **Part** button in the **Welcome** dialog box. The Part modeling environment is invoked.

Note: If SOLIDWORKS is already open and the **Welcome** dialog box does not appear on the screen, then you can invoke the **Welcome** dialog box by clicking on the **Welcome to SOLIDWORKS** tool in the **Standard** toolbar.

Section 2: Specifying Unit Settings

1. Move the cursor toward the lower right corner of the screen over the Status Bar and then click on the **Unit System** area, see Figure 2.252. The **Unit System** flyout appears.

2.252

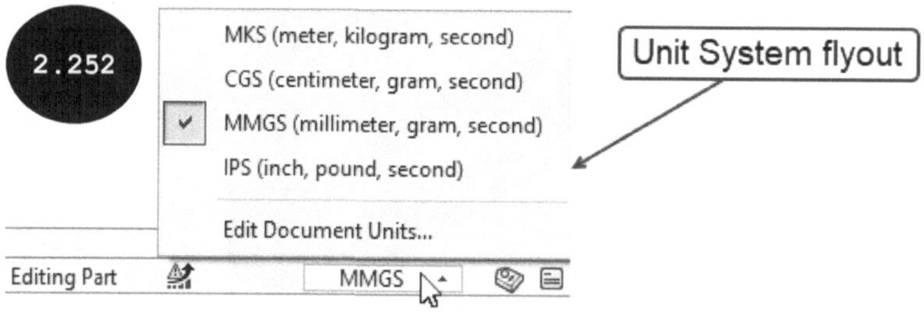

2. Ensure that the **MMGS (millimeter, gram, second)** option is tick-marked in the flyout as the unit system for the current part document.

Section 3: Creating the Base Flange

1. Click on the **Sheet Metal** tab in the CommandManager. The tools of the **Sheet Metal CommandManager** appear, see Figure 2.253.

2.253

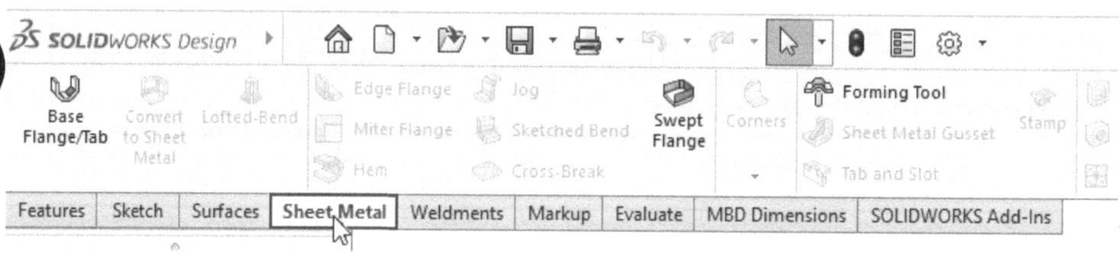

Note: If the **Sheet Metal** tab is not available in the CommandManager then right-click anywhere on the CommandManager. Next, click on the **Tabs > Sheet Metal** option in the shortcut menu that appears.

2. Click on the **Base Flange/Tab** tool in the **Sheet Metal CommandManager** to create the base flange. The **Message PropertyManager** appears, and you are prompted to either select a sketching plane for creating the sketch or an existing sketch. Also, three default planes, which are mutually perpendicular to each other appear in the graphics area.

3. Select the Right plane as the sketching plane in the graphics area for creating the sketch of the base flange. The Sketching environment gets invoked and the Right plane becomes normal to the viewing direction.

4. Create the sketch of the base flange in the drawing area by using the sketching tools, see Figure 2.254.

5. After creating the sketch of the base flange, exit the Sketching environment. The **Base Flange PropertyManager** appears. Also, the preview of the base flange with default thickness appears in the graphics area.

   Now, you need to define the sheet metal parameters in the **Base Flange PropertyManager** and the same will be used as the default parameters for the entire sheet metal component.

6. Select the **Mid Plane** option in the **End Condition** drop-down list of the **Direction 1** rollout for defining the depth of the base flange symmetrically about the sketching plane.

7. Enter **250** mm in the **Depth** field of the **Direction 1** rollout as the depth of the base flange. The preview of the base feature appears like the one shown in Figure 2.255.

2.254

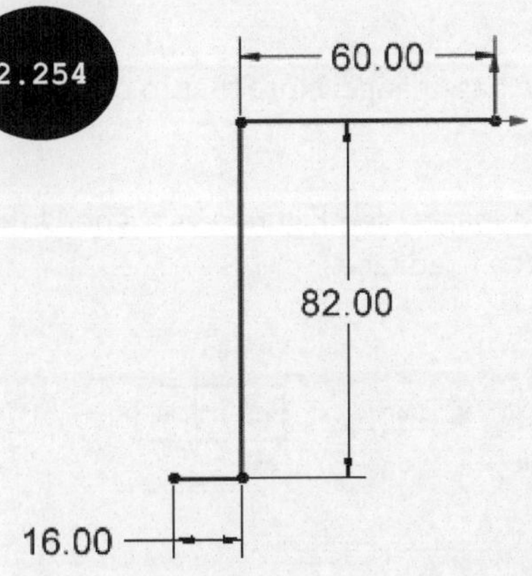

2.255

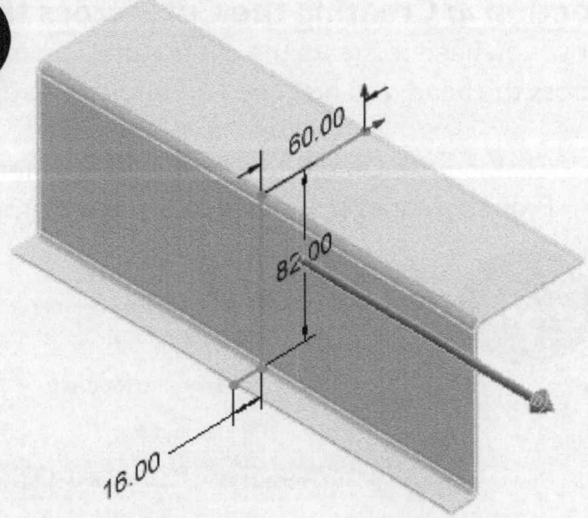

8. Enter **2** mm in the **Thickness** field of the **Sheet Metal Parameters** rollout as the thickness of the sheet metal component.

9. Enter **2.5** mm in the **Bend Radius** field of the **Bend Parameters** rollout as the default bend radius of the sheet metal component.

10. Select the **K-Factor** option in the **Bend Allowance Type** drop-down list of the **Bend Allowance** rollout for defining the bend allowance of the sheet metal component in the bent regions.

11. Enter **0.5** as the K-factor value in the **K-Factor** field of the **Bend Allowance** rollout.

12. Select the **Rectangular** option in the **Auto Relief Type** drop-down list of the **Auto Relief** rollout of the PropertyManager.

13. Ensure that the **Use relief ratio** check box is selected and then enter **1** in the **Ratio** field of the **Auto Relief** rollout.

14. Click on the green tick-mark button in the PropertyManager. The base flange of the sheet metal component gets created, see Figure 2.256.

2.256

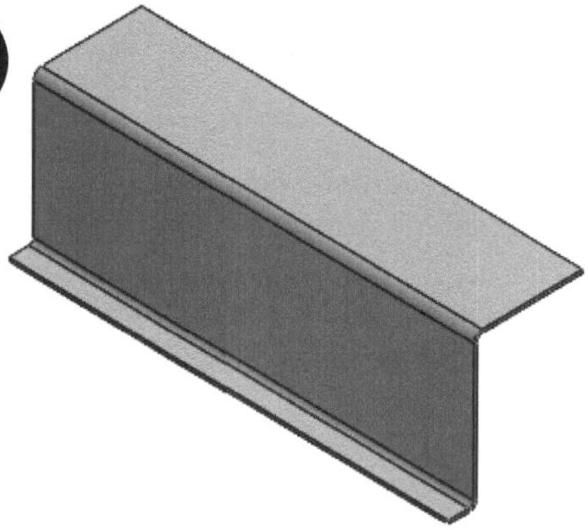

Section 4: Creating the Cut Across the Bend

Now, you need to create the cut feature across the bend of the base flange. Note that to create a cut across the bend, you first need to unfold or flatten the bend.

1. Click on the **Unfold** tool in the **Sheet Metal CommandManager**, see Figure 2.257. The **Unfold PropertyManager** appears, and you are prompted to select a fixed face.

2.257

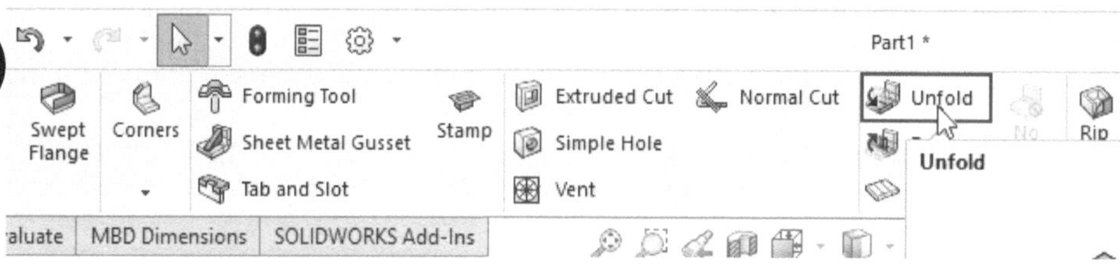

2. Click on the top planar face of the base flange as the fixed face, see Figure 2.258. The **Bends to unfold** field gets activated and you are prompted to select bends to be unfolded.

3. Click on the **Collect All Bends** button in the **Unfold PropertyManager**. All the bends get listed in the **Bends to unfold** field of the PropertyManager.

4. Click on the green tick-mark button in the PropertyManager. The selected bends get flattened in the graphics area, see Figure 2.259.

2.258

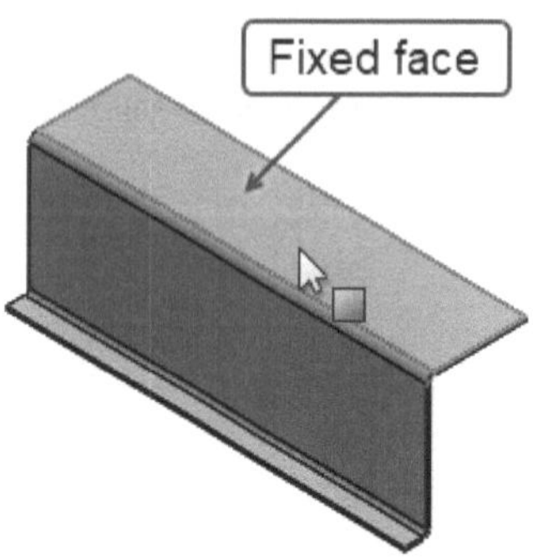

2.259

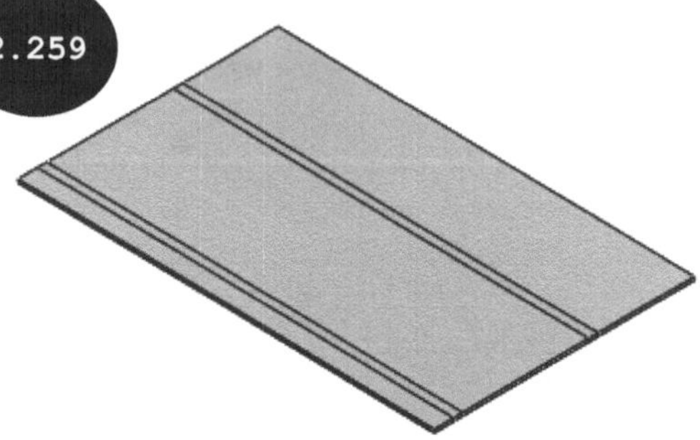

After unfolding the bends, you can create the cut feature across them.

5. Click on the **Extruded Cut** tool in the **Sheet Metal CommandManager** and then select the top face of the flattened sheet as the sketching plane. The Sketching environment gets invoked.

6. Create the sketch of the cut feature in the graphics area, see Figure 2.260.

2.260

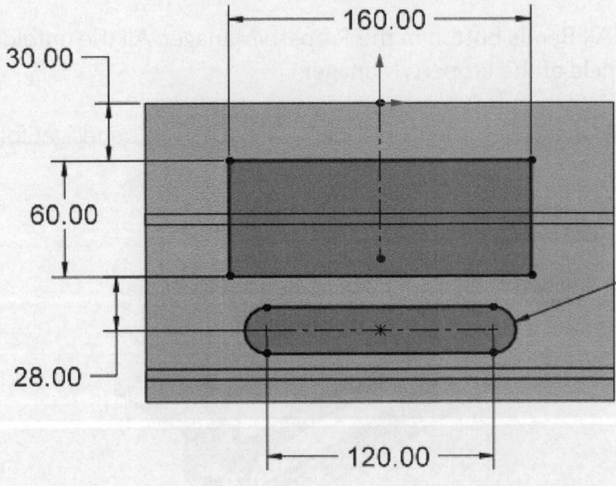

7. After creating the sketch, exit the Sketching environment. The **Cut-Extrude PropertyManager** appears. Next, change the orientation of the component to isometric.

8. Ensure that the **Link to thickness** check box is selected in the PropertyManager for linking the depth of the cut feature with the thickness of the sheet.

9. Click on the green tick-mark button in the PropertyManager. The cut feature is created, see Figure 2.261.

2.261

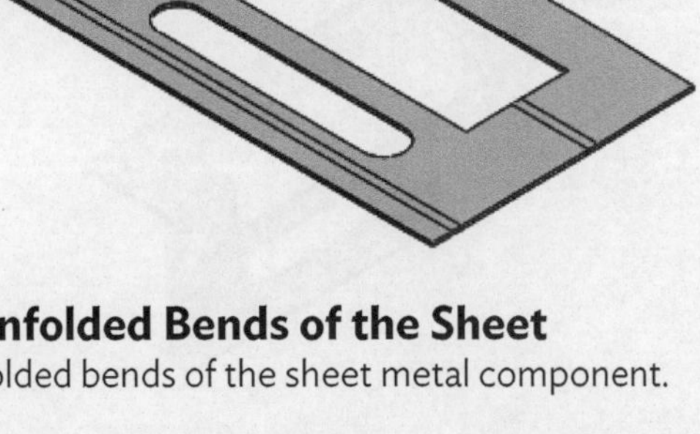

Section 5: Folding the Unfolded Bends of the Sheet

Now, you need to fold the unfolded bends of the sheet metal component.

1. Click on the **Fold** tool in the **Sheet Metal CommandManager**, see Figure 2.262. The **Fold PropertyManager** appears, and the fixed face of the sheet is selected, by default.

2.262

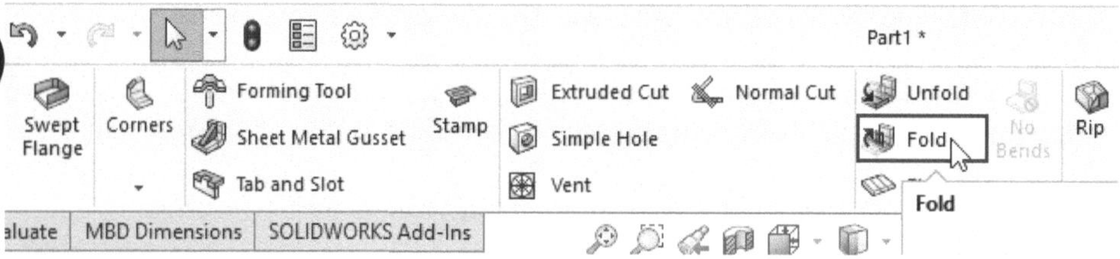

2. Click on the **Collect All Bends** button in the PropertyManager. All the unfolded bends get listed in the **Bends to fold** field of the PropertyManager.

3. Click on the green tick-mark button in the PropertyManager. The bends get folded in the graphics area, see Figure 2.263.

2.263

Section 6: Creating the Edge Flange

1. Click on the **Edge Flange** tool in the **Sheet Metal CommandManager**. The **Edge Flange PropertyManager** appears. Also, you are prompted to select an edge.

2. Select the upper edge of the previously created cut feature, see Figure 2.264. The preview of an edge flange appears along the entire length of the selected edge.

2.264

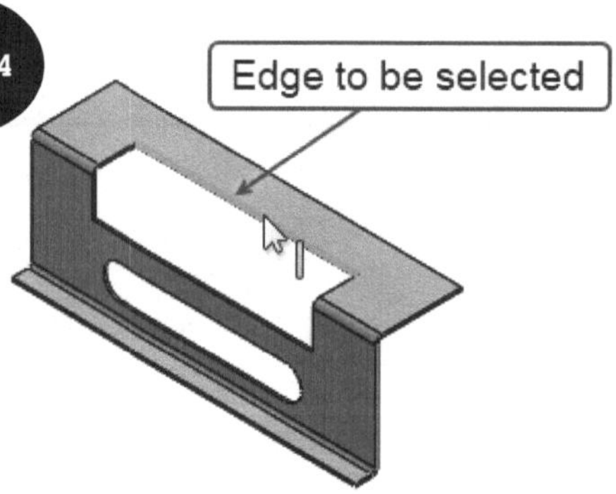

3. Move the cursor downward to a small distance and then click to define the length of the edge flange arbitrarily in the graphics area.

Now, you need to edit the width of the edge flange along the selected edge.

4. Click on the **Edit Flange Profile** button in the **Flange Parameters** rollout of the PropertyManager. The Sketching environment gets invoked with the display of the **Profile Sketch** dialog box.

5. Drag the side vertical entities of the flange profile (sketch) one by one to adjust the width of the profile like the one shown in the Figure 2.265.

6. Apply dimensions to the flange profile (sketch) in the graphics area, see Figure 2.266.

2.265

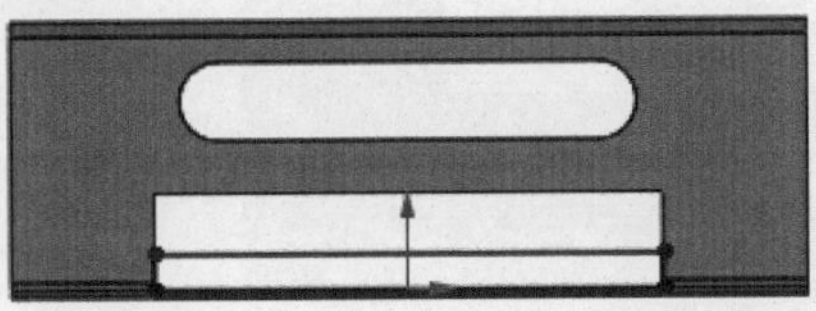

2.266

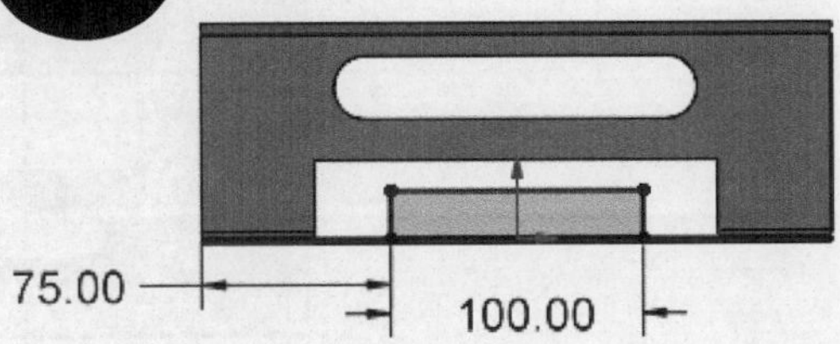

7. After editing the width of the edge flange along the selected edge, click on the **Back** button in the **Profile Sketch** dialog box to switch back to the **Edge Flange PropertyManager** for defining the remaining parameters of the edge flange.

8. Press CTRL + 7 keys to change the orientation of the model to isometric.

9. Enter **35** degrees in the **Flange Angle** field of the **Angle** rollout as the angle of the edge flange.

10. Ensure the **Blind** option is selected in the **End Condition** drop-down list of the **Flange Length** rollout.

11. Enter **20** mm in the **Length** field of the **Flange Length** rollout as the length of the edge flange.

12. Click on the **Outer Virtual Sharp** button in the **Flange Length** rollout to measure the length of the flange from the outer virtual sharp.

13. Click on the **Material Inside** button in the **Flange Position** rollout to add the flange thickness inside the maximum limit of the sheet.

14. Click on the green tick-mark button in the PropertyManager. The edge flange feature with specified parameters gets created, see Figure 2.267.

2.267

Section 7: Creating the Cut Feature

1. Click on the **Extruded Cut** tool in the **Sheet Metal CommandManager** and then select the top planar face of the previously created edge flange as the sketching plane.

2. Create the sketch of the cut feature (five circles of the same diameter and spacing) in the Sketching environment, see Figure 2.268. Note that you can create one circle and then pattern it to create the remaining instances.

2.268

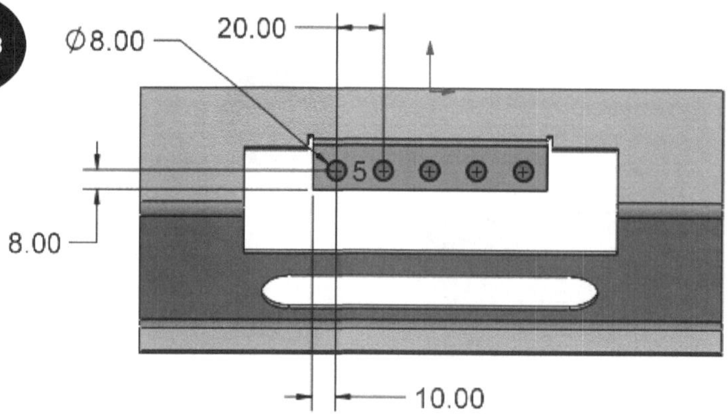

3. After creating the sketch of the cut feature, exit the Sketching environment. The **Cut-Extrude PropertyManager** appears.

4. Ensure that the **Link to thickness** check box is selected in the PropertyManager. Next, press the CTRL + 7 keys to change the orientation of the model to isometric.

5. Click on the green tick-mark button in the PropertyManager. The cut feature gets created, see Figure 2.269.

2.269

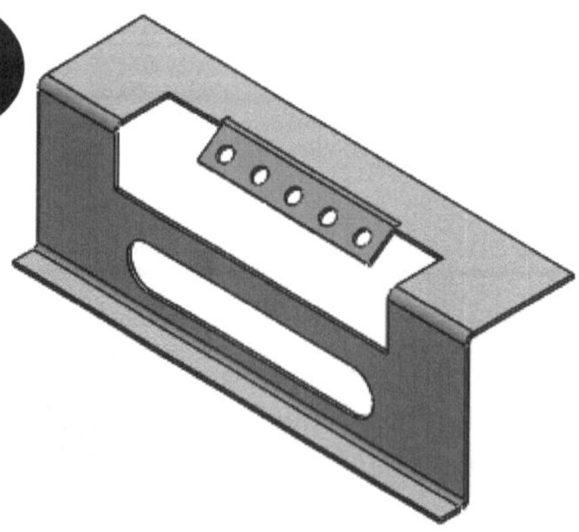

Section 8: Breaking Corners by Creating Fillets

Now, you need to break the corner edges of the edge flanges by creating chamfers.

1. Click on **Corners > Break-Corner/Corner-Trim** in the **Sheet Metal CommandManager**, see Figure 2.270. The **Break Corner PropertyManager** appears.

2.270

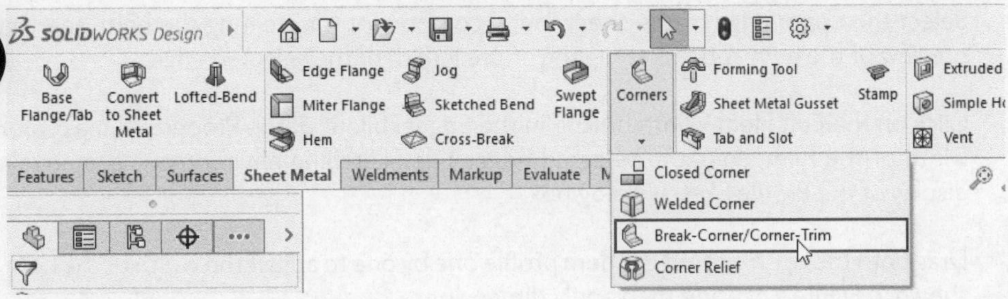

2. Select the upper two corner edges of the sheet metal component in the graphics area, see Figure 2.271.

3. Click on the **Fillet** button in the **Break type** area of the PropertyManager to create fillets on the selected edges.

4. Enter **10** mm in the **Radius** field of the PropertyManager.

5. Click on the green tick-mark button in the PropertyManager. The fillets are created on the selected corners, see Figure 2.272.

2.271

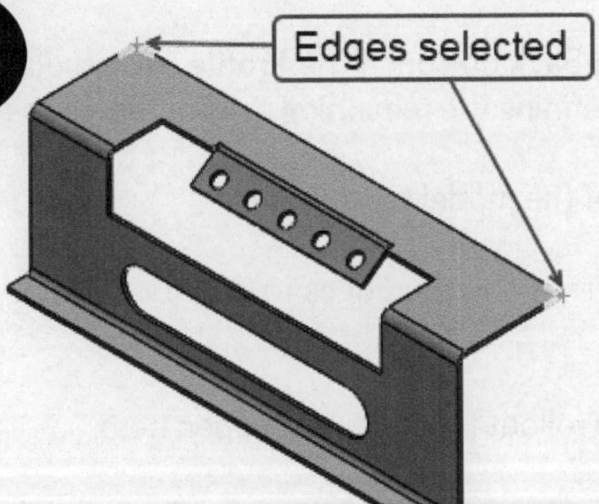

2.272

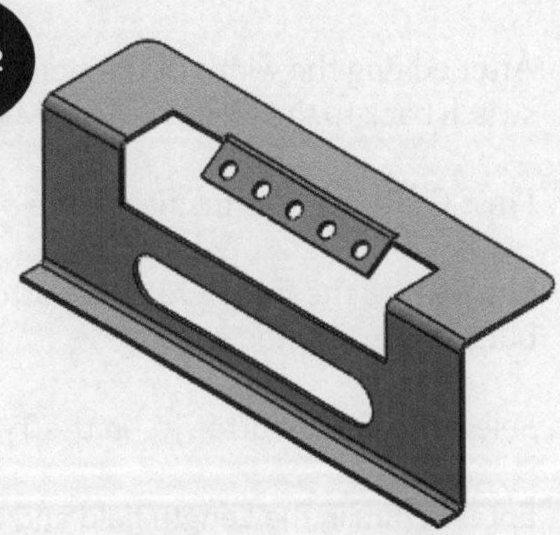

Section 9: Creating Hems

Now, you need to create hems on the edges of the sheet metal component.

1. Click on the **Hem** tool in the **Sheet Metal CommandManager**, see Figure 2.273. The **Hem PropertyManager** appears. Also, you are prompted to select edges for creating hems.

2.273

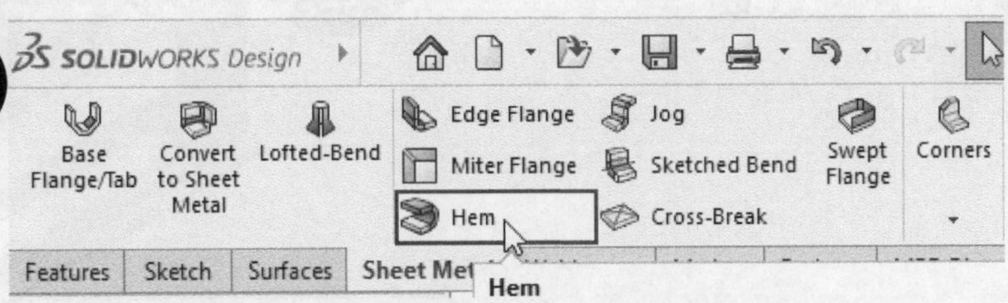

2. Select the upper edge of the sheet metal component for creating the hem, see Figure 2.274. A preview of the hem appears along the entire length of the selected edge.

3. Click on the **Edit Hem Width** button in the **Edges** rollout of the PropertyManager for editing the width of the hem along the selected edge. The Sketching environment gets invoked with the display of the **Profile Sketch** dialog box.

4. Drag both the open ends of the hem profile one by one to adjust the width of the hem like the one shown in Figure 2.275 and then apply dimensions.

2.274

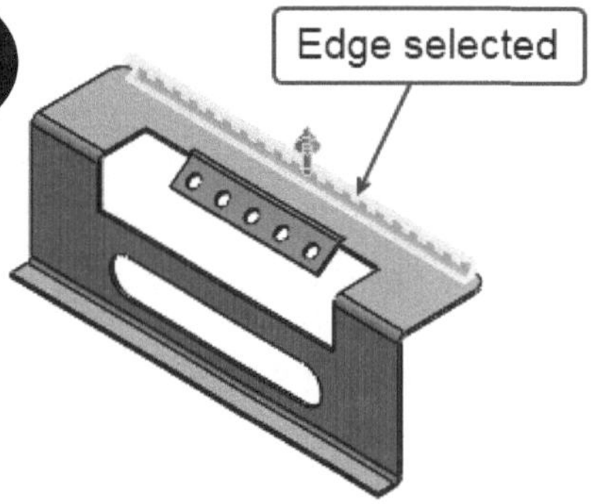

2.275

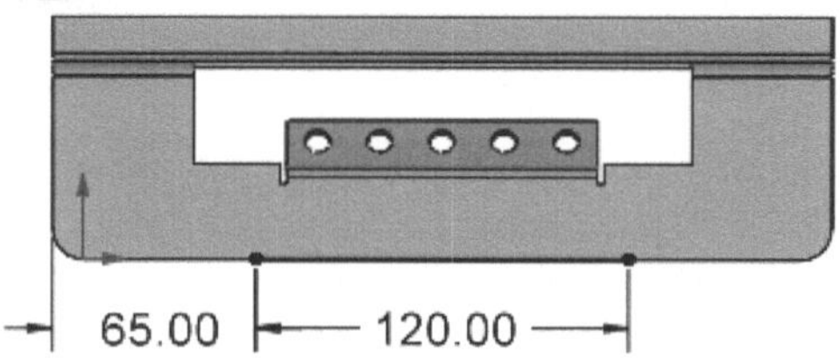

5. After editing the width of the hem, click on the **Back** button in the **Profile Sketch** dialog box to switch back to the **Hem PropertyManager** for defining the remaining parameters of the hem.

6. Press CTRL + 7 keys to change the orientation of the model to isometric.

7. Ensure that the **Bend Outside** button is activated in the **Edges** rollout for creating the hem outside the selected edge.

8. Select the **Open** button in the **Type and Size** rollout for creating an open hem.

9. Enter **12** mm in the **Length** field and **10** mm in the **Gap Distance** field of the **Type and Size** rollout of the PropertyManager, see Figure 2.276.

10. Click on the green tick-mark button in the PropertyManager. A hem with specified parameters gets created, see Figure 2.277.

2.276

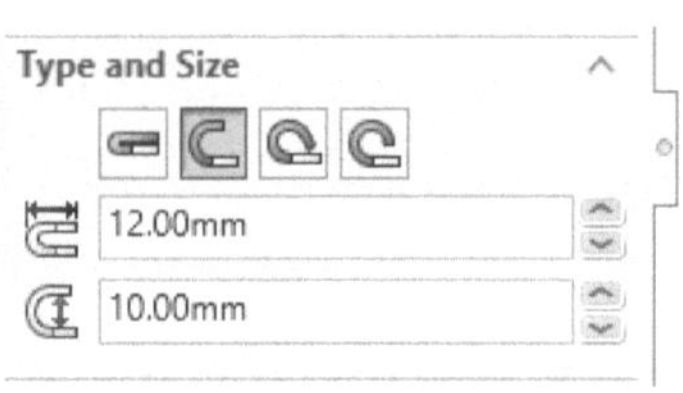

2.277

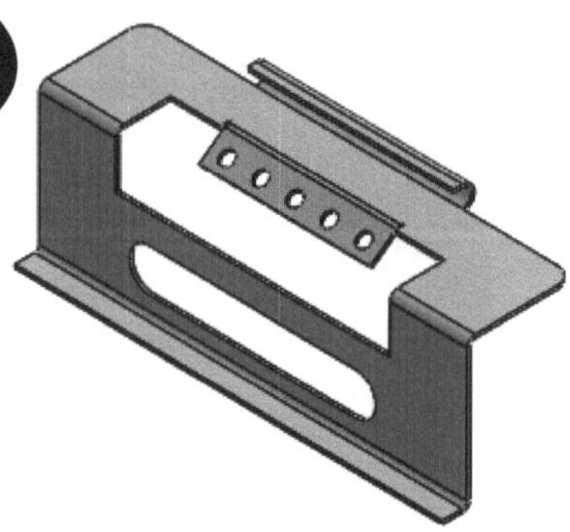

11. Similarly, create a tear drop hem of radius 0.375 mm and **200** degrees angle along the entire length of the bottom edge of the sheet metal component, see Figure 2.278.

2.278

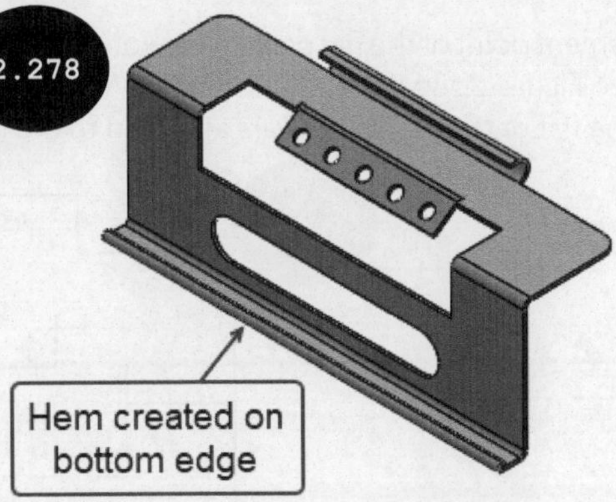

Section 10: Saving the Sheet Metal Component

1. Click on the **Save** tool in the **Standard** toolbar. The **Save As** dialog box appears.

2. Browse the **SOLIDWORKS Sheet Metal Design** folder in the local drive of your system. Note that you need to create this folder if not created earlier.

3. Enter **Tutorial 2** in the **File name** field of the dialog box and then click on the **Save** button. The sheet metal component is saved with the name Tutorial 2 at the specified location.

Section 11: Generating the Flat Pattern Drawing View

Now, you need to generate a drawing view of the flat pattern in the Drawing environment.

1. Click on the **New** tool in the **Standard** toolbar and then double-click on the **Drawing** button in the **New SOLIDWORKS Document** dialog box that appears. The **Sheet Format/Size** dialog box appears.

2. Select the **A3 (ANSI) Landscape** sheet size in the **Sheet Format/Size** dialog box and then click on the **OK** button. The Drawing environment gets invoked with the display of the **Model View PropertyManager** on the left side of the sheet.

3. Double-click on the **Tutorial 2** component in the **Open documents** field of the **Part/Assembly to Insert** rollout in the PropertyManager. A rectangular box representing the drawing view of the selected component is attached to the cursor. Also, the options of the PropertyManager get modified.

Note: The **Open document** field displays a list of components that are opened in the current session of SOLIDWORKS. If the component whose drawing view is to be generated is not listed in the **Open documents** field, then you need to click on the **Browse** button for selecting the component whose drawing view is to be generated.

4. Select the **Flat pattern** check box in the **More views** area of the **Orientation** rollout in the modified PropertyManager, see Figure 2.279.

5. Click to define the placement point of the flat pattern view anywhere on the sheet. The flat pattern view gets generated, see Figure 2.280. Also, the **Projected View PropertyManager** appears, and the projected view of the flat pattern view appears attached to the cursor.

2.279

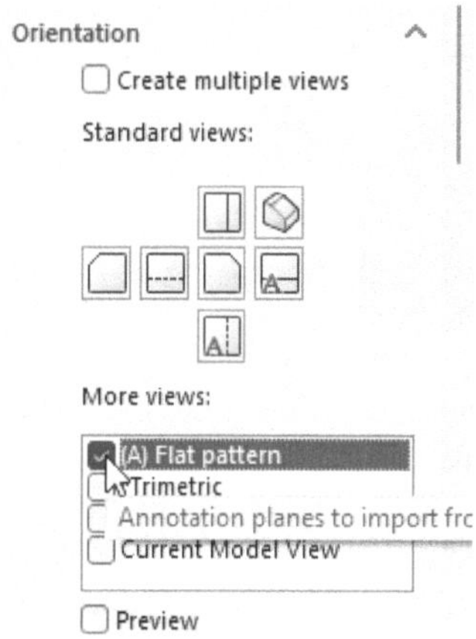

2.280

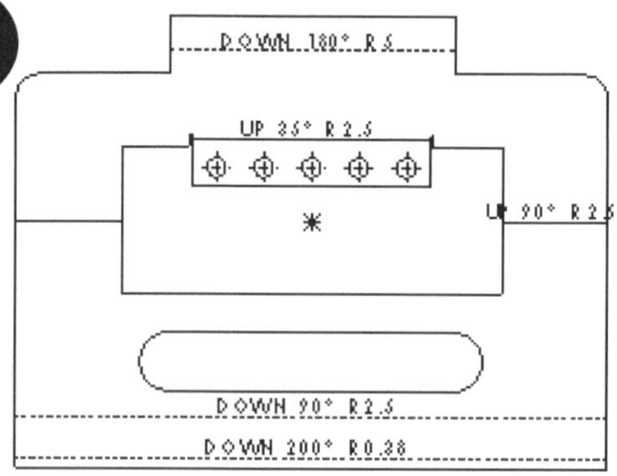

6. Press the ESC key to exit the placement of the projection views.

Note: If needed, you can create other drawing views of the sheet metal components on the drawing sheet. To learn about creating different drawing views of a component, refer to "**SOLIDWORKS 2026: A Power Guide for Beginners and Intermediate Users**" textbook by CADArtifex.

Section 12: Saving the Flat Pattern Drawing View

1. Click on the **Save** tool in the **Standard** toolbar. The **Save Modified Documents** dialog box appears. In this dialog box, click on the **Save All** button. The **Save As** dialog box appears.

2. Ensure that the **SOLIDWORKS Drawing (*.drw,*.slddrw)** option is selected in the **Save as type** drop-down list of the dialog box.

3. Click on the **Save** button in the dialog box. The flat pattern drawing view is saved in the **SOLIDWORKS Sheet Metal Design** folder with the name Tutorial 2.

4. Save the drawing view in the **SOLIDWORKS Sheet Metal Design** folder of the local drive of your system. Note that you need to create this folder if not created earlier.

Hands-on Test Drive 1

Create the sheet metal component shown in Figure 2.281. The different views, dimensions, and flat pattern of the sheet metal component are shown in Figure 2.282. The thickness of the sheet metal component is 1.5 mm, bend radius is 1.5 mm, and K-factor is 0.5. After creating the component, you need to generate its flat pattern. All dimensions are in mm.

2.281

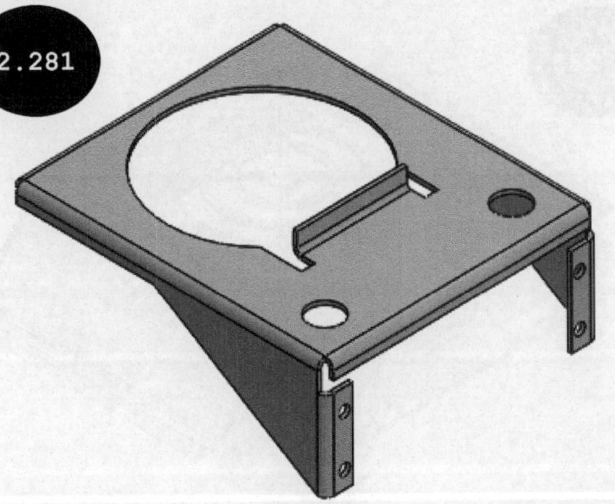

2.282

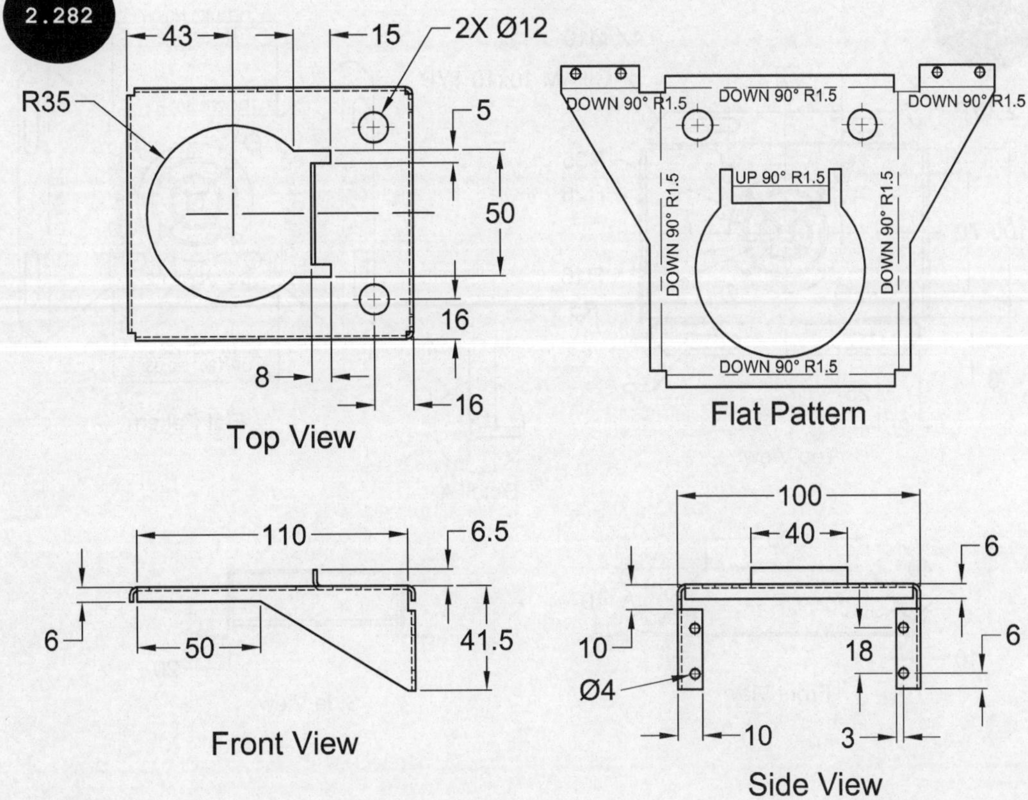

Hands-on Test Drive 2

Create the sheet metal component shown in Figure 2.283. The different views, dimensions, and flat pattern of the sheet metal component are shown in Figure 2.284. The thickness of the sheet metal component is 1.5 mm, bend radius is 2 mm, and K-factor is 0.5. After creating the component, you need to generate its flat pattern drawing view on A3 sheet size. All dimensions are in mm.

2.283

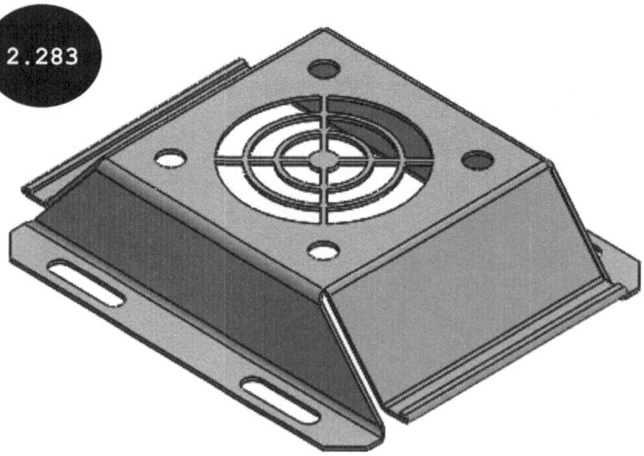

2.284

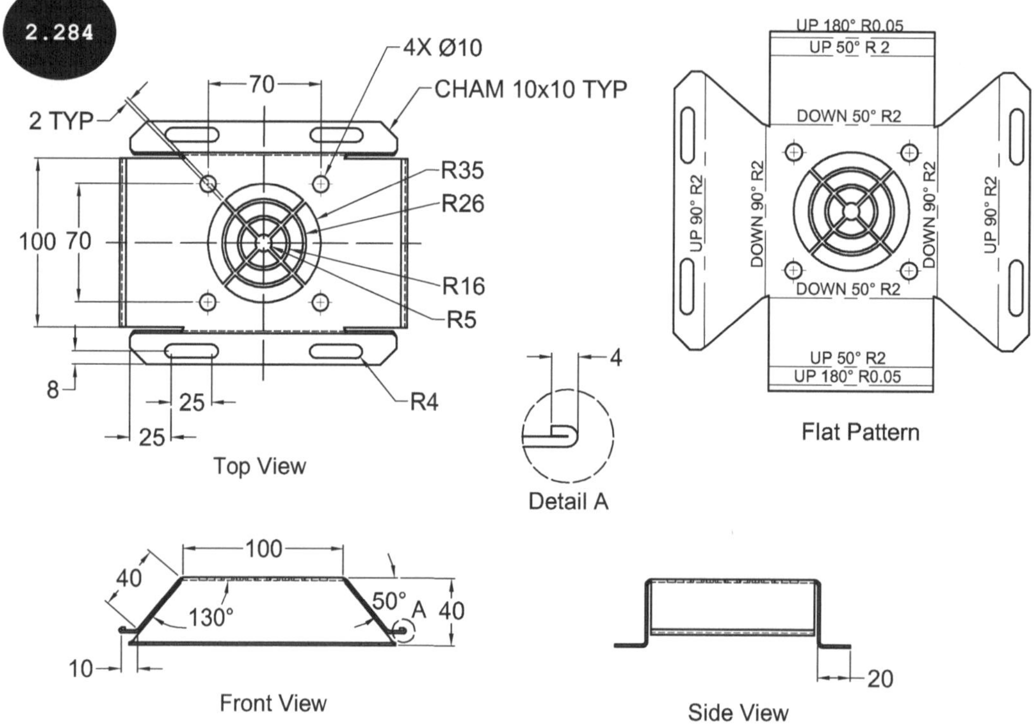

Hands-on Test Drive 3

Create the sheet metal component shown in Figure 2.285. The different views, dimensions, and flat pattern of the sheet metal component are shown in Figure 2.285. The thickness of the sheet metal component is 1 mm, bend radius is 2 mm, and K-factor is 0.5. After creating the component, generate its flat pattern layout. All dimensions are in mm.

2.285

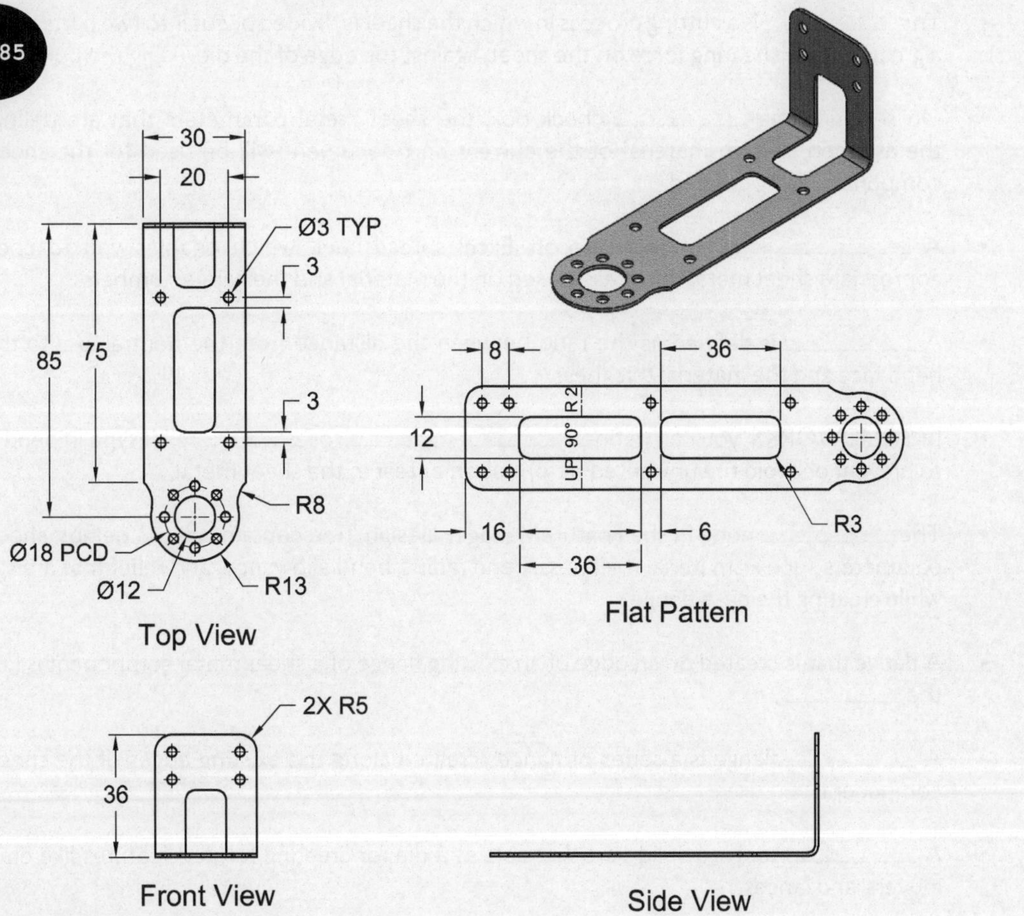

Summary

In this book, the basics of sheet metal design, various sheet metal parameters, and the method for creating a sheet metal component has been explained. A detailed discussion is provided on creating a base flange, a tab, a miter flange, a sketched bend, a jog bend, a hem, a lofted bend, an extruded cut, and a vent of a sheet metal component along with discussions on closing corners, welding corners and breaking corners of a sheet metal component. The method for the creation and insertion of forming tools is also explained in addition to converting a 3D solid or shelled part into a sheet metal component. Operations such as mirroring, patterning, flattening bends, folding bends, creating cuts across the bends, and generating a flat pattern of a sheet metal component are also discussed. The book also describes methods for defining sheet parameters to a custom material and generating the flat pattern drawing view of a sheet metal component in the Drawing environment.

Questions

Complete and verify the following sentences.

- A sheet metal component is a thin and flat piece of metal that has a uniform thickness ranging from ________ to ________ mm.
- The ________ is a cutting process in which the sheet is divided or cut into two parts by applying a great enough shearing force on the sheet, against the edge of the die, using the punch.
- On selecting the ________ check box, the sheet metal parameters that are defined with the assigned custom material of the current part document will be used for the sheet metal component being created.
- A ________ is simply a Microsoft Excel spreadsheet, which enables you to choose an appropriate sheet metal thickness, based on the material and the gauge numbers.
- A ________ is defined as the ratio between the distance from the neutral axis to the inner bend face and the material thickness.
- In SOLIDWORKS, you can define a ______, ______, or ______ relief type in bend regions to prevent or avoid the unwanted deformation or tear in the sheet metal.
- The ________ node in the FeatureManager Design Tree contains all the default sheet metal parameters such as material thickness, bend radius, bend allowance, and relief that are specified while creating the base flange.
- A flange that is created on an edge of an existing flange of a sheet metal component is known as the ________.
- A ________ flange is a series of flanges created along the existing edges of the sheet metal component.
- A ________ tool is a solid part that acts as a die for creating formed features like embosses, louvers, and lances.
- The ________ tool in the **Sheet Metal CommandManager** is used for generating the flat pattern layout of the sheet metal component.
- In SOLIDWORKS, you can break the corner edges of a sheet metal component by creating chamfers or fillets. (True/False)
- In a tool room, the most important thing that you need before creating a sheet metal component is the flat pattern layout of the sheet. (True/False)
- In SOLIDWORKS, you can create sheet metal components within the Part modeling environment. (True/False)

CHAPTER

3

Creating Surface Models

In this chapter, the following topics will be discussed:

- Introduction to Surface Modeling
- Getting Started with Surface Modeling
- Creating an Extrude Surface
- Creating a Revolve Surface
- Creating a Sweep Surface
- Creating a Loft Surface
- Creating a Filled Surface
- Creating a Planar Surface
- Offsetting a Surface
- Creating a Ruled Surface
- Creating a Flat Pattern of a Surface
- Extending a Surface
- Trimming a Surface
- Untrimming a Surface
- Deleting a Face
- Replacing a Face
- Deleting Holes in a Surface Body
- Creating a Freeform Surface
- Knitting Surfaces
- Adding Thickness to a Surface Model

Introduction to Surface Modeling

Surface modeling is a technique for creating complex shapes that are three-dimensional geometries of zero thickness. A geometry of zero thickness does not have any mass properties and is known as a surface. With the surface modeling technique, you can create a complex shape of a geometry that is not possible to create with solid modeling due to its limitations. After creating a surface model, it needs to be converted into a solid model, since anything with zero thickness and no mass, does not have any existence in the real world.

SOLIDWORKS uses two main techniques for modeling: Solid and Surface, see Figure 3.1. Most of the real world models are created by using the solid modeling technique. However, the complex shape models or geometries that are not possible to create as solid models, need to be created by using the Surface modeling technique. This chapter is focused on creating surface models.

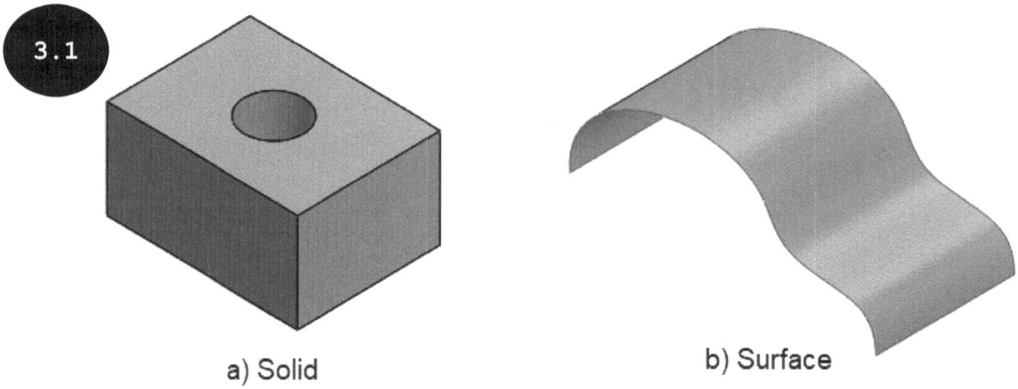

Note: To learn creating 3D solid models, assemblies, and 2D drawings, refer to "**SOLIDWORKS 2026: A Power Guide for Beginners and Intermediate User**" textbook by **CADArtifex**.

Getting Started with Surface Modeling

As discussed earlier, you can create surface models within the Part modeling environment by using various tools available in the **Surfaces CommandManager**. To display the tools of the **Surfaces CommandManager**, click on the **Surfaces** tab in the CommandManager, see Figure 3.2.

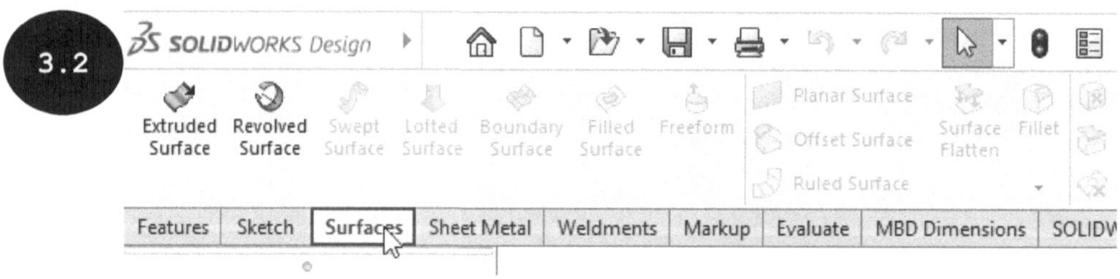

If the **Surfaces** tab is not available in the CommandManager then right-click anywhere on the CommandManager. Next, click on the **Tabs > Surfaces** option in the shortcut menu that appears, see Figure 3.3. The **Surfaces** tab becomes available in the CommandManager. Note that initially, most of the tools of the **Surfaces CommandManager** are not activated. These tools get activated as soon as you create a base feature of a surface model.

3.3

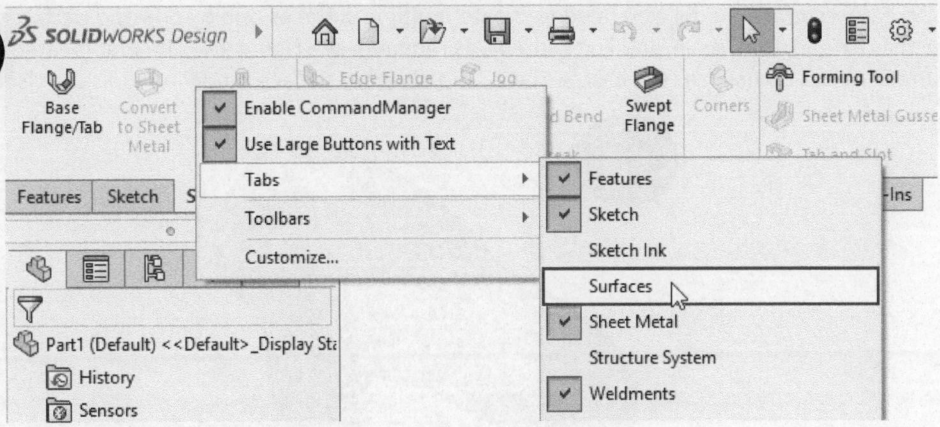

Note: In the shortcut menu shown in Figure 3.3, a tick-mark in front of the CommandManager name indicates that the respective CommandManager is already added. You can add any CommandManager that is not available by default, on clicking its name.

Some of the surface modeling tools such as **Extruded Surface, Revolved Surface, Swept Surface,** and **Lofted Surface** use one or more than one 2D sketch and work in the same manner as the solid modeling tools, with the only difference is that these tools are used for creating surfaces, refer to Figures 3.4 and 3.5. Figure 3.4 shows a 2D sketch and the resultant extrude surface. Figure 3.5 shows two sketches (path and profile) and the resultant sweep surface.

3.4

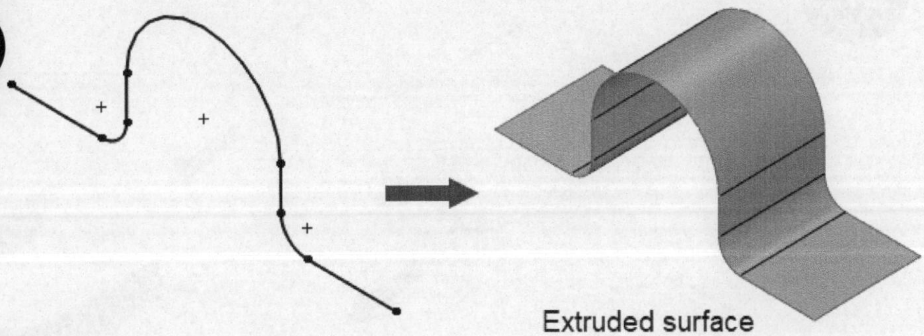

3.5

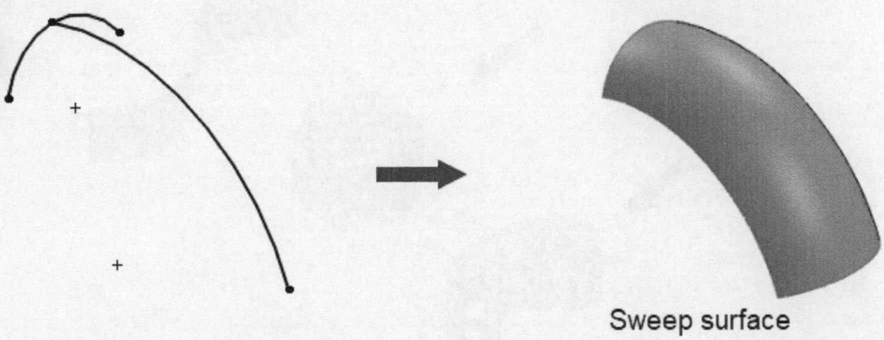

To create a surface model, you need to create multiple surfaces one by one and perform operations such as extend, trim, scale, and knit (stitch), as required, see Figure 3.6. The first created surface of a surface model is known as the base surface. The different surface modeling tools are discussed next.

3.6

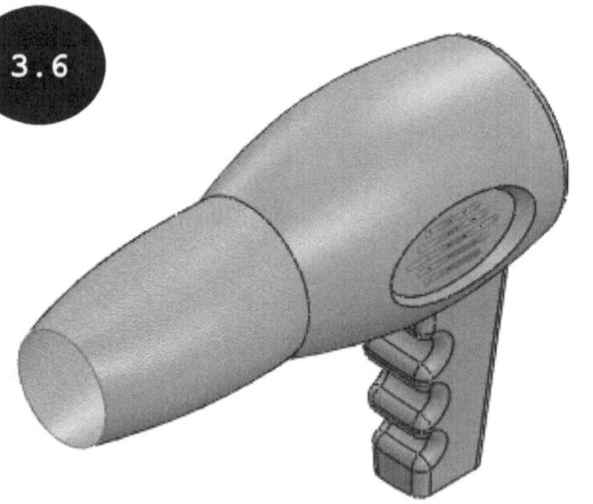

Creating an Extrude Surface

An extrude surface is created by extruding a closed or an open 2D sketch. Note that the sketch of the extrude surface defines its geometry. Figure 3.7 shows different extrude surfaces that are created from closed and open sketches, respectively. In SOLIDWORKS, you can create an extrude surface by using the **Extruded Surface** tool in the **Surfaces CommandManager**.

3.7

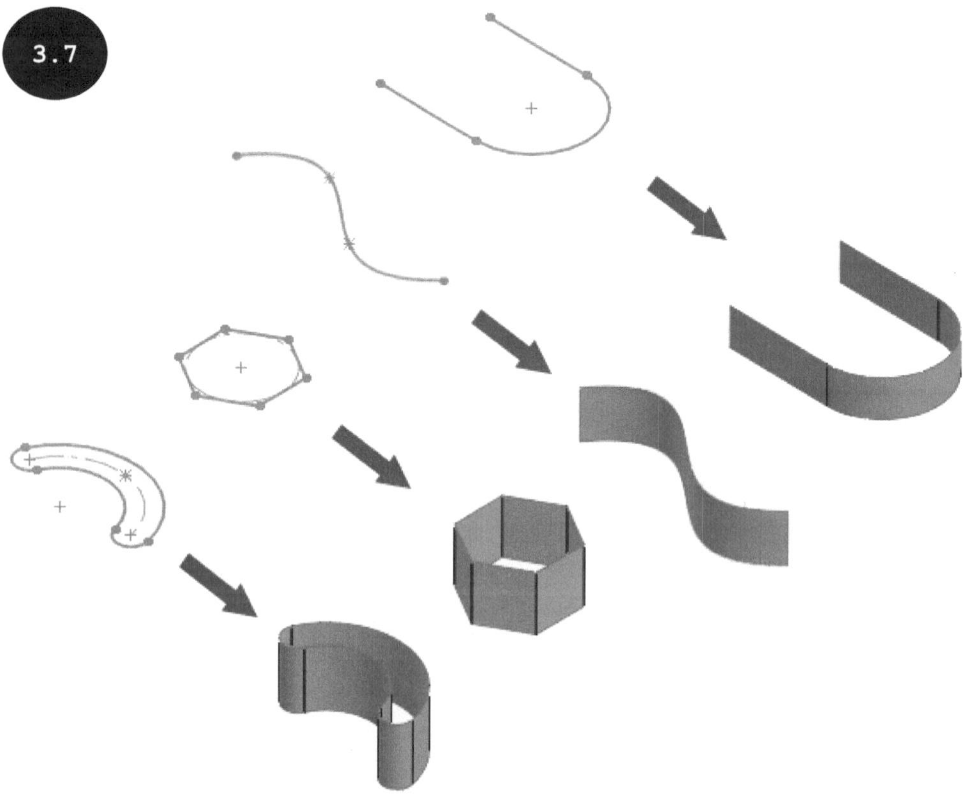

To create an extrude surface, invoke the Sketching environment by clicking on the **Sketch** tool in the **Sketch CommandManager**, (see Figure 3.8) and then select a plane as the sketching plane. The Sketching environment gets invoked and the selected plane gets oriented normal to the viewing direction, so that you can create a sketch easily by using the sketching tools available in the **Sketch CommandManager**.

3.8

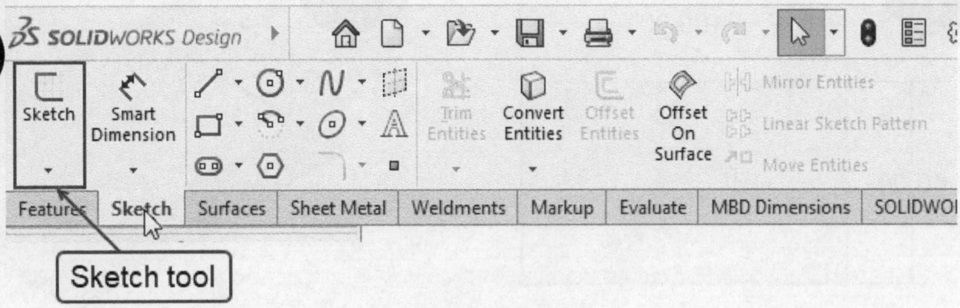

After creating a sketch by using the sketching tools, click on the **Surfaces** tab in the CommandManager for displaying the surface modeling tools in the **Surfaces CommandManager**, see Figure 3.9. Next, click on the **Extruded Surface** tool. The preview of an extrude surface appears in the graphics area with the default extrusion parameters. Also, the view orientation is changed to trimetric and the **Surface-Extrude PropertyManager** appears to the left of the graphics area, see Figure 3.10.

3.9

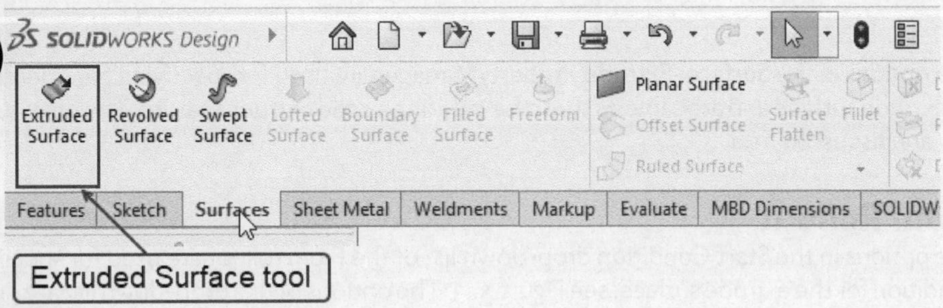

3.10

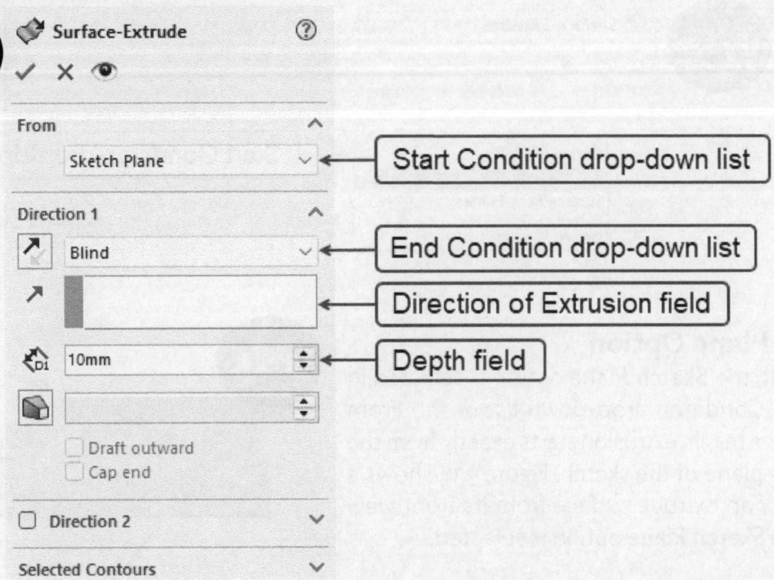

Figure 3.11 shows a rectangular sketch created on the Top Plane in the Sketching environment and Figure 3.12 shows a preview of the resultant extruded surface in Trimetric orientation.

3.11

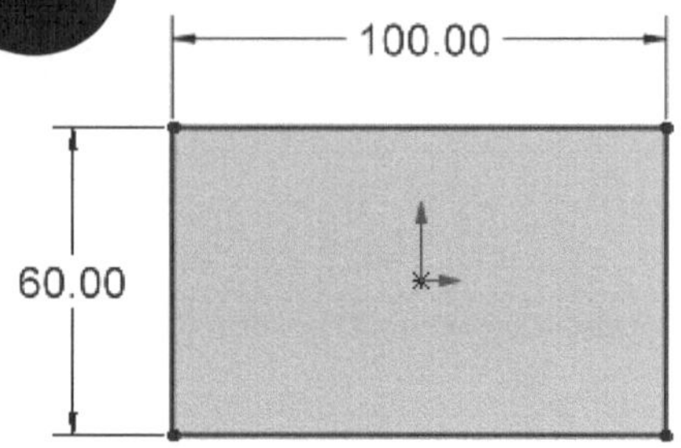

3.12

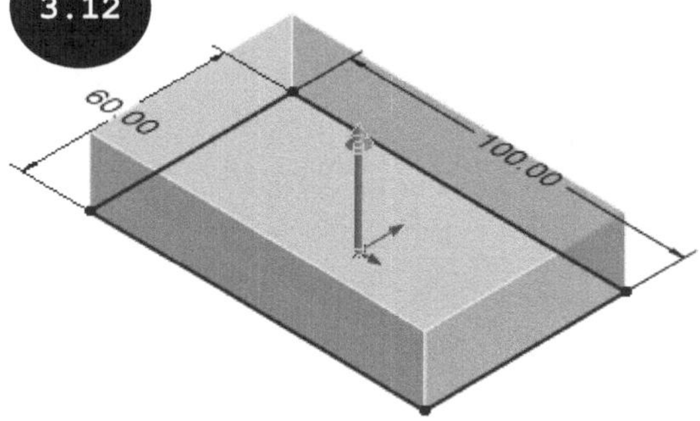

Note: After creating a sketch, you can also exit the Sketching environment to finish the creation of the sketch first by clicking on the **Exit Sketch** tool in the **Sketch CommandManager** and then invoking the **Extruded Surface** tool in the **Surfaces CommandManager** for extruding it.

The options in the **Surface-Extrude PropertyManager** are used for specifying parameters for creating an extrude surface and are same as those for creating a solid extrude feature. The options in this dialog box are discussed next.

From Rollout

The options in the **Start Condition** drop-down list of the **From** rollout are used for specifying the start condition for the extrude surface, see Figure 3.13. The options of this drop-down list are discussed next.

3.13

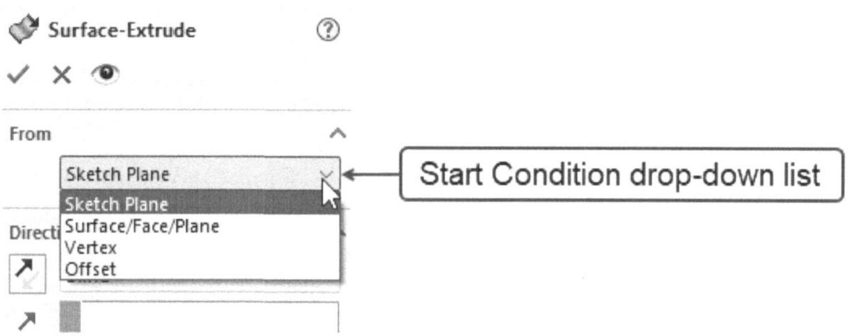

Sketch Plane Option

By default, the **Sketch Plane** option is selected in the **Start Condition** drop-down list of the **From** rollout. As a result, extrusion starts exactly from the sketching plane of the sketch. Figure 3.14 shows a preview of an extrude surface from its front view when the **Sketch Plane** option is selected.

3.14

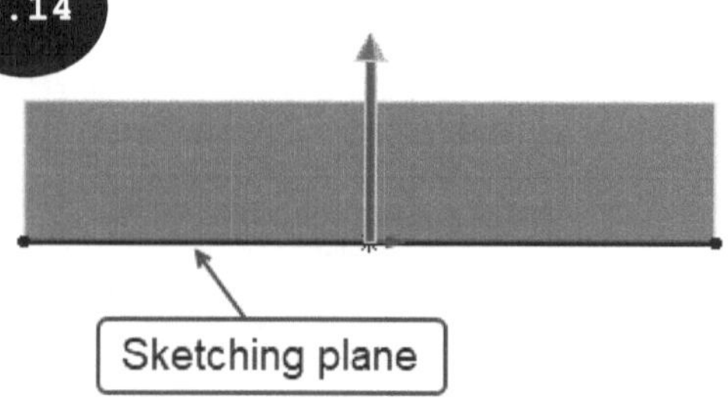

Offset Option

The **Offset** option is used for creating an extrude surface at an offset distance from the sketching plane. You can enter the required offset distance value in the **Enter Offset Value** field that appears in the rollout, see Figure 3.15. Alternatively, you can use the Spinner Up and Down arrows of the **Enter Offset Value** field to set the desired offset distance value. Figure 3.16 shows the preview of an extrude surface from its front view after specifying an offset distance. To reverse the offset direction, click on the **Reverse Direction** button in the **From** rollout.

3.15

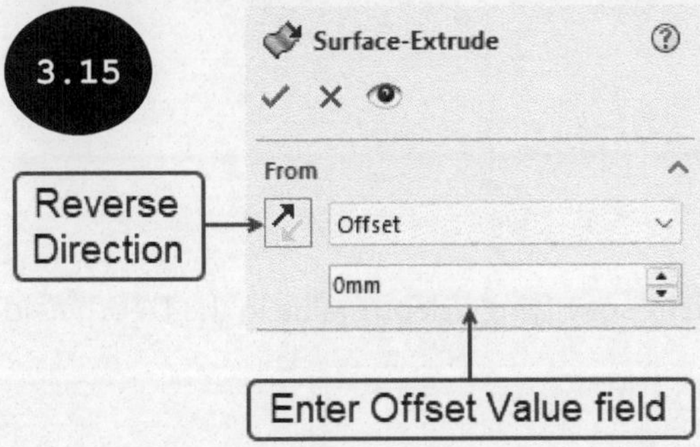

3.16

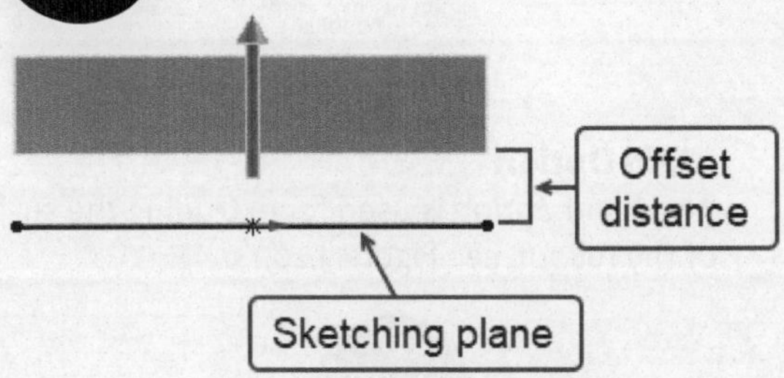

Surface/Face/Plane Option

The **Surface/Face/Plane** option is used for selecting an existing surface, a face, or a plane as the start condition of the extrusion from where extrusion starts. Figure 3.17 shows a sketch to be extruded and a surface to be selected as the start condition of extrusion. Figure 3.18 shows a preview of the resultant extrude surface after selecting the existing surface as the start condition.

3.17

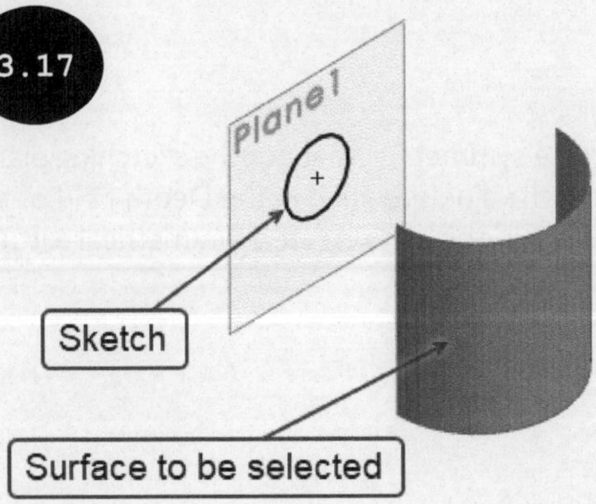

3.18

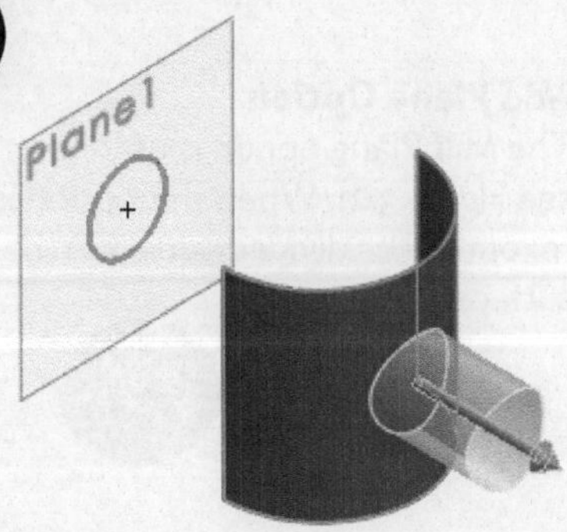

Vertex Option

The **Vertex** option is used for selecting a vertex of an existing object as the start condition of the extrusion.

Direction 1 Rollout

The options in the **Direction 1** rollout of the PropertyManager are used for defining extrusion parameters for extruding the sketch on one side (Direction 1) of the sketching plane. The options are discussed next.

End Condition Drop-down List

The options in the **End Condition** drop-down list are used for defining the end condition for the extrude surface in one side (Direction 1) of the sketching plane, see Figure 3.19. The options of this drop-down list are discussed next.

3.19

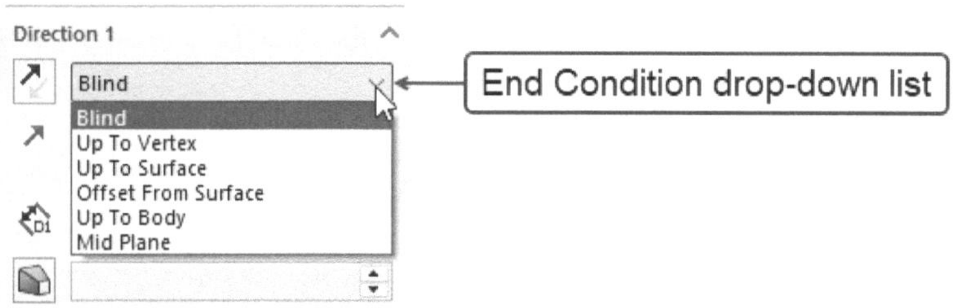

Blind Option

The **Blind** option is used for extruding the surface by specifying a depth value in the **Depth** field of the rollout, see Figure 3.20.

3.20

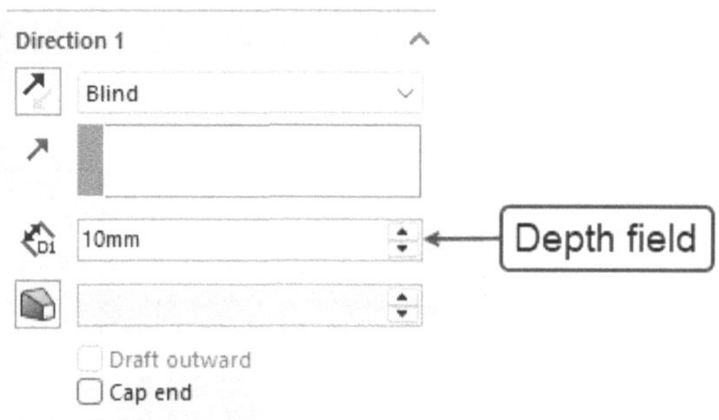

Mid Plane Option

The **Mid Plane** option is used for extruding the surface symmetrically about the sketching plane, see Figure 3.21. When this option is selected, the depth value specified in the **Depth** field of the rollout will be divided equally on both sides of the sketching plane to create a symmetrical extrude surface.

3.21

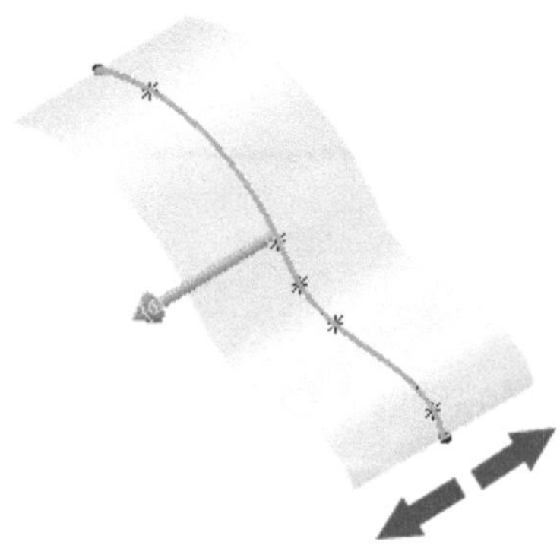

Up To Surface Option

The **Up To Surface** option is used for defining the end condition or termination of the extrusion up to an existing surface. Figure 3.22 shows a sketch to be extruded and a surface to be selected as the end condition of extrusion. Figure 3.23 shows a preview of the resultant extrude surface.

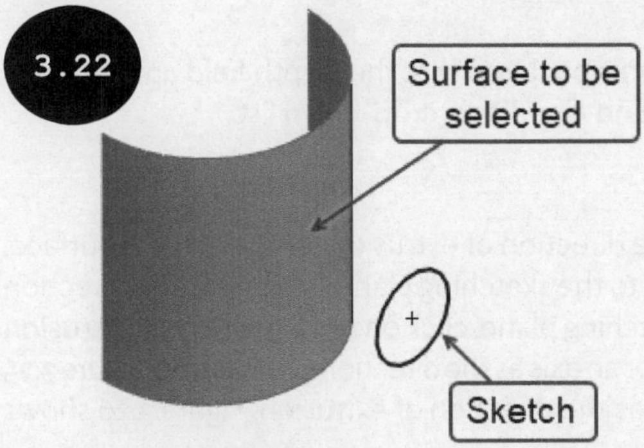

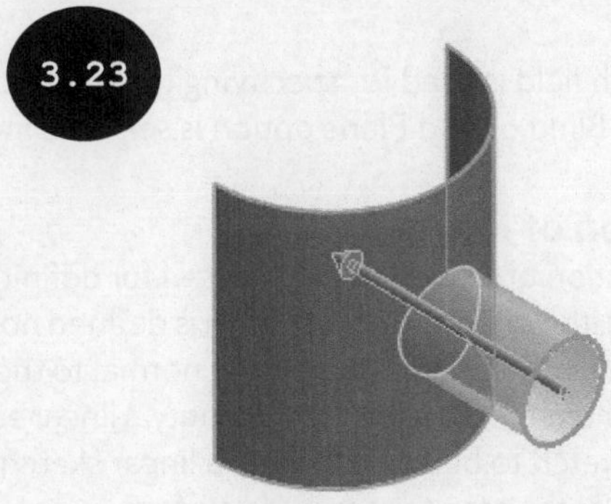

Offset From Surface

The Offset From Surface option is used for defining the end condition or termination of the extrusion at an offset distance from an existing surface, see Figure 3.24. After selecting this option, you can select an existing surface, a face, or a plane of the model as the end condition of the extrusion and then enter an offset distance value in the **Offset Distance** field that appears in the rollout. Note that the resultant extrude surface gets terminated at the specified offset distance from the selected surface. Figure 3.24 shows the preview of a surface whose end condition is defined at an offset distance from an existing surface.

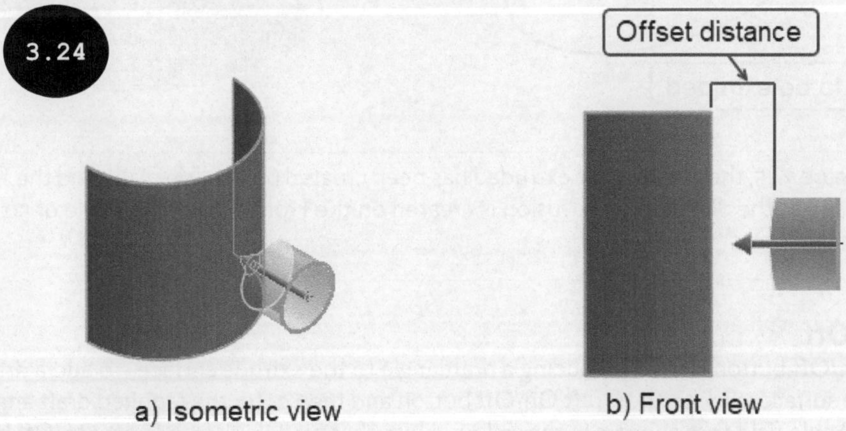

Up To Vertex Option

The Up To Vertex option is used for defining the end condition or termination of the extrusion by selecting a vertex of an existing object.

Up To Body Option

The Up To Body option is used for defining the end condition or termination of extrusion up to a body.

Reverse Direction

The **Reverse Direction** button in the **Direction 1** rollout is used for reversing the direction of extrusion from one side of the sketching plane to the other.

Depth

The **Depth** field is used for specifying the depth of extrusion. Note that the **Depth** field appears only when the **Blind** or **Mid Plane** option is selected in the **End Condition** drop-down list.

Direction of Extrusion

The **Direction of Extrusion** field is used for defining the direction of extrusion for the extrude surface. By default, the direction of extrusion is defined normal to the sketching plane. To specify the direction of extrusion other than the direction normal to the sketching plane, click on the **Direction of Extrusion** field and then select a linear sketch entity, a linear edge, or an axis as the direction of extrusion. Figure 3.25 shows a sketch to be extruded and a linear sketch line as the direction of extrusion. Figure 3.26 shows a preview of the resultant extrude surface.

3.25

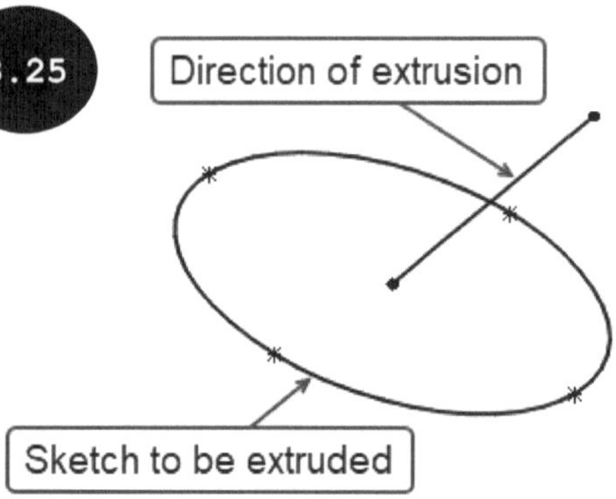

3.26

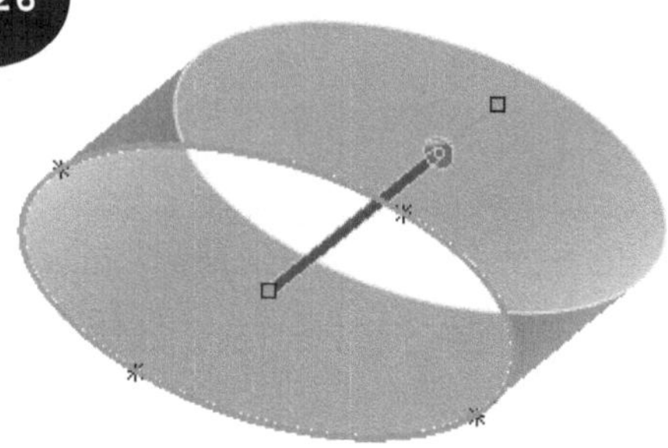

Tip: In Figure 3.25, the sketch to be extruded has been created on the Top plane and the sketch to be used as the direction of extrusion is created on the Front plane at an angle of 50 degrees from the X axis.

Draft On/Off

The **Draft On/Off** button is used for adding a draft angle to the extrude surface. To add a draft angle to an extrude surface, click on the **Draft On/Off** button and then enter the required draft angle value in the **Draft Angle** field that appears in the rollout. Note that by default, the **Draft On/Off** button is not activated. As a result, the resultant extrude surface is created without having any tapering in it.

You can enter a draft angle in the **Draft Angle** field. By default, the **Draft outward** check box is cleared in the rollout. As a result, the draft is added in the inward direction of the sketch, see Figure 3.27. If you select this check box, the draft will be added in the outward direction of the sketch, see Figure 3.28.

3.27

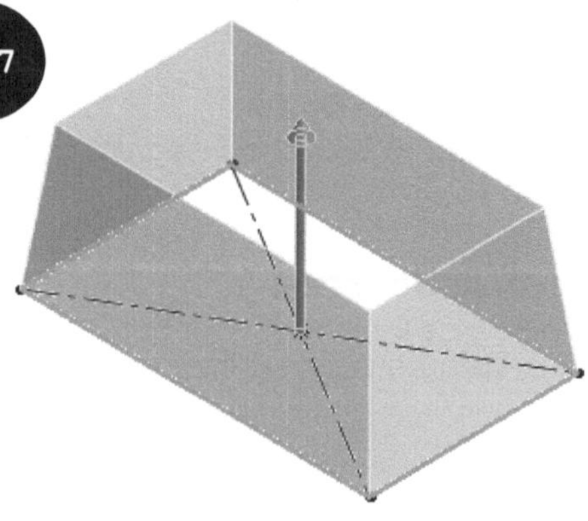

Cap end

The **Cap end** check box is used to close the open ends of the extrude surface, see Figure 3.29. This check box is enabled only while extruding a closed sketch.

3.28

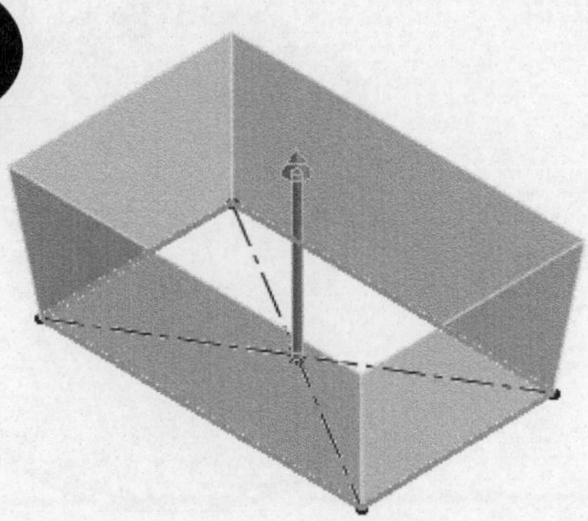

3.29

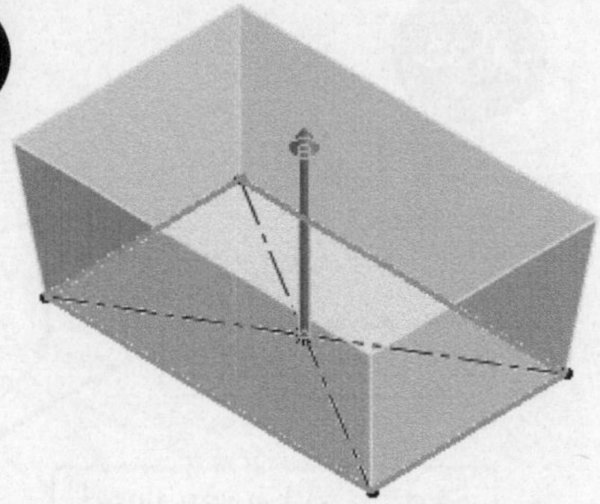

Direction 2

The options in the **Direction 2** rollout are same as those in the **Direction 1** rollout of the PropertyManager with the only difference that the options of the **Direction 2** rollout are used for specifying the end condition in the second direction (Direction 2) of the sketching plane. Figure 3.30 shows the expanded **Direction 2** rollout and Figure 3.31 shows the preview of an extrude surface, that is extruded on both sides of the sketching plane with different extrusion depths.

3.30

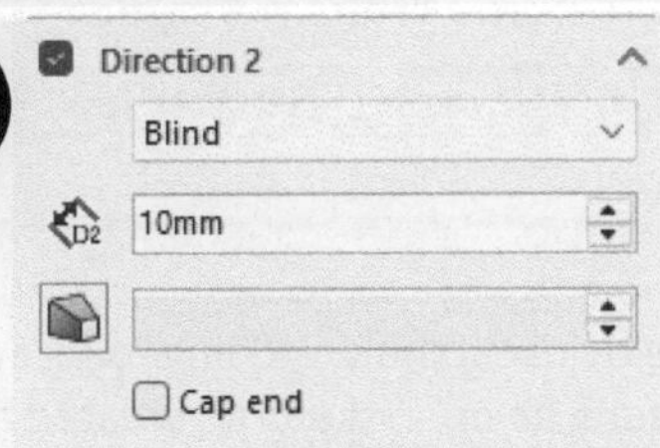

3.31

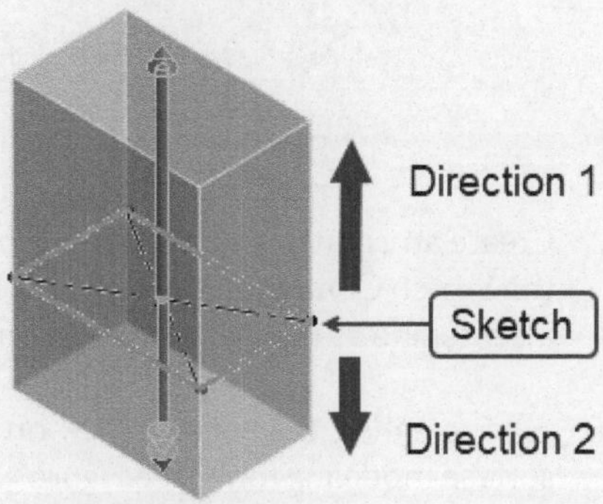

After specifying the required parameters for extruding the sketch, click on the green tick-mark ✓ button in the **Surface-Extrude PropertyManager** to accept the defined parameters and create the extrude surface.

Creating a Revolve Surface

A revolve surface is created by revolving an open or a closed sketch around an axis of revolution. Note that the sketch to be revolved should be on either side of the axis of revolution. You can use a line, a centerline, an axis, or a linear edge as the axis of revolution. In SOLIDWORKS, you can create a revolve surface by using the **Revolved Surface** tool in the **Surfaces CommandManager**. Figure 3.32 shows a revolve surface created by an open sketch. The method for creating a revolve surface is discussed below:

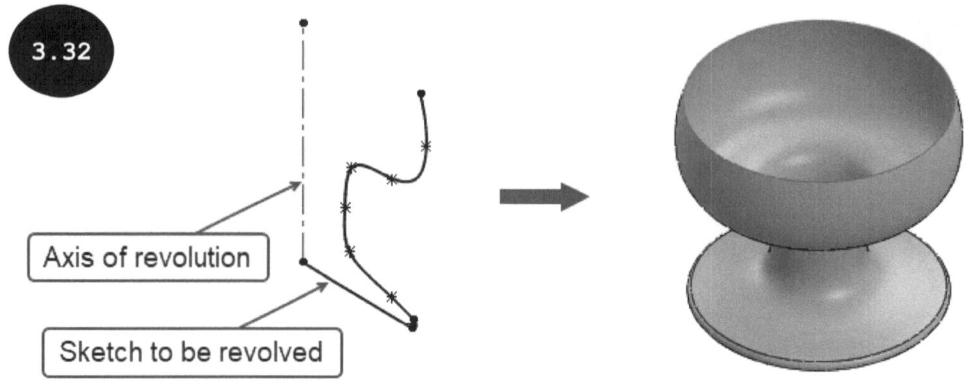

1. Invoke the Sketching environment by selecting a plane as the sketching plane using the **Sketch** tool of the **Sketch CommandManager**, see Figure 3.33.

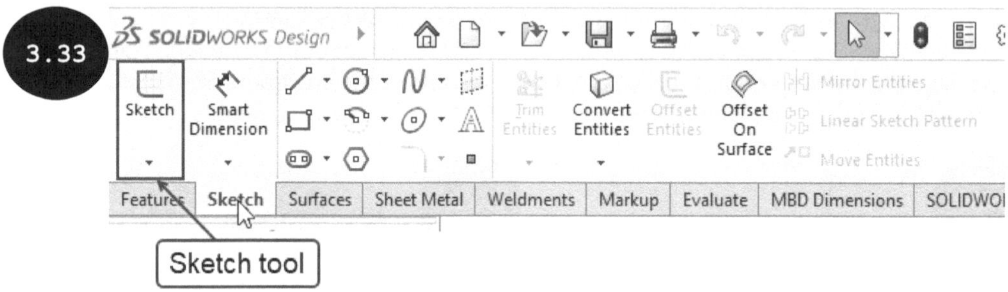

2. Create an open or a closed sketch of the revolve surface by using the sketching tools available in the Sketch CommandManager, see Figure 3.34. In this figure, an open sketch is created along with a centerline as the axis of revolution.

3. After creating the sketch, click on the **Surfaces** tab in the CommandManager to display the surface modeling tools, see Figure 3.35.

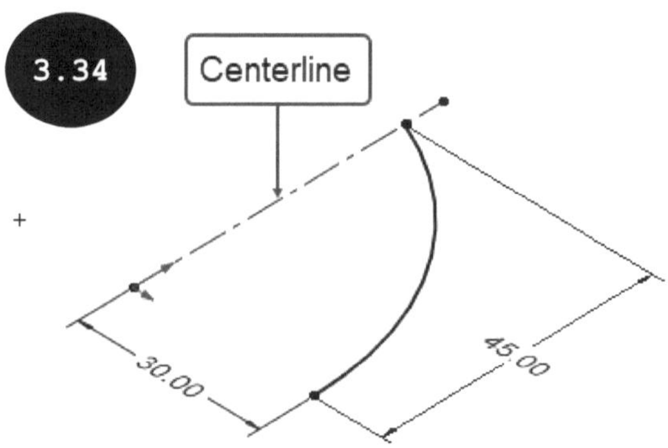

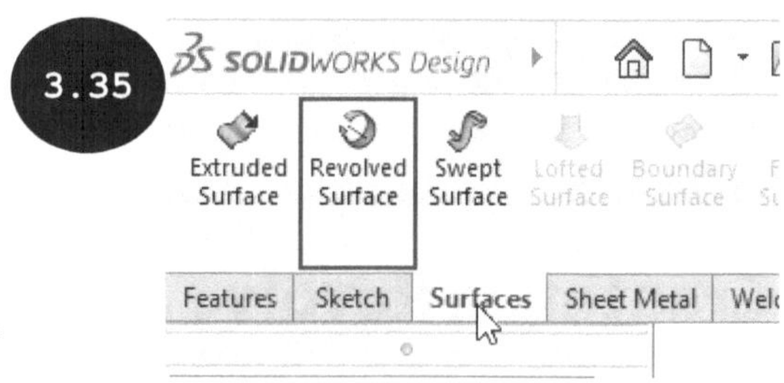

4. Click on the **Revolved Surface** tool in the **Surfaces CommandManager**. A preview of the revolve surface appears in the graphics area with default parameters, see Figure 3.36. Also, the **Surface-Revolve PropertyManager** appears on the left of the graphics area, see Figure 3.37.

3.36

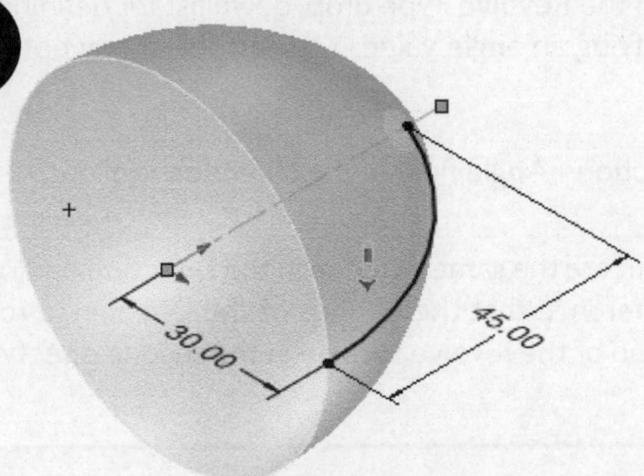

3.37

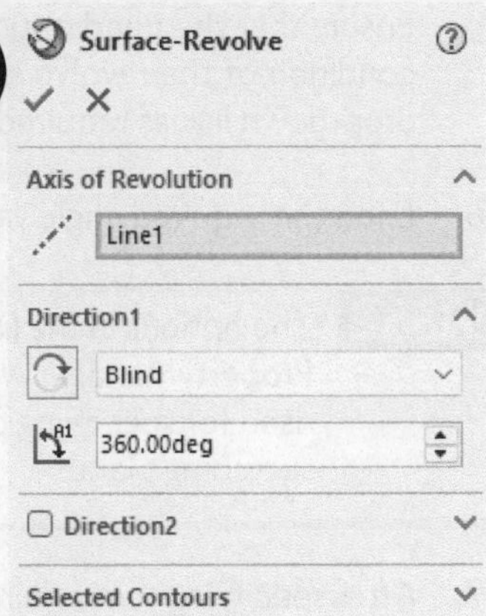

Axis of Revolution: The Axis of Revolution field in the **Surface-Revolve PropertyManager** is used for selecting an axis of revolution of the revolve surface.

Note: If the sketch to be revolved has only one centerline, then the centerline drawn will automatically be selected as the axis of revolution and the preview of the resultant revolve surface appears in the graphics area. However, if the sketch has two or more than two centerlines or does not have any centerline, then on invoking the **Revolved Surface** tool, the preview of the revolve surface does not appear and you are prompted to select an axis of revolution. You can select a linear sketch entity, a centerline, an axis, or an edge as the axis of revolution.

Revolve Type Drop-down list: The **Revolve Type** drop-down list of the **Direction 1** rollout is used for selecting a method for revolving the sketch. The options of this drop-down list are discussed below:

Blind: The **Blind** option is used for defining the end condition or termination of the revolve surface by specifying an angle value. By default, this option is selected in this drop-down list.

Mid Plane: The **Mid Plane** option is used for revolving a sketch symmetrically on both sides of the sketching plane about an axis of revolution, see Figure 3.38.

3.38

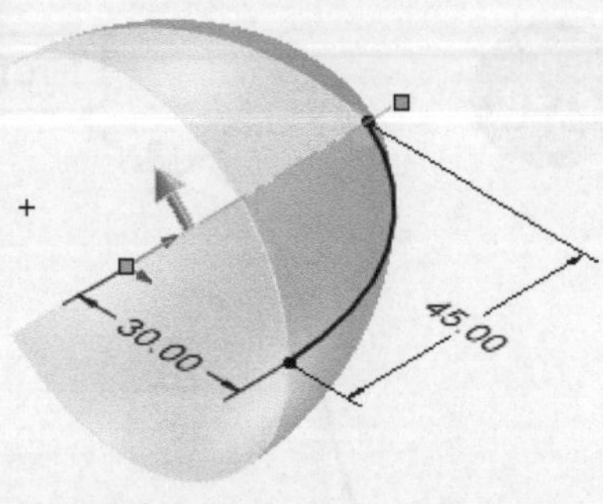

Note: The **Up To Vertex**, **Up To Surface**, and **Offset From Surface** options of the **Revolve Type** drop-down list are the same as discussed earlier while creating an extrude surface with the only difference that these options are used for creating a revolve surface.

5. Ensure that the **Blind** option is selected in the **Revolve Type** drop-down list for defining the end condition of the revolve surface by specifying an angle value. You can select any option in this drop-down list, as required.

6. Enter the required angle value in the **Direction 1 Angle** field of the **Direction 1** rollout.

Note: The options in the **Direction 2** rollout are the same as those in the **Direction 1** rollout of the PropertyManager with the only difference that the options of the **Direction 2** rollout are used for specifying the end condition of the revolve surface in the second direction of the sketching plane.

7. After specifying the required parameters for revolving a sketch, click on the green tick-mark ✓ button in the PropertyManager to accept the defined parameters and create a revolve surface, see Figure 3.39.

3.39

Creating a Sweep Surface

A sweep surface is created by sweeping an open or a closed sketch profile along a path. Figure 3.40 shows a profile and a path. Figure 3.41 shows the resultant sweep surface created by sweeping the profile along the path.

3.40

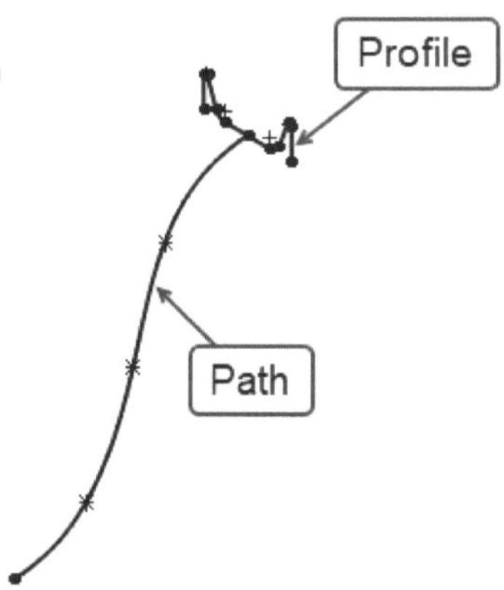

3.41

It is evident from the above figures that to create a sweep surface, you first need to create a profile and a path where the profile follows the path and creates a sweep surface. In SOLIDWORKS, you can create a sweep surface by using the **Swept Surface** tool available in the **Surfaces CommandManager**. The method for creating a sweep surface is given below:

1. Create an open or a closed sketch profile and path as individual sketches in the Sketching environment.
2. Click on the **Swept Surface** tool in the **Surfaces CommandManager**, see Figure 3.42. The **Surface-Sweep PropertyManager** appears, see Figure 3.43. Also, you are prompted to select a path, since the **Path** field is activated in the **Profile and Path** rollout, by default.

3.42

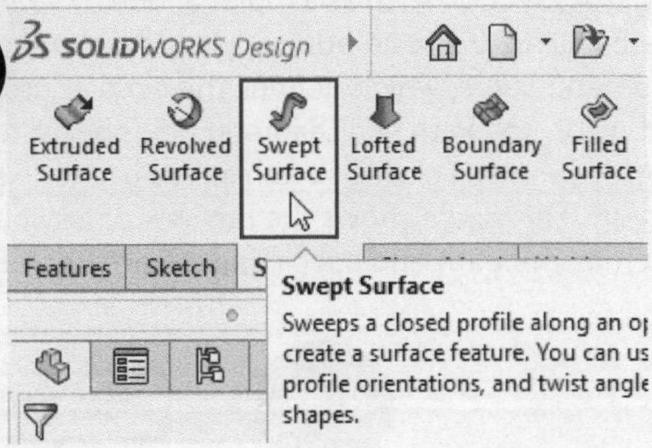

3.43

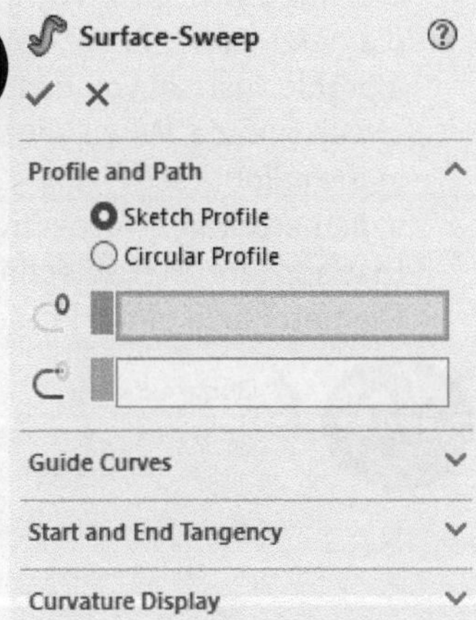

Sketch Profile: The Sketch Profile radio button is selected in the **Profile and Path** rollout, by default. As a result, the **Profile** and the **Path** fields are available in the PropertyManager, refer to Figure 3.43. The **Profile** field is used for selecting a profile of the sweep surface. You can select an open or a closed sketch, a face, a surface, or an edge as a profile. The **Path** field is used for selecting a path of the sweep surface. You can select an open or a closed sketch, an edge, or a curve as the path of the sweep surface. Figure 3.44 shows an open sketch as a path and an open sketch as a profile.

3.44

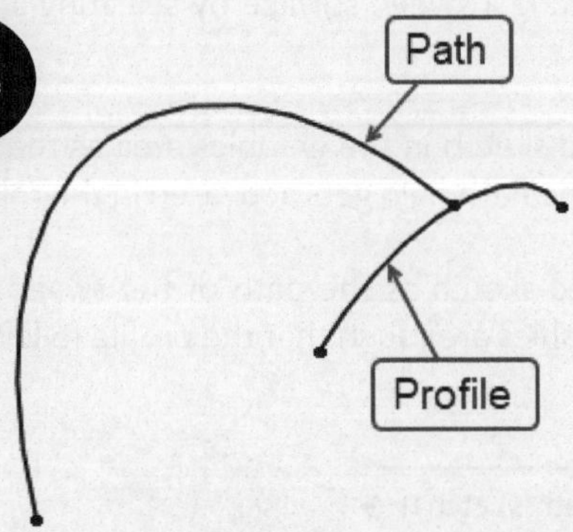

Note: The starting point of the path must intersect the plane of the profile. Also, the profile and path as well as the resultant sweep surface must not self-intersect.

Tip: In Figure 3.44, the plane of profile is created along the path. To learn about different methods for creating reference planes, refer to "**SOLIDWORKS 2026: A Power Guide for Beginners and Intermediate Users**" textbook by **CADArtifex**.

Circular Profile: The **Circular Profile** radio button of the **Profile and Path** rollout is used for creating a sweep surface that has a circular cross section such as a rod or a tube by specifying the diameter value. To create a sweep surface by using this radio button, you do not need to select a profile, instead you need to specify a diameter value, which defines the circular profile of the sweep surface. When you select this radio button, the **Path** and **Diameter** fields become available in the rollout (see Figure 3.45) for selecting an open or a closed sketch as the path and specifying a diameter value, respectively, see Figure 3.46. This figure shows the preview of a sweep surface that appears after selecting an open sketch as the path and specifying a diameter value in the **Diameter** field of the PropertyManager.

3.45

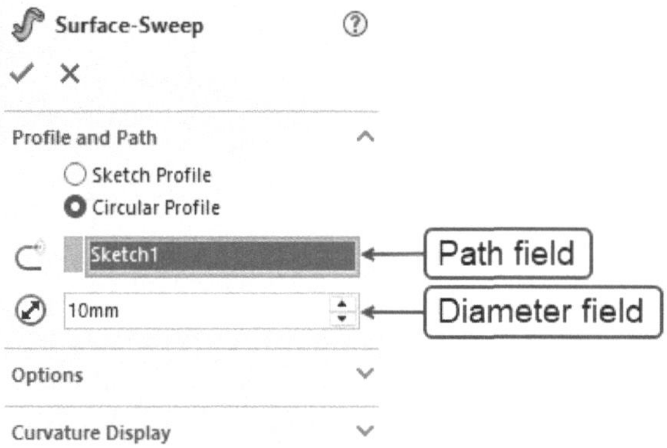

3.46

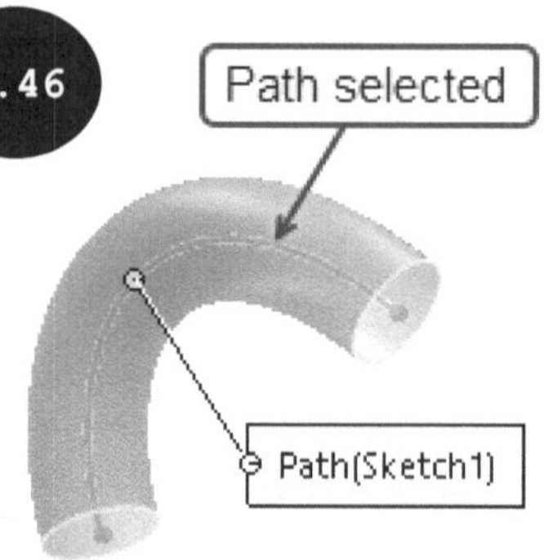

3. Ensure that the **Sketch Profile** radio button is selected in the **Profile** and **Path** rollout of the PropertyManager for creating a sweep surface by selecting a profile and a path in the graphics area.

4. Select an open or a closed sketch in the graphics area as the profile of the sweep surface. The profile gets selected and the **Path** field gets activated in the rollout, automatically.

5. Select an open or a closed sketch as the path of the sweep surface. The preview of a sweep surface appears in the graphics area such that the profile follows the path, see Figure 3.47.

3.47

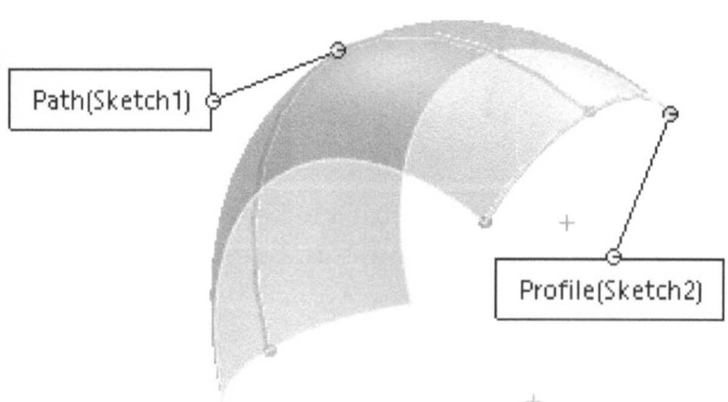

Note: If the profile is created between the endpoints of the path, (see Figure 3.48) then the preview of the sweep surface appears on either side of the profile, see Figure 3.49. You can select the required button: **Direction 1**, **Bidirectional**, or **Direction 2** that appears in the rollout for sweeping the profile on one side (Direction 1), both sides (Bidirectional), or other side (Direction 2) of the profile, respectively. Figure 3.50 shows the **Profile** and **Path** rollout with the display of **Direction 1**, **Bidirectional**, and **Direction 2** buttons. Figure 3.51 shows the preview of a sweep surface when the **Bidirectional** button is selected.

3.48

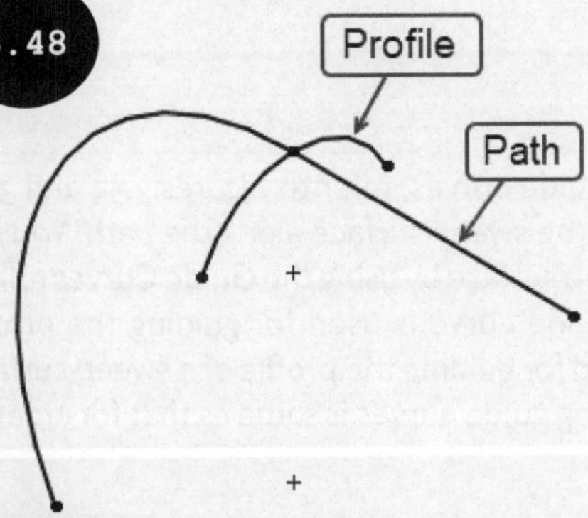

3.49

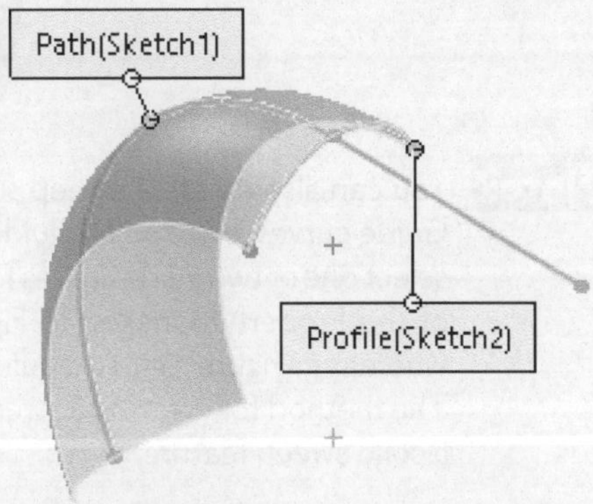

3.50

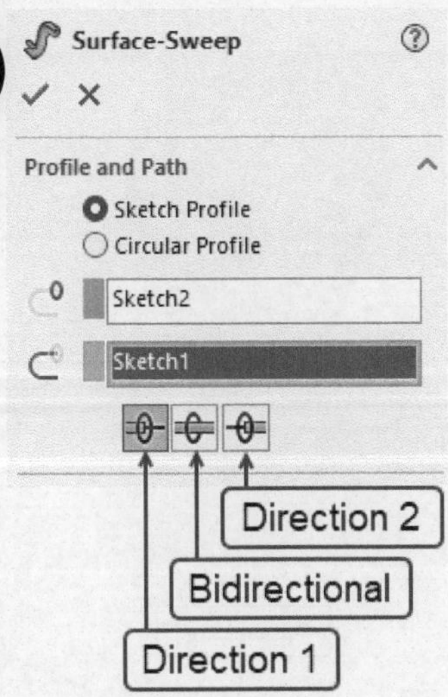

3.51

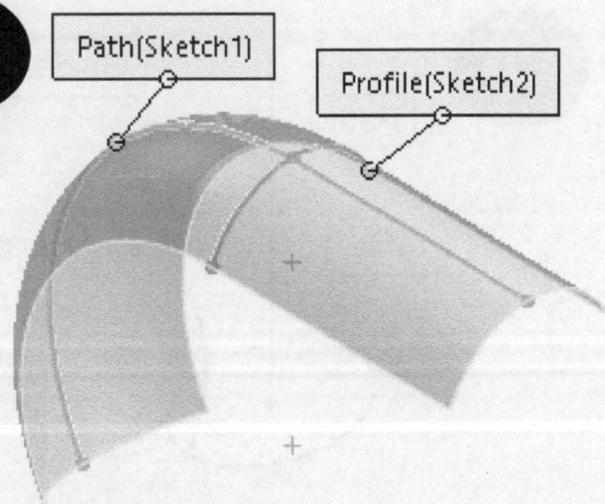

Options: The Options rollout of the PropertyManager is used for defining the profile orientation and twist along the path, and is same as that of creating a solid sweep feature. Figure 3.52 shows the expanded Options rollout.

3.52

6. Accept the default specified options in the **Options** rollout of the PropertyManager.

7. Click on the green tick-mark ✓ button in the PropertyManager to accept the preview of a sweep surface. A sweep surface gets created, see Figure 3.53.

3.53

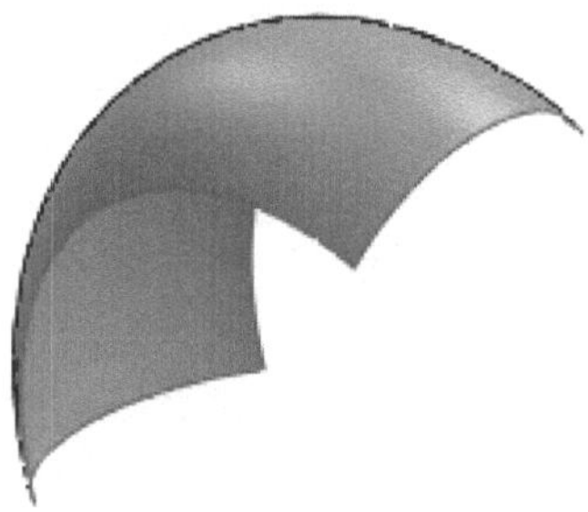

Note: You can also create a sweep surface by using guide curves, refer to Figures 3.54 and 3.55. Guide curves are used for guiding the profile of the sweep surface along the path. You can select one or two guide curves for creating a sweep surface by using the **Guide Curves** rollout of the PropertyManager. In Figure 3.54, one guide curve is used for guiding the profile, whereas in Figure 3.55, two guide curves are used for guiding the profile of a sweep surface. The method for creating a sweep surface by using guide curves is same as that for creating a solid sweep feature.

3.54

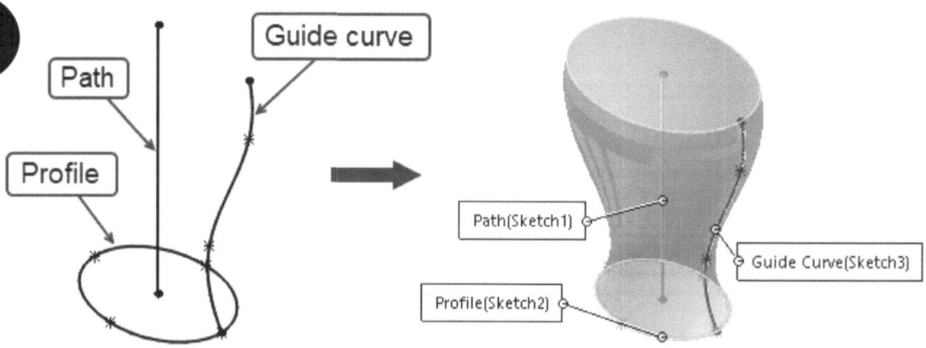

3.55

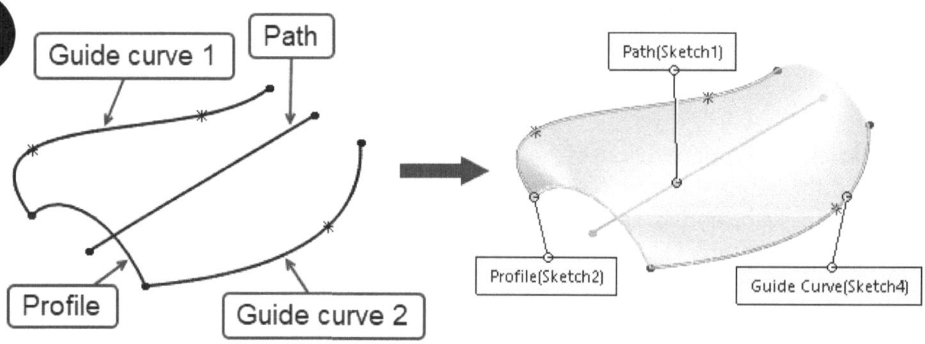

Creating a Loft Surface

A loft surface is created by lofting two or more than two open or closed sketch profiles such that the cross-sectional shape of the loft surface transits from one sketch profile to another. Figure 3.56 shows two open profiles (sections) created on different planes having an offset distance between each other. Figure 3.57 shows the resultant loft surface.

3.56

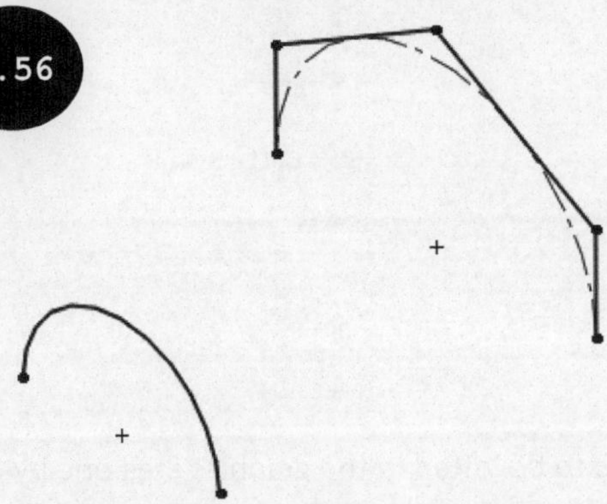

3.57

In SOLIDWORKS, you can create three types of loft surfaces: with profiles, with profiles and guide curves, and with profiles and centerline. The methods for creating different types of loft surfaces are discussed next.

Creating a Loft Surface with Profiles

1. Create two or more than two open or closed sketch profiles as different sketches one by one, refer to Figure 3.58.

3.58

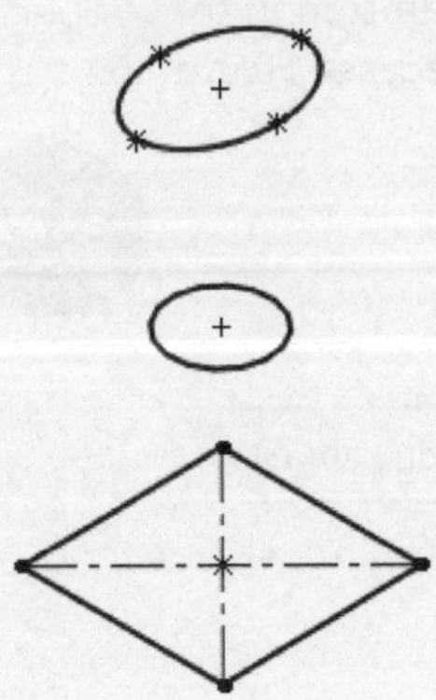

Note: In Figure 3.58, three closed sketch profiles are created on different planes having an offset distance between each other.

2. After creating sketch profiles to be lofted, click on the **Lofted Surface** tool in the **Surfaces CommandManager**, see Figure 3.59. The **Surface-Loft PropertyManager** appears, see Figure 3.60.

3.59

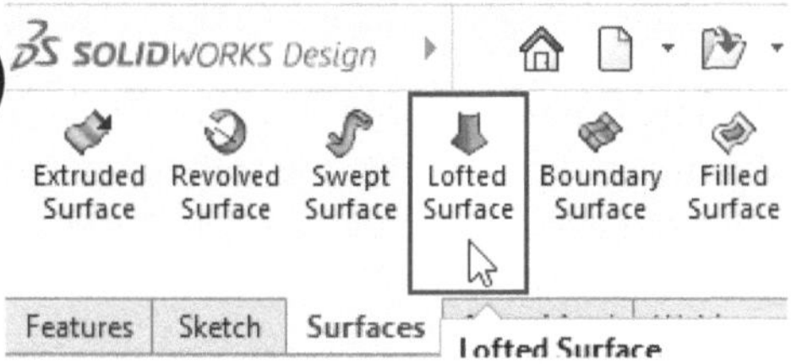

3.60

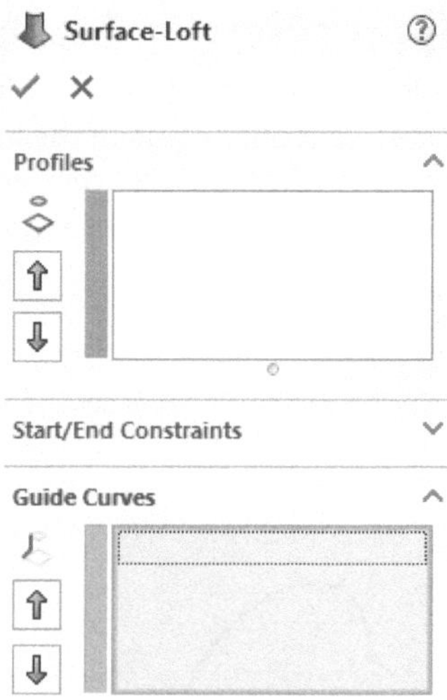

3. Select two or more open or closed sketch profiles to be lofted in the graphics area one by one. The preview of a loft surface appears with connectors, that connect the profiles, see Figure 3.61. Also, the names of the selected profiles appear in the **Profile** field of the rollout in an order in which they are selected. Note that you can change the order of selection by using the **Move Up** and **Move Down** buttons of the **Profiles** rollout.

Note: You can drag the connector points that appear in the preview of the loft feature to create a twist in the feature.

4. Click on the green tick-mark ✓ button in the PropertyManager to accept the preview of a loft surface. A loft surface gets created, see Figure 3.62.

3.61

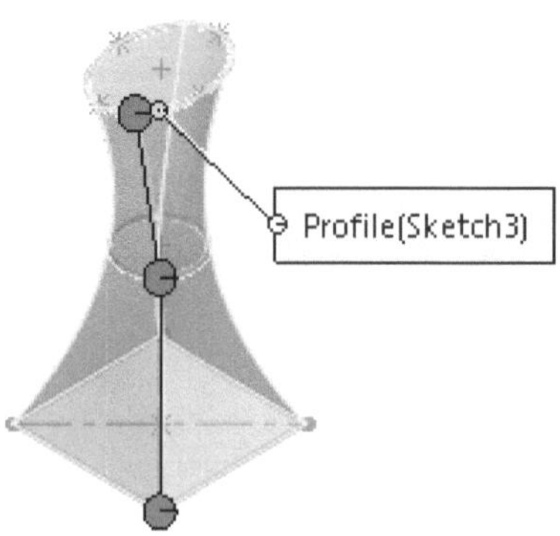

3.62

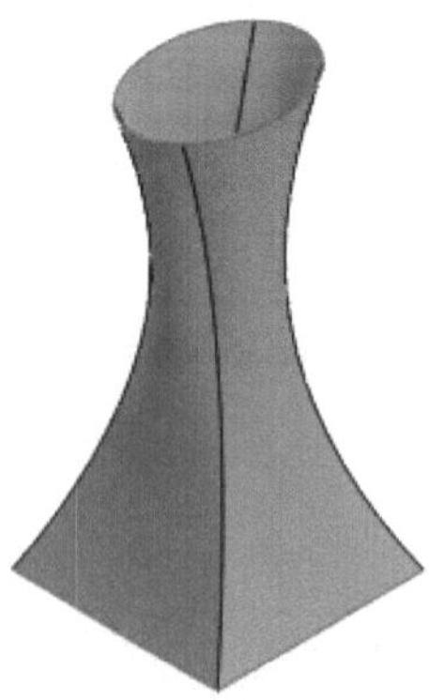

Creating a Loft Surface with Profiles and Guide Curves

In SOLIDWORKS, you can also create a loft surface with profiles and guide curves. Guide curves are used for guiding the cross-sectional shape of the loft surface, see Figures 3.63 and 3.64. In this figure, two profiles and two guide curves are selected to guide the cross-sectional shape of the loft surface. You can select one or more than one guide curve for controlling the shape of the loft surface. Note that the guide curves must intersect with the profiles of the loft surface. To create a loft surface with profiles and guide curves, follow the steps given below:

3.63

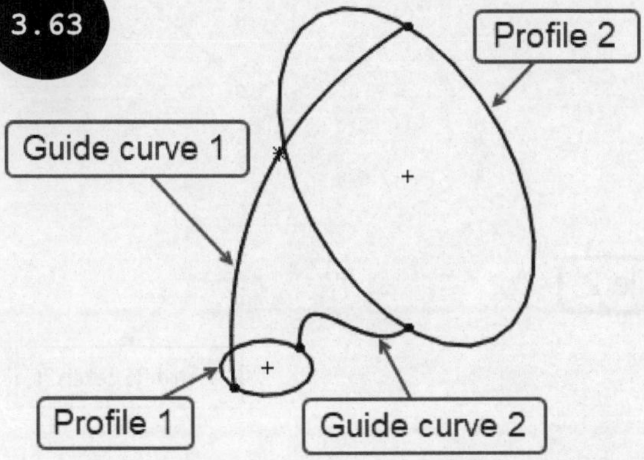

3.64

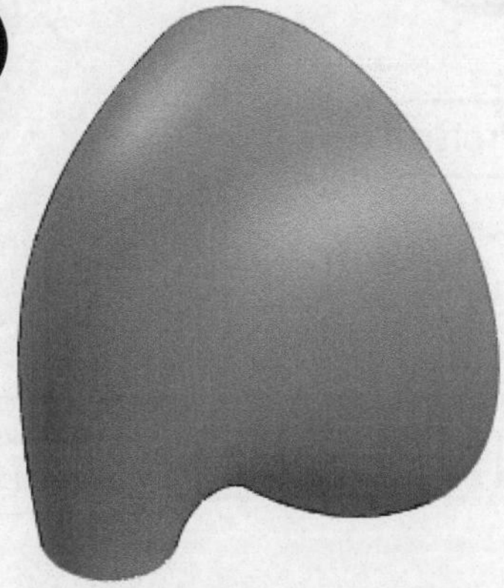

1. Create all the required sketch profiles and guide curves one by one, as different sketches for creating a loft surface, refer to Figure 3.63.

2. After creating sketch profiles and guide curves, click on the **Lofted Surface** tool in the **Surfaces CommandManager**, see Figure 3.65. The **Surface-Loft PropertyManager** appears, see Figure 3.66.

3.65

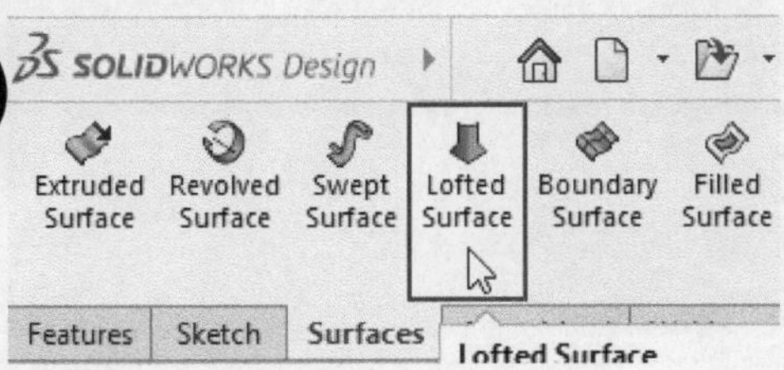

3.66

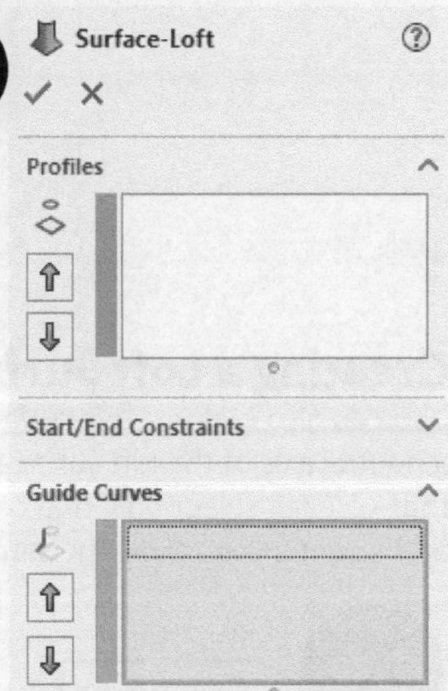

3. Select the sketch profiles of the loft surface one by one in the graphics area. The preview of a loft surface appears, see Figure 3.67. In this figure, two open profiles are selected. You can select multiple similar or dissimilar closed or open sketch profiles for creating a loft surface.

   Now, you can select the guide curves to guide the cross-sectional shape of the loft surface.

4. Click on the **Guide Curves** field in the **Guide Curves** rollout and then select the guide curves in the graphics area one by one. The preview of the loft surface gets modified such that the cross-sectional shape of the surface is guided by the selected guide curves, see Figure 3.68. In this figure, two guide curves are selected.

3.67

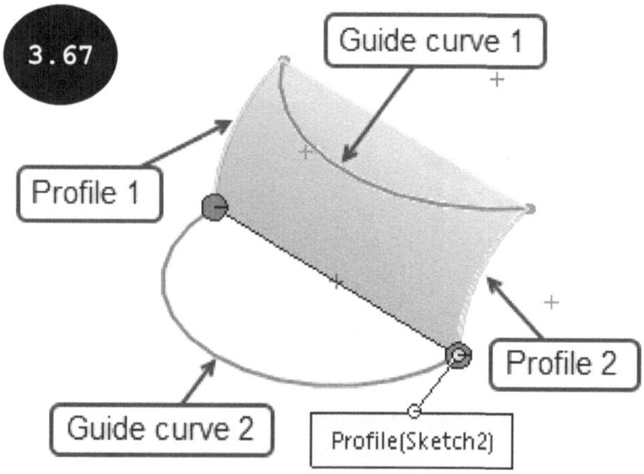

3.68

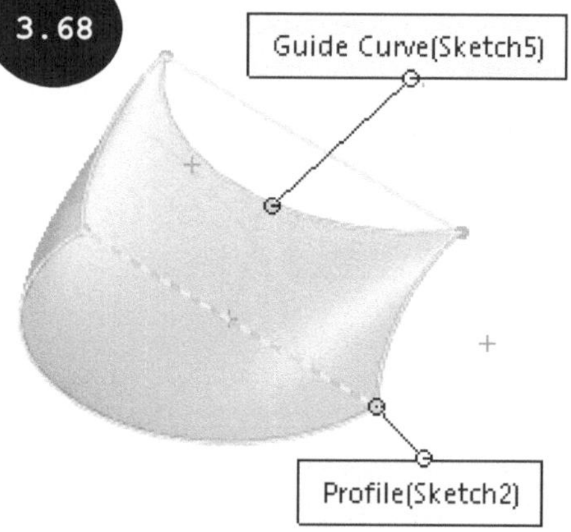

5. Click on the green tick-mark button in the PropertyManager to accept the preview of a loft surface. A loft surface with profiles and guide curves is created, see Figure 3.69.

3.69

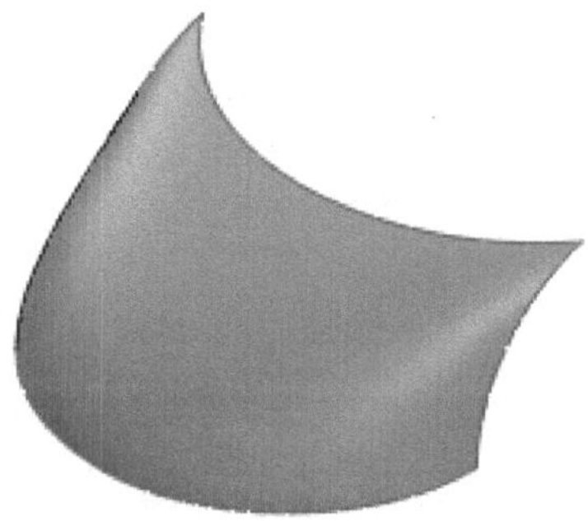

Creating a Loft Surface with Profiles and Centerline

You can also create a loft surface with profiles and a centerline. A centerline is used for maintaining a neutral axis of the loft surface and consistent transition between the profiles, see Figure 3.70. Note that you can select only one centerline to create a loft surface. To create a loft surface with profiles and a centerline, follow the steps given below:

3.70

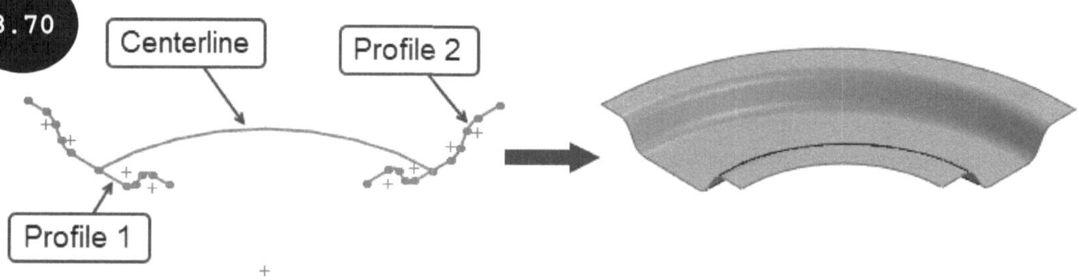

1. Create all the required sketch profiles and a centerline as different sketches one by one for creating a loft surface, refer to Figure 3.70.

2. Click on the **Lofted Surface** tool in the **Surfaces CommandManager**. The **Surface-Loft PropertyManager** appears.

3. Select the profiles of the loft surface in the graphics area one by one. The preview of a loft surface appears, see Figure 3.71.

3.71

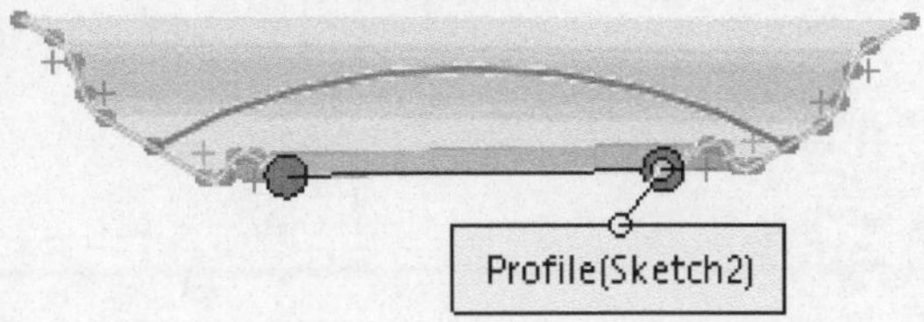

Now, you can select a centerline for maintaining a neutral axis of the loft surface.

4. Expand the **Centerline Parameters** rollout of the PropertyManager for selecting a centerline.

5. Select a centerline for the loft surface in the graphics area. The preview of a loft surface appears such that its intermediate sections become normal to the centerline, see Figure 3.72.

6. Click on the green tick-mark ✓ button in the PropertyManager to accept the preview of a loft surface. A loft surface with profiles and a centerline gets created, see Figure 3.73.

3.72

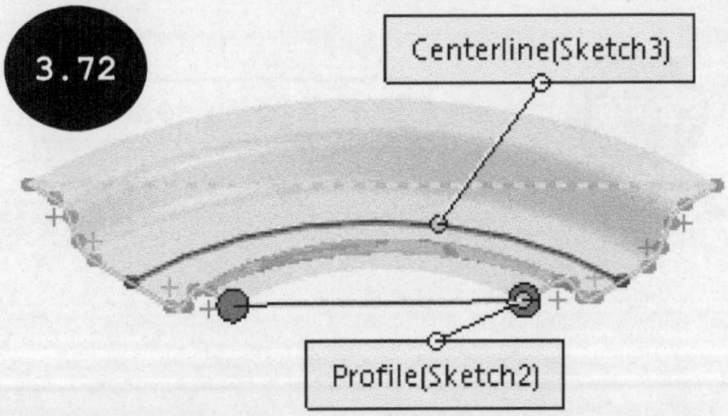

3.73

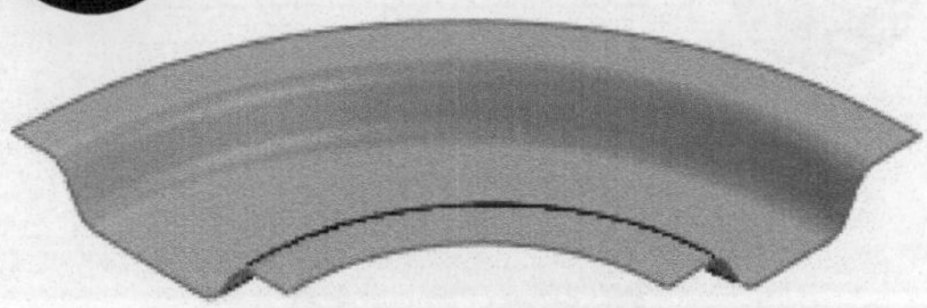

Creating a Filled Surface

A filled surface is used for filling a gap or an open area defined by end-to-end connected edges of an existing surface or a loop of 2D or 3D curves and sketches. It is also known as a boundary patch. Figure 3.74 shows a closed area to be filled and the resultant model after filling the closed area by creating a filled surface. The method for creating a filled surface is discussed below:

3.74

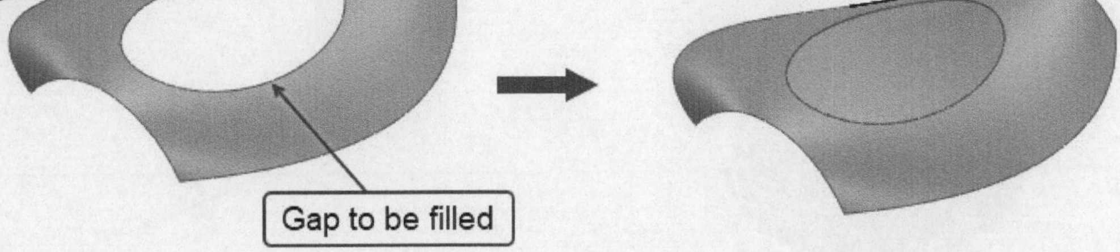

1. Click on the **Filled Surface** tool in the **Surfaces CommandManager**, see Figure 3.75. The **Fill Surface PropertyManager** appears, see Figure 3.76.

3.75

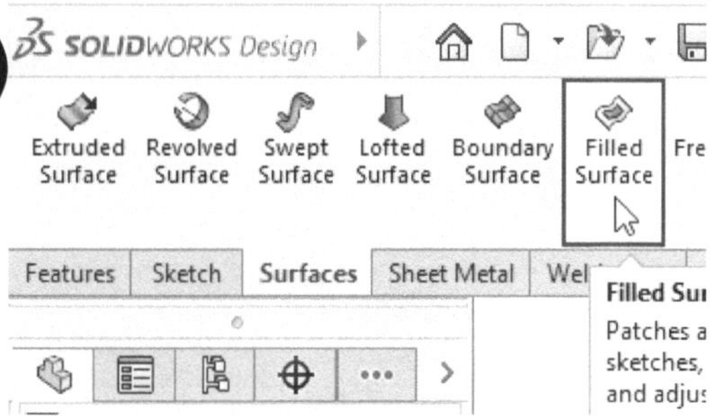

3.76

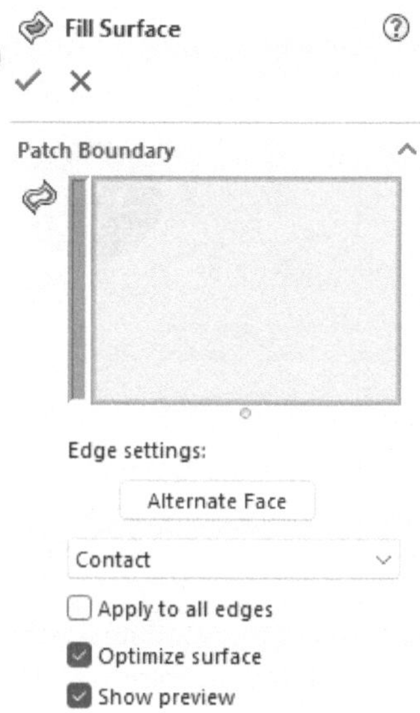

2. Select a loop of closed edges, curves, or sketches that define a gap or an open area to be filled, see Figures 3.77 and 3.78. A preview of the filled surface appears in the graphics area, see Figures 3.79 and 3.80.

3.77

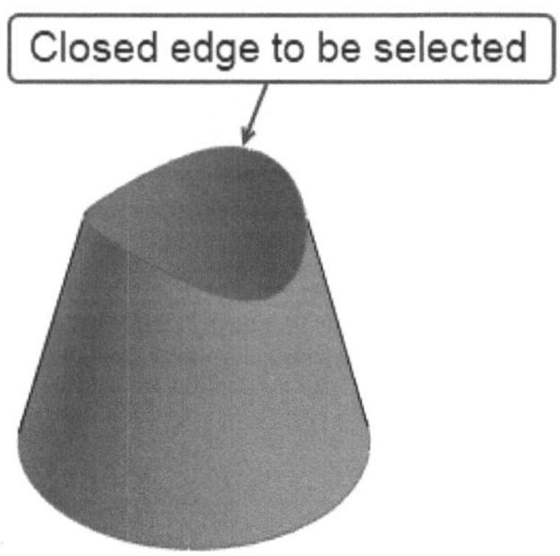

3.78

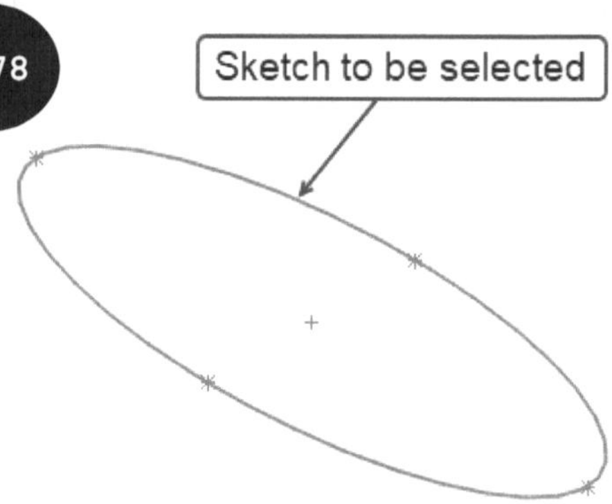

3.79

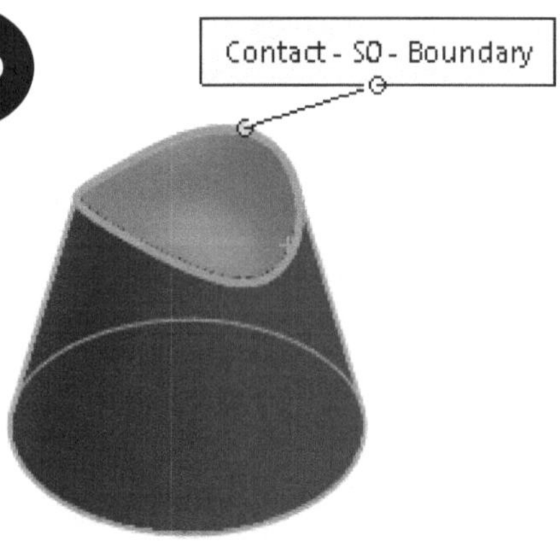

3.80

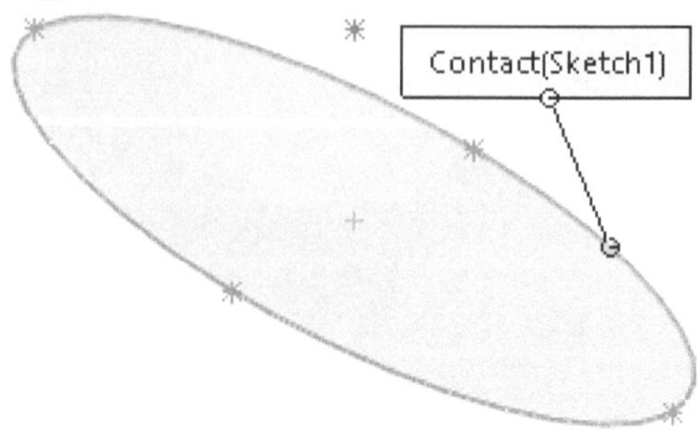

Alternate Face: The **Alternate Face** button is used for flipping the automatic selection of a reference face to control the curvature of the resultant filled surface. Note that the **Alternate Face** button is used only when creating a filled surface on a solid model.

Curvature Control: The options in the **Curvature Control** drop-down list are used for defining the type of control to be applied on the resultant filled surface. The **Contact** option is used for creating a filled surface within the defined boundary. The **Tangent** option is used for creating a filled surface by maintaining the tangency with the selected edges, see Figure 3.81. The **Curvature** option is used for creating a filled surface by maintaining the curvature continuity with the adjacent faces of the selected edges.

Optimize surface: The **Optimize surface** check box is used for creating a simplified filled surface along the selected edges. Note that a simplified filled surface is created in less time with faster model rebuild time. When this check box is cleared, the **Resolution Control** rollout displays in the PropertyManager with a Slider, see Figure 3.82. This Slider is used for specifying the resolution of the filled surface to be created. The higher the resolution, the better the quality of the filled surface. However, the time taken to rebuild the model will increase.

3.81

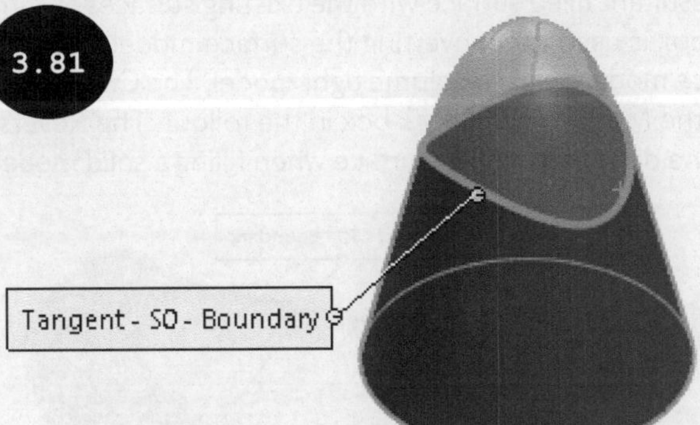

3.82

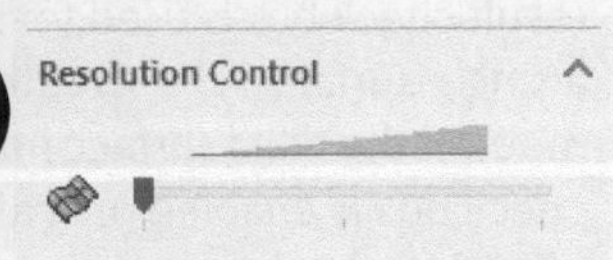

Show preview: The **Show preview** check box is used for displaying a shaded preview of the resultant filled surface in the graphics area.

Constraint Curves: The **Constraint Curves** rollout is used for selecting one or more splines or sketch points as the constraint curves for controlling the slope of the filled surface, see Figures 3.83 and 3.84. In Figure 3.83, a spline is selected as a constraint curve, and in Figure 3.84, a sketch point is selected as a constraint curve.

3.83

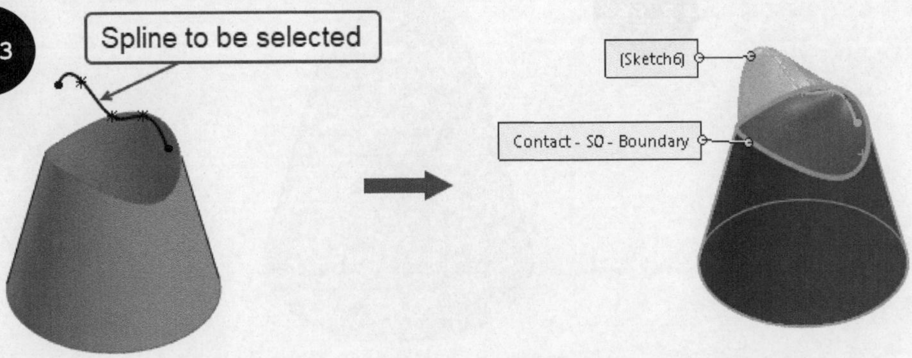

3.84

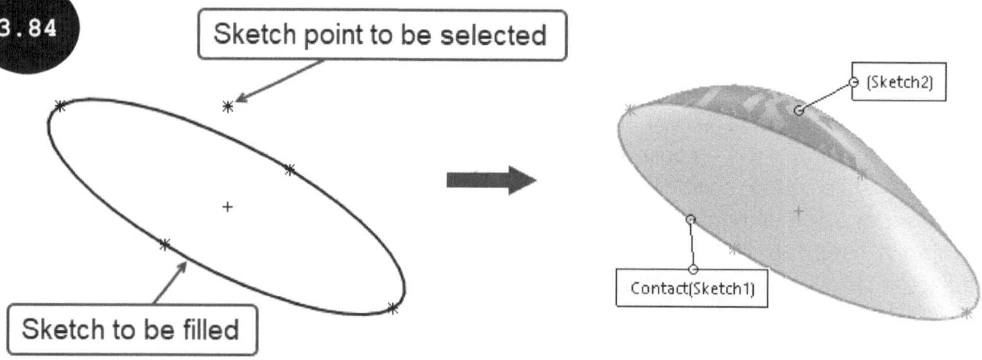

Options: The **Fix up boundary** check box in the **Options** rollout is used for automatically fixing issues (missing pieces) of an open boundary by making it a closed boundary for creating a filled surface, see Figure 3.85 This figure shows an open boundary with a missing surface piece and a preview of the resultant filled surface after selecting the **Fix up boundary** check box. The **Merge result** check box is used for merging the resultant filled surface with the existing surfaces to form a single surface. The **Create solid** check box is used for converting the surface model to a solid model if the filled surface makes the surface model a closed volume tight model. The **Create solid** check box is enabled only after selecting the **Merge result** check box in the rollout. The **Reverse direction** check box is used for reversing the direction of filled surface when filling a solid model.

3.85

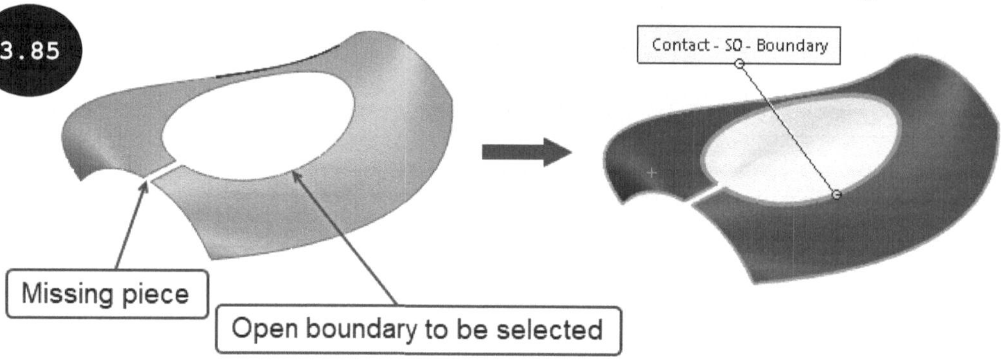

3. Click on the green tick-mark ✓ button in the PropertyManager to accept the preview of a filled surface. A filled surface is created, see Figure 3.86.

3.86

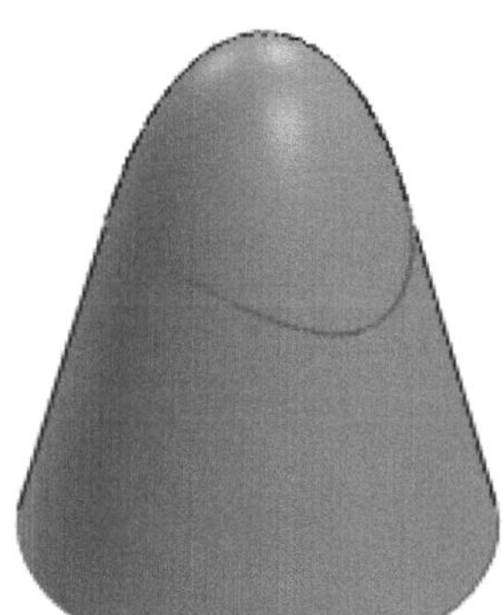

Creating a Planar Surface

A planar surface is used for filling a planar boundary or gap defined by a set of end-to-end connected edges of an existing surface or a loop of 2D closed sketches. It is also known as a planar patch. The main difference between the planar surface and the filled surface discussed earlier is that the planar surface uses a planar patch (2D) to fill a gap. It can't fill a gap that is defined by a 3D curve or a 3D sketch, unlike the filled surface. Figure 3.87 shows a set of end-to-end connected bottom edges to be selected as a planar boundary to be filled and the resultant planar surface created. The method for creating a planar surface is discussed below:

3.87

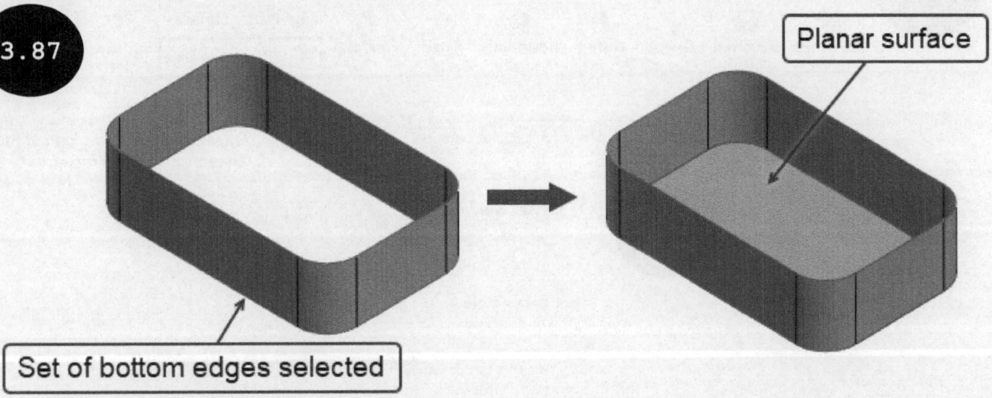

1. Click on the **Planar Surface** tool in the **Surfaces CommandManager**, see Figure 3.88. The **Planar Surface PropertyManager** appears, see Figure 3.89.

3.88

2. Select end-to-end connected edges of a surface or a 2D closed sketch as a planar boundary to be filled in the graphics area. A preview of a planar surface appears, see Figure 3.90.

3.89

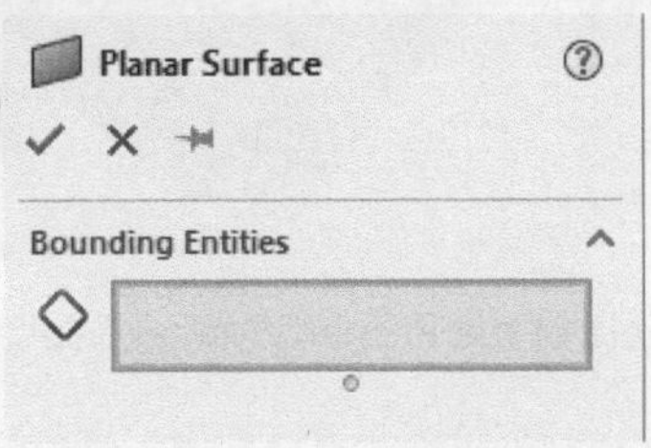

3.90

3. Click on the green tick-mark ✓ button in the PropertyManager to accept the preview of a planar surface. A planar surface is created.

Offsetting a Surface

In SOLIDWORKS, you can offset an existing surface at a specified offset distance and create a new surface. The method for offsetting a surface is discussed below:

1. Click on the **Offset Surface** tool in the **Surfaces CommandManager**, see Figure 3.91. The **Offset Surface PropertyManager** appears, see Figure 3.92.

3.91

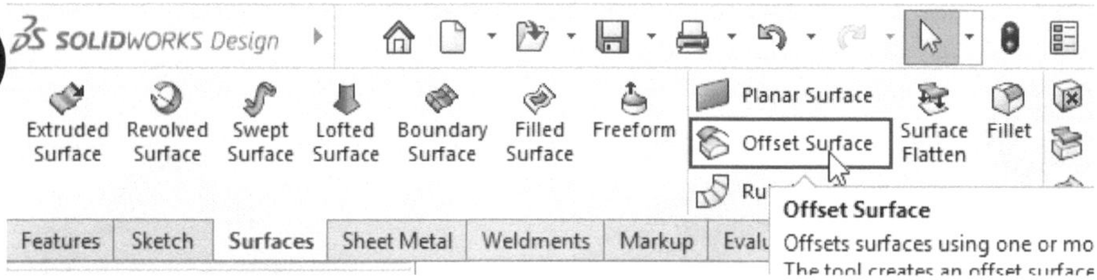

3.92

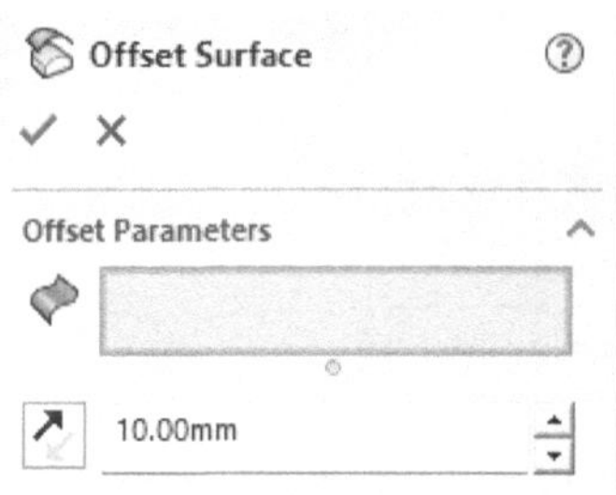

2. Select one or more surfaces to be offset in the graphics area, see Figure 3.93. A preview of an offset surface appears in the graphics area with the default specified offset distance, see Figure 3.94.

3.93

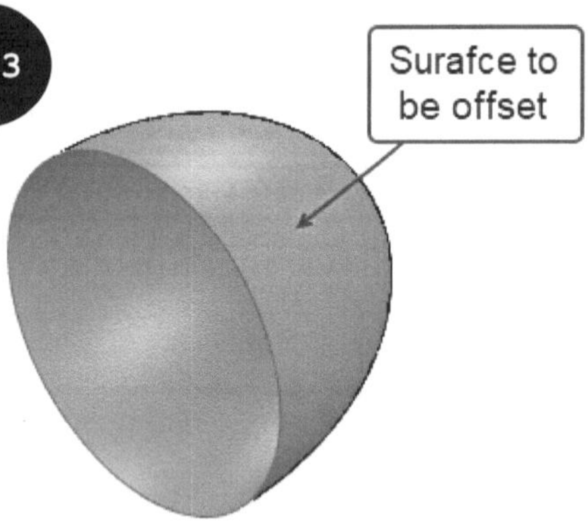

3.94

3. Enter an offset distance value in the **Offset Distance** field of the PropertyManager, as required.

4. Click on the **Flip Offset Direction** button to reverse the direction of the offset in the graphics area, if needed.

5. Click on the green tick-mark button in the PropertyManager. A new surface at a specified offset distance is created in the graphics area.

Creating a Ruled Surface

A ruled surface is created by adding an extension to existing surfaces along their edges at a specified distance and angle, see Figure 3.95. Generally, it is used as a parting surface while designing a mold for extracting the core and cavity. The method for creating a ruled surface is discussed below:

3.95

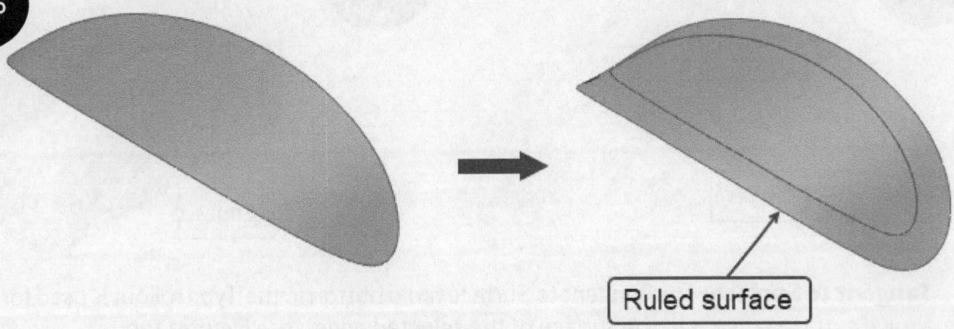

1. Click on the **Ruled Surface** tool in the **Surfaces CommandManager**, see Figure 3.96. The **Ruled Surface PropertyManager** appears, see Figure 3.97. Also, you are prompted to select edges for creating a ruled surface, since the **Edges** field is activated in the **Edge Selection** rollout of the PropertyManager, by default.

3.96

3.97

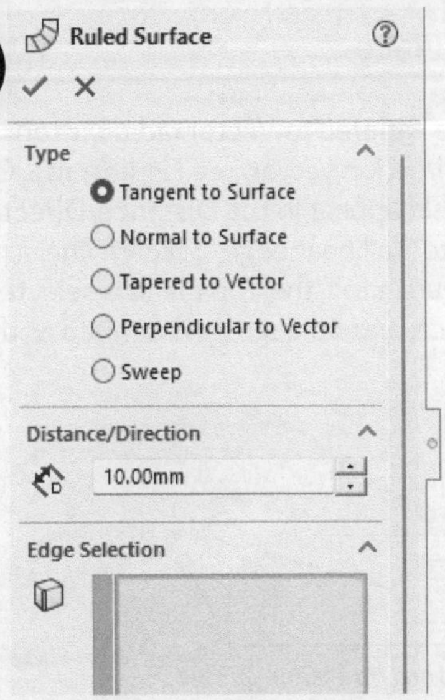

2. Click one or more edges of an existing surface to create a ruled surface. A preview of a ruled surface appears in the graphics area, see Figures 3.98 and 3.99. Also, the names of the selected edges appear in the **Edges** field of the **Edge Selection** rollout. In Figure 3.98, only 1 edge is selected and in Figure 3.99, a total of 8 edges are selected.

3.98

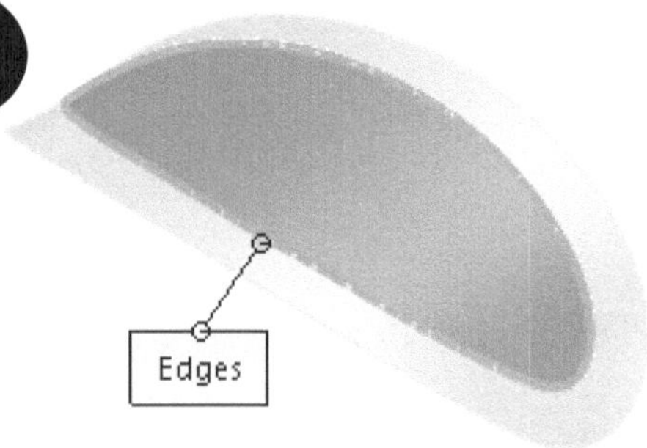

3.99

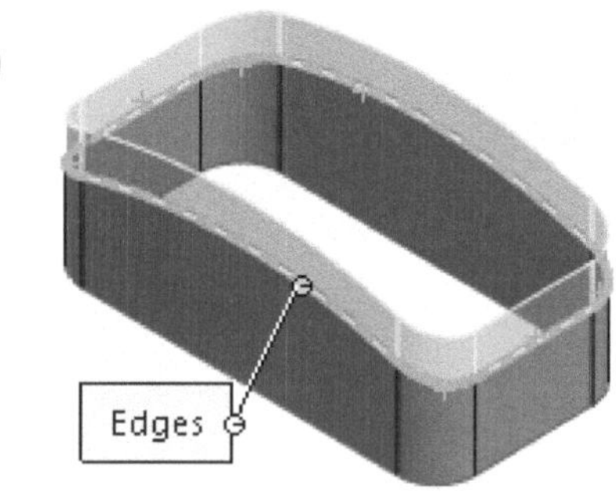

Tangent to Surface: The **Tangent to Surface** radio button in the **Type** rollout is used for creating a ruled surface tangent to the surface of the selected edges, see Figure 3.100.

Normal to Surface: The **Normal to Surface** radio button is used for creating a ruled surface normal to the surface of the selected edges, see Figure 3.101.

3.100

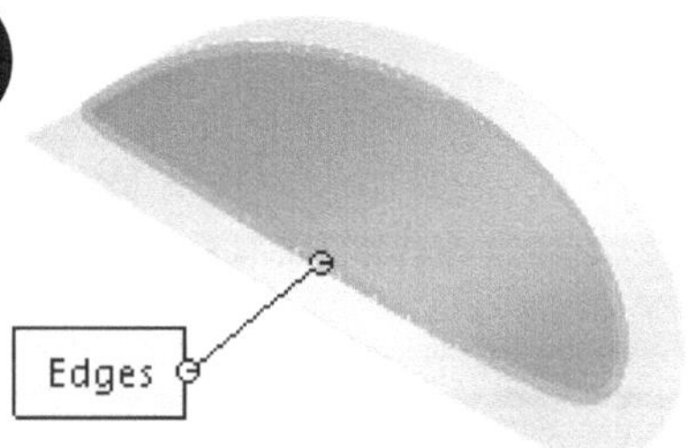

Tangent to surface

3.101

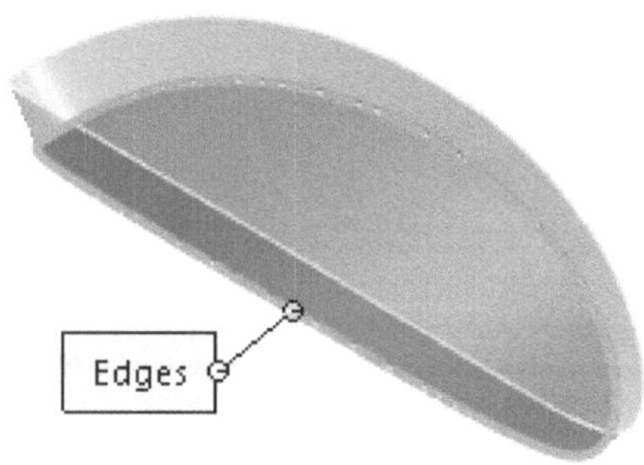

Normal to surface

Tapered to Vector: The **Tapered to Vector** radio button is used for creating a ruled surface at an angle to a user defined direction vector, see Figure 3.102. On selecting this option, the **Reference Vector** field and **Angle** field appear in the **Distance/Direction** rollout of the PropertyManager for selecting a direction vector (a linear edge, a sketch line, a plane, or an axis) and defining an angle value, respectively. In Figure 3.102, the Top plane is selected as a direction vector for defining the direction of a ruled surface, and 60 degrees is defined as the angle value.

3.102

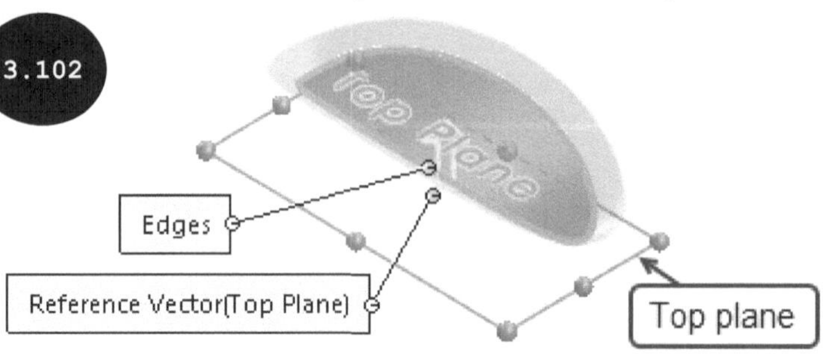

Perpendicular to Vector: The Perpendicular to Vector radio button is used for creating a ruled surface perpendicular to a direction vector (a linear edge, a line, a plane, or an axis) selected in the **Reference Vector** field of the **Distance/Direction** rollout.

Sweep: The Sweep radio button is used for creating a ruled surface sweep along a direction vector selected in the **Reference Vector** field.

3. Select the required option (**Tangent to Surface, Normal to Surface, Tapered to Vector, Perpendicular to Vector**, or **Sweep**) in the **Type** rollout of the PropertyManager as a type of a ruled surface to be created, as discussed above.

4. Enter the required extension distance value of the ruled surface in the **Distance** field of the **Distance/Direction** rollout.

5. Click on the **Reverse Direction** button in front of the **Distance** field in the **Distance/Direction** rollout to reverse the direction of the ruled surface, if needed.

Note: The availability of the **Reverse Direction** button depends upon the radio button selected in the **Type** rollout of the PropertyManager.

6. Click on the green tick-mark ✓ button in the PropertyManager. A ruled surface of specified distance and direction gets created.

Creating a Flat Pattern of a Surface

In SOLIDWORKS, you can create a flat pattern of a surface, see Figure 3.103. It defines the flattened shape and size of the surface. The method for creating a flat pattern of a surface is discussed below:

3.103

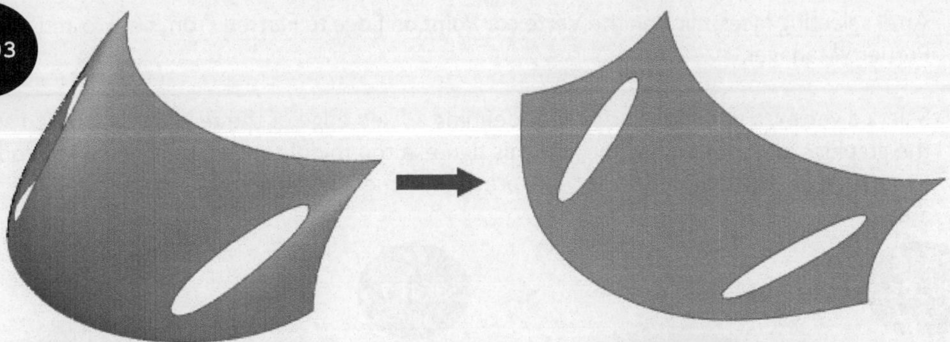

Flat pattern

1. Click on the **Surface Flatten** tool in the **Surfaces CommandManager**, see Figure 3.104. The **Flatten PropertyManager** appears, see Figure 3.105. Also, you are prompted to select a face or a surface, since the **Face/Surface to Flatten** field is activated in the **Selections** rollout of the PropertyManager, by default.

3.104

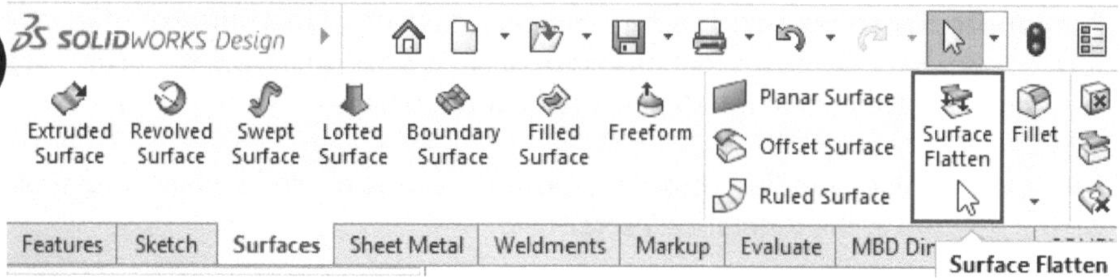

3.105

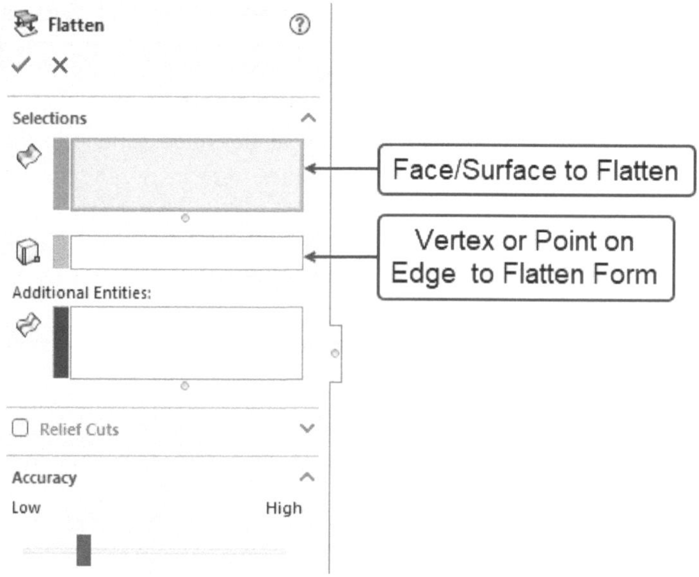

2. Select one or more faces as surface or surfaces to be flattened in the graphics area, see Figure 3.106. In this figure, four faces of a surface are selected.

3. After selecting faces, click on the **Vertex or Point on Edge to Flatten From** field to activate it in the PropertyManager.

4. Select a vertex, a point, or an edge for defining a fixed edge of the resultant flattened surface in the graphics area, see Figure 3.107. In this figure, a top middle vertex is selected for defining the fixed edge of the flattened surface. A preview of the flattened surface appears in the graphics area.

3.106

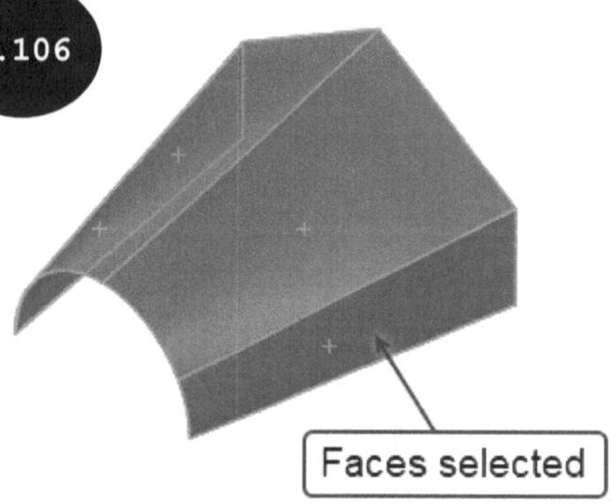

3.107

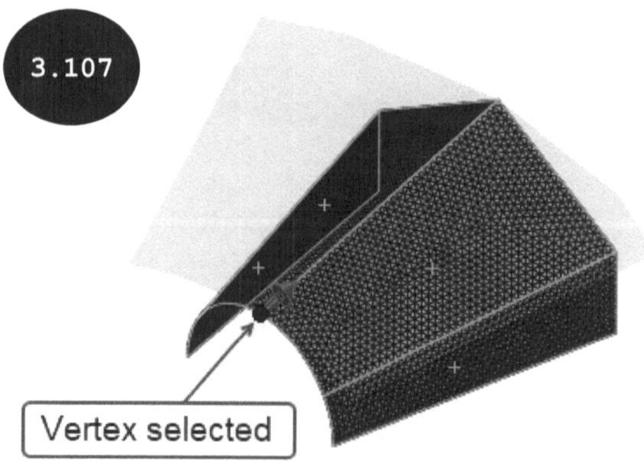

Additional Entities: The Additional Entities field is used for selecting edges of selected faces or surfaces to be included in the resultant flatten surface as sketches or curves.

Accuracy Slider: The Accuracy slider in the **Accuracy** rollout is used for defining the accuracy of the flattened surface. You can slide the slider between **Low** to **High** to specify the accuracy of the flattened surface.

5. Click on the green tick-mark button in the PropertyManager. The flat pattern of the selected faces or surfaces gets created in the graphics area, see Figure 3.108.

Note: You can hide the display of the original surface in the graphics area, see Figure 3.109. To do so, select a surface to be hidden in the graphics area or in the FeatureManager Design Tree and then click on the **Hide** tool in the Pop-up toolbar that appears.

3.108

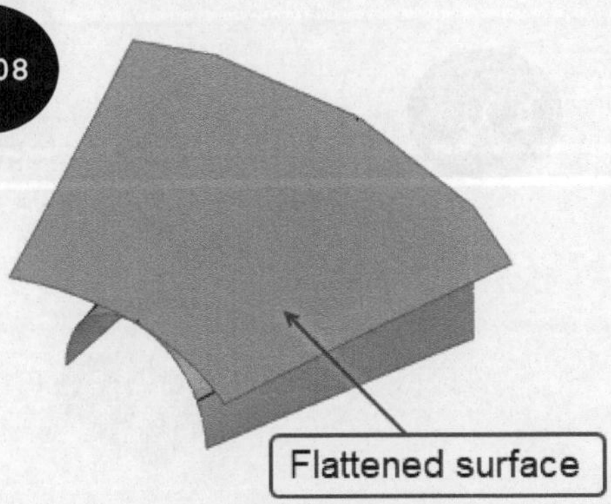

3.109

Extending a Surface

In SOLIDWORKS, you can extend a surface along one or more of its selected edges. The method for extending a surface is discussed below:

1. Click on the **Extend Surface** tool in the **Surfaces CommandManager**, see Figure 3.110. The **Extend Surface PropertyManager** appears, see Figure 3.111. Also, you are prompted to select one or more edges or faces, since the **Selected Face/Edges** field is activated in the **Edges/Faces to Extend** rollout, by default.

3.110

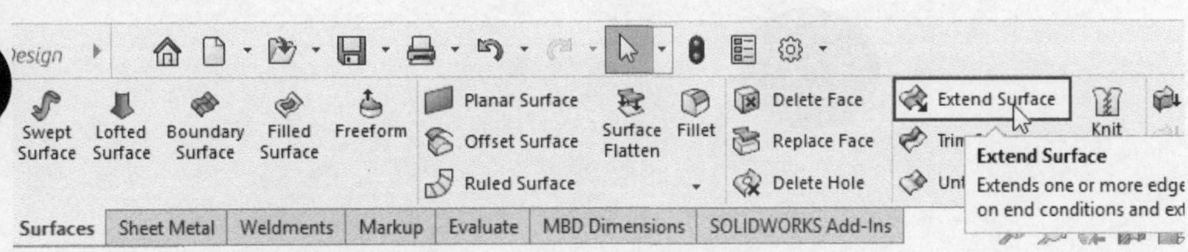

3.111

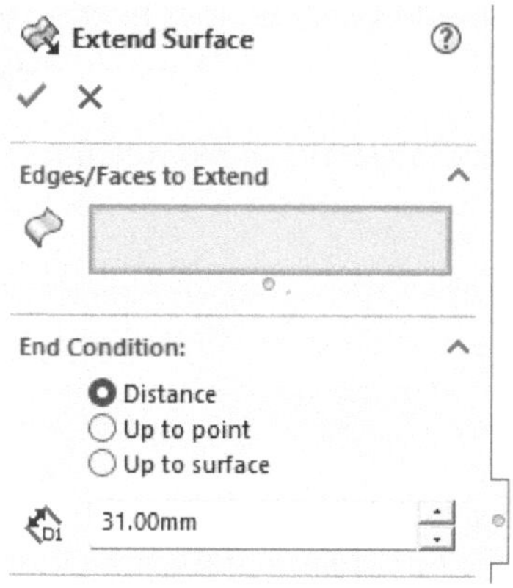

2. Select an edge or a face of a surface in the graphics area. A preview of an extended surface appears, see Figures 3.112 and 3.113. You can select one or more edges or faces to be extended, as required.

3.112

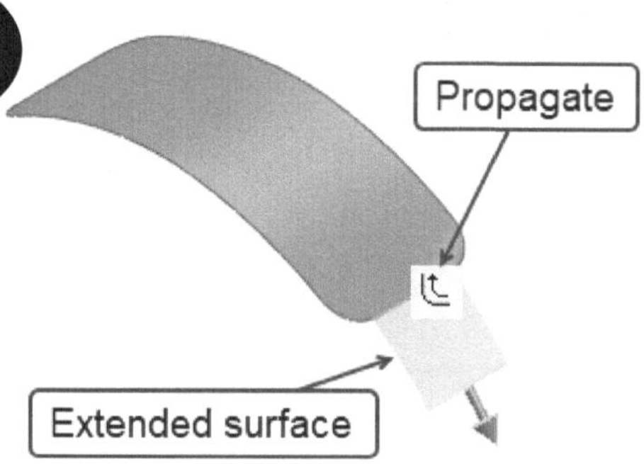

3.113

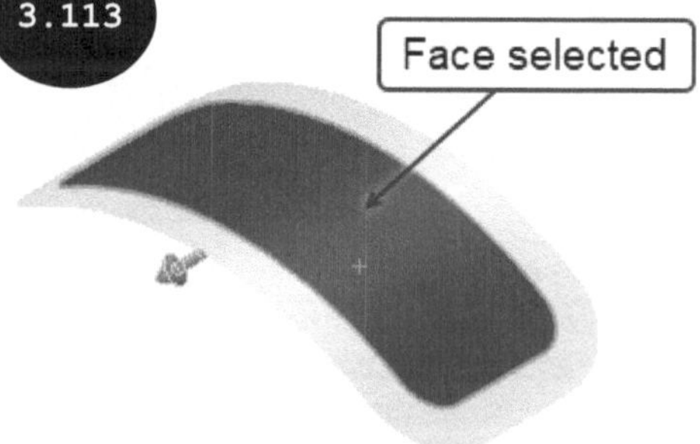

Note: On selecting an edge, the preview of an extended surface appears along the selected edge with the display of **Propagate** button in the graphics area, refer to Figure 3.112. On clicking this **Propagate** button, the extension of the surface appears along all the tangentially connected edges, see Figure 3.114. It is a toggle button.

On selecting a face, the extension of the surface appears along all its edges, refer to Figure 3.113.

3.114

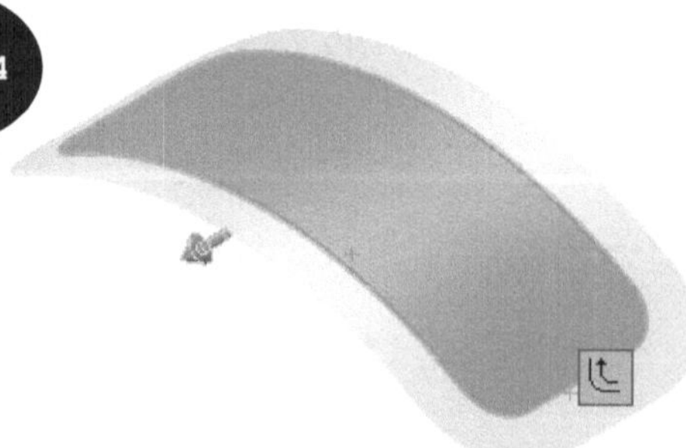

End Condition: The **Distance** radio button in the **End Condition** rollout is used for extending the surface by specifying a distance value in the **Distance** field of the rollout. The **Up to point** radio button is used for extending the surface up to a selected point or a vertex. On selecting this radio button, the **Vertex** field appears for selecting a point or a vertex for defining the end condition. The **Up to surface** radio button is used for extending the surface up to a selected surface or a face by using the **Surface/Face** field that appears in the rollout when this radio button is selected.

3. Select the required radio button (**Distance, Up to point**, or **Up to surface**) for defining the end condition of the extension, as discussed above.

Extension Type: The **Same surface** radio button in the **Extension Type** rollout is used for extending the surface along the selected edge by maintaining the same continuity as that of the geometry of the surface, see Figure 3.115. The **Linear** radio button is used for extending the surface linearly along the selected edge of the original surface, see Figure 3.116.

3.115

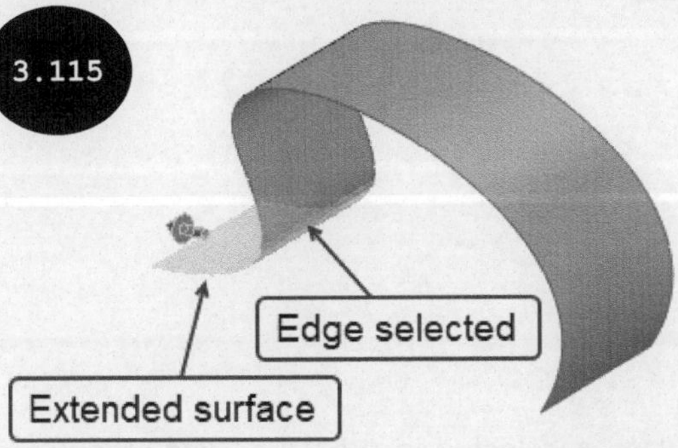

3.116

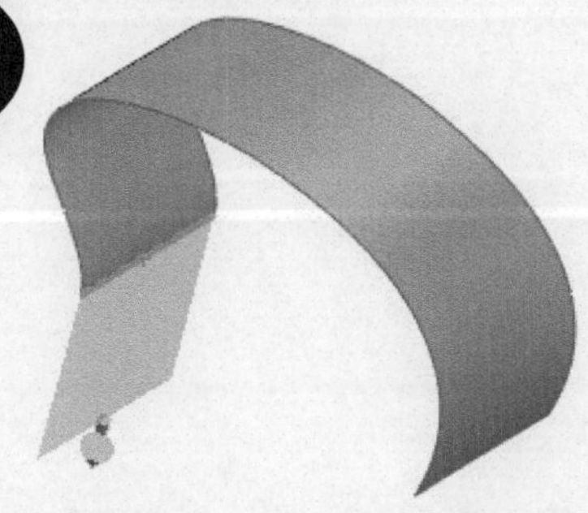

4. Select the required radio button (**Same surface** or **Linear**) as the extension type, as discussed above.

5. Click on the green tick-mark button in the PropertyManager. The surface gets extended along the selected edge or edges.

Trimming a Surface

You can trim a surface by removing a portion or an area using an object as a trim tool, see Figure 3.117. In this figure, a surface is selected as a trim tool. In SOLIDWORKS, you can trim a surface by using two methods: Standard and Manual. Both these methods for trimming a surface are discussed next.

3.117

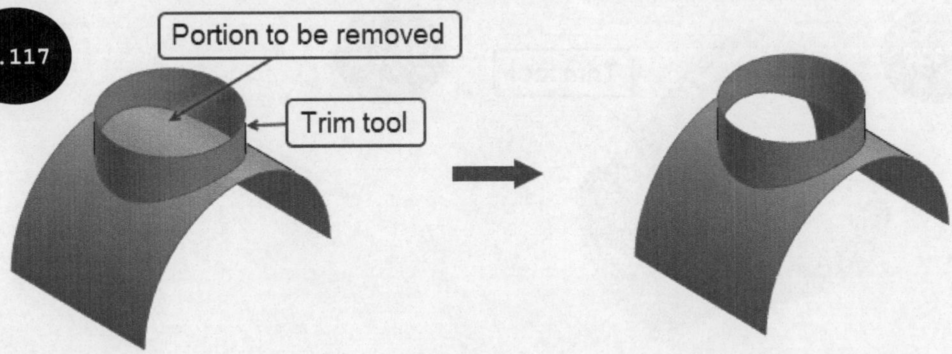

Trimming a Surface by using the Standard Method

1. Click on the **Trim Surface** tool in the **Surfaces CommandManager**, see Figure 3.118. The **Trim Surface PropertyManager** appears, see Figure 3.119.

3.118

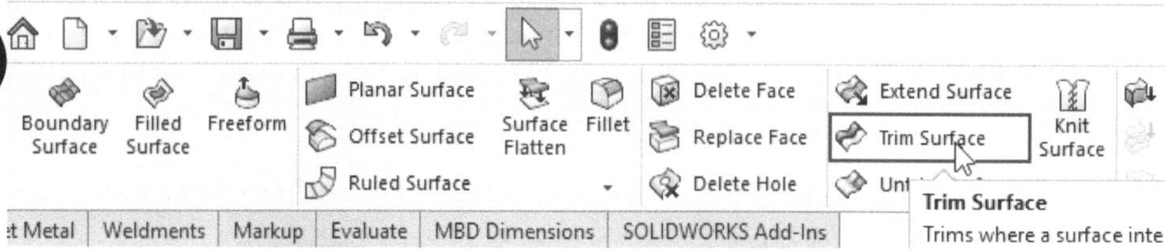

3.119

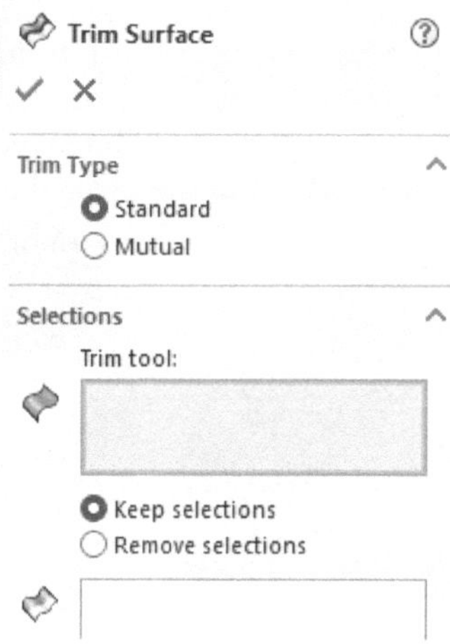

Standard: By default, the **Standard** radio button is selected in the **Trim Type** rollout as a trimming method. In this method, you need to select a trim tool for trimming a surface at its intersection. The method for trimming a surface by using the Standard method is discussed below:

2. Ensure that the **Standard** radio button is selected in the **Trim Type** rollout of the PropertyManager as the trimming method.

3. Select a surface, a curve, a sketch, or an edge as a trim tool, see Figures 3.120 and 3.121. In Figure 3.120, a surface is selected as a trim tool, and in Figure 3.121, a sketch is selected as a trim tool. The name of the object selected as a trim tool appears in the **Trim tool** field of the **Selections** rollout.

3.120

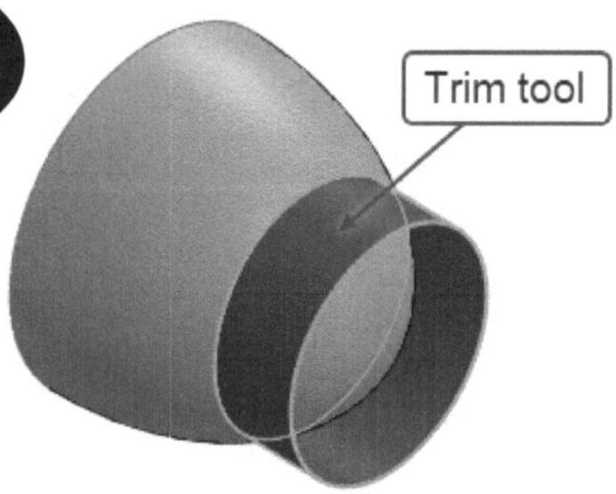

3.121

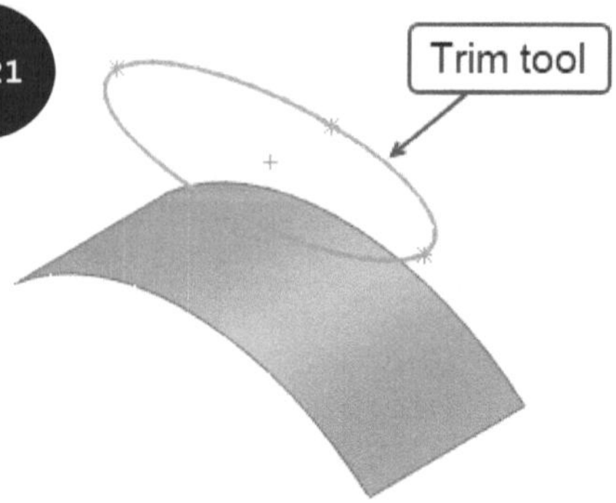

Keep selections: The **Keep selections** radio button is used for selecting a portion of a surface to be kept at the intersection with the trim tool selected.

Remove selections: The **Remove selections** radio button is used for selecting a portion of a surface to be removed at the intersection with the trim tool selected.

Surface Split Options: The **Natural** radio button in the **Surface Split Options** rollout is used for extending the end of the selected trim tool tangentially up to the next intersecting edge of the surface for keeping or removing either side of the surface, see Figure 3.122. The **Linear** radio button is used for extending the end of the selected trim tool linearly up to the nearest edge of the surface for keeping or removing either side of the surface, see Figure 3.123. Note that both these options work better if the trim tool does not completely pass through the surface.

3.122

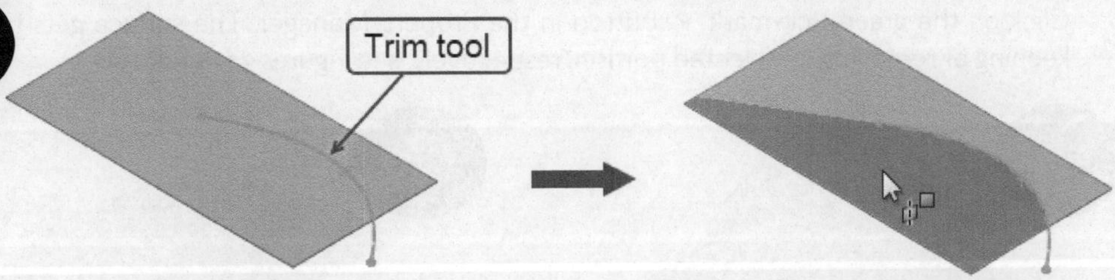

Natural radio button is selected

3.123

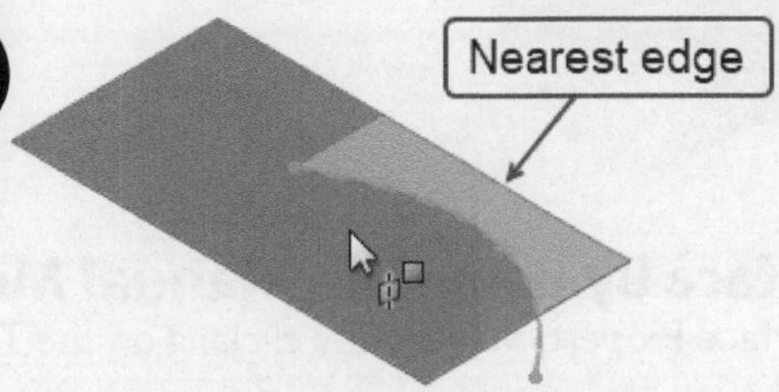

Linear radio button is selected

Note: If the **Split All** check box is selected, the surface gets split into multiple portions about the trim tool depending upon whether the **Natural** or **Linear** radio button is selected for keeping or removing one or more of its split portions.

4. Select the required radio button (**Keep selections** or **Remove selections**) in the **Selections** rollout.

5. Select a portion of a surface to be kept or removed at the intersection with the trim tool depending upon whether the **Keep selections** or **Remove selections** radio button is selected, see Figures 3.124 and 3.125.

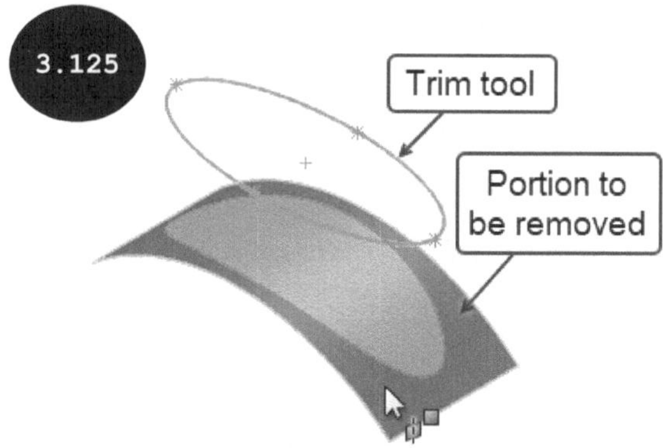

6. Click on the green tick-mark button in the PropertyManager. The surface gets trimmed by keeping or removing its selected portion, respectively, see Figures 3.126 and 3.127.

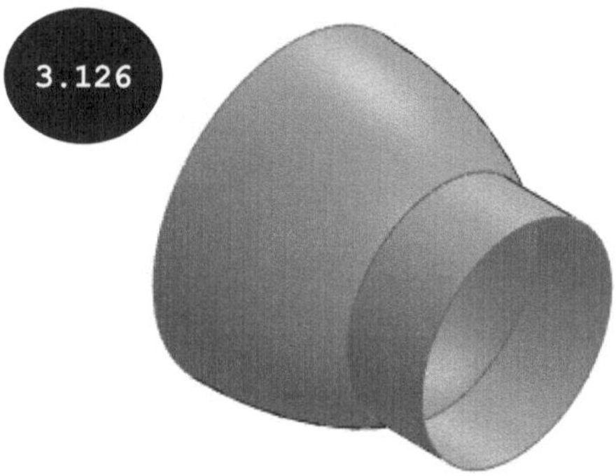

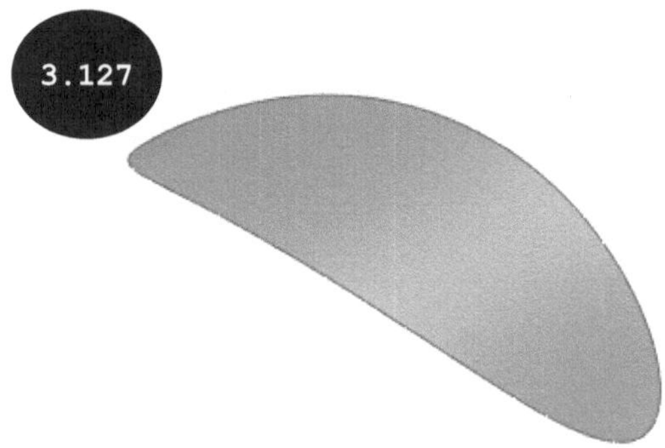

Trimming a Surface by using the Manual Method

1. Invoke the **Trim Surface PropertyManager** by clicking on the **Trim Surface** tool in the **Surfaces** CommandManager.

   Mutual: The **Mutual** radio button is used for trimming a portion of a surface at the intersection of two selected surfaces. In this method, you need to select two trimming surfaces in the graphics. The method for trimming a surface by using the Standard method is discussed below:

2. Select the **Mutual** radio button in the **Trim Type** rollout of the PropertyManager as the trimming method.

3. Select two surfaces in the graphics area one by one as the trimming surfaces, see Figure 3.128. The names of the selected surfaces appear in the **Surfaces** field of the Selections rollout.

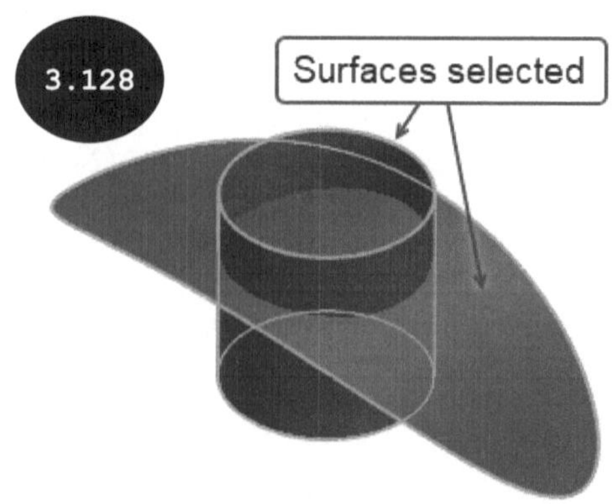

4. Select the required radio button (**Keep selections** or **Remove selections**) in the Selections rollout of the PropertyManager.

5. Select one or more portions of the selected surfaces to be kept or removed at the intersection depending upon whether the **Keep selections** or **Remove selections** radio button is selected, see Figures 3.129 and 3.130.

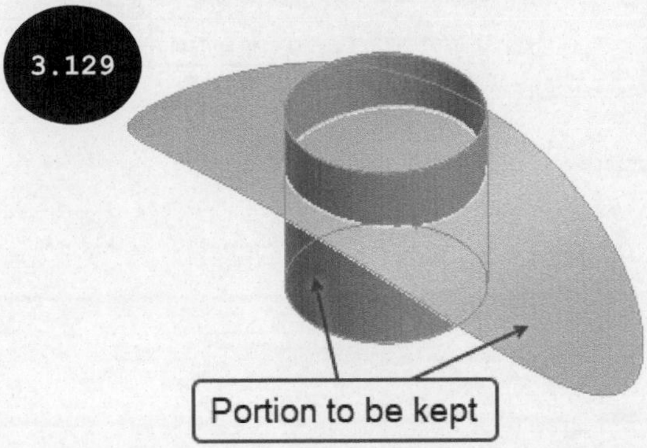

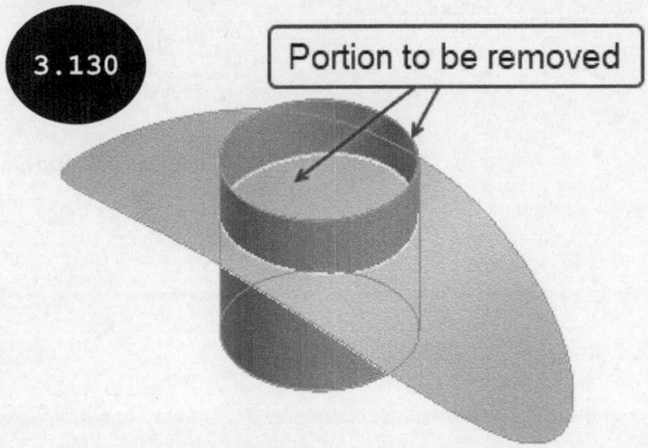

6. Click on the green tick-mark button in the PropertyManager. The surface gets trimmed by keeping or removing the selected portions, respectively, see Figure 3.131.

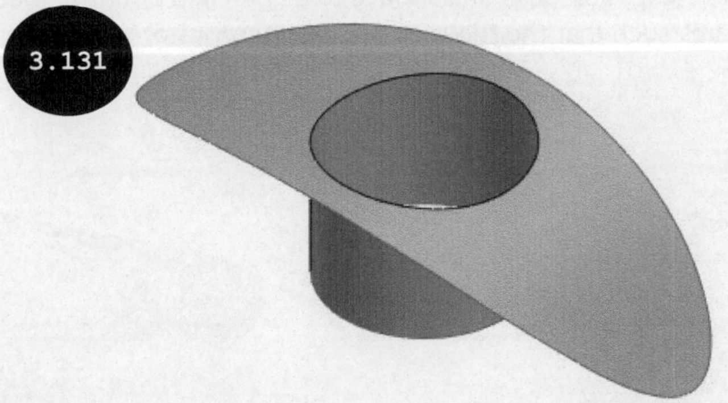

Untrimming a Surface

You can patch surface holes and external trimmed edges of a selected surface by using the **Untrim Surface** tool, see Figure 3.132. The method for patching or untrimming a surface is discussed below:

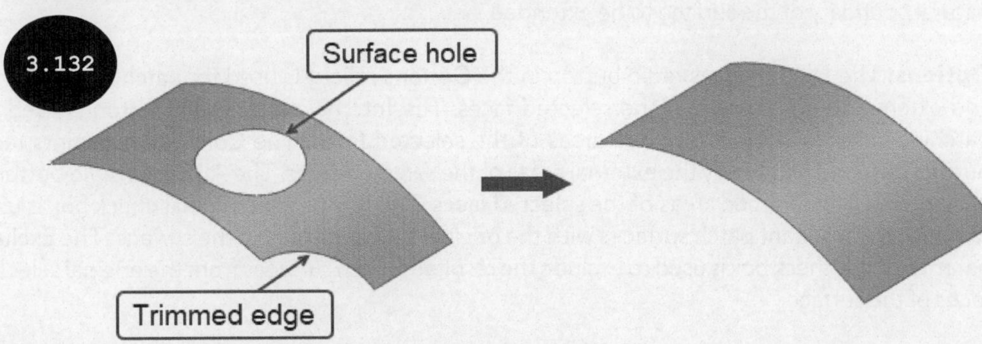

1. Click on the **Untrim Surface** tool in the **Surfaces CommandManager**, see Figure 3.133. The **Untrim Surface PropertyManager** appears, see Figure 3.134.

3.133

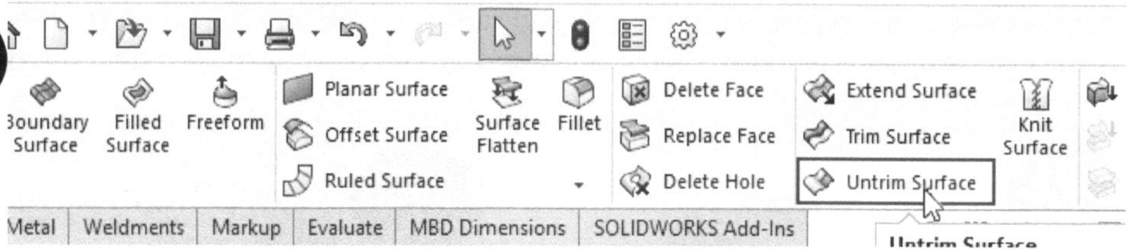

3.134

2. Select one or more edges or faces of a surface to be patched or untrimmed. A preview appears in the graphics area such that the trimmed areas or portions of the selected faces get patched, see Figure 3.135.

3.135

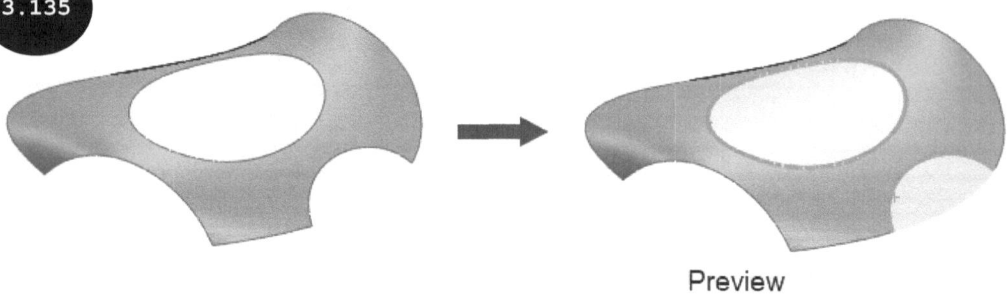

Distance: The **Distance** field in the **Selections** rollout is used for entering a percentage of the natural boundary of the surface to be extended.

Options: The **Extend edges** radio button in the **Options** rollout is used for patching all internal and external trimmed areas of the selected faces. The **Internal edges** radio button is used for patching only the internal trimmed areas of the selected faces. The **Connect endpoints** radio button is used to patch only the external areas of the selected faces. The **All Edges** radio button is used to patch all trimmed areas of the selected faces. The **Merge with original** check box is used to merge the resultant patch surfaces with the original selected faces of the surface. The **Exclude parent surface** check box is used to exclude the resultant patch surfaces from the original selected faces of the surface.

3. Ensure that the **Extend edges** radio button is selected in the **Options** rollout of the PropertyManager for patching all internal and external trimmed areas of the selected surface.

4. Click on the green tick-mark button in the PropertyManager. The surface gets patched, see Figure 3.136.

3.136

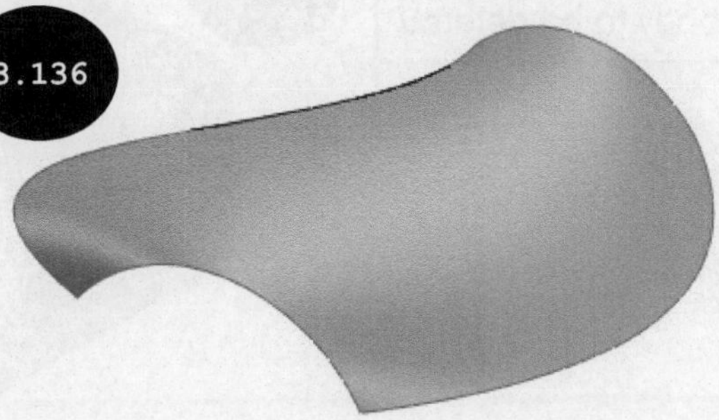

Deleting a Face

You can delete one or more faces of a surface or a solid body by using the **Delete Face** tool. Note that after you delete the face of a solid body, it becomes a surface body. The method for deleting the face of a surface and solid bodies is discussed below:

1. Click on the **Delete Face** tool in the **Surfaces CommandManager**, see Figure 3.137. The **Delete Face PropertyManager** appears, see Figure 3.138.

3.137

3.138

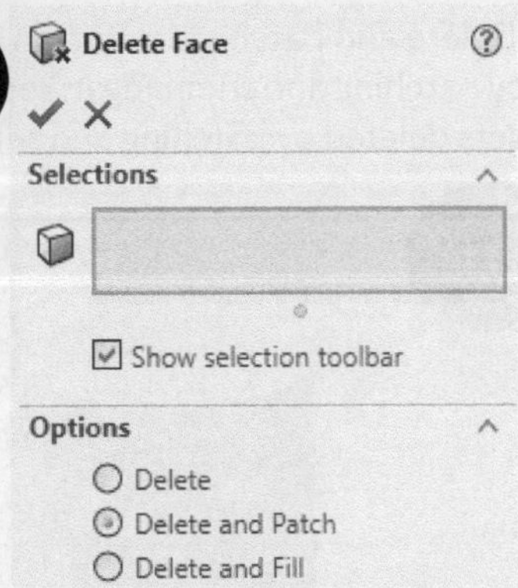

2. Select a face of a surface or a solid body to be deleted, see Figures 3.139 and 3.140. The name of the selected face appears in the **Faces to delete** field of the PropertyManager. You can select one or more faces of a surface body to be deleted. Note that you cannot delete all the faces of a surface body.

Tip: A surface body is created by merging multiple individual surfaces together by using the **Knit Surface** tool. You will learn about knitting multiple surfaces to form a single surface body later in this chapter.

3.139

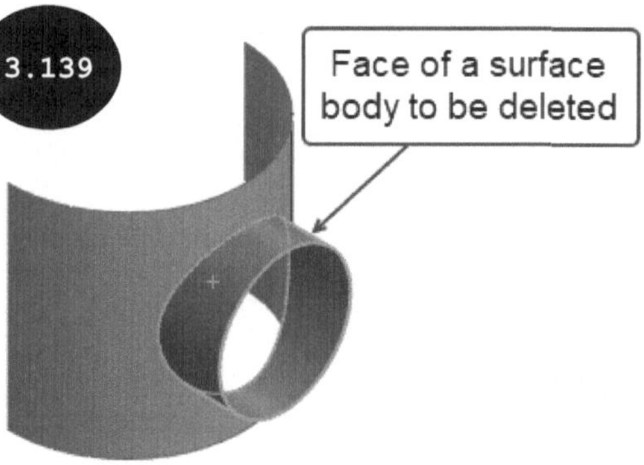

3.140

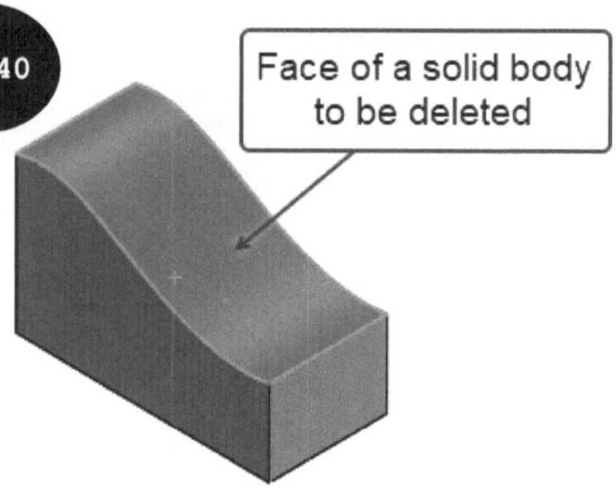

Delete: The **Delete** radio button is used for deleting one or more faces of a surface or a solid body without patching and trimming it, see Figures 3.141 and 3.142. Also, it converts the solid body into a surface body after deleting one or more of its faces.

3.141

3.142

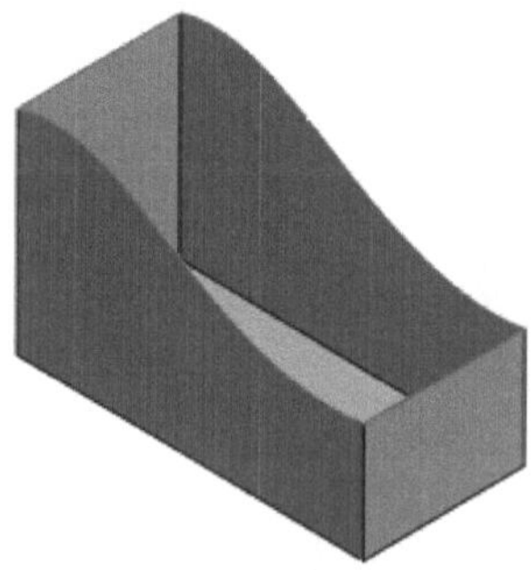

Delete and Patch: The **Delete and Patch** radio button is used for deleting one or more faces of a surface or a solid body by patching and trimming it, see Figures 3.143. In this figure, the selected face of the surface body gets deleted by patching and trimming it.

3.143

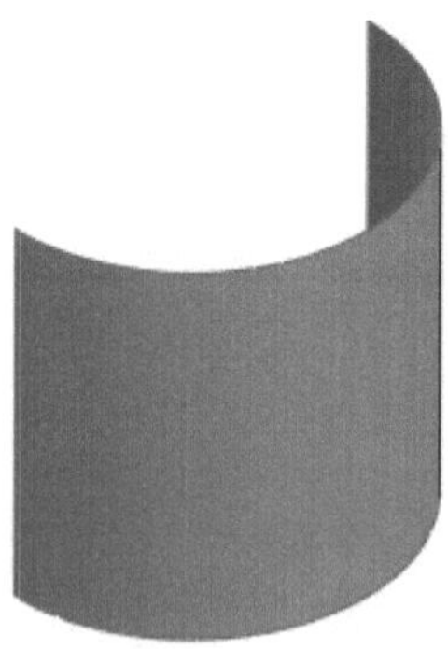

Delete and Fill: The **Delete and Fill** radio button is used for deleting multiple faces of a solid or a surface body by generating a new single face, see Figure 3.144. This figure shows a surface body before and after deleting its three faces by generating a single face when the **Tangent fill** check box is cleared. The **Tangent fill** check box appears in the rollout when the **Delete and Fill** radio button is selected. When the **Tangent fill** check box is selected the generated single face maintains tangency with its adjacent faces.

3.144

3. Click on the green tick-mark ✓ button in the PropertyManager. The selected face or faces get deleted.

Replacing a Face

In SOLIDWORKS, you can replace the face of a surface or a solid body with a new surface body by using the **Replace Face** tool. The method for replacing a face is discussed below:

1. Click on the **Replace Face** tool in the **Surfaces CommandManager**, see Figure 3.145. The **Replace Face PropertyManager** appears, see Figure 3.146.

3.145

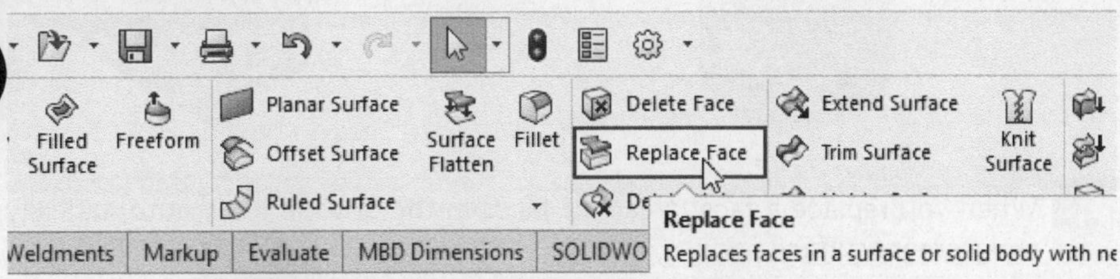

3.146

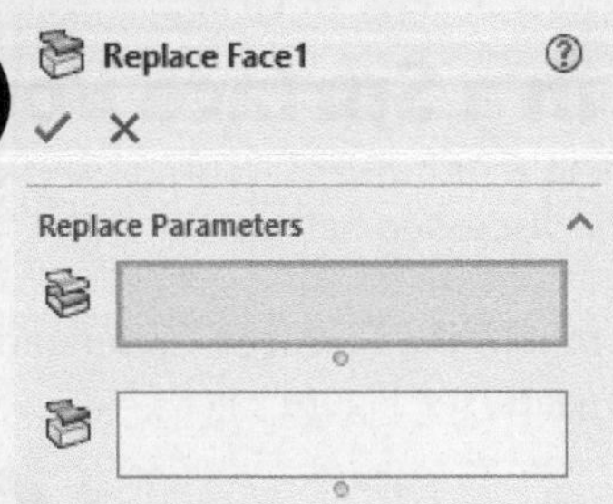

2. Select a face of a surface body or a solid body to be replaced in the graphics area, see Figures 3.147 and 3.148. In Figure 3.147, a face of a surface body is selected and in Figure 3.148, a face of a solid body is selected. The selected face gets highlighted in the graphics area and its name appears in the **Target faces for replacement** field in the PropertyManager.

3. Click on the **Replacement surface(s)** field in the PropertyManager and then select a replacement surface body in the graphics area, see Figures 3.147 and 3.148.

3.147

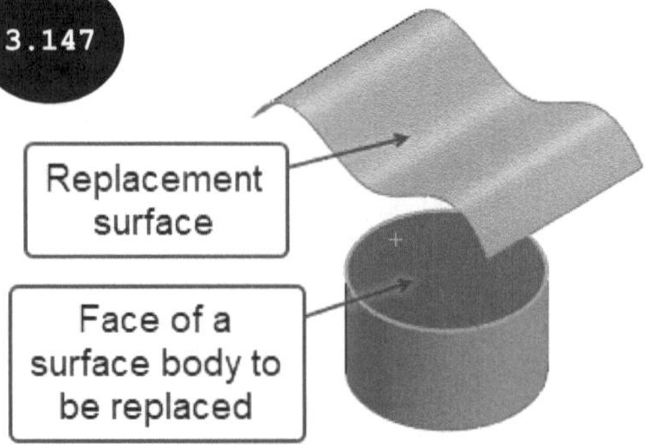

3.148

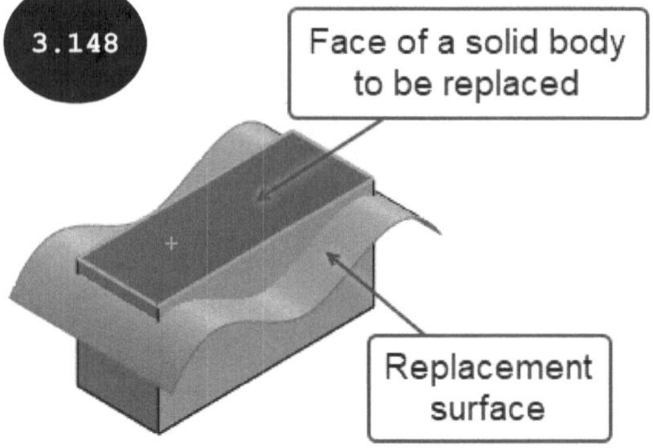

4. Click on the green tick-mark ✓ button in the PropertyManager. The selected face gets replaced with the replacement face of the surface, see Figures 3.149 and 3.150.

3.149

3.150

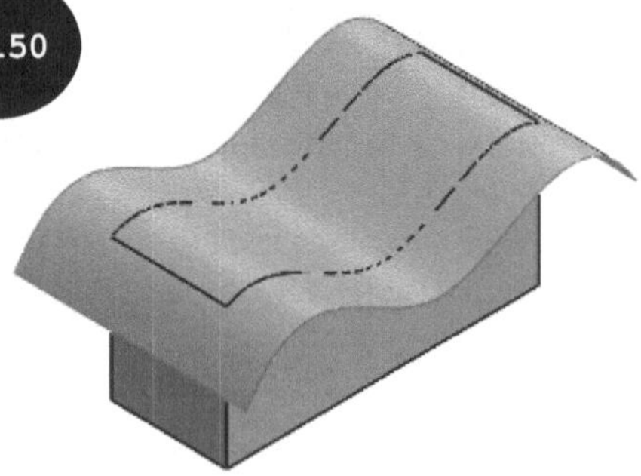

Tip: When you replace a face, adjacent faces in the original body automatically adjust to the replacement surface body.

Deleting Holes in a Surface Body

You can delete closed cut instances or holes of a surface by using the **Delete Hole** tool. The method for deleting holes on a surface is discussed below:

1. Click on the **Delete Hole** tool in the **Surfaces CommandManager**, see Figure 3.151. The **Delete Hole PropertyManager** appears, see Figure 3.152.

3.151

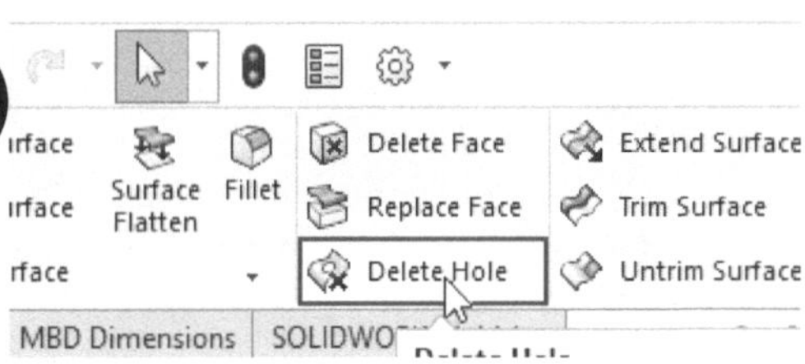

3.152

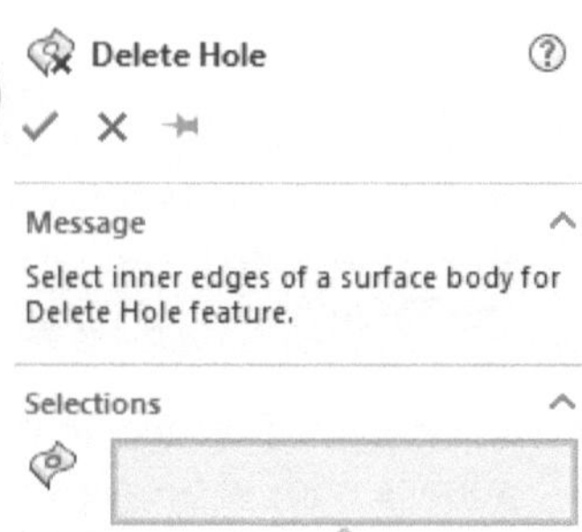

2. Select edges of the closed cut instances or holes of the surface to be deleted, see Figure 3.153. The preview appears in the graphics area such that the selected closed cut instances or holes get patched. Also, the names of the selected edges appear in the **Selected Edges to remove** the field of the PropertyManager.

3. Click on the green tick-mark button in the PropertyManager. The selected closed cut instances or holes get deleted, see Figure 3.154.

3.153

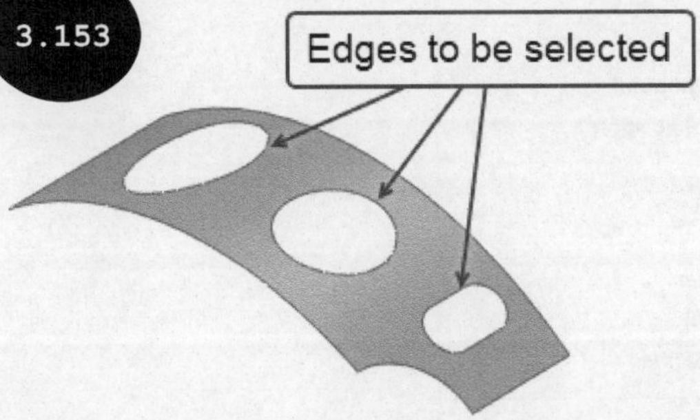

3.154

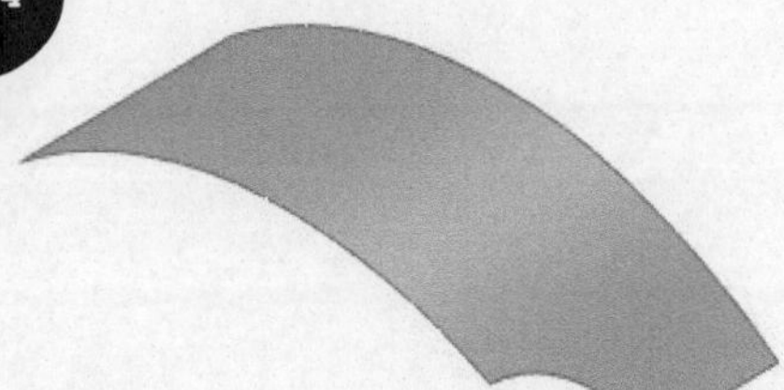

Creating a Freeform Surface

In SOLIDWORKS, you can deform or modify a face of a surface or solid body by creating control curves and control points and then pushing and pulling the control points, see Figure 3.155. The method for creating a freeform surface is discussed below:

3.155

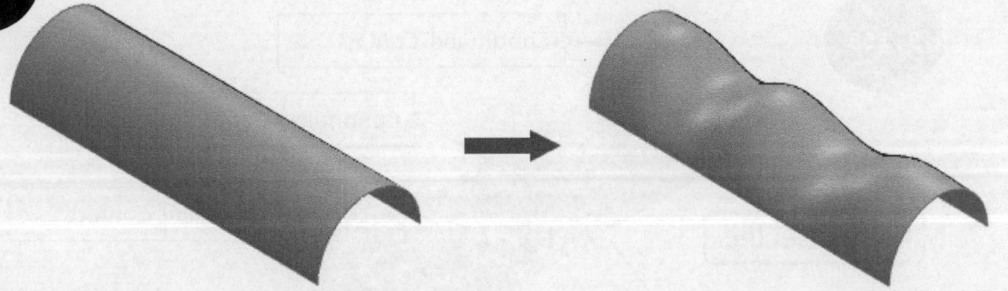

1. Click on the **Freeform** tool in the **Surfaces CommandManager**, see Figure 3.156. The **Freeform PropertyManager** appears, see Figure 3.157.

3.156

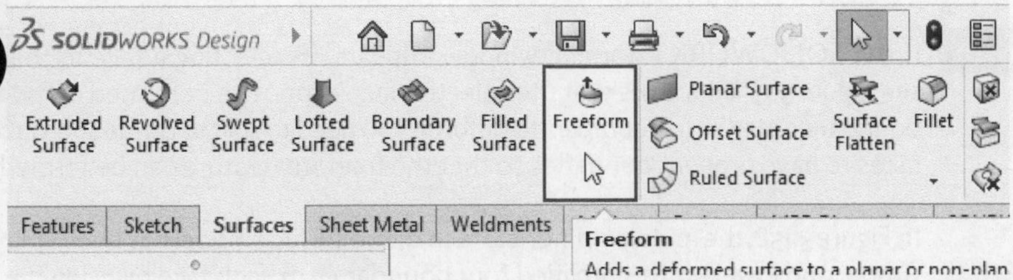

3.157

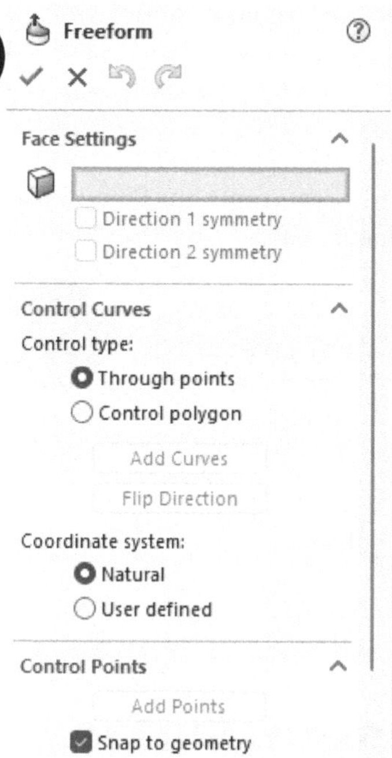

2. Select a face of a surface body to be deformed or modified in the graphics area. The mesh preview of the selected face appears in the graphics area, see Figure 3.158. Also, continuity callouts appear along each boundary (edge) of the selected face for controlling the relation of the face being modified along its respective boundary.

3.158

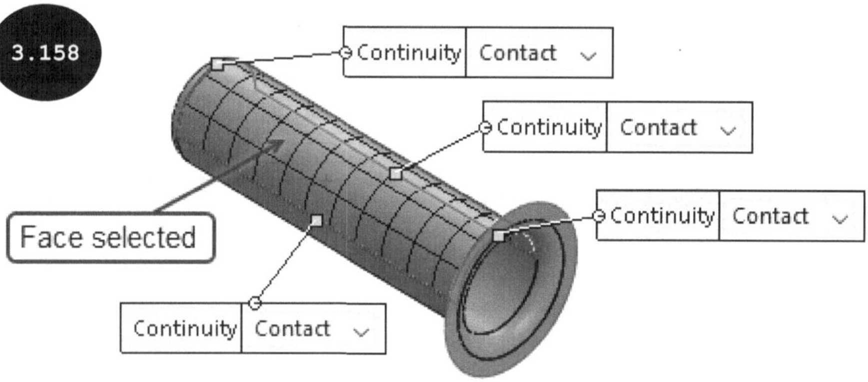

Note: If the **SOLIDWORKS** warning window appears on selecting a face in the graphics area, see Figure 3.159, it means that the selected face cannot be deformed or modified, since its boundaries may be too complex to deform. You need to split to divide such faces into smaller faces to have proper boundaries so that the freeform feature can be formed.

In Figure 3.158, the middle cylindrical face of the surface model has been split into two faces (upper and lower) with simplified four boundaries to each face by using the **Split** tool.

3.159

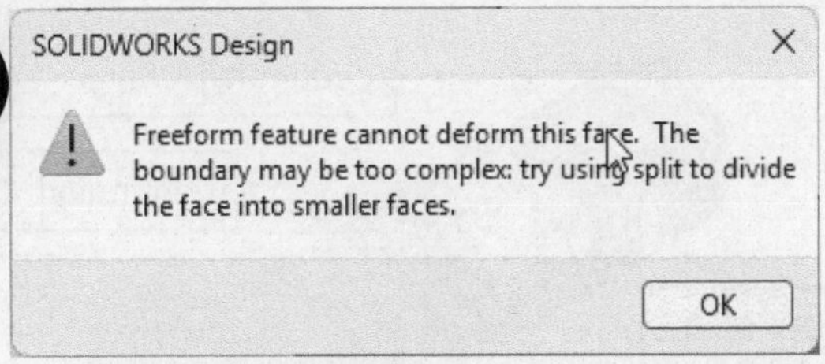

Continuity Callouts: By default, the **Contact** option is selected in the continuity callouts that appear along each boundary (edge) of the selected face in the graphics area. As a result, on modifying the face, the contact continuity will be maintained along the original boundary of the face. Similarly, the **Tangent** option is used for maintaining the tangent continuity along the original boundary. The **Curvature** option is used for maintaining the curvature continuity along the original boundary. The **Moveable** option is used for modifying the original boundary without maintaining the tangent continuity with the selected face. The **Moveable/Tangent** option is used for modifying the original boundary while maintaining the tangent continuity parallel to its face.

Direction 1 symmetry: On selecting the **Direction 1 symmetry** check box in the **Face Settings** rollout, a mirror symmetry gets added in Direction 1 and is represented by a mirroring plane at the middle of the selected face in Direction 1. As a result, on modifying the geometry on one side of the mirroring plane, the mirrored geometry on the other side of the mirroring plane also gets modified simultaneously.

Direction 2 symmetry: On selecting the **Direction 2 symmetry** check box, a mirror symmetry gets added in Direction 2 of the selected face.

3. Select the **Direction 1 symmetry**, **Direction 2 symmetry**, or both of these check boxes for adding the mirror symmetry either in Direction 1, Direction 2, or both the directions, respectively. If you do not want to add any mirror symmetry in any direction, ensure that both the check boxes are cleared in the **Face Settings** rollout of the PropertyManager.

Add Curves: The **Add Curves** button in the **Control Curves** rollout is used for adding control curves along the selected face.

Flip Direction: The **Flip Direction** button is used for reversing the direction to add a control curve along Direction 1 to Direction 2 or vice-versa. Note that the **Flip Direction** button is enabled only when the **Add Curves** button is activated for adding a control curve.

4. Click on the **Add Curves** button in the **Control Curves** rollout to add a control curve on the selected face.

5. Move the cursor over the selected face, and the preview of a control curve appears, see Figure 3.160. You can reverse the direction of adding the control curve from Direction 1 to Direction 2 or vice-versa by clicking on the **Flip Direction** button that can be enabled below the **Add Curves** button in the rollout, if needed.

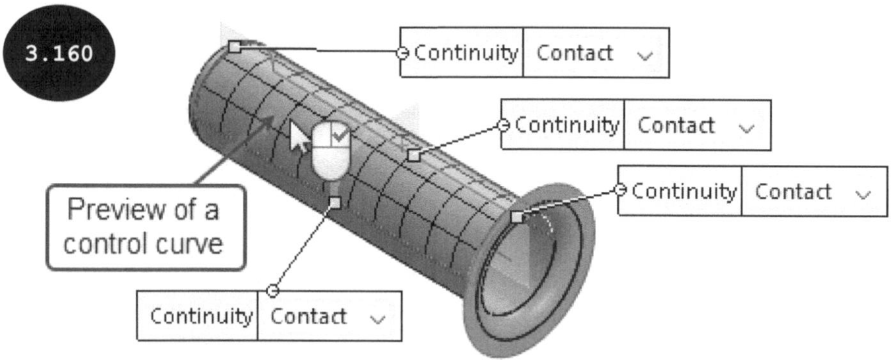

6. Click to define the position of the control curve at the required location on the selected face. A control curve gets added at the specified location. You can create multiple control curves one after another by clicking the left mouse button.

7. After adding a control curve, right-click to add control points on the control curve. Alternatively, you can also click on the **Add Points** button in the **Control Points** rollout of the PropertyManager to add control points.

8. Move the cursor over the control curve, the preview of a control point appears attached to the cursor along the curve, see Figure 3.161.

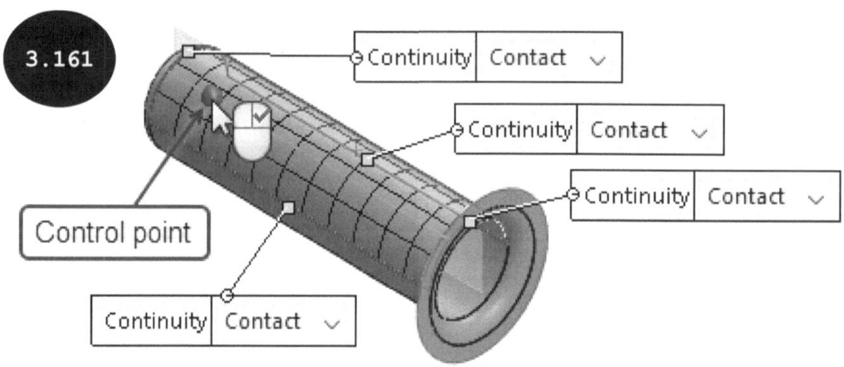

9. Click the left mouse button at a required location along the control curve. A control point at the specified location is added along the control curve.

10. Similarly, you can add multiple control points along the control curve as required, by clicking the left mouse button, see Figure 3.162. In this figure, 6 control points are added along a control curve.

3.162

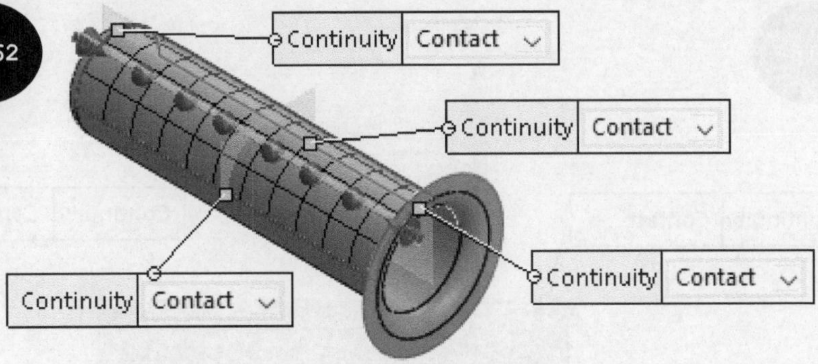

11. After adding control points, right-click over the control curve to exit the addition of control points and switch to the editing mode.

    Now, you can deform or modify the selected face by pulling and pushing the control points.

12. Move the cursor over a control point and then click on it when the move symbol appears. The Triad with X, Y, and Z axes appears on the selected control points, see Figure 3.163.

3.163

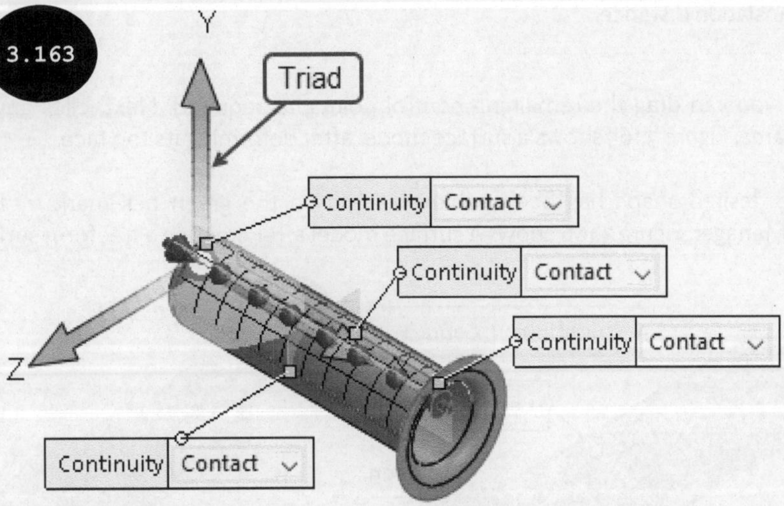

Note: The Triad helps to constrain the push or pull directions. You can also drag the control point directly for deforming the selected face.

13. Drag the required axis of the Triad to a specific translation distance along the direction of the axis for deforming the selected face by pressing and holding the left mouse button, see Figure 3.164. In this figure, the orientation of the surface model has been changed to the Front view. Next, release the left mouse button.

3.164

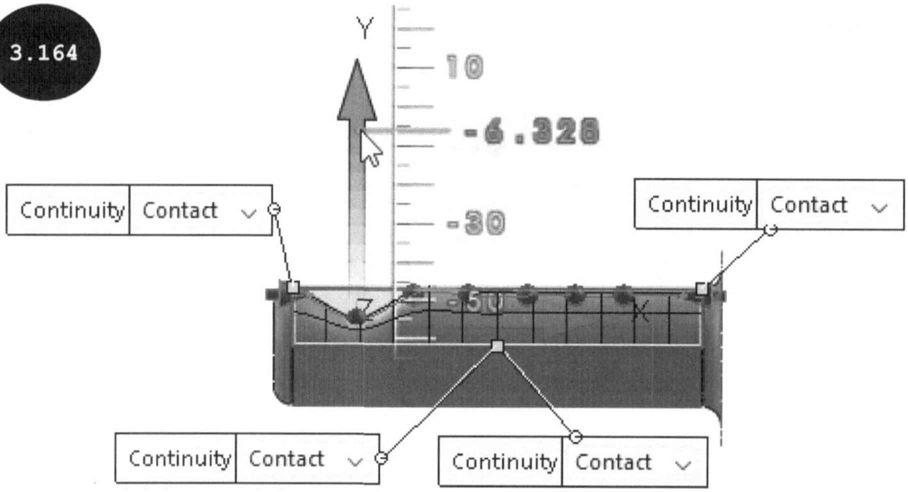

Note: You can also enter the required translation distance in the **Triad X Direction, Triad Y Direction,** and **Triad Z Direction** fields in the **Control Points** rollout of the PropertyManager. You can also drag the respective thumbwheel at the bottom of these fields for defining the translation distance.

14. Similarly, you can drag the remaining control points, as required. Next, click anywhere in the graphics area. Figure 3.165 shows a surface model after deforming its top face.

15. After the desired shape has been achieved, click on the green tick-mark ✓ button in the PropertyManager. Figure 3.166 shows a surface model after creating a freeform surface.

3.165

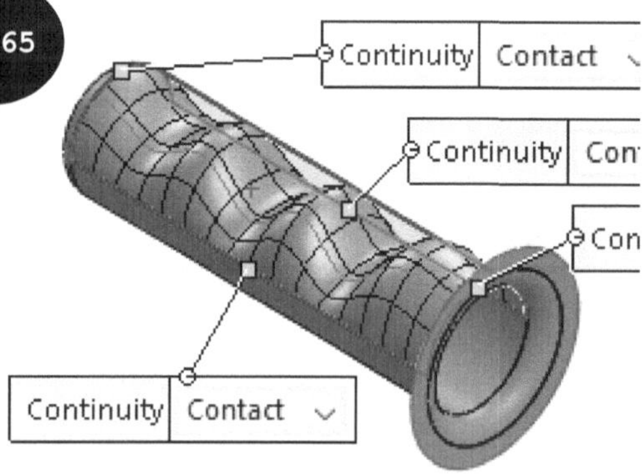

3.166

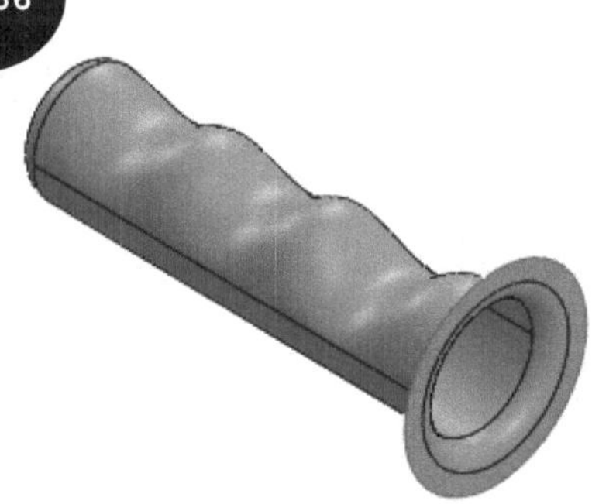

Knitting Surfaces

In SOLIDWORKS, after creating multiple surfaces one after another to create a surface model of a desired shape, you need to knit these individual surfaces together to form a single surface. You can knit surfaces together by using the **Knit Surface** tool. Note that the surfaces to be knit together must have contact with each other. The method for knitting surfaces is discussed below:

1. Click on the **Knit Surface** tool in the **Surfaces CommandManager**, see Figure 3.167. The **Knit Surface PropertyManager** appears, see Figure 3.168. Also, you are prompted to select surfaces and faces to knit, since the **Surfaces and Faces to Knit** field is activated in the **Selections** rollout, by default.

3.167

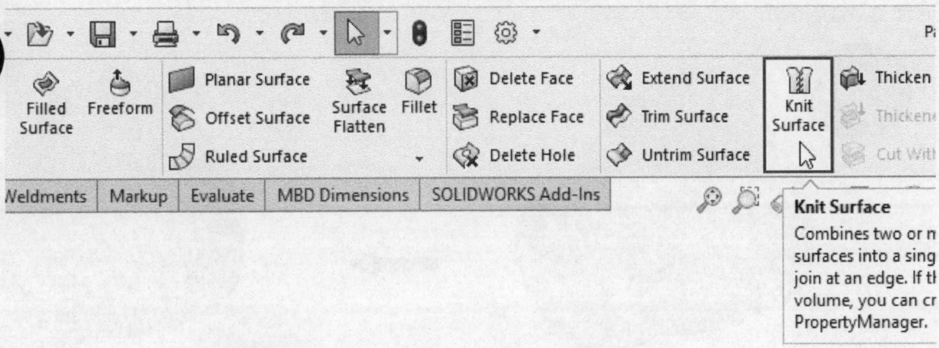

3.168

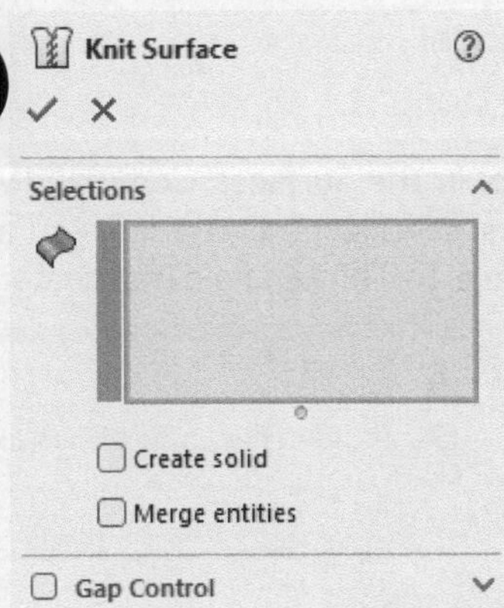

2. Select surfaces to be stitched one by one in the graphics area. The surfaces get selected and are highlighted in the graphics area. Also, the names of the selected surfaces appear in the **Surfaces and Faces to Knit** field.

   Create solid: The Create solid check box is used for creating a solid model from enclosed surfaces that are selected to knit.

   Merge entities: The Merge entities check box is used for merging faces with the same underlying geometry.

3. If needed, select the **Gap Control** check box for defining the knitting tolerance and allowable gap range for knitting selected surfaces.

4. Click on the green tick-mark ✓ button in the PropertyManager. All individually selected surfaces get knit together and form a single surface model.

Adding Thickness to a Surface Model

After creating a single surface model by knitting individual surfaces, you can add thickness to make it a solid model of specified thickness, see Figure 3.169. This figure shows a surface model and the resultant solid model after adding thickness. The method for adding thickness to a surface model is discussed below:

3.169

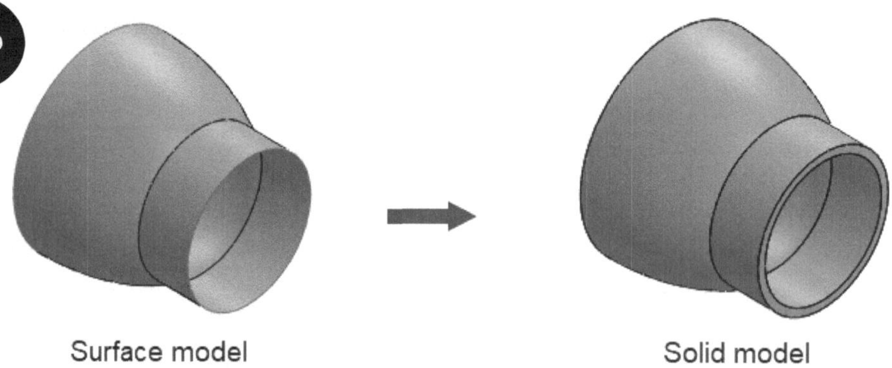

1. Click on the **Thicken** tool in the **Surfaces CommandManager**, see Figure 3.170. The **Thicken PropertyManager** appears, see Figure 3.171. Also, you are prompted to select a surface to be thickened, since the **Surface To Thicken** field is activated in the PropertyManager, by default.

3.170

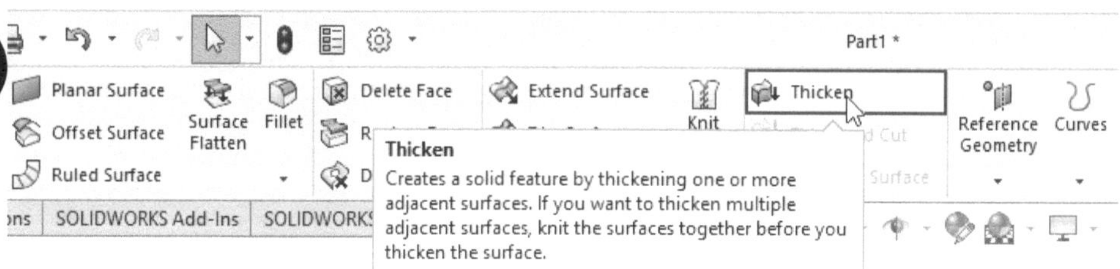

3.171

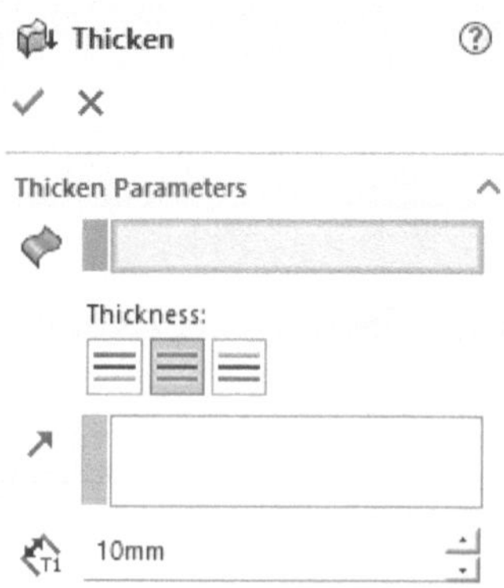

2. Select a surface body to be thickened in the graphics area. The preview of a thickened (solid) model appears in the graphics area with the default specified thickness value, see Figure 3.172.

3.172

3. Enter the thickness value in the **Thickness** field of the PropertyManager. The preview of a thickened (solid) model gets modified accordingly in the graphics area.

4. Click on the **Thicken Side 1**, **Thicken Both Sides**, or **Thicken Side 2** button in the PropertyManager to add thickness to one side, symmetrically on both sides or the second side of the surface, respectively.

Note: You can also define thickness direction other than normal to the selected surface by using the **Direction of Thicken** field of the PropertyManager. On activating this field, you can select a plane, a linear sketch entity, an edge, or an axis to define the direction of thickness.

5. Click on the green tick-mark ✓ button in the PropertyManager. A solid model of specified thickness gets created, see Figure 3.173.

3.173

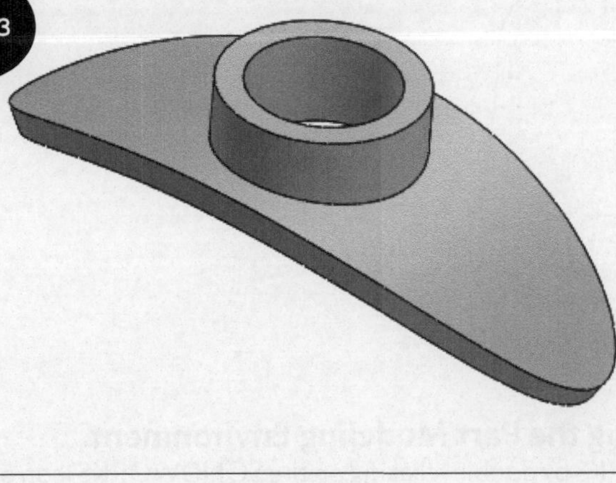

Tutorial 1

Create the surface model of a Mouse as shown in Figure 3.174. After creating the model, you need to convert it into a solid model by adding a thickness of 1 mm. The different views of the model are given in the same figure. The given dimensions are for your reference. You can assume the missing dimensions for achieving the overall shape of the model.

3.174

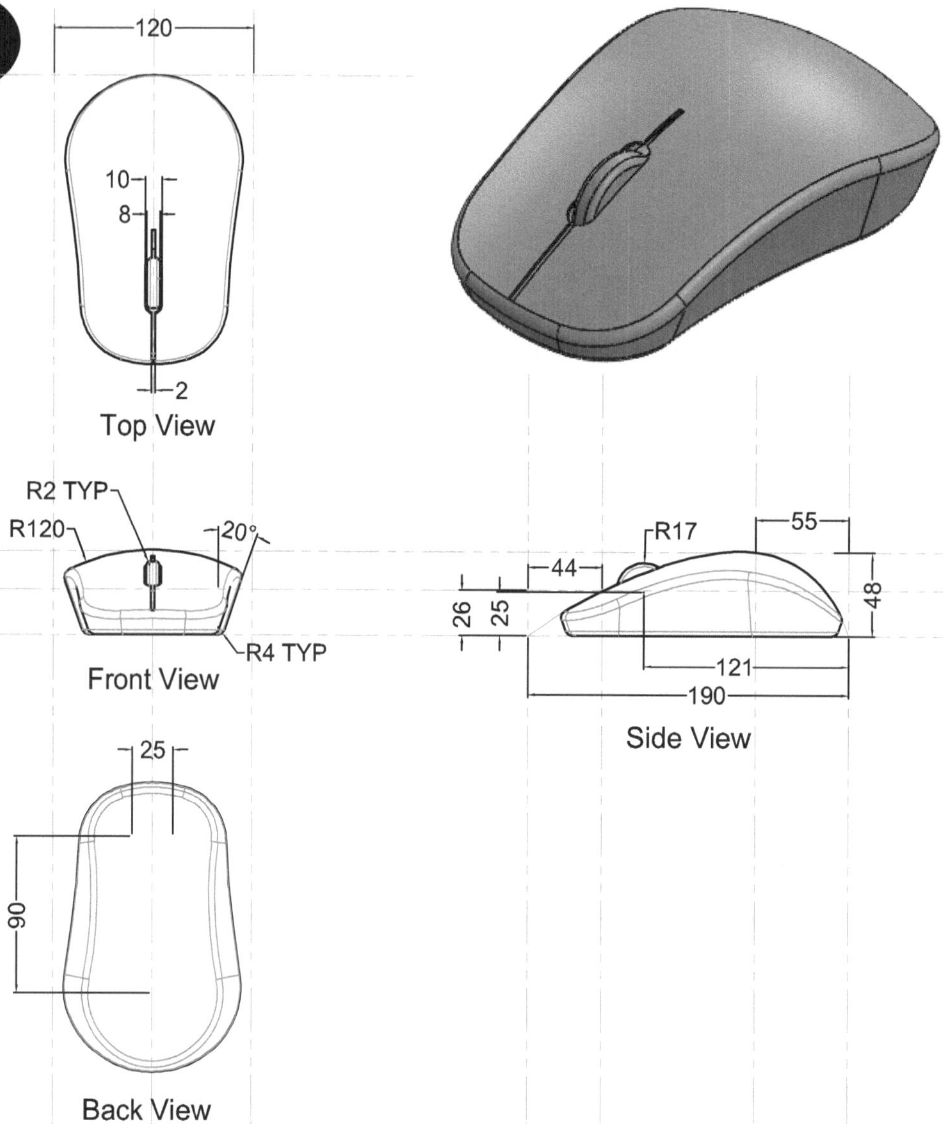

Section 1: Invoking the Part Modeling Environment

1. Start SOLIDWORKS by double-clicking on the SOLIDWORKS icon on your desktop. The startup user interface of SOLIDWORKS appears along with the **Welcome** dialog box.

Note: If SOLIDWORKS is already open and the **Welcome** dialog box does not appear on the screen, then you can invoke the same by clicking on the **Welcome to SOLIDWORKS** tool in the **Standard** toolbar.

2. Click on the **Part** button in the **Welcome** dialog box. The Part modeling environment is invoked.

Tip: You can also invoke the Part modeling environment by using the **New SOLIDWORKS Document** dialog box. To do so, click on the **New** tool in the **Standard** toolbar. The **New SOLIDWORKS Document** dialog box appears. In this dialog box, ensure that the **Part** button is selected and then click on the **OK** button.

Section 2: Specifying Unit Settings

1. Move the cursor toward the lower right corner of the screen over the Status Bar and then click on the **Unit System** area. The Unit System flyout appears, see Figure 3.175.
2. Ensure that the **MMGS (millimeter, gram, second)** option is tick-marked in the flyout.

3.175

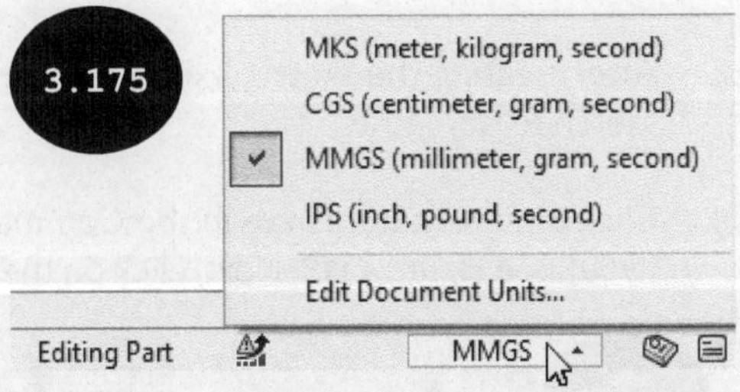

Tip: A tick-mark in front of any unit system in the **Unit System** flyout indicates that it is selected as the unit system for the current document of SOLIDWORKS. You can also open the **Document Properties - Units** dialog box to specify the unit system for the current document by clicking on the **Edit Document Units** option in the flyout.

Section 3: Creating the Base Surface - Sweep Surface

To create a sweep surface, you first need to create a path and a profile as individual sketches.

1. Click on the **Sketch** tab in the CommandManager, then click on the **Sketch** tool, see Figure 3.176. The three default planes, which are mutually perpendicular to each other appear.

3.176

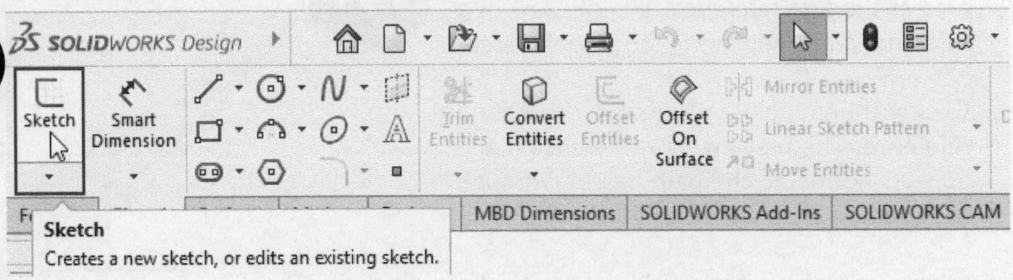

2. Select the Right Plane as the sketching plane in the graphics area. The Sketching environment gets invoked and the selected Right Plane becomes normal to the viewing direction.

3. Create the path of the sweep surface by using the **Spline** tool, see Figure 3.177. To fully define the sketch, you need to apply a horizontal relation between the endpoints of the curve and the origin.

3.177

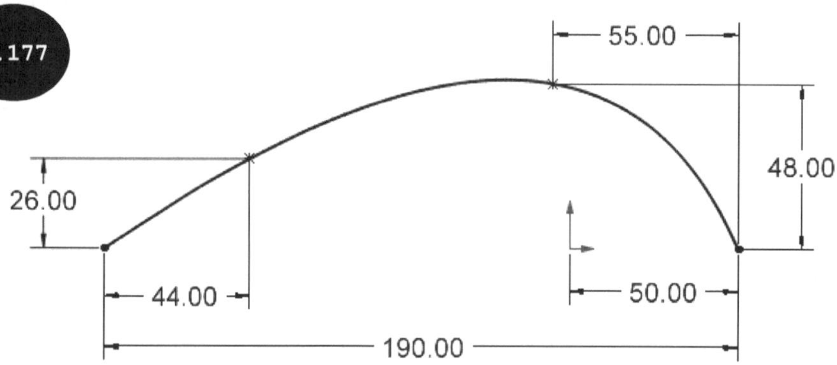

4. After creating the sketch, exit the Sketching environment. Next, change the orientation of the sketch to isometric.

5. Click on the **Features** tab in the CommandManager and then invoke the **Reference Geometry** flyout, see Figure 3.178. Next, click on the **Plane** tool. The **Plane PropertyManager** appears.

3.178

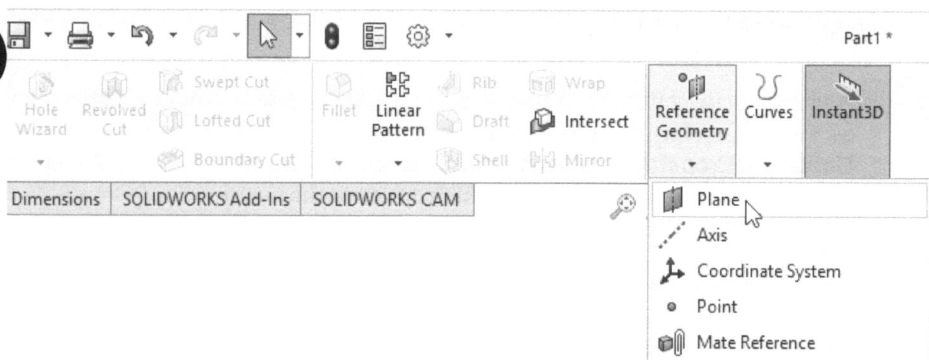

6. Select the sketch of the path in the graphics area as the first reference. The preview of a reference plane appears in the graphics area.

7. Click on the endpoint of the path as the second reference. The preview of a reference plane appears normal to the path passing through the selected endpoint, see Figure 3.179.

8. Click on the green tick-mark in the PropertyManager. A reference plane normal to the path and passing through the selected endpoint is created.

3.179

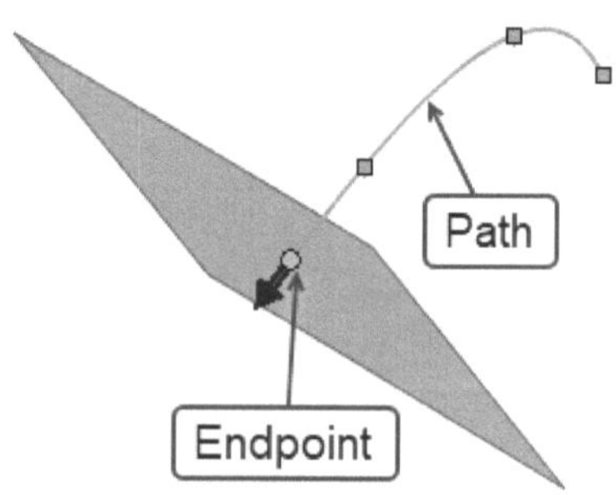

Now, you can create the profile of the sweep surface.

9. Invoke the Sketching environment by selecting the newly created plane as the sketching plane and then create an open profile of the sweep surface by using the sketching tools, see Figure 3.180. Next, exit the Sketching environment.

Note: In Figure 3.180, a coincident relation is applied between the arc and the origin. Also, a vertical relation is applied between the origin and the center point of the arc. Also, a horizontal relation is applied between the endpoints of the arc to make the sketch fully defined. Note that to select the origin, you may need to rotate the sketch in the graphics area by pressing and holding the middle mouse button.

10. Change the view orientation to isometric. Figure 3.181 shows the path and the profile of the sweep surface.

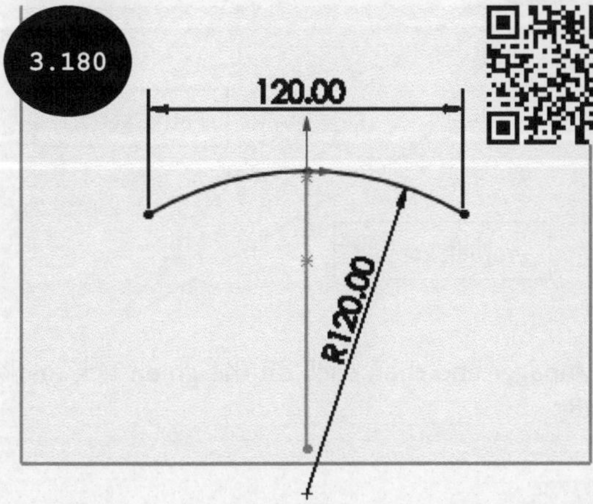

3.180

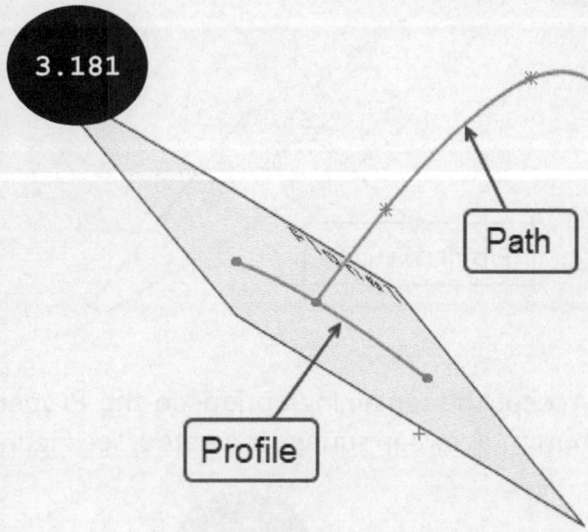

3.181

Now, you can create a sweep surface.

11. Click on the **Surfaces** tab in the CommandManager, see Figure 3.182. The tools of the **Surfaces CommandManager** appear.

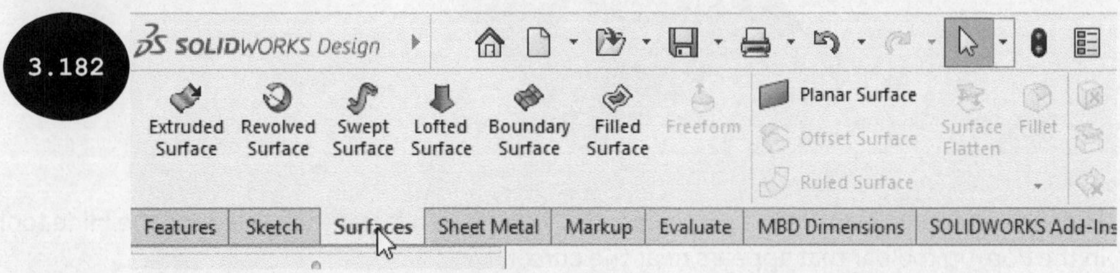

3.182

Note: If the **Surfaces** tab is not available in the CommandManager then right-click anywhere on the CommandManager. Next, click on the **Tabs > Surfaces** option in the shortcut menu that appears.

12. Click on the **Swept Surface** tool in the **Surfaces CommandManager**. The **Surface-Sweep PropertyManager** appears.

13. Ensure that the **Sketch Profile** radio button is selected in the **Profile and Path** rollout of the PropertyManager.

14. Select the profile of the sweep surface in the graphics area. The profile gets selected, see Figure 3.183. Also, the **Path** field gets activated automatically in the PropertyManager and you are prompted to select a path of the sweep surface.

15. Select the path of the sweep surface in the graphics area. The preview of a sweep surface appears such that the profile follows the path, see Figure 3.184.

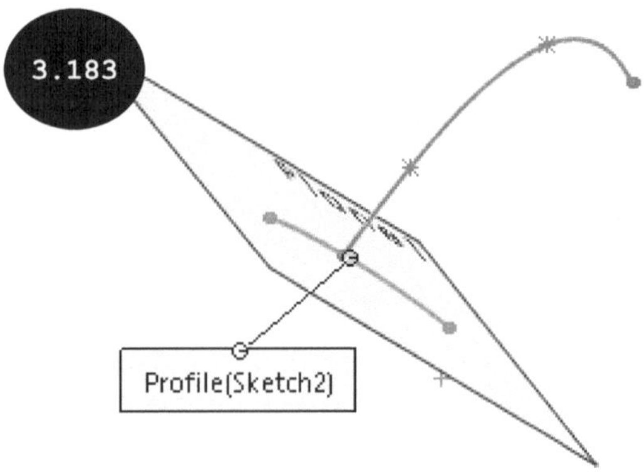

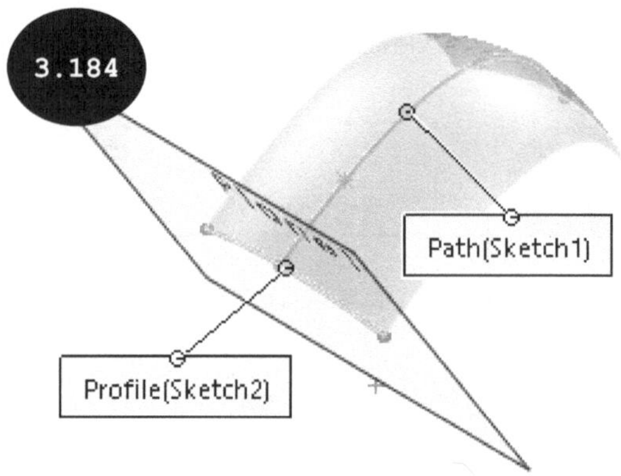

16. Accept the remaining options in the PropertyManager and then click on the green tick-mark button. A sweep surface is created, see Figure 3.185.

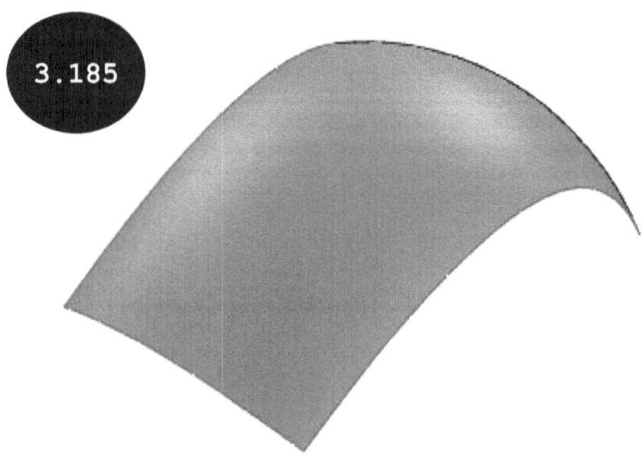

17. Hide the reference plane in the graphics area by clicking on it and then selecting the **Hide** tool in the Pop-up toolbar that appears near the cursor.

Section 4: Creating the Second Surface - Extrude Surface

1. Click on the **Sketch** tab in the CommandManager and then click on the **Sketch** tool, see Figure 3.186. You are prompted to select a sketching plane.

3.186

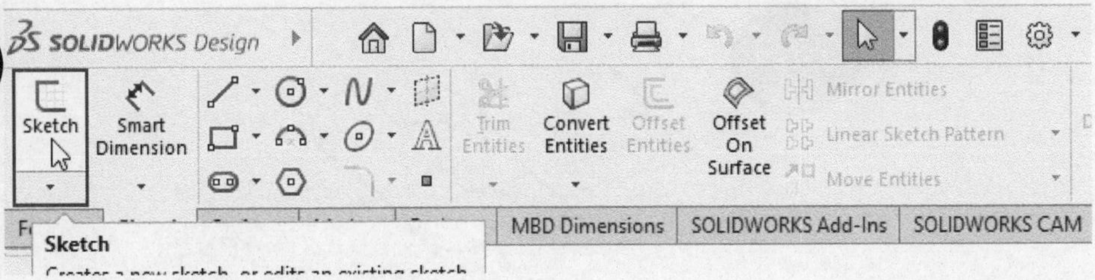

2. Expand the FeatureManager Design Tree and then select the Top plane as the sketching plane. The Sketching environment gets invoked.

3. Create the sketch of the extrude surface by using the sketching tools, see Figure 3.187.

3.187

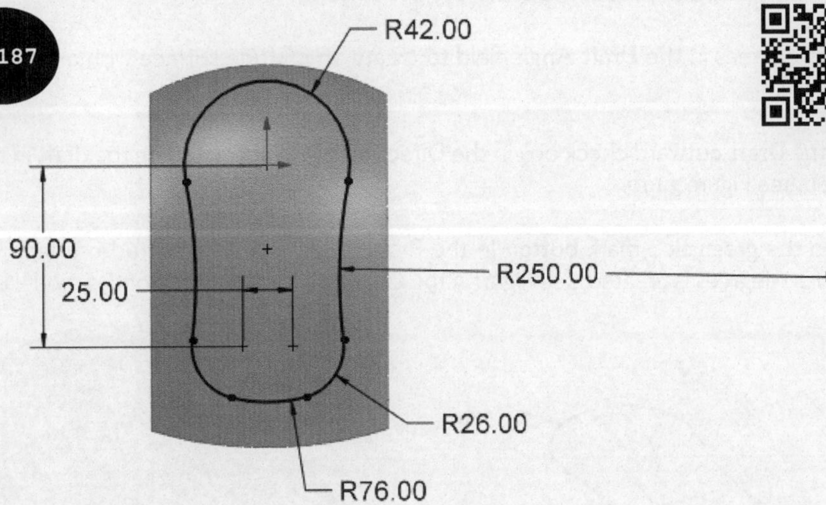

4. Click on the **Surfaces** tab in the CommandManager and then click on the **Extruded Surface** tool, see Figure 3.188. The **Surface-Extrude PropertyManager** appears. Also, the preview of an extrude surface appears with default parameters in the graphics area.

3.188

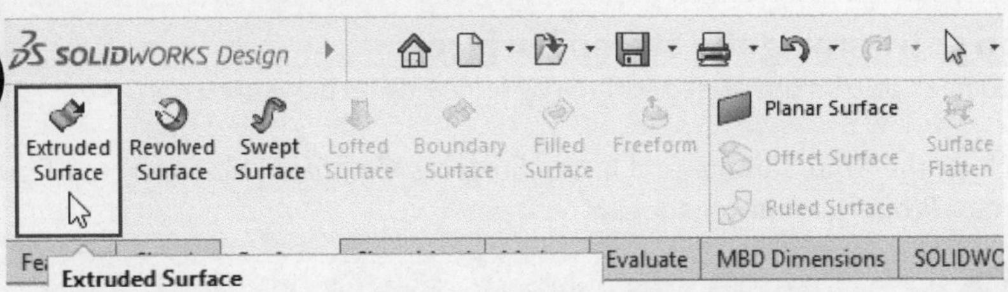

5. Select the **Up To Surface** option in the **End Condition** drop-down list of the **Direction 1** rollout. The **Face/Plane** field appears in the rollout and you are prompted to select a face or a plane as the end condition.

6. Select the previously created sweep surface in the graphics area. The preview of an extrude surface appears such that it gets terminated at the selected surface, see Figure 3.189.

3.189

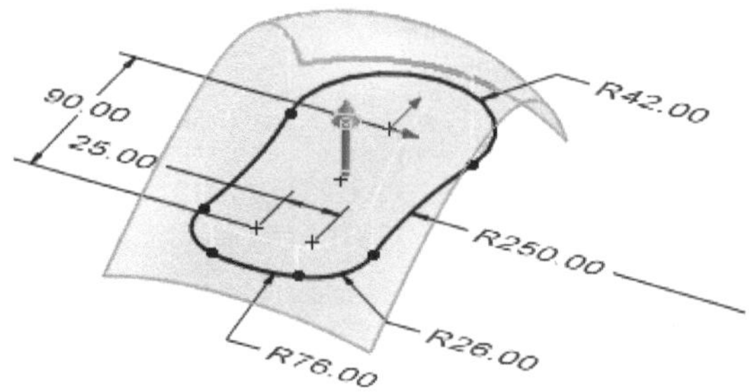

7. Click on the **Draft On/Off** button in the **Direction 1** rollout of the PropertyManager. The **Draft Angle** field appears in front of the **Draft On/Off** button.

8. Enter **20** degrees in the **Draft Angle** field to create an extrude surface with a specified draft or taper angle.

9. Select the **Draft outward** check box in the **Direction 1** rollout for adding the draft in the outward direction, see Figure 3.190.

10. Click on the green tick-mark button in the PropertyManager. An extrude surface with a draft angle of 20 degrees is created, see Figure 3.191. Change the orientation of the model to isometric.

3.190

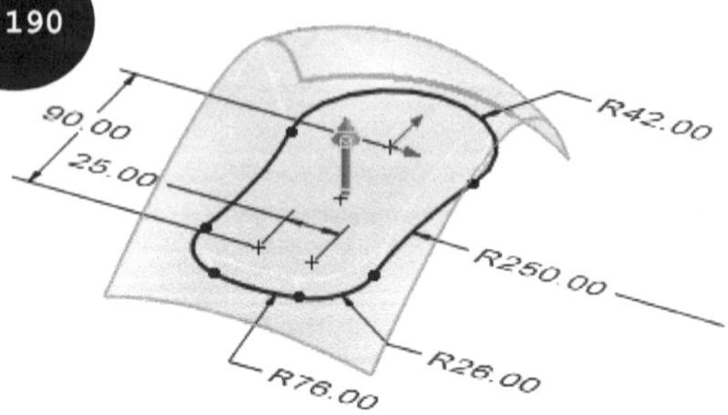

3.191

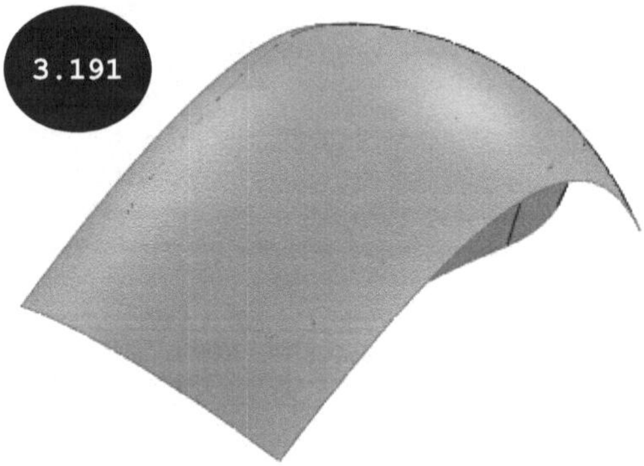

Section 5: Trimming the Sweep Surface

Now, you need to trim the sweep surface by removing its unwanted portion.

1. Click on the **Trim Surface** tool in the **Surfaces CommandManager**, see Figure 3.192. The **Trim Surface PropertyManager** appears.

3.192

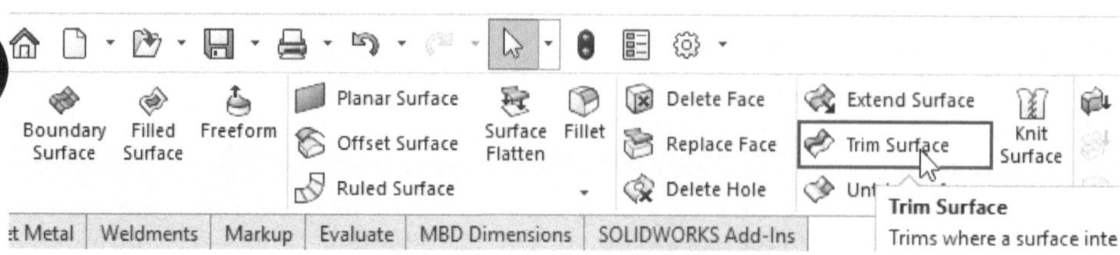

2. Ensure that the **Standard** radio button is selected in the **Trim Type** rollout of the PropertyManager.

3. Select the previously created extrude surface as the trim tool in the graphics area, see Figure 3.193. The name of the selected surface appears in the **Trim tool** field of the **Selections** rollout.

3.193

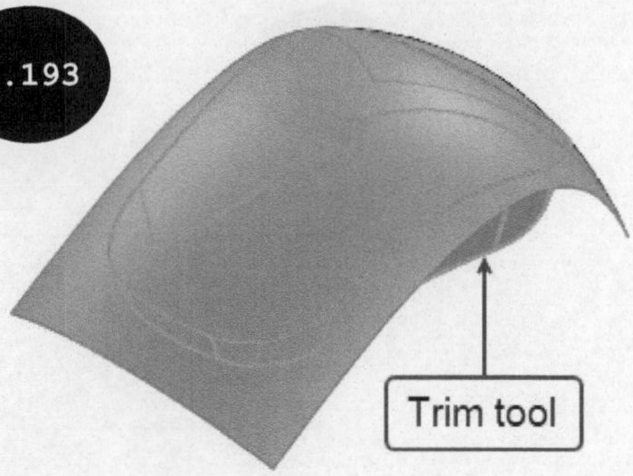

4. Select the **Remove selections** radio button in the **Selections** rollout for removing selected portions of the surface at the intersection with the trim tool.

5. Select the outer portion of the sweep surface as the portion to be removed in the graphics area, see Figure 3.194. The name of the selected portion appears in the **Pieces to Remove** field of the **Selections** rollout.

3.194

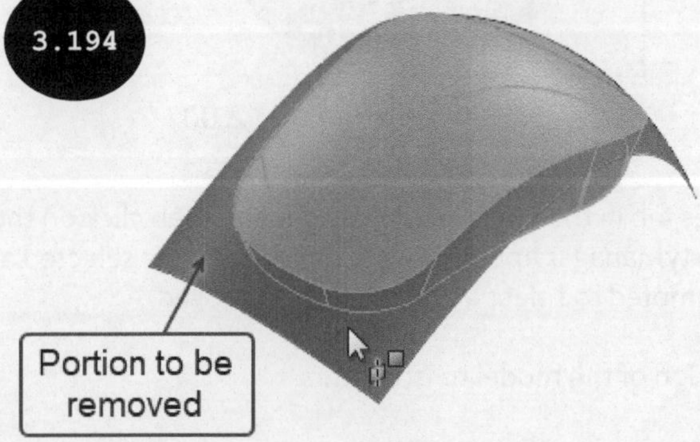

6. Click on the green tick-mark button in the PropertyManager. The sweep surface gets trimmed such that its selected portion gets removed from the intersection of the trim tool, see Figure 3.195.

3.195

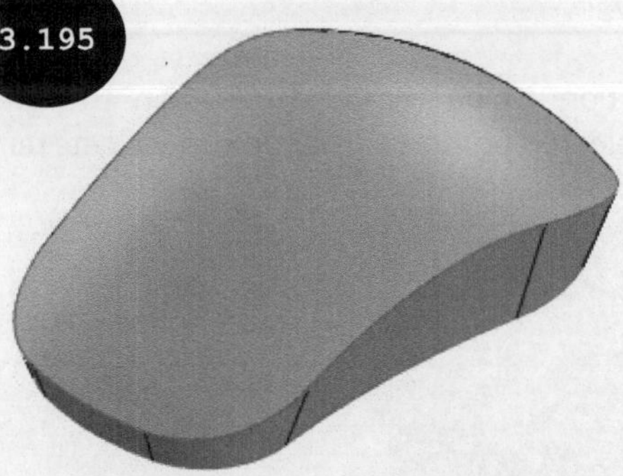

Section 6: Trimming the Top Surface of the Model

Now, you need to trim the top surface of the model by using a sketch as the trim tool.

1. Invoke the Sketching environment by selecting the Top plane as the sketching plane and then create a sketch by using the sketching tools, see Figure 3.196.

3.196

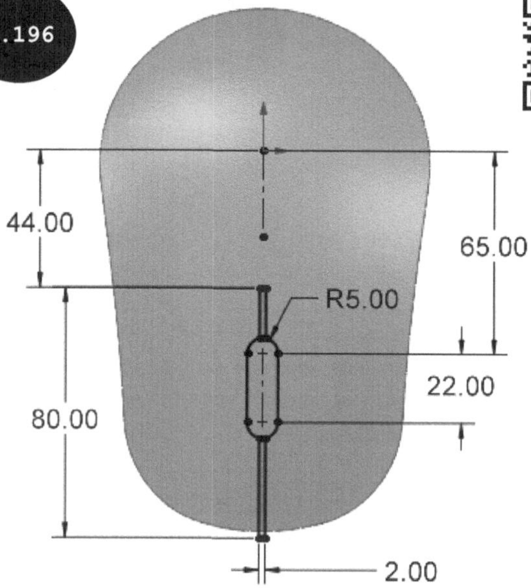

2. Click on the **Surfaces** tab in the CommandManager and then click on the **Trim Surface** tool. The **Trim Surface PropertyManager** appears. Also, the sketch gets selected automatically as the trim tool and you are prompted to select a portion to be removed.

3. Change the orientation of the model to isometric.

4. Ensure that the **Remove selections** radio button is selected in the **Selections** rollout of the PropertyManager.

5. Select the inner portion of the top surface that lies inside the trim tool as the portion to be removed, see Figure 3.197.

6. After selecting the portion to be removed, click on the green tick-mark button in the PropertyManager. The selected portion of the top surface gets removed, see Figure 3.198.

3.197

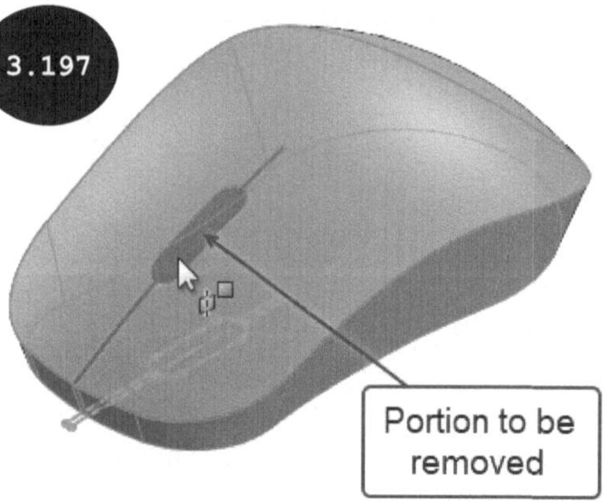

3.198

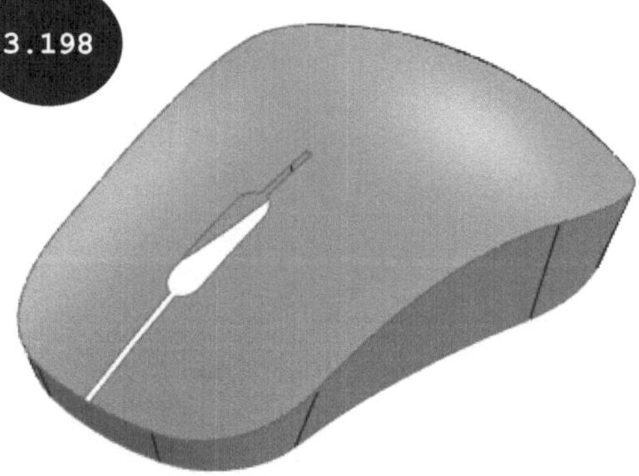

Section 7: Creating a Planar Surface

Now, you need to create the bottom side of the model by creating a planar surface.

1. Click on the **Planar Surface** tool in the **Surfaces CommandManager**, see Figure 3.199. The **Planar Surface PropertyManager** appears.

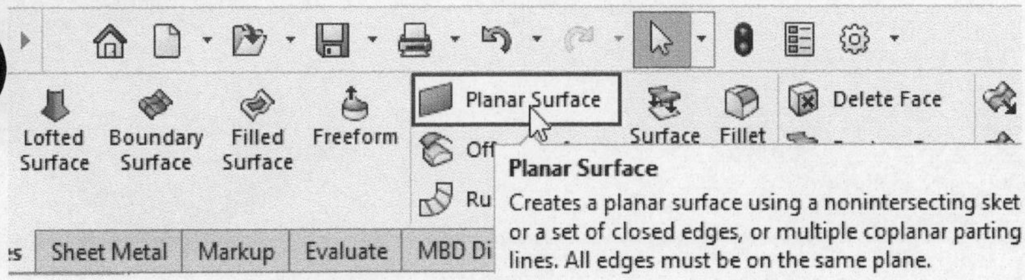

3.199

2. Rotate the model and then select all its bottom edges (6 edges), see Figure 3.200. The preview of a planar surface appears in the graphics area.

3. Click on the green tick-mark button in the PropertyManager. A planar surface gets created and the bottom side of the model gets closed, see Figure 3.201. This figure shows the rotated view of the model so that the planar surface can be viewed.

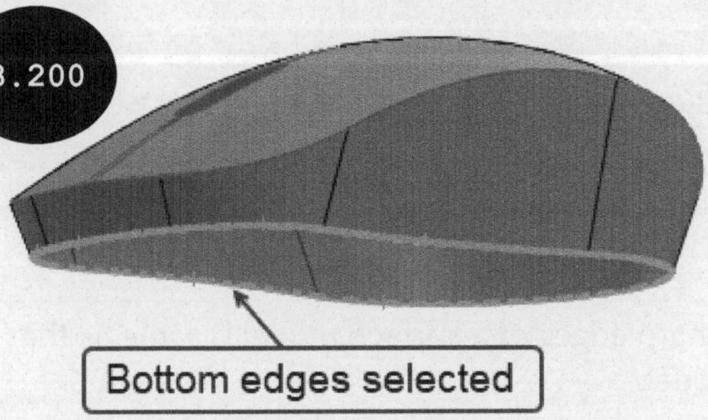

3.200

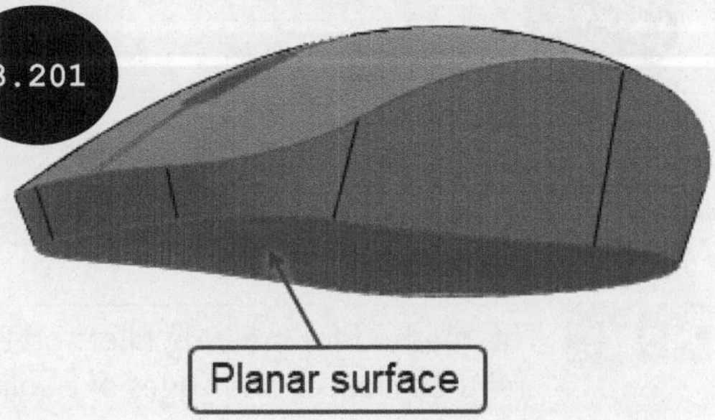

3.201

Section 8: Knitting or Stitching Surfaces

Now, you need to knit or stitch all the individual surfaces together to form a single surface.

1. Click on the **Knit Surface** tool in the **Surfaces CommandManager**, see Figure 3.202. The **Knit Surface PropertyManager** appears.

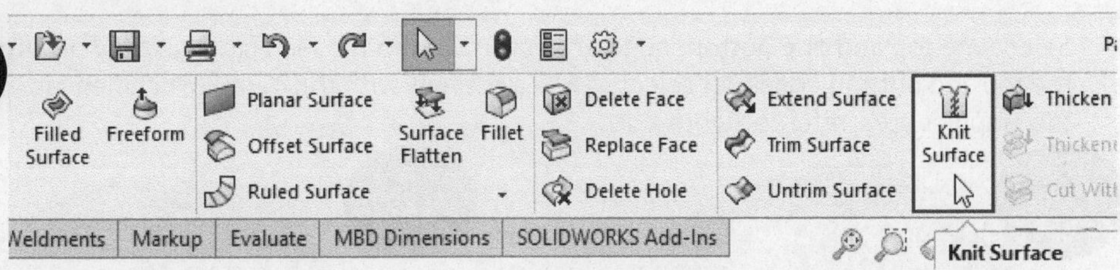

3.202

2. Select all the individual surfaces of the model in the graphics area one by one. The surfaces get selected and highlighted in the graphics area, see Figure 3.203.

3. Click on the green tick-mark button in the PropertyManager. The selected surfaces get stitched together and form a single surface model, see Figure 3.204. Also, the **Surface Bodies** node in the FeatureManager Design Tree displays a single surface body.

3.203

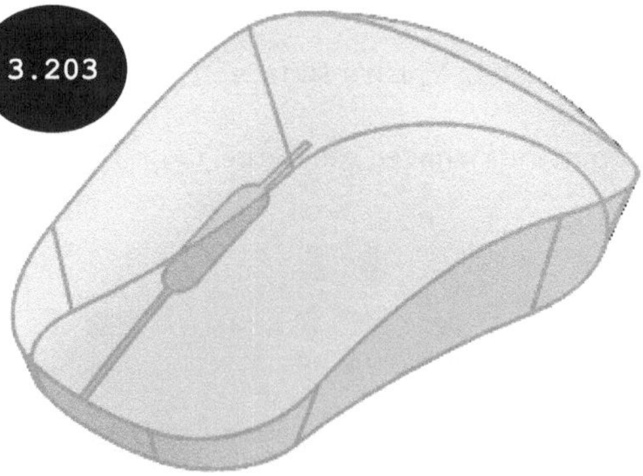

3.204

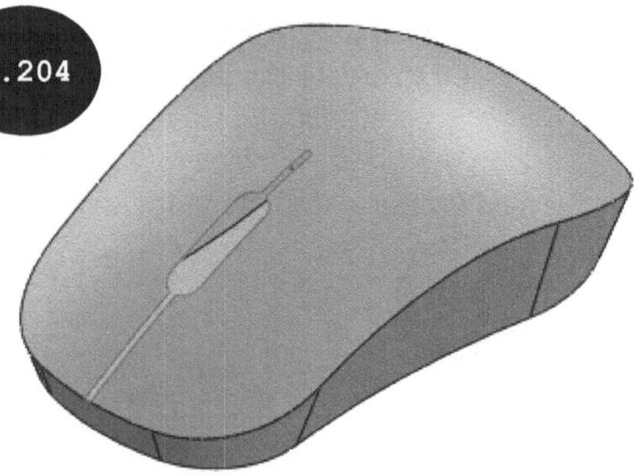

Section 9: Creating Fillets

Now, you need to remove the sharp corners of the surface model by creating fillets.

1. Click on the **Fillet** tool in the **Surfaces CommandManager**, see Figure 3.205. The **Fillet PropertyManager** appears.

3.205

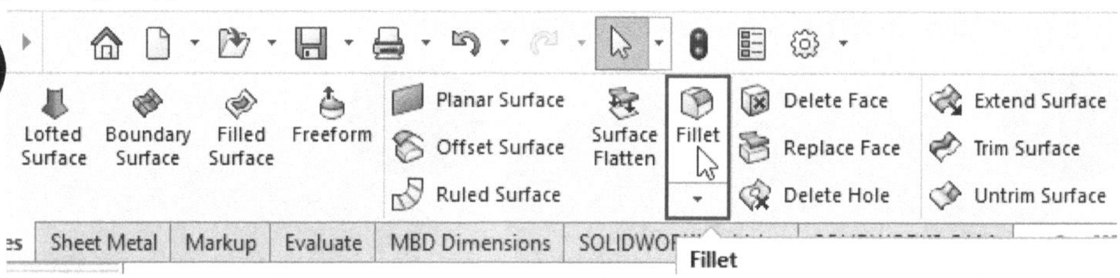

Note: The method for creating fillets on the sharp edges of a surface model is same as that for creating fillets on the edges of a solid model.

2. Ensure that the **Constant Size Fillet** button is activated in the **Fillet Type** rollout of the **Fillet PropertyManager** for creating a constant radius fillet.

3. Ensure that the **Tangent propagation** check box is selected in the **Items To Fillet** rollout for applying fillet to all the edges that are tangent to a selected edge.

4. Select one top and one bottom edge of the surface model, see Figure 3.206. The closed loops of the top and bottom edges get selected and a preview with the default specified radius appears in the graphics area, refer to Figure 3.207.

3.206

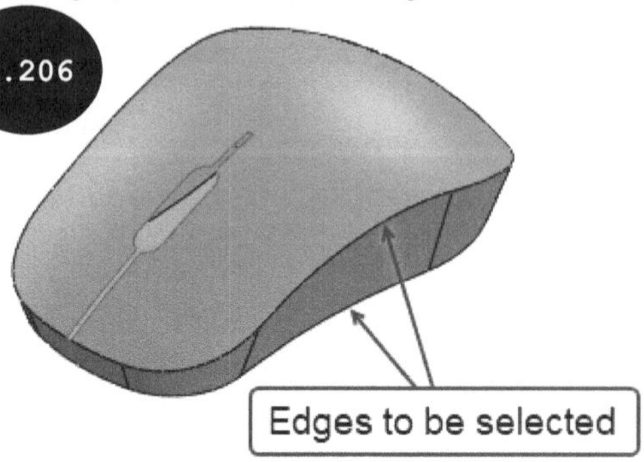

3.207

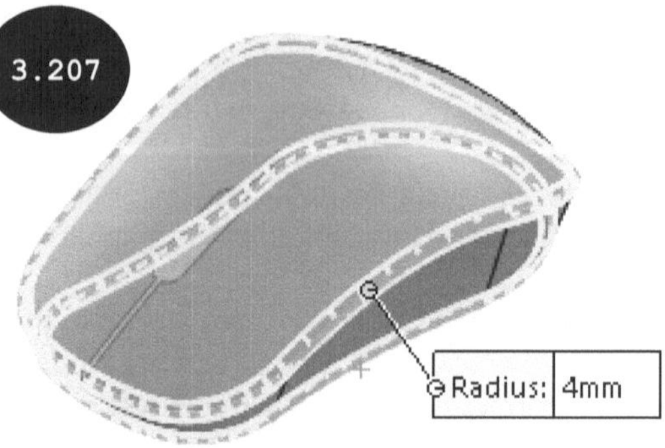

5. Ensure that the **Symmetric** option is selected in the **Fillet Method** drop-down list of the **Fillet Parameters** rollout for creating a fillet, that is symmetric on both sides of the edges selected.

6. Enter **4 mm** in the **Radius** field of the **Fillet Parameters** rollout as the radius of the fillet. A preview of the fillet of a specified radius appears on both the selected edges.

7. Accept the remaining default specified options and then click on the green tick-mark button in the PropertyManager. The fillet of a specified radius gets created on the selected edges of the surface model, see Figure 3.208.

3.208

Section 10: Adding Thickness

After creating a surface model, you need to add thickness to make a solid model.

1. Click on the **Thicken** tool in the **Surfaces CommandManager**, see Figure 3.209. The **Thicken PropertyManager** appears.

3.209

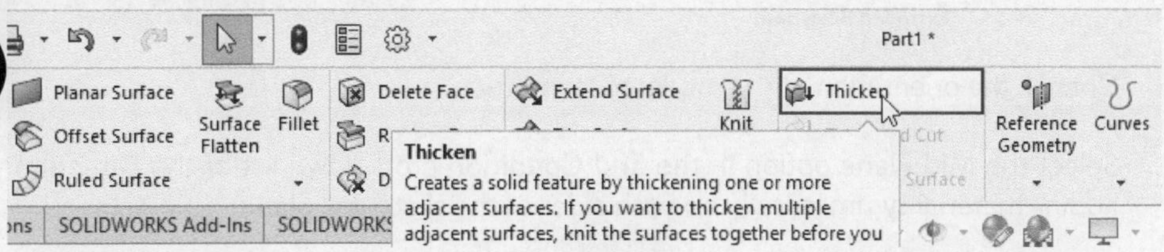

2. Select the surface model in the graphics area.

3. Ensure that the **Thicken Side 1** button is activated in the **Thickness** area of the PropertyManager for adding thickness towards the inner side of the surface model.

4. Enter **1** in the **Thickness** field of the PropertyManager as the thickness to be added.

3.210

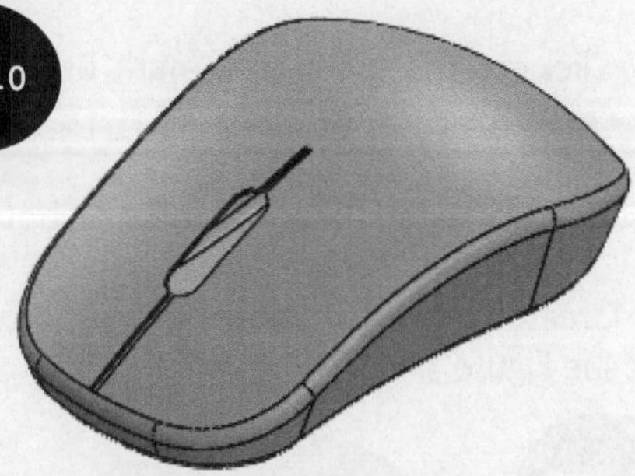

5. Click on the green tick-mark button in the PropertyManager. A solid model with a uniform thickness of 1 mm is created, see Figure 3.210.

Section 11: Creating a Solid Extrude Feature

Now, you need to create the wheel of the mouse model as a solid extrude feature.

1. Invoke the Sketching environment by selecting the Right plane as the sketching plane and then create two circles as the sketch of the wheel, see Figure 3.211. Note that you need to expand the FeatureManager Design Tree to select the Right plane.

3.211

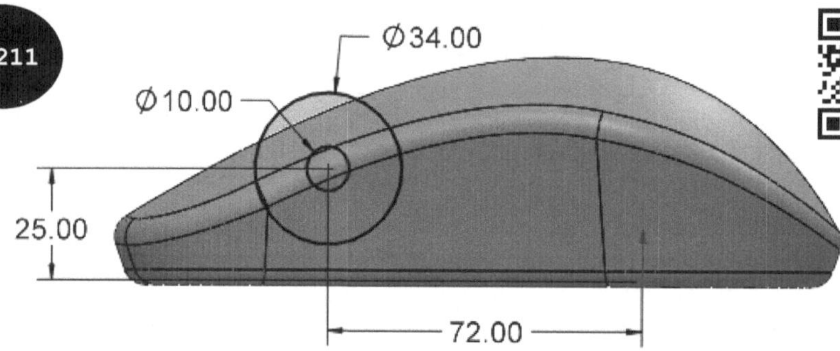

2. Click on the **Features** tab in the CommandManager and then click on the **Extruded Boss/Base** tool for creating a solid extrude feature, see Figure 3.212. The **Boss-Extrude PropertyManager** appears. Also, the preview of an extrude feature with default parameters appears.

3.212

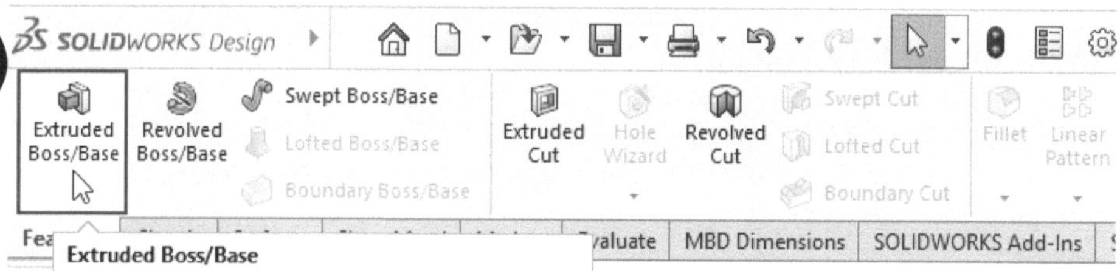

3. Change the orientation of the model to isometric.

4. Select the **Mid Plane** option in the **End Condition** drop-down list of the **Direction 1** rollout for adding material symmetrically on both sides of the sketching plane.

5. Enter **8 mm** in the **Depth** field of the **Direction 1** rollout as the depth of extrusion.

6. Click on the green tick-mark button in the PropertyManager. A solid extrude feature gets created, see Figure 3.213.

   Now, you need to create a fillet on both the sharp edges of the previously created extrude feature.

7. Create a fillet of radius 2 mm on both edges of the previously created extrude feature, see Figure 3.214.

3.213

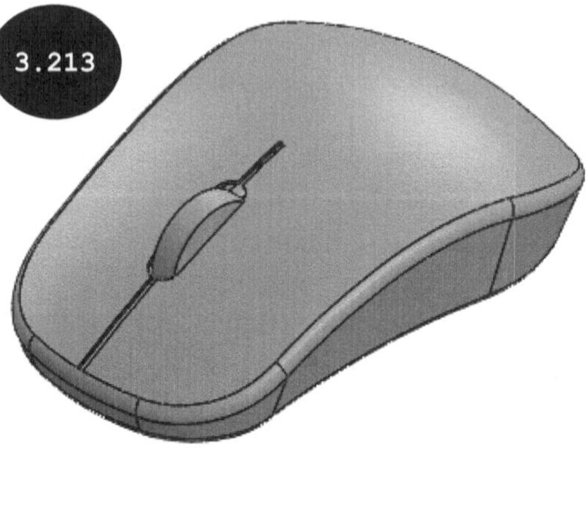

3.214

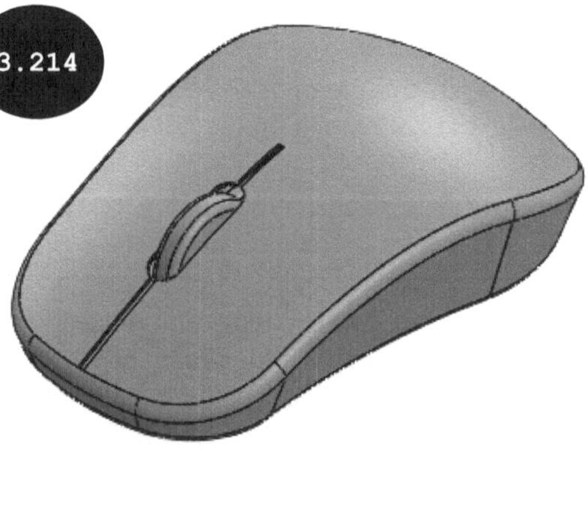

Section 12: Saving the Model

1. Click on the **Save** tool in the **Standard** toolbar. The **Save As** dialog box appears.
2. Browse to the local drive of your system and create a folder with the name **SOLIDWORKS Surface Design.**
3. Double-click on the newly created folder **"SOLIDWORKS Surface Design"** to access it.
4. Enter **Tutorial 1** in the **File name** field of the dialog box as the name of the model.
5. Click on the **Save** button in the dialog box. The model gets saved with the name Tutorial 1 inside the SOLIDWORKS Surface Design folder.

Tutorial 2

Create a surface model of an earphone as shown in Figure 3.215. After creating the model, you need to convert it into a solid model by adding a thickness of 1 mm. The different views of the model are given in the same figure. The given dimensions are for your reference. You can assume the missing dimensions for achieving the overall shape of the model.

3.215

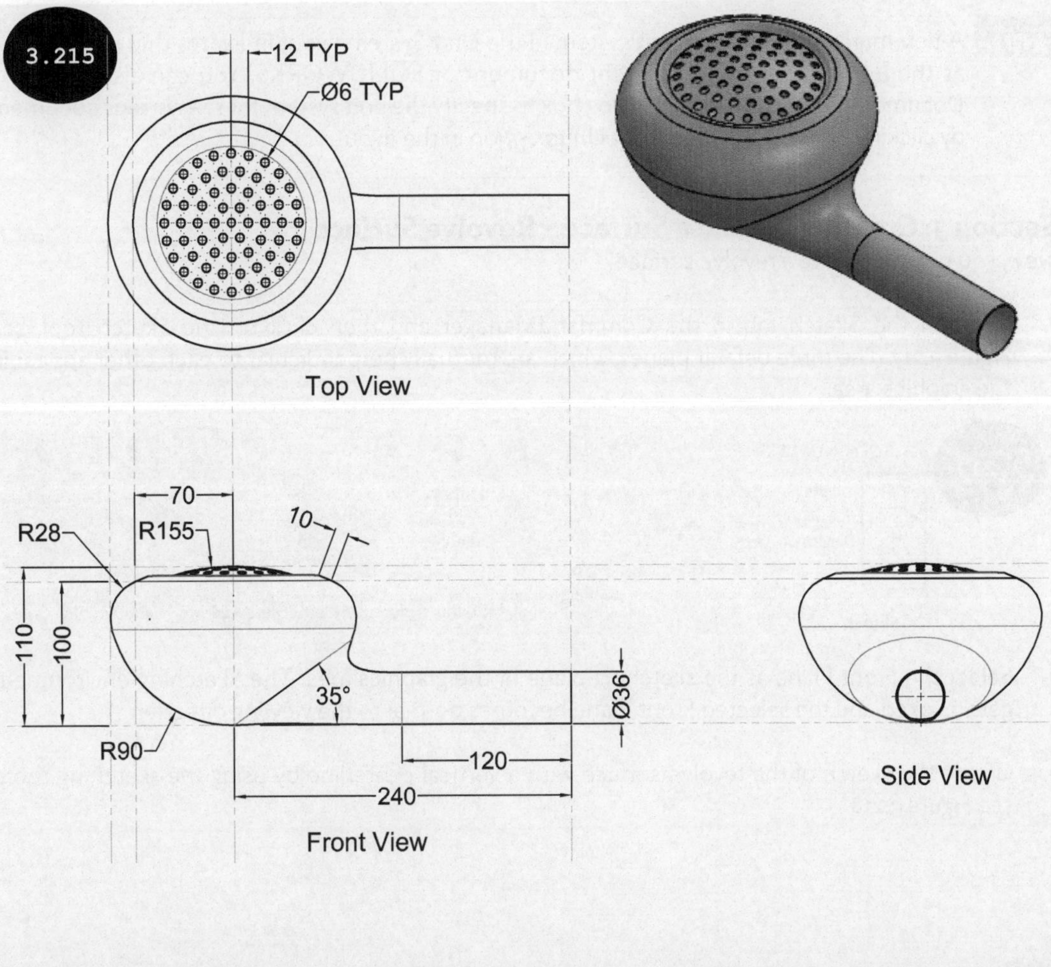

Section 1: Invoking the Part Modeling Environment

1. Start SOLIDWORKS by double-clicking on the SOLIDWORKS icon on your desktop. The startup user interface of SOLIDWORKS appears along with the **Welcome** dialog box.

Note: If SOLIDWORKS is already open and the **Welcome** dialog box does not appear on the screen, then you can invoke the same by clicking on the **Welcome to SOLIDWORKS** tool in the **Standard** toolbar.

2. Click on the **Part** button in the **Welcome** dialog box. The Part modeling environment is invoked.

Section 2: Specifying Unit Settings

1. Move the cursor toward the lower right corner of the screen over the Status Bar and then click on the **Unit System** area. The **Unit System** flyout appears, see Figure 3.216.

2. Ensure that the **MMGS (millimeter, gram, second)** option is tick-marked in the flyout.

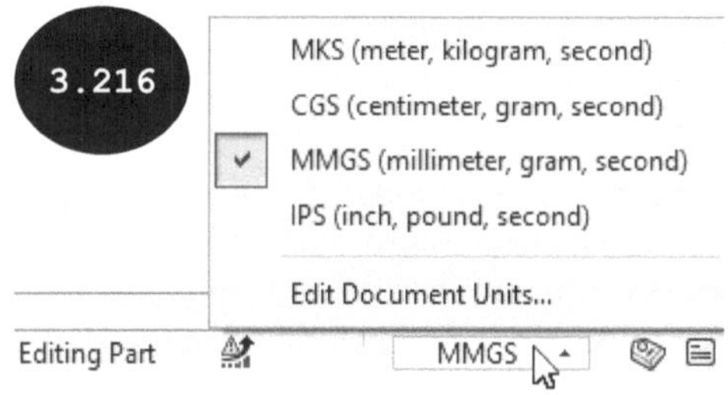

3.216

Tip: A tick-mark in front of any unit system in the **Unit System** flyout indicates that it is selected as the unit system for the current document of SOLIDWORKS. You can also open the **Document Properties - Units** dialog box to specify the unit system for the current document by clicking on the **Edit Document Units** option in the flyout.

Section 3: Creating the Base Surface - Revolve Surface

Now, you need to create a revolve surface.

1. Click on the **Sketch** tab in the CommandManager and then click on the **Sketch** tool, see Figure 3.217. The three default planes, which are mutually perpendicular to each other appear in the graphics area.

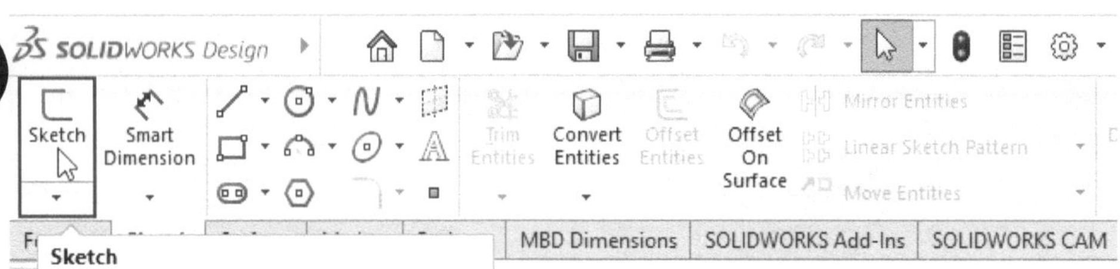

3.217

2. Select the Front Plane as the sketching plane in the graphics area. The Sketching environment gets invoked and the selected Front Plane becomes normal to the viewing direction.

3. Create the sketch of the revolve surface with a vertical centerline by using the sketching tools, see Figure 3.218.

3.218

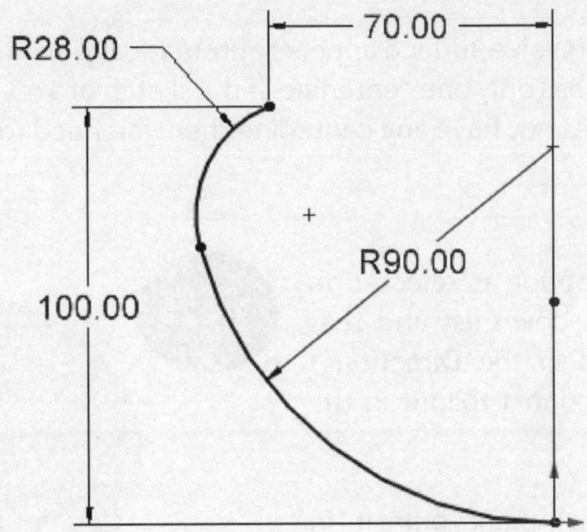

Note: In Figure 3.218, the tangent relation is applied between the arcs of the sketch. Also, the vertical relation is applied between the origin and the center point of arc having 90 mm radius for making the sketch fully defined.

4. Click on the **Surfaces** tab in the CommandManager and then click on the **Revolved Surface** tool, see Figure 3.219. The preview of a revolve surface appears in the graphics area, see Figure 3.220. Also, the **Surface-Revolve PropertyManager** appears to the left of the screen.

3.219

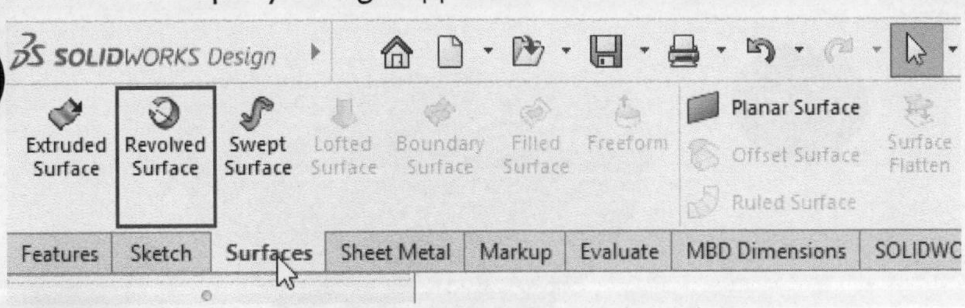

3.220

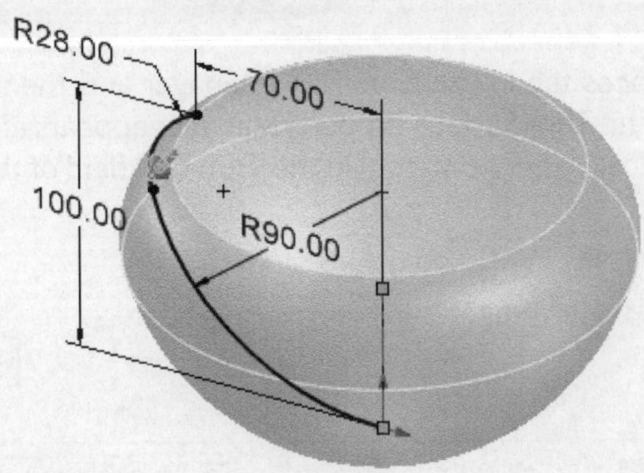

Note: The preview of a revolve surface appears automatically on invoking the **Revolved Surface** tool, if the sketch has only one centerline. If the sketch of a revolve surface has two or more centerlines or does not have any centerline then you need to select an axis of revolution, manually.

5. Ensure that the **Blind** option is selected in the **Revolve Type** drop-down list and that **360 degrees** is entered in the **Direction 1 Angle** field of the **Direction 1** rollout in the PropertyManager.

6. Click on the green tick-mark button in the PropertyManager. A revolve surface is created, see Figure 3.221.

3.221

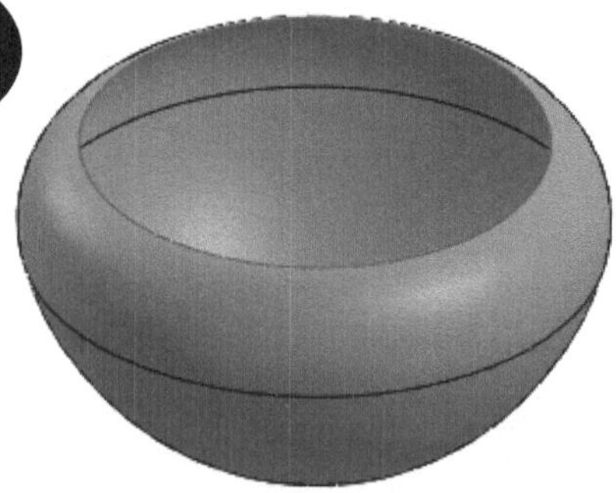

Section 4: Trimming a Surface

Now, you need to trim the previously created surface by using a sketch as the trim tool.

1. Invoke the Sketching environment by selecting the Front plane as the sketching plane and then create an inclined line of any length that passes throughout the model, see Figure 3.222. Note that you need to expand the FeatureManager Design Tree to select the Front plane as the sketching plane.

3.222

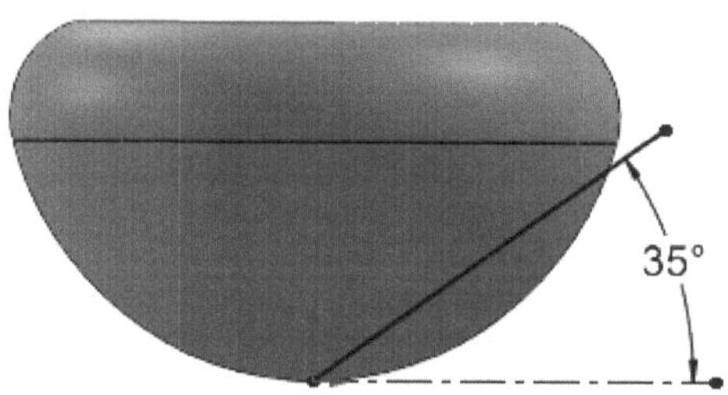

2. Click on the **Surfaces** tab in the CommandManager and then click on the **Trim Surface** tool, see Figure 3.223. The **Trim Surface PropertyManager** appears and the sketch (inclined line) gets selected automatically as the trim tool in the **Trim tool** field of the PropertyManager.

3.223

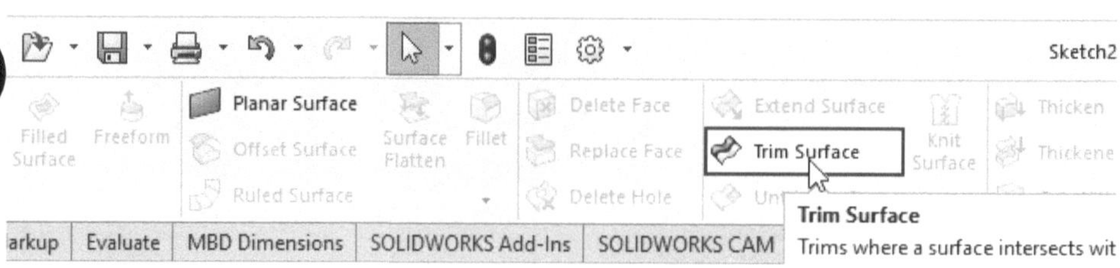

3. Change the orientation of the model to isometric.

4. Ensure that the **Remove selections** radio button is selected in the **Selections** rollout for selecting a portion of a surface to be removed.

5. Select a portion of the surface that is at the lower side of the trim tool as the portion to be removed, see Figure 3.224.

6. After selecting the portion to be removed, click on the green tick-mark button in the PropertyManager. The selected portion of the surface gets removed, see Figure 3.225.

3.224

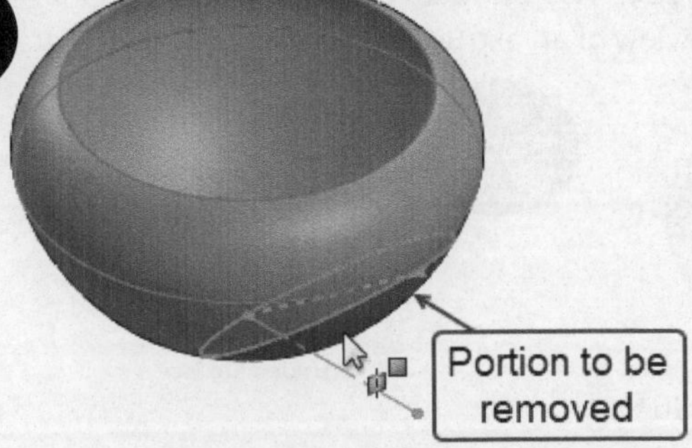

3.225

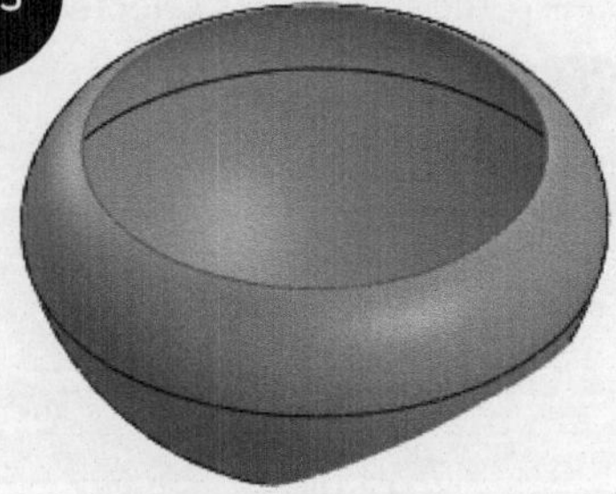

Section 5: Creating the Second Surface - Extrude Surface

Now, you need to create an extrude surface. To create this extrude surface, first, you need to create a reference plane at an offset distance of 240 mm from the Right plane.

1. Invoke the **Reference Geometry** flyout in the **Surfaces CommandManager** and then click on the **Plane** tool, see Figure 3.226. The **Plane PropertyManager** appears.

2. Expand the FeatureManager Design Tree, which is now at the top left corner of the graphics area, and then click on **Right Plane** as the first reference. The preview of a reference plane appears at an offset distance in the graphics area, see Figure 3.227.

3.226

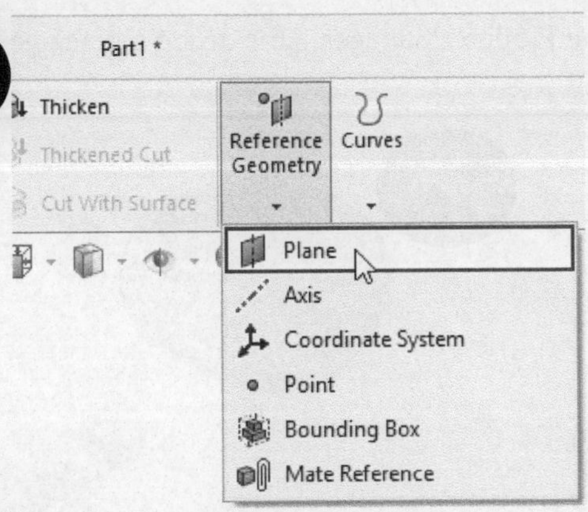

3.227

3. Enter **240 mm** in the **Offset distance** field of the **First Reference** rollout in the PropertyManager.

4. Click on the green tick-mark button in the PropertyManager. A reference plane is created at the specified offset distance from the Right plane.

After creating a reference plane, you can create a sketch of the extrude surface on it.

5. Invoke the Sketching environment by selecting the newly created reference plane as the sketching plane and then create a circle as the sketch of the extrude surface, see Figure 3.228.

6. After creating the sketch, click on the **Surfaces** tab in the CommandManager and then click on the **Extruded Surface** tool, see Figure 3.229. The **Surface-Extrude PropertyManager** appears. Also, the sketch gets selected and the preview of an extrude surface appears in the graphics area.

3.228

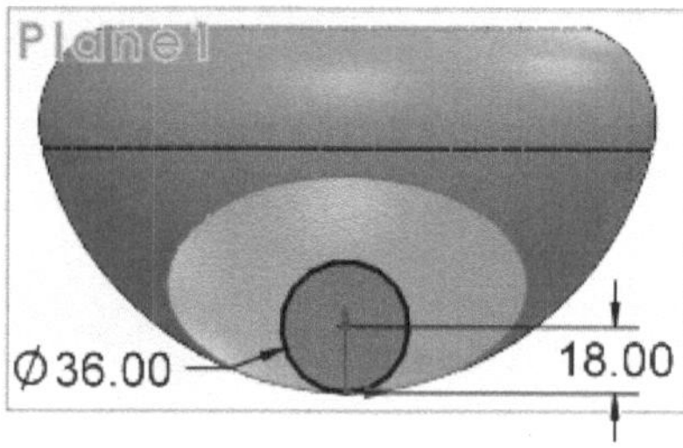

3.229

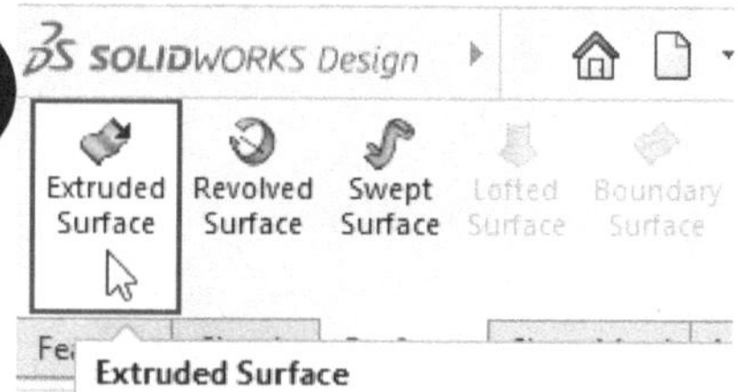

Note: In Figure 3.228, a vertical relation is applied between the origin and the center point of the circle for making the sketch fully defined.

7. Enter **120 mm** as the depth of extrusion in the **Depth** field of the **Direction 1** rollout.

8. Click on the **Reverse Direction** button in the **Direction 1** rollout to reverse the direction of extrusion towards the first created revolve surface of the model. A preview of the extrude surface appears similar to the one shown in Figure 3.230.

9. Click on the green tick-mark button in the PropertyManager. An extrude surface gets created, see Figure 3.231.

3.230

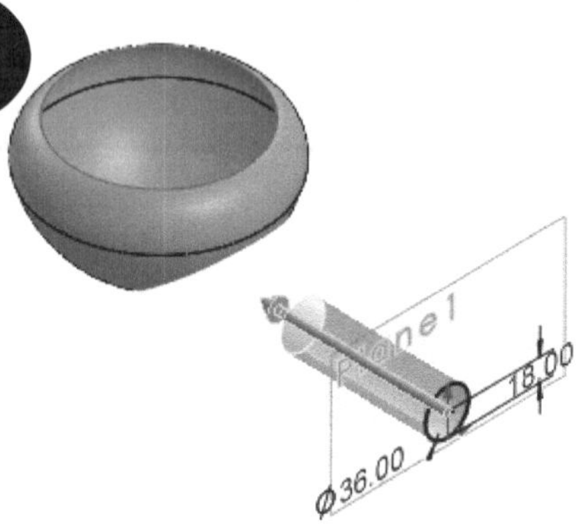

3.231

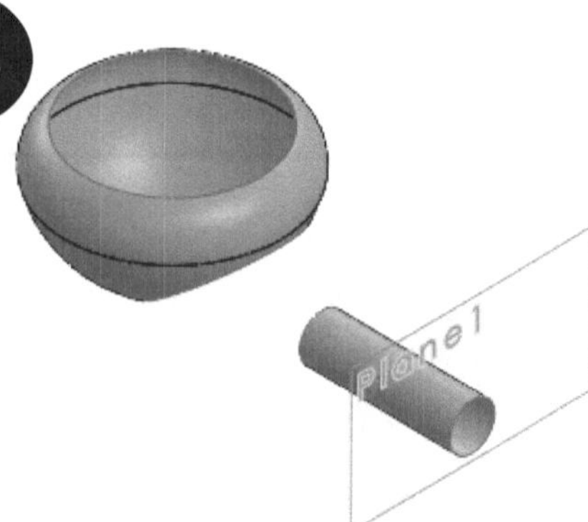

10. Hide the reference plane in the graphics area by clicking on it and then selecting the **Hide** tool in the Pop-up toolbar that appears near the cursor.

Section 6: Creating the Third Surface - Loft Surface

1. Click on the **Lofted Surface** tool in the **Surface CommandManager**, see Figure 3.232. The **Surface-Loft PropertyManager** appears and you are prompted to select profiles for creating a loft surface, since the **Profile** field is activated in the PropertyManager, by default.

3.232

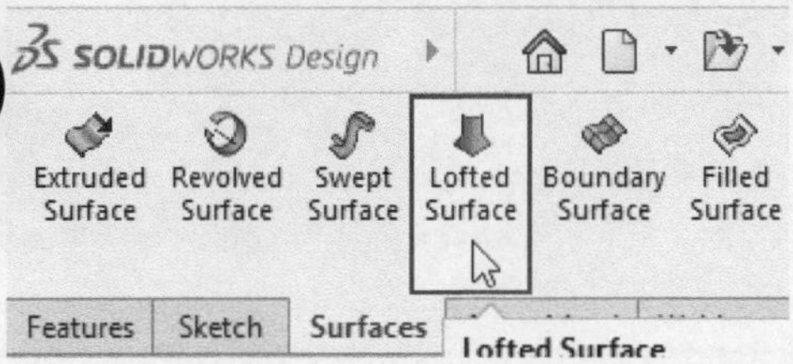

2. Select a circular edge of the previously created extrude surface as the first profile (Profile 1) and the bottom circular edge of the revolve surface as the second profile (Profile 2) one by one in the graphics area, Figure 3.233. The preview of a loft surface appears, see Figure 3.234.

3.233

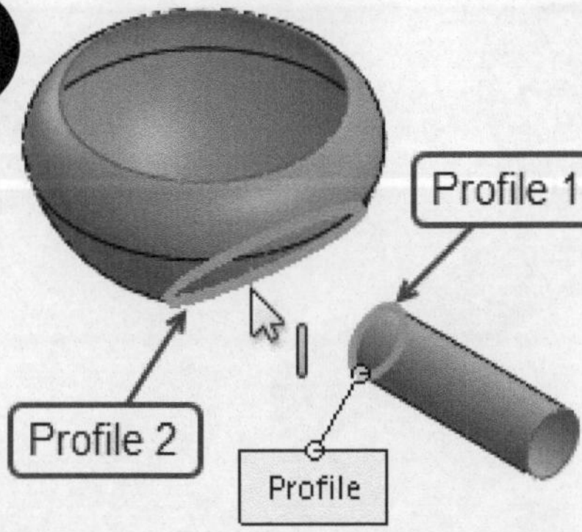

3.234

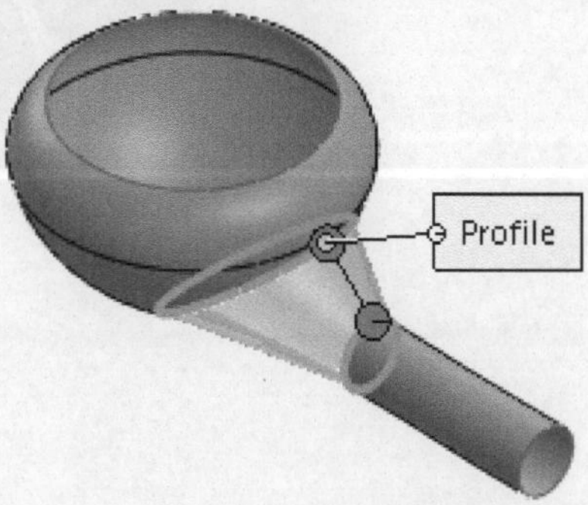

3. Expand the **Start/End Constraints** rollout by clicking on the down arrow at its title bar, see Figure 3.235.

4. Select the **Curvature To Face** option in the **Start constraint** and **End constraint** drop-down lists, see Figure 3.236.

5. Enter **3** in the **Start Tangent Length** field and **1.5** in the **End Tangent Length** field of the **Start/End Constraints** rollout, see Figure 3.236. Figure 3.237 shows a preview of the loft feature from the Front view after defining the curvature continuity for both the start and end profiles.

3.235

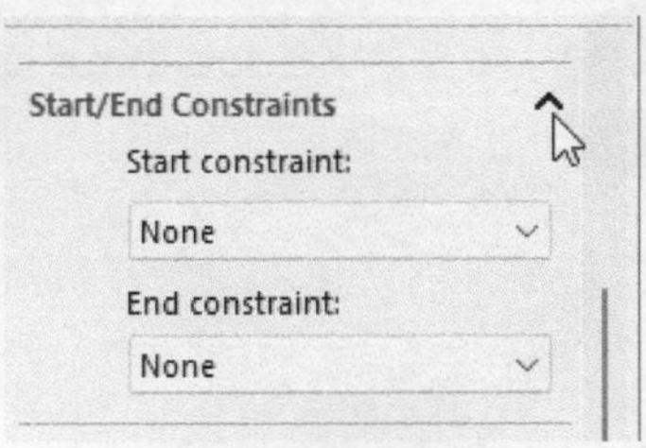

3.236

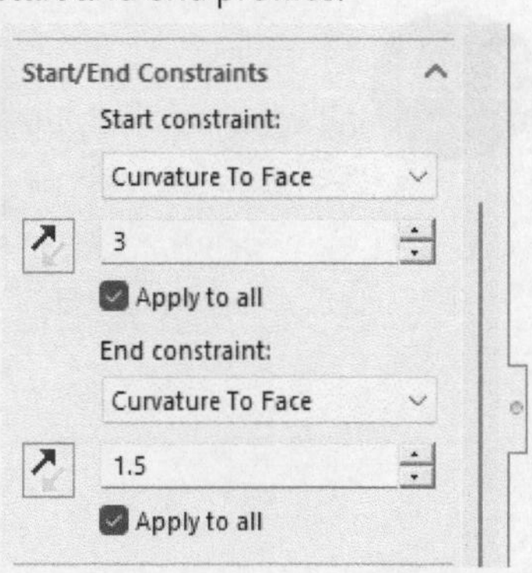

3.237

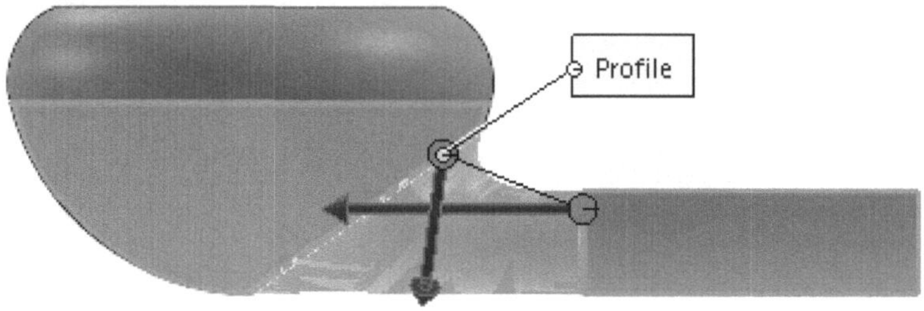

6. Click on the green tick-mark button in the PropertyManager. A loft surface gets created, see Figure 3.238.

3.238

Section 7: Extending a Surface

Now, you need to extend the revolve surface of the model from its top circular edge.

1. Click on the **Extend Surface** tool in the **Surfaces CommandManager**, see Figure 3.239. The **Extend Surface PropertyManager** appears. Also, you are prompted to select a face or edge(s) to be extended, since the **Selected Face/Edges** field is activated in the **Edges/Faces to Extend** rollout of the PropertyManager, by default.

2. Select the top circular edge of the revolve surface to be extended, refer to Figure 3.240. A preview of an extended surface appears in the graphics area.

3.239

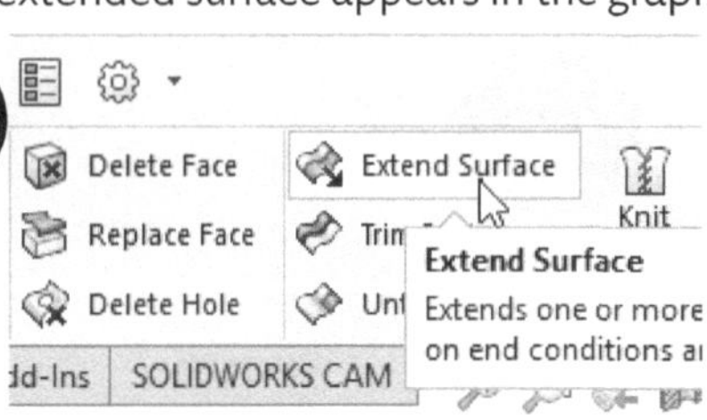

3.240

3. Ensure the **Distance** radio button is selected in the **End Condition** rollout for extending the surface by specifying a distance value.

4. Enter **10** mm in the **Distance** field of the **End Condition** rollout as the extension distance of the surface.

5. Ensure that the **Linear** radio button is selected in the **Extension Type** rollout for extending the surface linearly along the selected edge of the original surface.

3.241

6. Click on the green tick-mark button in the PropertyManager. The surface gets extended, see Figure 3.241.

Section 8: Creating the Fourth Surface - Revolve Surface

1. Invoke the Sketching environment by selecting the Front plane as the sketching plane and then create an arc as the sketch of the revolve surface with a vertical centerline, see Figure 3.242.

3.242

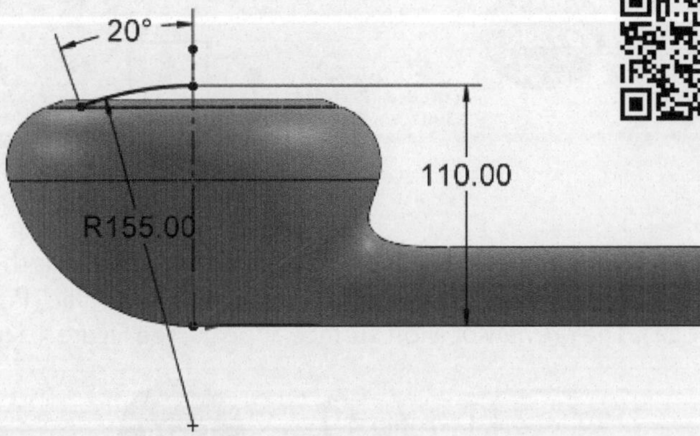

2. After creating the sketch, click on the **Surfaces** tab in the CommandManager and then click on the **Revolved Surface** tool, see Figure 3.243. The **Surface-Revolve PropertyManager** appears. Also, the vertical centerline of the sketch gets selected automatically as the axis of revolution and the preview of a revolve surface appears in the graphics area, see Figure 3.244.

3.243

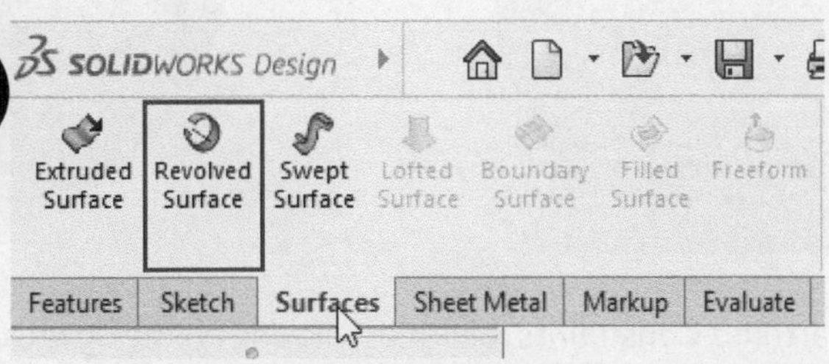

3. Ensure that the **Blind** option is selected in the **Revolve Type** drop-down list and that **360 degrees** is entered in the **Direction 1 Angle** field of the **Direction 1** rollout in the PropertyManager.

4. Click on the green tick-mark button in the PropertyManager. A revolve surface gets created, see Figure 3.245.

3.244

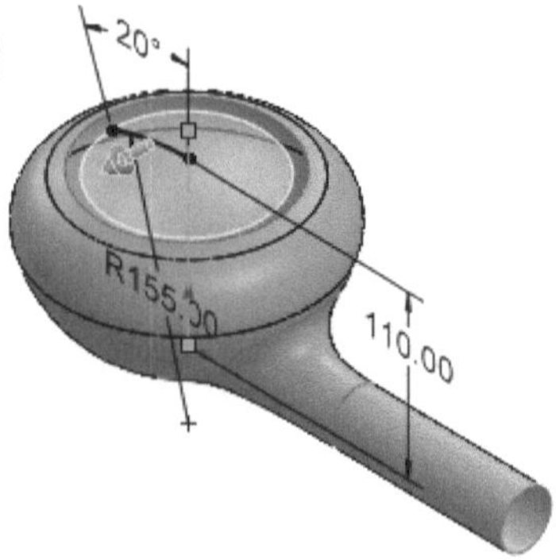

3.245

Section 9: Creating the Fifth Surface - Loft Surface

1. Click on the **Lofted Surface** tool in the **Surface CommandManager**, see Figure 3.246. The **Surface-Loft PropertyManager** appears and you are prompted to select profiles.

3.246

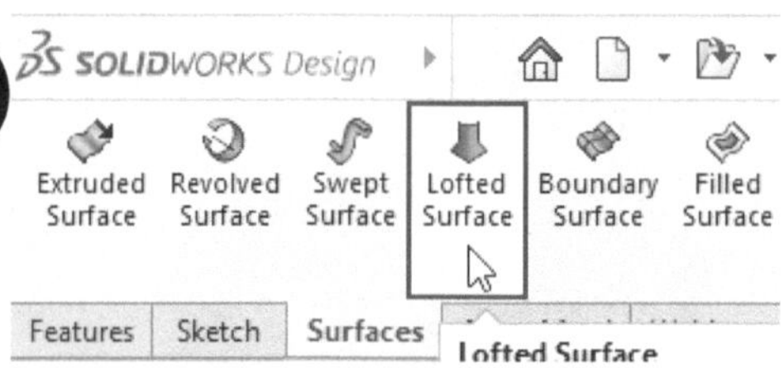

2. Select the circular edge of the previously created revolve surface as the first profile (Profile 1) and the top circular edge of the extended surface as the second profile (Profile 2) in the graphics area, see Figure 3.247. The preview of a loft surface appears, see Figure 3.248.

3.247

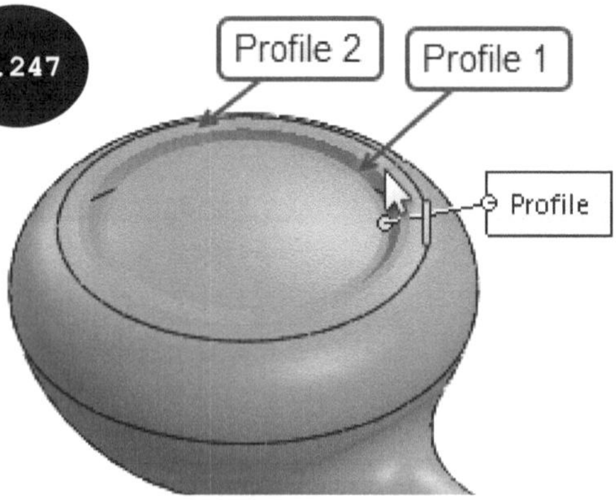

3.248

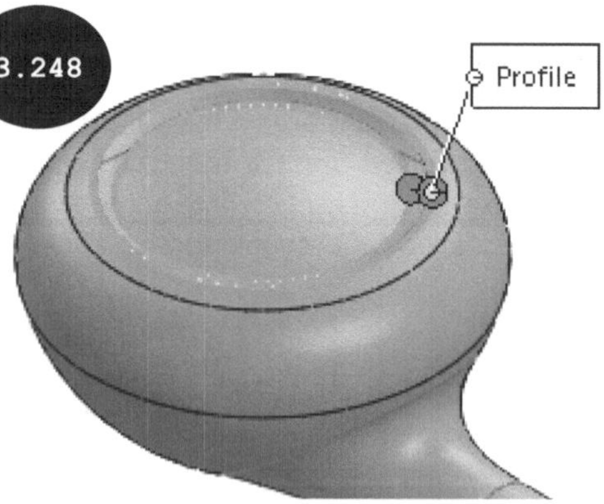

3. Expand the **Start/End Constraints** rollout by clicking on the down arrow at its title bar.

4. Select the **Curvature To Face** option in the **Start constraint** and **End constraint** drop-down lists, see Figure 3.249.

5. Enter 1 in the **Start Tangent Length** field and 1 in the **End Tangent Length** field of the **Start/End Constraints** rollout, see Figure 3.249.

6. Click on the green tick-mark button in the PropertyManager. A loft surface gets created, see Figure 3.250.

3.249

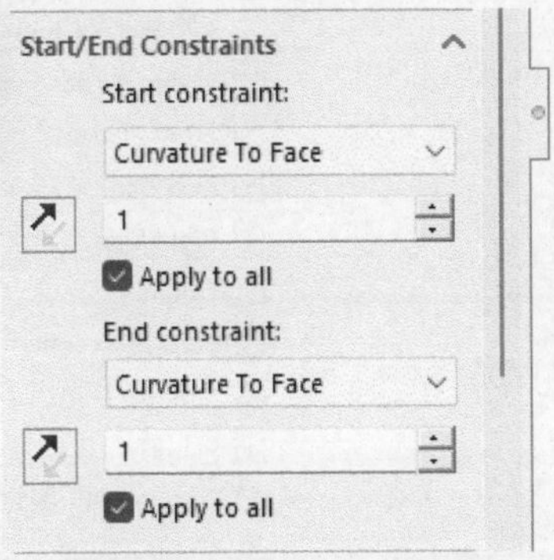

3.250

Section 10: Knitting or Stitching Surfaces

Now, you need to knit or stitch all the individual surfaces together to form a single surface.

1. Click on the **Knit Surface** tool in the **Surfaces CommandManager**, see Figure 3.251. The **Knit Surface PropertyManager** appears.

3.251

2. Select all the individual surfaces of the model in the graphics area one by one. The surfaces get selected and highlighted in the graphics area, see Figure 3.252.

3.252

3. Click on the green tick-mark button in the PropertyManager. The selected surfaces get stitched together and form a single surface model, see Figure 3.253. Also, the **Surface Bodies** node in the FeatureManager Design Tree displays a single surface body, see Figure 3.254.

3.253

3.254

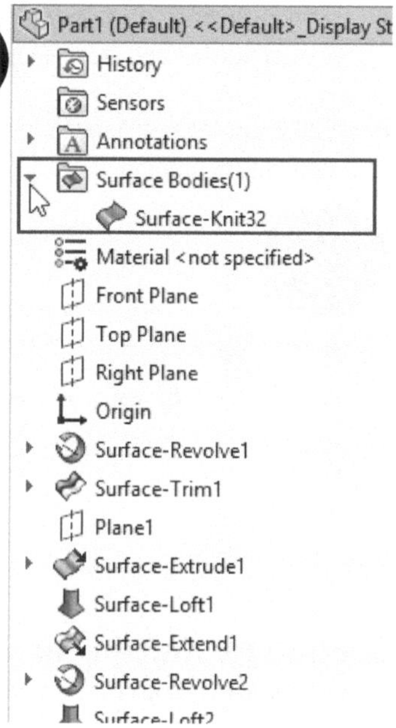

Section 11: Adding Thickness

After creating a surface model, you need to add thickness to make a solid model.

1. Click on the **Thicken** tool in the **Surfaces CommandManager**, see Figure 3.255. The **Thicken PropertyManager** appears.

3.255

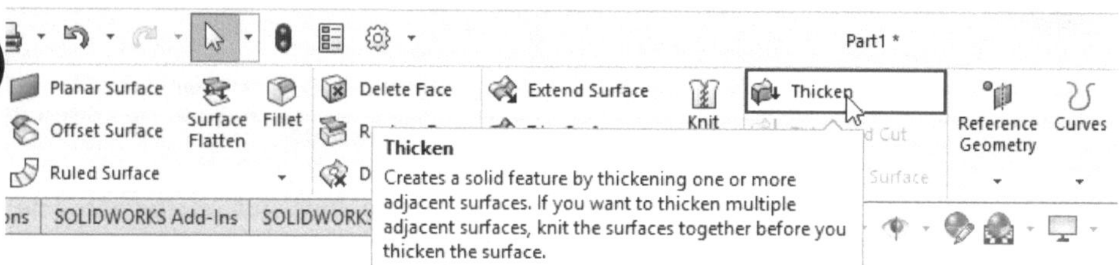

2. Select the surface model in the graphics area.

3. Ensure that the **Thicken Side 2** button is activated in the **Thickness** area of the PropertyManager for adding thickness towards the inner side of the surface model.

4. Enter **1** in the **Thickness** field of the PropertyManager as the thickness to be added.

5. Click on the green tick-mark button in the PropertyManager. A solid model with uniform thickness of 1 mm is created, see Figure 3.256.

Section 12: Creating an Extrude Cut Feature

Now, you need to create an extrude cut feature.

1. Create a reference plane at an offset distance of 120 mm from the Top plane in the upward direction by using the **Plane** tool, see Figure 3.257.

3.256

3.257

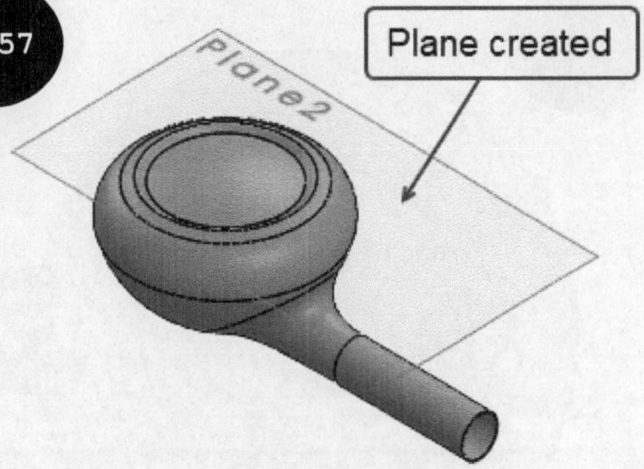

2. Invoke the Sketching environment by selecting the newly created reference plane as the sketching plane.

   Now, you can create a sketch of the extrude cut feature.

3. Create five circles of equal diameter measuring 6 mm with uniform spacing of 12 mm between each other, see Figure 3.258. In this figure, one circle of diameter 6 mm is created at the origin and then its linear pattern is created in one direction to create other instances of the circles.

3.258

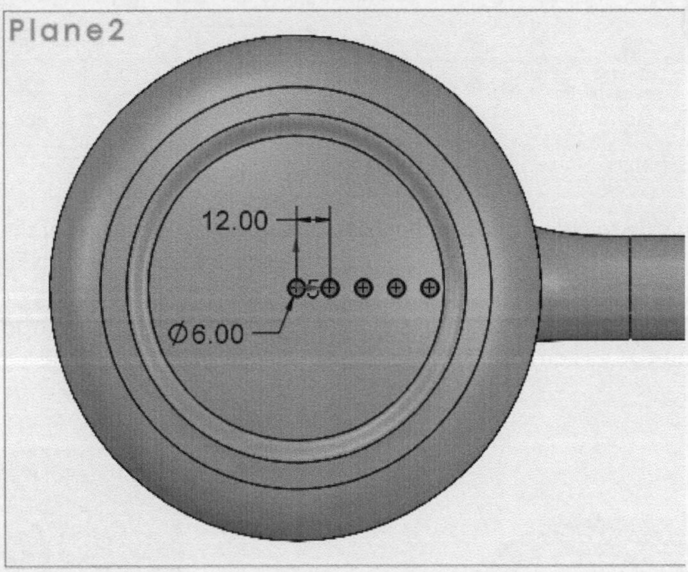

4. Create a circular pattern of all the previously created circles individually except the circle created at the origin, see Figures 3.259 and 3.260. Note that you need to create a circular pattern around the origin. In Figure 3.259, the circular pattern of the inner circle is created around the origin with 6 instances. Figure 3.260 shows the resultant sketch after creating circular patterns of all the circles one by one with increments of 6 instances (6, 12, 18, and 24) in every circular pattern.

3.259

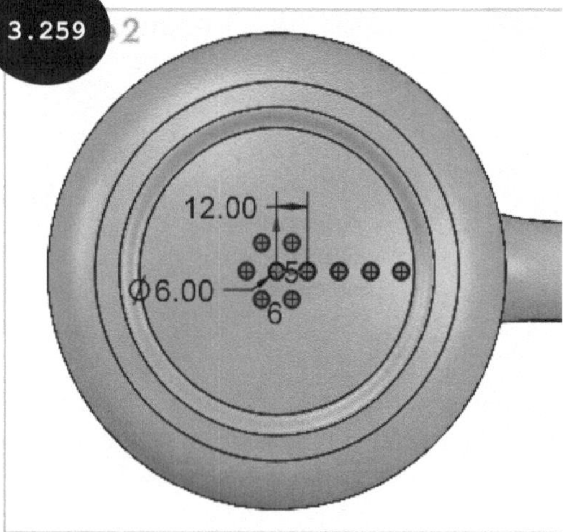

3.260

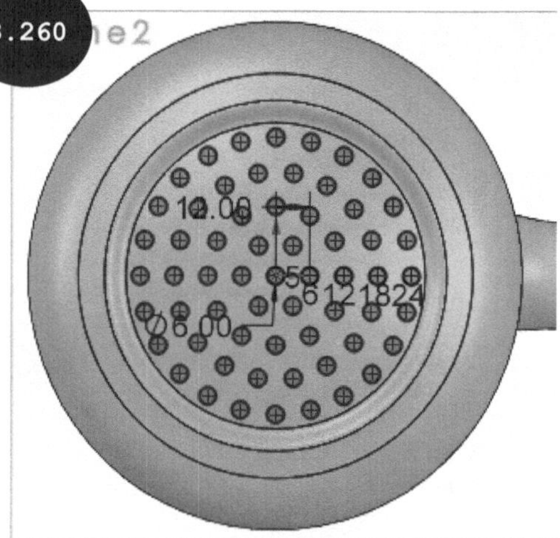

5. Click on the **Features** tab in the CommandManager and then click on the **Extruded Cut** tool, see Figure 3.261. The **Cut-Extrude PropertyManager** appears. Next, change the orientation of the model to isometric.

3.261

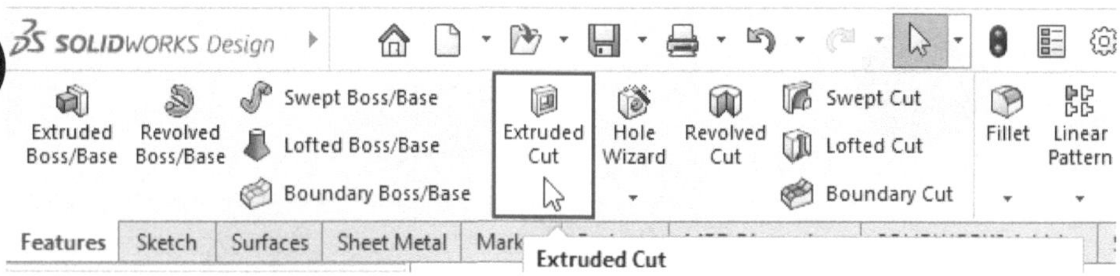

6. Select the **Up to Next** option in the **End Condition** drop-down list of the **Direction 1** rollout. The preview of an extrude cut feature appears similar to the one shown in Figure 3.262.

7. Click on the green tick-mark button in the PropertyManager. An extrude cut feature is created, see Figure 3.263. Hide the reference plane in the graphics area.

3.262

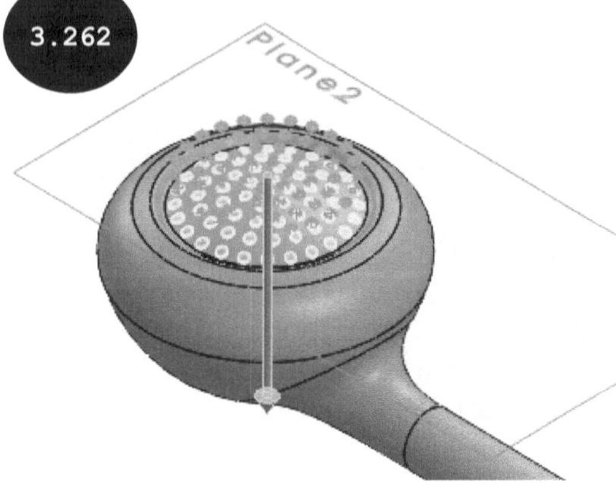

3.263

Section 13: Saving the Model

1. Click on the **Save** tool in the **Standard** toolbar. The **Save As** dialog box appears.
2. Browse the **SOLIDWORKS Surface Design** folder in the local drive of your system. You need to create this folder, if not created earlier.
3. Enter **Tutorial 2** in the **File name** field of the dialog box as the name of the model.
4. Click on the **Save** button in the dialog box. The model gets saved with the name Tutorial 2 inside the SOLIDWORKS Surface Design folder.

Hands-on Test Drive 1

Create a surface model of a hair dryer as shown in Figure 3.264. After creating the model, you need to convert it into a solid model by adding a thickness of 1 mm. The given dimensions are for your reference. You can assume the missing dimensions for achieving the overall shape of the model.

3.264

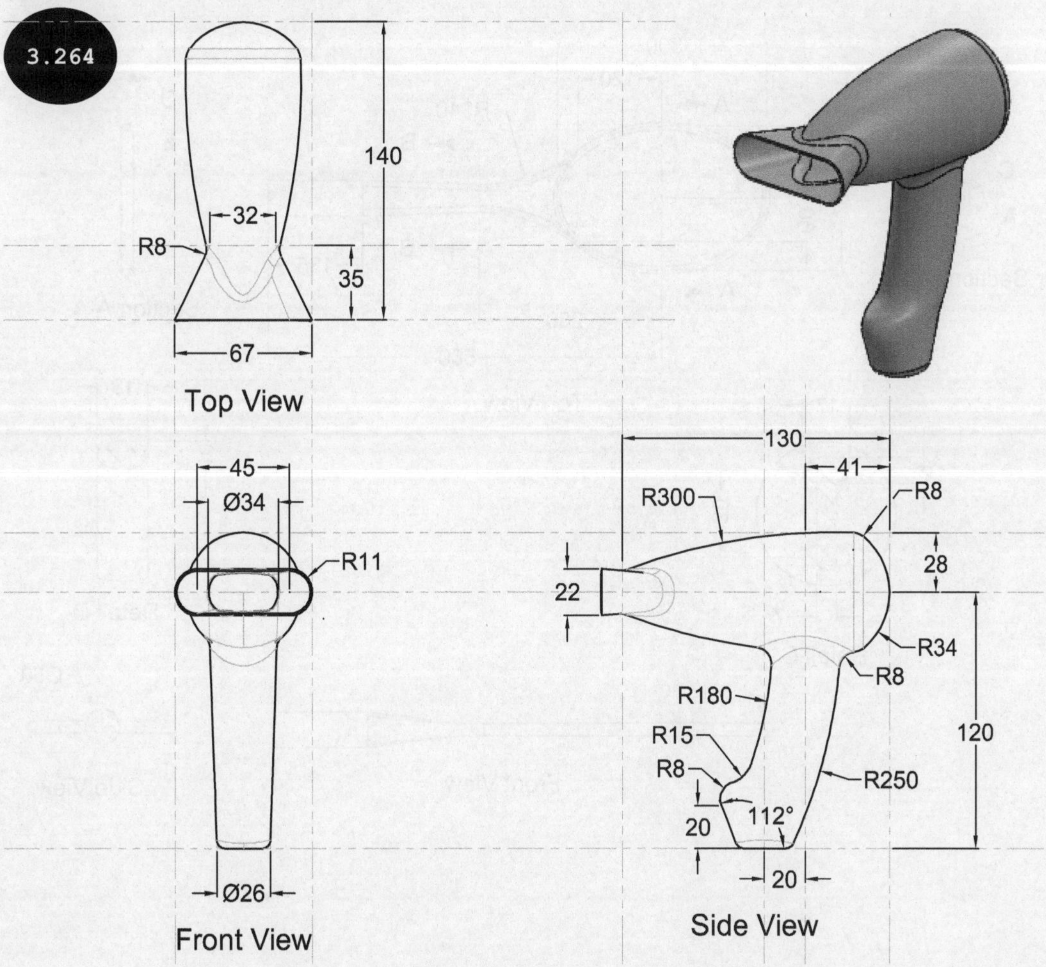

Hands-on Test Drive 2

Create a surface model as shown in Figure 3.265. The given dimensions are for your reference. You can assume the missing dimensions for achieving the overall shape of the model. After creating the surface model, you need to convert it into a solid model from the inside.

Hint: *You can convert enclosed surfaces into a solid model while knitting them into a single surface by selecting the* ***Create solid*** *check box in the* ***Knit Surface PropertyManager****.*

3.265

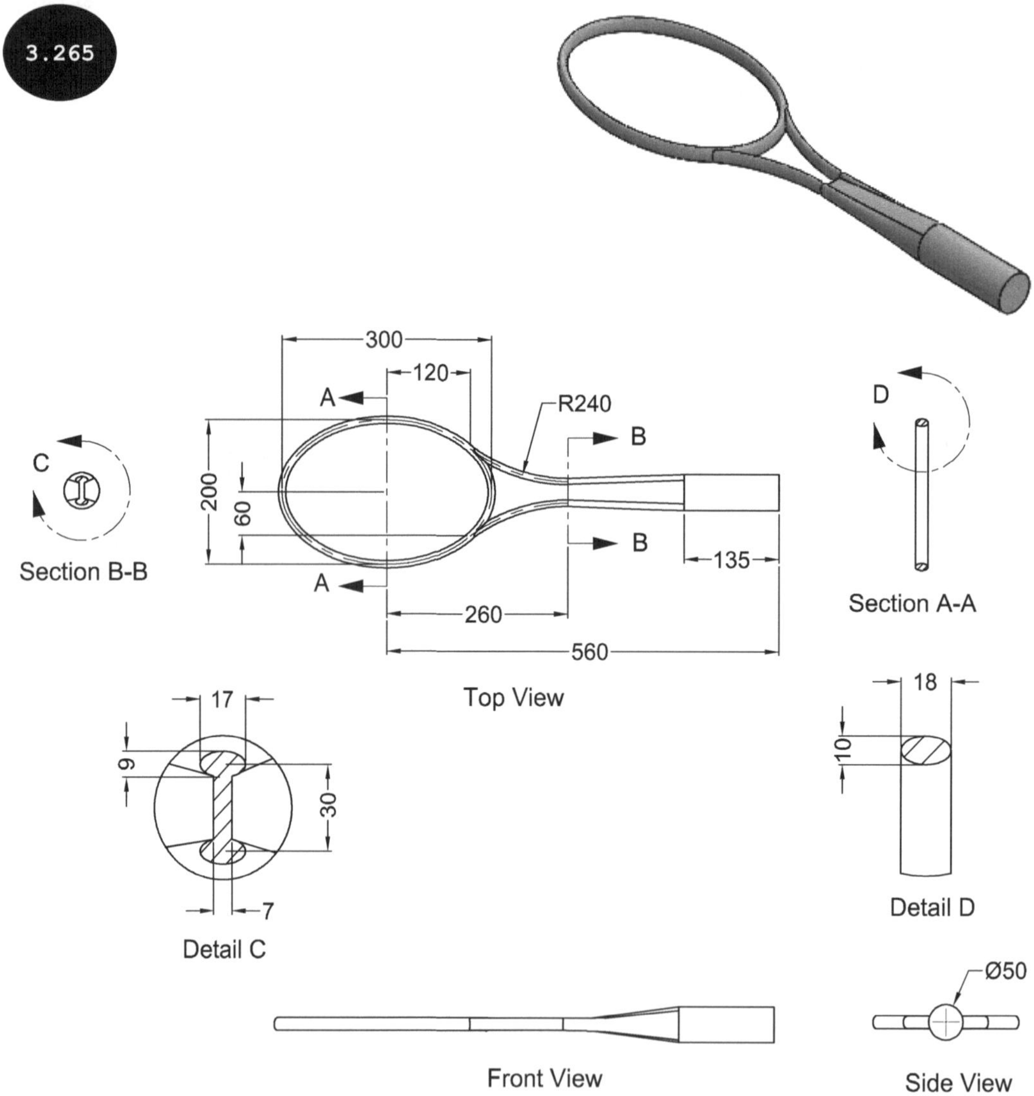

Summary

In this chapter, you have learned the basics of surface modeling for creating complex shape three-dimensional geometries of zero thickness. The chapter discusses in detail about creating different surface geometries such as extrude, revolve, sweep, loft, planar, and ruled. Operations such as extending, offsetting, trimming, untrimming, deleting, and replacing a surface are also discussed. The chapter also described methods for creating a freeform surface and knitting individual surfaces together to form a single surface. The method for converting a knitted surface model into a solid model by adding a thickness is also discussed.

Questions

Complete and verify the following sentences:

- A geometry of zero thickness does not have any mass properties and is known as a _________.
- An _________ surface is created by extruding a closed or an open 2D sketch, normal to the sketching plane.
- A _________ surface is created by sweeping an open or a closed sketch profile along a path.
- Surface modeling is a technique for creating complex shape, and three-dimensional geometries of _________ thickness.
- The _________ tool is used for offsetting an existing surface at a specified offset distance and creating a new surface.
- A _________ surface is created by adding extension to existing surfaces along their edges at a specified distance and angle.
- The _________ tool is used for creating a flat pattern of a surface.
- The _________ tool is used for deforming or modifying the face of a surface by creating control curves and control points, then pushing and pulling the control points.
- You can patch surface holes and external trimmed edges of a selected surface by using the _________ tool.
- The _________ tool is used for combining or joining multiple individual surfaces together to form a single surface.
- If the selected surfaces are to be knitted form a closed watertight volume, then the resultant stitched body will be created as a solid body in the graphics area. (True/False)

- You cannot select a sketch as the trim tool for trimming a surface. (True/False)
- The surfaces to be knitted together must have contact with each other. (True/False)
- You can unstitch or break already stitched surfaces into individual surfaces. (True/False)

INDEX

INDEX

D

E

F

G

H

I

J

K

L

M

N

O

P

R

S

Other Publications by CADArtifex

Some of the other Publications by CADArtifex are given below:

AutoCAD Textbooks

AutoCAD 2026: A Power Guide for Beginners and Intermediate Users
AutoCAD 2025: A Power Guide for Beginners and Intermediate Users
AutoCAD 2024: A Power Guide for Beginners and Intermediate Users
and more

AutoCAD For Architectural Design Textbooks

AutoCAD 2023 for Architectural Design: A Power Guide for Beginners and Intermediate Users
AutoCAD 2022 for Architectural Design: A Power Guide for Beginners and Intermediate Users
and more

Autodesk Fusion 360 Textbooks

Autodesk Fusion 360: A Power Guide for Beginners and Intermediate Users (8th Edition)
Autodesk Fusion 360: A Power Guide for Beginners and Intermediate Users (7th Edition)
Autodesk Fusion 360: A Power Guide for Beginners and Intermediate Users (6th Edition)
and more

Autodesk Fusion 360 Surface and T-Spline Textbooks

Autodesk Fusion 360 Surface Design and Sculpting with T-Spline Surfaces (8th Edition)
Autodesk Fusion 360 Surface Design and Sculpting with T-Spline Surfaces (7th Edition)
and more

Autodesk Inventor Textbooks

Autodesk Inventor 2026: A Power Guide for Beginners and Intermediate Users
Autodesk Inventor 2025: A Power Guide for Beginners and Intermediate Users
Autodesk Inventor 2024: A Power Guide for Beginners and Intermediate Users
and more

FreeCAD Textbooks

FreeCAD 1.0: A Power Guide for Beginners and Intermediate Users
FreeCAD 0.21: A Power Guide for Beginners and Intermediate Users
and more

Onshape Textbooks

Onshape 2025: A Power Guide for Beginners and Intermediate Users
and more

PTC Creo Parametric Textbooks

Creo Parametric 12.0: A Power Guide for Beginners and Intermediate Users
Creo Parametric 11.0: A Power Guide for Beginners and Intermediate Users
and more

SOLIDWORKS Textbooks

SOLIDWORKS 2026: A Power Guide for Beginners and Intermediate User
SOLIDWORKS 2025: A Power Guide for Beginners and Intermediate User
SOLIDWORKS 2024: A Power Guide for Beginners and Intermediate User
and more

SOLIDWORKS Sheet Metal and Surface Design Textbooks

SOLIDWORKS Sheet Metal and Surface Design 2026 for Beginners and Intermediate Users
SOLIDWORKS Sheet Metal and Surface Design 2025 for Beginners and Intermediate Users
and more

SOLIDWORKS Simulation Textbooks

SOLIDWORKS Simulation 2026: A Power Guide for Beginners and Intermediate User
SOLIDWORKS Simulation 2025: A Power Guide for Beginners and Intermediate User
SOLIDWORKS Simulation 2024: A Power Guide for Beginners and Intermediate User
and more

Exercises Books

100 AutoCAD Exercises - Learn by Practicing (2 Edition)
Autodesk Inventor Exercises - Learn by Practicing
Autodesk Fusion 360 Exercises Learn by Practicing (2023-24)
SOLIDWORKS Exercises - Learn by Practicing (3 Edition)

Video Courses by CADArtifex

CADArtifex offers a range of video courses designed to support students, educators, and professionals in developing practical CAD skills through structured, project-based learning. Available video courses include:

- SOLIDWORKS Mastery Pack – 11 Courses in 1 | Complete Beginner to Industry Training
- Fusion 360 Mastery Pack: Design, Sculpt & Build Real Projects (6-in-1 Course Combo)
- Learn SOLIDWORKS Sheet Metal: From Concept to Creation
- Complete Fusion 360 All-in-One Course for Beginners (2025)
- Fusion 360 Surface Design & T-Spline Sculpting
- Complete FreeCAD for Beginners – No Experience Needed
- Complete Onshape for Beginners: Project-Based Approach
- Master Autodesk Inventor: From Basics to Advanced
- Mastering AutoCAD 2D & 3D for Beginners

For full course details and access, visit: ***cadartifex.com***
